THEORETICAL FOUNDATIONS OF NURSING PRACTICE

College of Health Sciences and Nursing

Custom Edition for University of Phoenix

PEARSON

Custom
Publishing

PEARSON CUSTOM PUBLISHING
75 Arlington Street, Suite 300, Boston, MA 02116
A Pearson Education Company

Contents

Section 2

$\mathcal{S}$ection 3

$\mathcal{S}$ection 4

$\mathcal{S}$ection 5

$\mathcal{S}$ection 6

SECTION

The Structure of
Nursing Knowledge:
Analysis and Evaluation
of Practice, Middle-Range,
and Grand Theory

Ann L. Whall

The structure of knowledge within the discipline of nursing holds within it explanations that clarify the present and hold promise for the future. This section explores the structure of nursing knowledge and the interrelationships of nursing models, middle-range theory, and nursing practice theory. Ways in which each of these three levels of theory might be analyzed and evaluated are also proposed.

*T*he Structure of Nursing Knowledge: The Perspective, Domains, Persistent Questions, and Truth Criteria of Nursing

Rosemary Ellis was a clear-thinking, futuristic scholar who concerned herself with major questions regarding the structure of nursing knowledge. This author, as a member of a nursing theory think tank with Ellis, noted her belief that by addressing structural questions first, one

Taken from: *Conceptual Models of Nursing: Analysis and Application,* Third Edition by Fitzpatrick and Whall.

might better understand current questions and issues. Understanding garnered from these discussions and other unpublished works of Ellis is used to address the current fit between nursing conceptual models and other theoretical levels within nursing (Algase & Whall, 1993, 1995).

Nursing science, according to Ellis, is composed of both processes and products of nursing's scholarly endeavors; thus, debates about products are one type of process needed to refine products of the discipline (Whall, 1989). Disciplines that are perhaps more "product" focused, such as chemistry, view science in a more positivistic way, that is, that valid scientific products are perceived through the senses (e.g., weighing measuring). Historians, on the other hand, hold that it is the manner or process by which knowledge is produced that should be a major focus. These views are both seen within nursing. Perhaps because of our need to have our "lived experience" straddle physically based as well as spiritually relevant and artfully applied approaches with patients, nursing science is focused on both products and processes.

According to Ellis, the major components of the structure of the discipline of nursing are *perspective, domains, persistent questions, truth criteria,* and the *community of scholars.* There are other elements, as outlined by Phoenix (1964), but Ellis often focused on these five components.

The domains of the discipline are the subjects or content areas upon which nursing practice is focused. One might conceptualize this content using older terms (e.g., *medical surgical nursing* or *pediatrics*) or using more contemporary terms (e.g., *long-term care* and *critical care*). It is very important to realize that no one discipline "owns" any particular area of knowledge; in the marketplace of ideas, any area may be claimed by a given discipline. Knowledge across disciplines is gradually modified and then becomes accepted within other disciplines. For example, blood pressure monitoring and electrocardiography were first part of medical knowledge and then became part of nursing. Nursing focuses upon caregiving, but so also do other disciplines, such as social work. Thus, the domains or components of knowledge found within any one discipline have a history, fluctuate, may be shared with other disciplines, and can only be relatively identified as specific to a particular discipline at a point in time.

The perspective of a discipline is perhaps the most fascinating structural element that Ellis discussed, for it is composed in large part of historical and traditional precedents, philosophical and ethical components, visionary ideals, and commonly accepted practices. Generally accepted beliefs within the discipline thus form its perspective. The disciplinary perspective is very important because it can be used to identify and sanction what can be considered "nursing" theory, "nursing" research, and "nursing" practice.

The perspective is related to a discipline's domains, for the perspective is used to evaluate the content of the domains. An example of this evaluative function is the debate over advanced-practice knowledge within nursing. In-depth physical assessment knowledge, which was once the preserve or domain of physicians, has gradually became part of the primary assessment of advanced-practice nursing. A debate within nursing between traditionalists and visionaries has stimulated opposing views with regard to the assessment. One group sees in-depth physical assessment as a normal extension of the domain of nursing, believing that as technology advances, domains are modified. This "avant-garde" group believes that although this assessment procedure is used in many disciplines, the perspective of a given discipline determines how and why it is applied. The perspectives of all disciplines are thus in flux, but also contain stable elements.

The persistent questions within the discipline may be found in its practice, education, and research discussions, and involve the products of nursing science: Was the action ethical? or Was the holistic perspective of nursing evident? These questions may also address trends in research over time: How often are questions of social support, life stress, and environmental management seen in nursing research? Questions regarding trends are thus used to evaluate whether nursing research is carrying out the traditional perspective of nursing.

The truth criteria used to evaluate nursing products are traditional as well as evolving. The analysis and evaluation guidelines used in this text and in its prior editions to address nursing conceptual models are one example of nursing's truth criteria. Likewise, the criteria used in this section to assess middle-range and practice theory are also a type of truth criteria. Questions used by national accrediting bodies, state boards, institutional review boards, and human subjects review groups also represent nursing's institutionalized truth criteria.

The community of scholars are members of the discipline who aim to develop the discipline by broadening nursing's knowledge base through such endeavors as research and scholarly discussions and debates. The community of scholars, in Ellis' view, should be involved in questions that address issues at the "cutting edge" of the discipline.

Ellis believed one threat to the community of scholars was that their "scholarly" pursuits and debates might become so esoteric that they would become estranged from nursing practice. An example in nursing of such estrangement was the debate over the relative usefulness of the philosophical view known as *logical positivism* (Whall, 1989). Scholars within nursing debated with much vigor the relevance of logical positivism, a philosophy in which a nonempirical focus is viewed as nonscientific. Acceptance of this position by nursing, which has set an historical precedent for consideration of the spirituality of clients, was unthinkable. Eventually logical positivism was rejected as untenable for nursing (Webster et al., 1981).

This entire debate, however, was unheard and unknown by most practicing nurses, who never considered rejecting the spiritual aspect of care. The situation points out Ellis' concern that the community of scholars could become of marginal importance to the discipline if they focused on issues not central to nursing. Nursing scholars, therefore, must continually check the relevance of their scholarly debates; at times they will lead nursing, at times they may follow, but in Ellis' view these scholars need to maintain relevancy by keeping in touch with nursing practice.

*A*nalysis and Evaluation of Three Levels of Knowledge in Nursing

Even though the debates about positivism were somewhat irrelevant to practicing nurses, they led to other discussions of theoretical nursing knowledge. In the 1950s and 1960s, there was a rejection of nursing as a proper university department (Whall, 1989). Although almost impossible to believe in the 1990s, the fact is that nursing was seen by some university governing boards as a "trade" that was primarily supportive of and related to medicine. In the 1950s, many nursing texts were, in fact, written by physicians, a situation that led to the universities' concerns about nursing as a distinct discipline. Compounding the problem was nursing's seeming inability to identify a comprehensive body of nursing knowledge.

Nevertheless, those nursing programs that were able to achieve university status began by asking nursing students to define nursing's essence. Resulting from these discussions were many of the nursing conceptual models of the 1950s to the present. These models served as a vehicle for nursing's study of the nature of theory and led to the study of the disciplinary structure of nursing. Related to the structural discussions was the emergence of various philosophy of science issues, such as the philosophical classification of nursing science. The nursing models, therefore, served as the impetus for a "giant leap forward" in the development of nursing as a discipline. The advent of the first journal, *Nursing Research,* in 1952 also served a similar function, for nursing science could not be creditable until its research was published in peer-reviewed journals.

Today, however, other discrete theoretical entities besides nursing models exist. Middle-range and practice theory are now considered as having status within nursing equal to that of the nursing conceptual models. It is still true, however, that the nursing models are the only systematically examined level of theory, as witness this and other texts. But middle-range and practice theory have other advantages; for example, they have more readily defined concepts with easily understood empirical referents. These types of theory are discussed here in hierarchical order.

Practice Theory

Practice theory, also called microlevel theory and/or prescriptive theory, is more specific than middle-range theory and produces specific directions for practice. Research on decubitus ulcers, on nasal gastric suction, on mouth care, and on urinary catheterization, for example, can be readily identified as producing practice theory. Practice theory is also produced by other methods, such as induction from practice and deduction from middle-range theory, as well as from research on nursing models. Many of nursing's early guidelines for care, which are found in hospital procedure books, were really theory generated from practice. Much of this theory was developed from practice trial and error.

Merton (1977) stated that middle-range theory may fall within or be congruent with several more abstract grand theories that are themselves incongruent with each other; so too may practice theories fit within a given middle-range theory that is itself incongruent with other middle-range theories. For example, one decubitus ulcer theory might be congruent with two middle-range theories of elder care, which in themselves have conflicting assumptions.

The guidelines for analysis and evaluation of practice theory are in the form of questions that will lead to practice actions (Table 1–1). These guidelines do not address the analysis of the four metaparadigm concepts of person, environment, health, and nursing; rather these concepts are implicit in the questions asked. Because practice theory is designed for immediate application to practice, questions regarding the match or fit with existing empirical data are important. Likewise, the relevance and adequacy for immediate application to practice of concept definitions are important. Operational definitions, descriptors of how to apply practice theory, are very important for practice theory. Thus the adequacy of operational definitions is addressed.

The interrelationships of statements or propositions found within practice theory should also be addressed, perhaps using theoretical substruction (Dulock & Holzemer, 1991). Gaps and inconsistencies in the theory would thus become understood and problems with the adequacy of the theory become evident.

The internal analysis of practice theory may be approached by diagramming the sign (i.e., positive, negative, or unknown) of the interrelationship of all concepts found within the theory, as described by Hardy (1974) long ago. In this way, lapses and inconsistencies in the completeness of the concept structure are addressed. Propositional adequacy of the overall theory is important, and at the practice level it may be argued that more explicit statements, such as those that are necessary, sufficient, and directional in nature, are most important (Hardy, 1974). Associational statements are also needed, but if these predominate, practice directions may not be specific enough.

The internal analysis and evaluation of practice theory considers gaps and inconsistencies within the theory. In part, this is answered via the diagramming of concepts and the analysis of propositions identified above. In addition, the overall theory is considered for problems involving completeness of thought and inconsistent conclusions.

The assumptions of the theory are also considered in light of the historical and current perspectives of nursing. The current perspective may be deduced from nursing models, which

TABLE 1–1   Criteria for the Analysis and Evaluation of Practice Theory

Basic Considerations

1. Definitional adequacy: Can the concepts be readily operationalized?
2. Empirical adequacy: Are the operationalized concepts congruent with empirical data?
3. Statement/propositional adequacy: Do the statements lead to clear directives for nursing care? Are the statements sufficient to the practice task at hand and not contradictory in nature?

Internal Analysis and Evaluation

1. Consideration of completeness and consistency: Are there gaps or inconsistencies within the theory that may lead to prescriptive conflicts and difficulties?
2. Assumptions of theory: Are these beliefs congruent with nursing's historical perspective? Are these assumptions congruent with existing ethical standards and social policy? Are these assumptions in conflict with given cultural groups?

External Analysis and Evaluation

1. Analysis of existing standards: Is the practice theory produced congruent with existing nursing standards? Is the practice theory produced congruent with care standards produced external to nursing (e.g., Agency for Health Care Policy Research guidelines)?
2. Analysis of nursing practice and education: Is the practice theory produced consistent with existing standards of education within nursing? Is the theory produced related to nursing diagnoses and nursing intervention practices?
3. Analysis of research: Is the practice theory supported by existing research internal and external to nursing?

are of prime importance in determining whether nursing's historical perspective is evident. If there are conflicts with the practice theory and nursing's historical perspective, then an assessment of the outcomes of the theory is needed. As with middle-range theory, practice theory may fit within nursing models that are themselves incongruent with each other; if this occurs, the choices made should be evident. Assumptions of practice theory are also relevant to ethical and cultural implications of the theory. Application of practice theory that is in conflict with given cultural standards is arguably unethical. This assessment thus has practice application implications in nursing.

The external analysis and evaluation have to do with comparison of standards of care, produced externally or internally to nursing, with the practice theory. Likewise, nursing research is examined and the question of its support for the theory, its neutrality, or its opposition to the theory is evaluated.

In summary, the body of nursing knowledge is so extensive today that analysis and evaluation of all levels of theory is necessary. Because a more interlocking body of knowledge in nursing may for the first time in history be possible to attain, assessment of the fit between the levels of theory found within nursing needs to be addressed. With such assessment, nursing knowledge may be greatly expanded and clarified. At the least, such assessment will lead to better understanding of the strengths and weaknesses of nursing's knowledge base, as well as the portions of theory that need to be better developed. Analysis of each theoretical level should also lead to more knowledgeable "consumers" of nursing theory.

Middle-Range Theory

There are many examples in which middle-range theory is the stimulus for or the outcome of research; for example, family theory produced in nursing is inherently middle range in nature. Merton (1957) discussed middle-range theory at length and stated that middle-range theory lies somewhere between the most abstract ideas (e.g., nursing models) and more circumscribed concrete ideas (e.g., care procedures, which deal with very specific topics). Intervention research in nursing often produces this most specific type of theory, as does practice itself.

That there are many methods by which levels of theory may be produced (Walker & Avant, 1995). For example, there is "armchair" theorizing, theorizing from practice situations or phenomena, developing and testing theory inductively, and deductively joining statements from several existing theories (Whall, 1986). For the purposes of this discussion, however, we are focusing on the nature of the theory produced by these methods and not on the methods per se.

The analysis and evaluation of middle-range theory uses a modification of the guidelines (or truth criteria) used for analysis and evaluation of the nursing conceptual models (Table 1–2). However, the metaparadigm concepts (person, environment, health, and nursing) have been eliminated from this analysis. Questions of more immediate relevance, such as the fit of the middle-range theory with the existing nursing perspective and domains, are asked. The more global metaparadigm concepts found in the models are not always implicit in middle-range theory, although they may be inferred. Likewise, middle-range concepts have more specific empirical referents (or can be understood through human sense data) than the more abstract models.

Theoretical statements found in middle-range theory may be categorized using the system of Hardy (1974) or identified as ranging from causal to associative in nature. Theoretical state-

---

TABLE 1–2   Criteria for the Analysis and Evaluation of Middle-Range Theory

Basic Considerations

1. What are the definitions and relative importance of major concepts?
2. What is the type and relative importance of major theoretical statements and/or propositions?

Internal Analysis and Evaluation

1. What are the assumptions underlying the theory? What is the relationship to philosophy of science positions?
2. Are concepts related/not interrelated via statements? Is there any resulting loss of information?
3. Is there internal consistency and congruency of all component parts of the theory?
4. What is the empirical adequacy of theory? Has it been examined in practice and research and has it held up to this scrutiny?

External Analysis and Evaluation

1. What is the congruence with related theory and research internal and external to nursing?
2. What is the congruence with the perspective of nursing, the domains, and the persistent questions?
3. What ethical, cultural, and social policy issues are related to the theory?

ments or propositions of middle-range theory should be assessed for their relative importance as well as for missing linkages between concepts. Theoretical substruction (Dulock & Holzemer, 1991), or the diagramming of all relationships found in a theory, may be used for this purpose. Missing relationships between concepts are also identified. For this purpose, a matrix is made of the sign of all the concepts, that is, one asks whether the relationship is positive, negative, or unknown (Hardy, 1974). A decision is made as to the relative importance of any missing concepts (i.e., whether missing data make the theory unclear). Assumptions derived from the middle-range theory are also analyzed by asking what is assumed to exist as a basis for the theory, and what situation exists during the theory and after the theoretical action is concluded. Philosophy of science views are also discerned. Questions are asked about what the theory asserts to be true, what beliefs underlie the theory, and which positions within the philosophy of science the theory represents. These questions lead to further insights regarding congruence between statements and concepts of the theory.

The internal consistency (e.g., consistent usage of terms) of middle-range theories is usually less of a problem than that of more global discussions found in grand theories. Nevertheless, assessing all concepts to determine whether inconsistency in definitions occurs across the theory will assist with the evaluation of clarity. Empirical adequacy, the inherent ability to operationalize and measure aspects of a theory, is also very important in middle-range theory. Operational definitions are needed for empirical adequacy, and these too are evaluated (i.e., are they adequate and readily applied?).

External analysis of middle-range theory has to do with its congruence with more global theories and with other related middle-range theories. Questions are asked as to the nursing perspective represented: Is the nursing perspective represented consistent with the *historical* view, for example, that found within nursing conceptual models? Because middle-range theory is more readily applied than grand theory, its ethical, cultural, and social policy stances are crucial. Does the theory seem relevant to various cultural groups? Are there ethical concerns in this regard? What would be the result should social policy be based upon this theory? Finally, assessment is made of congruence with the perspective espoused by nursing, as well as with the domains of nursing that are currently accepted: Where does the theory lead nursing? What research or other empirical examination is needed to more fully develop the theory?

Because a goal of many disciplines is the interlocking of all products found in its body of theoretical knowledge, the congruence of middle-range nursing models is assessed. According to Merton (1977), it is likely that any one middle-range theory can fit within or be congruent with several grand theories (such as the nursing models). Merton asserts that middle-range theories thus may fit within several grand theories that are incongruent with each other. Thus, groups of middle-range theories may be congregated within several nursing models and, therefore, produce interlocking levels of knowledge. The body of knowledge within nursing would thus be strengthened by such analysis and evaluation.

$\mathcal{N}$ursing Models: Analysis and Evaluation

The nursing models examined in this text will continue to have a major influence on nursing. For example, products of the discipline should be examined in light of nursing models that have been developed over a long period of nursing history. The nursing conceptual models are assessed from a postmodern view, that is, with the belief that these models are in and of themselves important, are free to vary between each other, and may be utilized as sources of either practice or middle-range theory. Unlike disciplines in which grand theories do not continue to be influential, in nursing, conceptual models continue to guide various programs of research, as discussed in each of the sections of this text. The guidelines presented for these models highlight the differences of each of the models as well as similarities across models.

Because, as Dubin (1978) has described, nursing conceptual models are composed of summative units, or very abstract concepts, partial relationship statements or propositions usually join these concepts. Oftentimes the assumptions of the models are in essence the general beliefs or understanding of nursing theorists. The guidelines presented in Table 1–3, therefore, are not only analysis guidelines but also evaluation guidelines that can continue to be used by students as a model continues to be developed.

As nursing conceptual models are composed of the major paradigm concepts found within nursing, that is, person, environment, health, and nursing, as well as additional concepts specific to the model, the first question addressed is the definition of these concepts. Besides asking about the definition of person, as defined throughout the model, the interrelationships of person with the other concepts within the model, for example, are addressed. Oftentimes the way in which person is discussed in other concepts within the model fills out the description that the theorist wishes to give.

It is important to realize that although the term *person* is used within most of the models, the term *recipient of care* could be equally well used. By this is meant that the recipient of care can be more than a single individual. It may be a family, it may be a community, or it may be a group with which the nurse is working.

TABLE 1–3   Guidelines for Analyzing Nursing Models

Introduction to the Model

Basic Paradigm Concepts Included in the Model

1. What are the definitions of person, nursing, health, and environment?
2. What are the additional understandings of person?
3. What are the additional understandings of nursing?
4. What are the additional understandings of health?
5. What are the additional understandings of environment?
6. What are the interrelationships among concepts of person, nursing, health, and environment?
7. What are the descriptions of other concepts found in the model?

Internal Analysis and Evaluation

1. What are the underlying assumptions of the model?
2. What are the definitions of any other components of the model?
3. What is the relative importance of basic concepts or other components of the model?
4. What are the analyses of internal and external consistency?
5. What are the analyses of adequacy?

External Analysis

1. Is nursing research based upon the model or related to the model?
2. Is nursing education based upon the model or related to the model?
3. Is nursing practice based upon the model or related to the model?
4. What is the relationship, if any, to existing nursing diagnoses and interventions systems?

It is also important to understand whether *nursing* is used as a verb or as a noun, and within what context it is used in either of these two ways. The description of nursing in terms of the actions taken, of the goals of nursing, and of the view of society is next addressed. How this view is alike or different from other commonly accepted views of nursing, such as that found within current organizations, is addressed. Finally, the way in which nursing addresses the care of individuals, families, groups, and communities is compared.

Health is addressed within each nursing conceptual model in overt or covert ways. If the definition of health is given, is health seen as the goal of nursing, is a definition of health from another source used, and are these definitions and discussion of the concept of nursing congruent with one another? If health is seen as some sort of steady state, then are the propositional statements regarding health consistent with the steady-state perspective, or is health seen as an open, ever-evolving state that is related to all aspects of humans and their environment? The way in which the nurse acts to bring about health is of major interest to the analyses.

The way in which environment is defined is extremely important to nursing. Florence Nightingale, in essence, saw nursing as a science of environmental management. Nightingale's early emphasis upon environment brought nursing to the realization that there are physical and emotional environments as well as other kinds of environments. It is of interest in the analysis to determine the way in which the theorist defines environment; to determine if it is directional, linear, open, or closed; and if it is interrelated with the other metaparadigm concepts.

The interrelationships amongst the four metaparadigm concepts are of interest because they identify the relative importance of each of these concepts. If, for example, a greater amount of time is spent within the model discussing person versus nursing, then there may be some difficulty for practice applications of the model. If the interrelationships are of equal importance, is there some implied hierarchy as these concepts are addressed? The importance of these four major concepts can be fairly well determined by reading through all portions of the model to determine how each of these concepts is described.

Within each model are found additional concepts that describe the other elements of importance. Oftentimes, the other major concepts that the theorist uses really define the model. Next, the interrelationships amongst the major concepts of the model, other than the four metaparadigm concepts, are addressed. Are these well defined? Are these relationships and various outcomes of the relationships described in detail? Is more detail needed?

In the internal analysis and evaluation, the underlying assumptions on which the model is based are important. Underlying assumptions provide data as to the nature of science ascribed to, for example, pragmatism or realism. The philosophical underpinnings of the model should guide the relationship statements provided. In addition, it should be determined whether there is conflict between the philosophical position suggested and the overall perspective of nursing. A portion of the model analysis should address this.

Many times theories or subtheories are presented within a given nursing model. In what way are these elements or related elements congruent with the overall nursing model? Is, for example, a certain subtheory identified but not further explored? If this is the case, then both the internal and external consistency of the model is affected. If a feature of the model that is presented is not discussed, one would assume this to be of lesser importance.

Internal consistency has to do with the uniformity of discussion throughout the model. Are the concepts used in the same way at the beginning as they are at the end of the model? Are the propositional statements consistent with the assumptions of the model? Are the propositional statements and concepts consistent with one another and with the assumptions of the model? Each of these points leads to a decision regarding the level of internal consistency.

External consistency is addressed; for example, do the authors or theoreticians view the world in a manner consistent with views external to the model? Is the model view consistent with other nursing conceptual models, with other statements found within nursing, with such elements such as the role of the nurse, and with nursing intervention classification systems? Each of these questions addresses the external consistency of the model.

Pragmatic adequacy is addressed; for example, does the model suggest doable activities for nursing? Empirical adequacy asks, in essence, "Can model elements be measured?" The level of abstraction of the model certainly affects usefulness and measurement: the more abstract the model, the more difficulty with use and measurement. If the concepts are highly abstract, it is often difficult to "bring them down" to a practice or more concrete level without using a good deal of interpretation. Nursing models having concepts that are very much "rooted in the senses," or observable, however, may be difficult to relate back to the philosophical assumptions of the model. Finally, the external analysis of the nursing model has to do with the way that it has been used in research, education, and practice.

Although nursing diagnoses are not often stated within the nursing models, there are portions within every nursing model that have to do with practice. Often these sections of the model lend themselves to nursing diagnoses that may be derived from the model. These nursing diagnoses, however, may not be congruent with external nursing diagnosis systems. For example, using Martha Rogers' model, one might identify a problem with an individual's environment. Although Rogers herself never used the term *nursing diagnosis* with her model, a diagnosis relating to the environment might be derived. Therefore, where possible, the authors of the sections found in this text identify nursing diagnoses that might be derived from the model. Not included in this text, but a step related to derived nursing diagnoses, is identification of nursing interventions that are compatible with the nursing model. Because the models presented here vary with respect to derivation of nursing diagnoses and interventions, it is left up to the reader in many instances to determine possible diagnoses and interventions related to the model.

One final note is that in this postmodern era, it is realized that some of these analytical and evaluative questions may be less suitable for a given model. When this is the case, the rationale as to why each question is unsuitable is important, for this analysis sheds light not only upon the model but also upon the evaluation criteria. It is hoped that the reader will enjoy this updated and more relevant journey through nursing theory presented in the sections that follow.

$\mathcal{R}$eferences

Algase, D., & Whall, A. (1993). Rosemary Ellis' views on the substantive structure of nursing. *IMAGE: Journal of Nursing Scholarship, 25* (1), 69–72.

Algase, D., & Whall, A. (1995). Analytic questions for emerging doctoral programs in nursing: An approach to develop culturally sensitive nursing content. In *Proceedings, nursing forum on doctoral education.* Dearborn, MI, June 1995, sponsored by the University of Michigan, School of Nursing.

Dubin, R. (1978). *Theory building.* New York: Macmillan.

Dulock, H., & Holzemer, W. (1991). Substruction: Improving the linkage from theory to method. *Nursing Science Quarterly, 4* (2), 83–87.

Hardy, M. (1974). Theories: Components, development, evaluation. *Nursing Research, 23,* 100–107.

Merton, R. (1977). *On sociological theory.* New York: Free Press.

Phoenix, P. (1964). *Realms of meaning.* New York: McGraw–Hill.

Webster, G., Jocax, S., & Baldwin, B. (1981). Nursing theory and the ghost of the received view. In J. C. McCloskey & H. C. Grace (Eds.), *Current issues in nursing.* Boston: Blackwell Scientific, (pp. 29–30).

Walker, L., & Avant, K. (1995). *Strategies for theory construction in nursing.* Norwalk, CT: Appleton & Lange.

Whall, A. (1989). *The influence of logical positivism on nursing practice. IMAGE: Journal of Nursing Scholarship, 21* (4), 243-245.

Whall, A. (1986). *Family therapy theory for nursing: Four approaches.* Norwalk, CT: Appleton & Lange.

An Introduction to Nursing Theory

Janet S. Hickman

The purpose of this section is to provide the learner with the tools necessary for understanding and evaluating the nursing theories presented in this book. These tools include learning the language and definitions of theoretical thinking, acquiring a perspective of the historical development of nursing theories, and learning a method to analyze and evaluate nursing theories.

The Language of Theoretical Thinking

Concepts

The basic unit in the language of theoretical thinking is the *concept*. Webster (1991) defines a concept as something conceived in the mind—a thought or a notion. Concepts are words that represent reality and enhance our ability to communicate about it. Concepts may be empirical or abstract, depending on their ability to be observed in the real world. Concepts are said to be *empirical* when they can be observed or experienced through the senses. A stethoscope is an example of an empirical concept; it can be seen and touched. *Abstract* concepts are those that are not observable, such as hope and infinity. All concepts become abstractions in the absence of the object. For example, once you have become familiar with a stethoscope, you are able to see the concept of a stethoscope in your mind without having one physically present.

Taken from: *Nursing Theories: The Base for Professional Nursing Practice*, Fourth Edition by George.

Abstractions such as hope or infinity are more difficult to picture, because one has never had the opportunity to observe or experience them through the senses.

To understand the presentations of nursing theories in this book, it will be of critical importance to look at the definitions of the concepts provided. Some of the theories will use concepts that you are familiar with, but they may be used in unfamiliar ways; others will introduce new concepts.

There is general agreement in the literature that nursing is concerned with four major concepts: person, health, environment, and nursing. Together these concepts make up the meta-paradigm of nursing. A meta-paradigm identifies the core content of a discipline.

In the meta-paradigm of nursing, each of the four concepts is presented as an abstraction. *Person* may represent one individual, a family, a community, or all of mankind. In this context, *person* is the recipient of nursing care. *Health* represents a state of well-being mutually decided on by the client and the nurse. *Environment* may represent the immediate surroundings, the community, or the universe and all it contains. *Nursing* is the science and art of the discipline.

All the nursing theories presented in this book address the concepts of the meta-paradigm of nursing. Some theories speak explicitly to these concepts, others only imply their presence.

Theories

Concepts are the elements used to generate theories. Kerlinger (1973) defines a theory as a set of interrelated concepts, definitions, and propositions that present a systematic way of viewing facts/events by specifying relations among the variables, with the purpose of explaining and predicting the fact/event. This definition can be broken down to the key ideas of *interrelated concepts, propositions specifying relations among the variables,* and *a stated purpose of explaining or predicting facts/events.* Simply stated, a theory suggests a direction in how to view facts and events.

Chinn and Kramer (1991) define theory as "a creative and rigorous structuring of ideas that project a tentative, purposeful, and systematic view of phenomena" (p. 79). An additional element of this definition is a focus on the tentative nature of theory. Theories cannot be equated with scientific laws, which predict the results of given experiments 100 percent of the time. Laws are the basis of most of the natural sciences. Because nursing is a human science, the rigor and objectivity of the laboratory are both inappropriate and impossible to duplicate. In the future, the predictability of nursing theories will become more reliable as the research base from which theories develop and in which theories are tested grows.

Meleis (1991) defines nursing theory as ". . . an articulated and communicated conceptualization of invented or discovered reality (central phenomena and relationships) in or pertaining to nursing for the purpose of describing, explaining, predicting, or prescribing nursing care" (p. 17). This definition adds the importance of communicating nursing theory and the purpose of prescription of nursing care.

Theories are composed of concepts (and their definitions) and propositions. Propositions explain the relationships between the concepts. For example, Nightingale *proposed* a beneficial relationship between fresh air and health. Theories are based on stated assumptions presented as givens. Theoretical assumptions, such as a value statement or ethic, may be taken as "truth" because they cannot be empirically tested. A theory may be presented as a model that provides a diagram or map of the theory's content.

Barnum (1994) states that a complete nursing theory is one that has context, content, and process. *Context* is the environment in which the nursing act takes place. *Content* is the subject of the theory. *Process* is the method by which the nurse acts in using the theory. The nurse acts on, with, or through the content elements of the theory.

Although some texts differentiate between "theories" and "conceptual models" of nursing, most authors believe that this is an artificial distinction. Meleis (1991) goes so far as to say, "These differences are tentative at best and hair-splitting, unclear, and confusing at worst" (p. 16). For the purposes of this text, the existing nursing conceptualizations presented *are* theories.

Levels of Theory

The level of a theory refers to the scope, or range, of phenomena to which the theory applies. The level of abstraction of the concepts in the theory is closely tied to its scope. Chinn and Kramer (1991) state that "theory may be characterized as *micro, macro, molecular, midrange, molar, atomistic,* and *holistic*" (p. 123). Micro, molecular, and atomistic suggest relatively narrow-range phenomena, whereas macro, holistic, and molar imply that the theory covers a broad scope. These labels are arbitrary and may differ in different disciplines. *Grand theory* is also a term used in the literature, meaning theory that covers broad areas of concern within a discipline. *Metatheory* is a term used to label theory about the theoretical process and theory development.

Another way of looking at levels of theory is to look at what it is that the theory does. For Dickoff, James, and Wiedenbach (1968), theory develops on four levels: factor-isolating, factor-relating, situation-relating, and situation-producing. Level 1, factor-isolating, is descriptive in nature. It involves naming or classifying facts/events. Level 2, factor-relating, requires correlating or associating factors in such a way that they meaningfully depict a larger situation. Level 3, situation-relating, explains and predicts how situations are related. Level 4, situation-producing, requires sufficient knowledge about how and why situations are related, so that when the theory is used as a guide, valued situations can be produced (Dickoff & James, 1968). When using this method, one speaks of the relative power of the theory, with Level 4 being the most powerful because it controls (or does more than describe, explain, or predict).

Worldviews

A worldview is one's philosophical frame of reference in looking at one's world. The worldview of the philosophy of science is that of logical empiricism. This worldview requires that all truths must be confirmed by sensory experiences. Logical empiricism requires objectivity and is relatively value free. Objectivity requires study of the smallest parts of phenomena by using the scientific method (Riegal et al., 1992). In this worldview, the whole is equal to the sum of its parts. In the literature, this worldview is also called the *received view* or the *positivist view*. It is from this view of nursing science that the nursing process was created.

One of the worldviews that opposes logical empiricism is that of the human science or the perceived view. A human science worldview focuses on human beings as wholes and on their lived experiences within a given context (Meleis, 1991).

Parse posits two worldviews of nursing related to the received and the perceived views. The description of the totality paradigm reflects the received view, whereas the description of the simultaneity paradigm reflects the perceived view (Parse, 1987). A basic difference in these paradigms is the perception of person. The totality paradigm looks at the bio-psycho-social-spiritual aspects of person, whereas the simultaneity paradigm views person as an irreducible whole in constant interrelationship with the universe. Theorists of the totality paradigm tend to define health as a state of well-being as measured against norms; simultaneity theorists view health as something the client determines individually.

Cyclical Nature of Theory, Research, and Practice

It is important to understand that theory, research, and practice have an impact on one another in a cyclical way. Middle-range theory can be tested in clinical practice. The testing process for theory is clinical research. The research process may validate the theory, cause it to be modified, or invalidate it. The more research that is conducted about a specific theory, the more useful the theory is to practice. Practice is based on the theories of the discipline that are validated through research (see Figure 1–1). Research findings are published in the periodical literature as well as in books.

Research may be based on the received or perceived worldview. Received view research is quantitative; statistical data represent empirical facts and events. The methodology of the research is based on the scientific method. Perceived view research is qualitative in nature and is based on the thoughts, feelings, and beliefs of the research subjects. A number of methodologies have been proposed to conduct qualitative research.

According to Haase and Meyers (1988), quantitative and qualitative approaches differ in the following ways:

1. Quantitative methods assume a singular reality, whereas qualitative methods assume multiple interrelated realities.

2. Quantitative methods assume that objective reality is the appropriate domain. Qualitative methods assume that subjective experiences are also legitimate.

3. Quantitative methods are reductionistic, whereas the opposite methods take an ecological view—that is, they attempt to gain a full understanding of the reality.

4. Quantitative methods reveal the whole through its parts. Qualitative methods assume that the whole is greater than its parts.

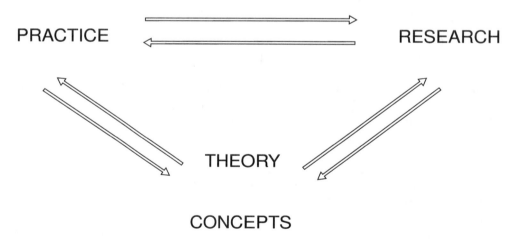

FIGURE 1–1

Cyclical Nature of Theory, Research, and Practice.

5. Quantitative methods assume that discrepancies are to be accounted for or eliminated. Qualitative methods recognize that discrepancies may be existentially real.

Historical Perspective

The history of theory development and theoretical thinking in nursing began with the writings of Florence Nightingale and continues in the 1990s. This section highlights significant events in this history.

Florence Nightingale

Nightingale's (1859/1992) *Notes on nursing* presents the first nursing theory that focuses on the manipulation of the environment for the benefit of the patient. Although Nightingale did not present her work as a "nursing theory," it has directed nursing practice for more than 100 years.

The Columbia School—The 1950s

In the 1950s the need to prepare nurses at the graduate level for administrative and faculty positions was recognized. Columbia University's Teachers College developed graduate education programs to meet these functional needs. The first theoretical conceptualizations of nursing science came from graduates of these programs. These include Peplau, Henderson, Hall, and Abdellah.

Theorists of the Columbia School operated from a biomedical model that focused primarily on what nurses do, on their functional roles. They considered patient problems and needs to be the practice focus. Independent of the Columbia theorists, Johnson (at the University of California, Los Angeles) suggested that nursing knowledge is based on a theory of nursing diagnosis that is different from medical diagnosis (Meleis, 1991).

The Yale School—The 1960s

In the 1960s theoretical thinking in nursing moved from focusing on a problem/need and the functional roles to focusing on the relationship between the nurse and the patient. The Yale School's theoretical position was influenced by the Columbia Teacher's College graduates who became faculty members there (Henderson, Orlando, and Wiedenbach).

Theorists of the Yale School view nursing as a process rather than an end in itself. They look at how nurses do what they do and how the patient perceives his or her situation. Theorists of this school include Orlando and Wiedenbach. Independent of the Yale School, Levine (1967) presented her four conservation principles of nursing.

In 1967 Yale faculty—Dickoff, James, and Wiedenbach (two philosophers and a nurse)—presented a definition of nursing theory and goals for theory development in nursing. Their paper was published in *Nursing Research* a year later and has become a classic document in the history of theoretical thinking in nursing (Dickoff et al., 1968).

It is important to note that it was during the 1960s that federal monies were made available for doctoral study for nurse educators. The resulting doctorally prepared individuals because the next wave of nurse theorists.

The 1970s

The 1970s were the decade in which many nursing theories were first presented. Most of these theories have been revised since their original presentations. Table 1–4 lists the theoretical publications of this decade.

The 1980s

In the 1980s, many nursing theories were revised on the basis of research findings that expanded them. In addition, the works of Dorothy Johnson, Rosemarie Rizzo Parse, Madeleine Leininger, and Erickson, Tomlin and Swain were added to the body of theoretical thought in nursing. The theoretical publications of the 1980s are presented in Table 1–5.

The 1990s

In the 1990s, research studies that test and expand nursing theory are numerous. *Nursing Science Quarterly* (edited by Rosemarie Rizzo Parse and published by Chestnut House) is devoted exclusively to the presentation of theory-based research findings and theoretical topics.

Rogers published "Nursing: Science of Unitary, Irreducible, Human Beings: Update 1990," the latest refinement of her theory, in *Visions of Rogers' science-based nursing,* edited by Barrett. Barrett's (1990) text contains twenty-four additional chapters about Rogers' theory and its implications for practice, research, education, and the future.

In 1992 Parse changed the language of her theory from Man-Living-Health to the theory of Human Becoming (Parse, 1992). She explained that the reason for the change is that contemporary dictionary definitions of "man" tend to be gender-based, as opposed to meaning *mankind.* The assumptions and principles of the theory remain the same, only the language is new.

In 1993 Boykin and Schoenhofer published their theory of *Nursing as Caring.* They presented this theory as a grand theory with caring as a moral imperative for nursing.

TABLE 1–4   Nursing Theories of the 1970s

Theorist	Year	Title
M. Rogers	1970	*An introduction to the theoretical basis of nursing*
I. King	1971	*Toward a theory for nursing: General concepts of human behavior*
D. Orem	1971	*Nursing: Concepts of practice*
M. Levine	1973	*Introduction to clinical nursing*
B. Neuman	1974	*The Betty Neuman Health-Care Systems Model: A total person approach to patient problems*
C. Roy	1976	*Introduction to nursing: An adaptation model*
J. Paterson & L. T. Zderad	1976	*Humanistic nursing*
M. Newman	1979	*Theory development in nursing*
J. Watson	1979	*Nursing: The philosophy and science of caring*

TABLE 1–5 Nursing Theories of the 1980s		
Theorist	**Year**	**Title(s)**
New		
Johnson	1980	The behavioral model for nursing
R. Parse	1981	*Man-living-health: A theory for nursing*
	1985	Man-living-health: A man-environment simultaneity paradigm
	1987	*Nursing science: Major paradigms, theories, critiques*
	1989	Man-living-health: A theory of nursing
H. Erickson, E. Tomlin, & M. Swain	1983	*Modeling and role modeling*
Revised/evolving		
M. Leininger	1980	Caring: A general focus of nursing and health care services
	1981	The phenomenon of caring: Importance, research, questions and theoretical considerations
	1988	Leininger's theory of nursing: Cultural care diversity and universality
D. Orem	1980	*Nursing: Concepts of practice,* 2nd ed.
	1985	*Nursing: Concepts of practice,* 3rd ed.
	1991	*Nursing: Concepts of practice,* 4th ed.
M. Rogers	1980	Nursing: A science of unitary man
	1983	Science of unitary human beings: A paradigm for nursing
	1989	Nursing: A science of unitary human beings
C. Roy	1980	The Roy Adaptation Model
	1981	*Theory construction in nursing: An adaptation model*
	1984	*Introduction to nursing: An adaptation model,* 2nd ed.
	1989	The Roy Adaptation Model
I. King	1981	*A theory for nursing: Systems, concepts, process*
	1989	King's general systems framework and theory
B. Neuman	1982	*The Neuman Systems Model*
	1989	*The Neuman Systems Model,* 2nd ed.
M. Newman	1983	Newman's health theory
	1986	*Health as expanding consciousness*
J. Watson	1985	*Nursing: Human science and human care*
	1989	Watson's philosophy and theory of human caring in nursing
M. Levine	1989	The conservation principles: Twenty years later

In 1994 Margaret Newman's second edition of her theory of health as expanding consciousness was published. This publication provided an update of her earlier work.

In 1995 Betty Neuman published her latest version of the Neuman systems model. This version is also an update rather than a major change in content.

Meleis (1992) presents six characteristics of the discipline of nursing that direct theory development in the twenty-first century:

1. The discipline of nursing is the human science underlying the discipline that is predicated on understanding the meanings of daily lived experiences as they are perceived by the members or the participants of the science.

2. There is increased emphasis on practice-orientation.

3. Nursing's mission is to develop theories to empower nurses, the discipline, and clients.

4. It is accepted that women may have different strategies and approaches to knowledge development than men do.

5. Nursing attempts to understand consumers' experiences for the purpose of empowering them to receive optimum care and to maintain optimum health.

6. The effort to broaden nursing's perspective includes efforts to understand the practice of nursing in third world countries (pp. 112–114).

Meleis (1992) forecasts that nursing theories will become theories for health, developed by nurses, physicians, occupational therapists and others. She also forecasts that the domain of nursing that focuses on environment-person interactions, energy levels, human responses, and caring will have long been accepted as a central and complementary perspective in providing health care to clients. She states that neglected aspects of care, such as advocacy, comfort, rest, access, sleep, trust, grief, symptom distress, harmony, and self-care will receive attention and will lead to collaborative programs of research and theory building.

Meleis (1992) also states that qualitative and quantitative research are *equally* essential for the development of the discipline of nursing. Theories may be single domain theories that describe, explain, or predict a phenomenon within a specific descriptive and explanatory context, or they may be prescriptive. Prescriptive theories reflect guidelines for caregivers and for providing appropriate actions. Meleis describes predictive theories of the future as having three components: levels and types of energy, mind-body wholeness, and environment-person connections.

*C*ategories of Theories

Nursing theories may be assigned to the categories of needs/problems, interaction, systems, and energy field. Assignment to a category is arbitrary, for many theories have elements of other categories within them. The nursing theories discussed in this text may be categorized as shown in Table 1–6.

Simply stated, needs/problem-oriented theorists focus on the needs and problems that clients have and seek to meet or correct them by using the nursing process. Interaction-oriented theorists focus on the communication process in the meeting of clients' needs. Systems theorists suggest that man is composed of many parts or subsystems that, when added together, are more than and different from their sum. Energy-field theorists believe that persons are energy fields in constant interaction with their environment or universe.

TABLE 1–6 Categories of Nursing Theories	
Needs/Problem-Oriented Theorists	**Interaction-Oriented Theorists**
Nightingale	Peplau
Abdellah	Orlando
Henderson	Wiedenbach
Orem	King
Hall	Paterson & Zderad
Watson	Erickson, Tomlin, & Swain
	Boykin & Schoenhofer
Systems-Oriented Theorists	**Energy Field Theorists**
Johnson	Rogers
Roy	Parse
Neuman	Newman
Levine	
Leininger	

Characteristics of a Theory

Torres (1990) presented the following characteristics of a theory:

1. **Theories can interrelate concepts in such a way as to create a different way of looking at a particular phenomenon.** Theories are constructed from concepts, which are mental images representing reality. Torres (1990) states that a theory must identify more than one concept and that the relationship between these concepts must be clear. The concepts need to be explicitly defined so that one can picture the events and experiences that the theory is designed to describe, explain, or predict. For example, a needs-oriented theorist might identify the concepts of "self-care deficit" and "nursing." The concept of self-care deficit may be described as a client who experiences an inability to perform health promotion activities. Nursing may be defined in terms of actions that can be taken to assist the client to perform health promotion activities. Theories guide practice by directing the nurse to look for needs or deficits that the client may have.

2. **Theories must be logical in nature.** Torres (1990) defines logic as orderly reasoning. Interrelationships of concepts must be sequential and consistently used within the theory. There should not be any contradictions between the definitions of concepts, their relationships within the theory, and the goals of the theory. These relationships and goals should flow directly from the theoretical assumptions. For example, if "man-universe" is defined to be in continuous interaction, this concept must be consistent in *all* parts of the theory, from the assumptions to the practice methodology.

3. **Theories should be relatively simple yet generalizable.** A theory may be defined as "tight," or *parsimonious*, if it is stated in the most simple terms possible but at the same time describes, explains, or predicts a wide range of possible experiences in nursing practice. A theory of communication that can be explained simply and generalized to all person-to-person interactions would be considered parsimonious.

4. **Theories can be the bases for hypotheses that can be tested or for theory to be expanded.** Quantitative research tests hypotheses in clinical practice and uses statistical analyses to arrive at findings. These findings represent the testing of the precision of the theory in describing, explaining, or predicting reality. Qualitative research expands theory by using a different research methodology that focuses on the lived experiences of persons. These findings represent determining, identifying, and exploring themes in the reality lived by the persons who participate in the studies.

5. **Theories contribute to and assist in increasing the general body of knowledge within the discipline through the research implemented to validate them.** Theories that can be tested, whether by quantitative or qualitative research methods, contribute to the general body of knowledge of the discipline of nursing. Validation of the theories enhances the ability of the nurse to describe, explain, predict, or control nursing practice.

6. **Theories can be used by practitioners to guide and improve their practice.** Torres (1990) states that one of the most significant characteristics of a theory is its usefulness to the practitioner. Theories guide practice by describing, explaining, or predicting events in clinical practice.

7. **Theories must be consistent with other validated theories, laws, and principles but will leave open unanswered questions that need to be investigated.** Torres (1990) states that the logic of theories and their assumptions must be based on underlying laws, previously validated knowledge, and humanitarian values that are generally accepted as good and right. However, the tentative nature of theory continues to raise questions that challenge aspects of knowledge that have not yet been challenged.

The authors of this text will compare the work of each nurse theorist with these characteristics of a theory.

A nalysis and Evaluation of Theory

There is a variety of methods for analyzing and evaluating nursing theories. Generally speaking, analysis of a theory refers to examining the content of the theory, whereas evaluation refers to a critique or judgment about the theory.

Chinn and Kramer (1991) offer a fairly simple approach to theory analysis and evaluation. They suggest that one should consider the following five criteria: clarity (semantic and structural), simplicity, generality, empirical applicability, and consequences.

Fawcett (1989) differentiates between analysis and evaluation. She developed this framework for analysis and evaluation of conceptual models, but it can readily be applied to theories. For analysis, Fawcett proposes a consideration of the historical evolution of the theory, the approach to model development, content, and source of concern. For evaluation, she proposes evaluation of the explicitness of the assumptions, degree of comprehensiveness of content, logical congruence, ability of the model to test and generate hypotheses, how much the model contributes to nursing's knowledge development and social conditions.

Barnum (1990) proposes evaluative criteria for internal criticism (internal construction) and external criticism (the theory and its relationships to people, nursing, and health). The criteria for internal criticism are clarity, consistency, adequacy, logical development, and levels of theory development. The criteria for external criticism are reality convergence, utility, significance, discrimination, scope of the theory, and complexity.

Meleis (1991) suggests a model that defines evaluation as encompassing description, analysis, critique, and testing. This model is too detailed for presentation here. The reader is referred to the reference citation for further study about this model.

S ummary

When concepts are interrelated, they provide the building blocks of theory. Theories guide nursing practice by describing, explaining, or predicting phenomena. Nursing theories interrelate the four concepts of the meta-paradigm of nursing; person, environment/society, health, and nursing. Nursing research using quantitative and qualitative methods expands or tests theory.

Theory development in nursing began with Nightingale and was revived in the 1950s. Nursing theories can be arbitrarily categorized into theories which are oriented to needs, interactions, systems, and energy fields.

The characteristics of a theory were discussed and methods for analysis and evaluation were presented in this section.

R eferences

Barnum, B. J. S. (1994). *Nursing theory: Analysis, application, and evaluation* (4th ed.). Philadelphia: Lippincott.

Barrett, E. A. M. (1990). *Visions of Rogers' science based nursing.* New York: National League for Nursing.

Boykin, A., & Schoenhofer, S. (1993). *Nursing as Caring: A model for transforming practice.* New York: National League for Nursing.

Chinn, P. L., &: Kramer, M. K. (1991). *Theory and nursing: A systematic approach* (3rd ed.). St. Louis: Mosby.

Dickoff, J., & James, P. (1968). A theory of theories: A position paper. *Nursing Research, 17,* 197–203.

Dickoff, J., James, P., & Wiedenbach, E. (1968). Theory in a practice discipline, Part 1—Practice-oriented theory. *Nursing Research, 17,* 415–435.

Erickson, H. C., Tomlin, E. M., & Swain, M. A. P. (1983). *Modeling and role-modeling.* Lexington, SC: Pine Press.

Fawcett, J. (1989). *Analysis and evaluation of conceptual models of nursing* (2nd ed.). Philadelphia: Davis.

Haase, J. E., & Meyers, S. T. (1988). Reconciling paradigm assumptions of qualitative and quantitative research. *Western Journal of Nursing Research, 10,* 132.

Johnson, D. E. (1980). The Behavioral System Model for Nursing. In J. P. Riehl, & C. Roy (Eds.), *Conceptual models for nursing practice* (2nd ed.) (pp. 207–216). New York: Appleton-Century-Crofts. [out of print]

Kerlinger, F. N. (1973). *Foundations of behavioral research* (2nd ed.). New York: Holt, Rinehart & Winston.

King, I. (1971). *Toward a theory for nursing: General concepts of human behavior.* New York: Wiley. [out of print]

King, I. M. (1981). *A theory for nursing: System, concepts, process.* New York: Wiley. (Reissued 1991, Albany, NY: Delmar.)

King, I. M. (1989). King's general systems framework and theory. In J. Riehl-Sisca (Ed.), *Conceptual models for nursing practice* (3rd ed.) (pp. 149–158). Norwalk, CT: Appleton & Lange.

Leininger, M. M. (1980). Caring: A central focus of nursing and health care services. *Nursing and Health Care, 1,* 135–143.

Leininger, M. M. (1981). The phenomenon of caring: Importance, research questions, and theoretical considerations. In M. M. Leininger (Ed.), *Caring: An essential human need* (pp. 3–15). Thorofare, NJ: Slack. [out of print]

Leininger, M. M. (1988). Leininger's theory of nursing: Culture care diversity and universality. *Nursing Science Quarterly, 1,* 152–160.

Levine, M. E. (1967). The four conservation principles. *Nursing Forum, 6,* 45–59.

Levine, M. E. (1973). *Introduction to clinical nursing.* Philadelphia: Davis. [out of print]

Levine, M. E. (1989). The conservation principles: Twenty years later. In J. Riehl-Sisca (Ed.), *Conceptual models for nursing practice* (3rd ed.) (pp. 325–337). Norwalk, CT: Appleton & Lange.

Meleis, A. I. (1991). *Theoretical nursing: Development and progress* (2nd ed.). Philadelphia; Lippincott.

Meleis, A. I. (1992). Directions for nursing theory development in the 21st century. *Nursing Science Quarterly, 5,* 112–117.

Neuman, B. (1974). The Betty Neuman Health Care Systems Model: A total person approach to patient problems. In J. P. Riehl, & C. Roy (Eds.), *Conceptual models for nursing practice,* (pp. 99–114). New York: Appleton-Century-Crofts. [out of print]

Neuman, B. (1982). *The Neuman systems model.* Norwalk, CT: Appleton-Century-Crofts. [out of print]

Neuman, B. (1989). *The Neuman systems model* (2nd ed.). Norwalk, CT: Appleton & Lange. [out of print]

Neuman, B. (1995). *The Neuman systems model* (3rd ed.) Norwalk, CT: Appleton & Lange.

Newman, M. A. (1979). *Theory development in nursing.* Philadelphia: Davis.

Newman, M. A. (1983). Newman's health theory. In I. W. Clements, & F. B. Roberts (Eds.), *Family health: A theoretical approach to nursing care* (pp. 161–175). New York: Wiley. [out of print]

Newman, M. A. (1986). *Health as expanding consciousness.* St. Louis: Mosby.

Newman, M. A. (1994). *Health as expanding consciousness* (2nd ed.). New York: National League for Nursing.

Nightingale, F. (1992). *Notes on nursing.* (Com. ed.). Philadelphia: Lippincott. (Original work published in 1859.)

Orem, D. (1971). *Nursing: Concepts of practice.* New York; McGraw-Hill. [out of print]

Orem, D. (1980). *Nursing: Concepts of practice* (2nd ed.). New York: McGraw-Hill. [out of print]

Orem, D. (1985). *Nursing: Concepts of practice* (3rd ed.). New York: McGraw-Hill. [out of print]

Orem, D. (1991). *Nursing: Concepts of practice* (4th ed.). St. Louis: Mosby.

Parse, R. R. (1987). *Nursing science: Major paradigms, theories, and critiques.* Philadelphia: Saunders.

Parse, R. R. (1989). Man-Living-Health: A theory of nursing. In J. Riehl-Sisca (Ed.), *Conceptual models for nursing practice* (3rd ed.) (pp. 253–257). Norwalk, CF: Appleton & Lange.

Parse, R. R. (1992). Human Becoming: Parse's theory of nursing. *Nursing Science Quarterly, 5,* 35–42.

Paterson, J. G., & Zderad, L. T. (1976). *Humanistic nursing.* New York: Wiley. (Reissued 1988, New York: National League for Nursing.)

Riegal, B., Omery, A., Calvillo, E., Elsayed, N. G., Lee, P., Shuler, P., & Siegal, B. E. (1992). Moving beyond: A generative philosophy of science. *Image, 24*, 115–120.

Rogers, M. E. (1970). *An introduction to the theoretical basis of nursing.* Philadelphia: Davis. [out of print]

Rogers, M. E. (1980). Nursing: A science of unitary man. In J. P. Riehl, & C. Roy (Eds.), *Conceptual models for nursing practice* (2nd ed.) (pp. 329–337). New York: Appleton-Century-Crofts. [out of print]

Rogers, M. E. (1983). Science of unitary human beings: A paradigm for nursing. In I. W. Clements, & F. B. Roberts (Eds.), *Family health: A theoretical approach to nursing care* (pp. 219–228). New York: Wiley. [out of print]

Rogers, M. E. (1989). Nursing: A science of unitary human beings. In J. Riehl-Sisca (Ed.), *Conceptual models for nursing practice* (3rd ed.) (pp. 181–188). Norwalk, CT: Appleton & Lange.

Rogers, M. E. (1990). Nursing: Science of unitary, irreducible human beings. In E. A. M. Barrett (Ed.), *Visions of Rogers' science based nursing* (pp. 5–11). New York: National League for Nursing.

Roy, C. (1976). *Introduction to nursing: An adaptation model.* Englewood Cliffs: Prentice-Hall. [out of print]

Roy, C. (1980). The Roy Adaptation Model. In J. P. Riehl, & C. Roy (Eds.), *Conceptual models for nursing practice* (2nd ed.) (pp. 179–188). New York: Appleton-Century-Crofts. [out of print]

Roy, C. (1984). *Introduction to nursing: An adaptation model* (2nd ed.). Norwalk, CT: Appleton-Century-Crofts.

Roy, C. (1989). The Roy Adaptation Model. In J. Riehl-Sisca (Ed.), *Conceptual models for nursing practice* (3rd ed.) (pp. 105–114). Norwalk, CT: Appleton & Lange.

Roy, C., & Roberts, S. (1981). *Theory construction in nursing: An adaptation model.* Englewood Cliffs: Prentice-Hall. [out of print]

Torres, G. (1990). The place of concepts and theories within nursing. In J. B. George (Ed.), *Nursing theories: The base for professional nursing practice* (3rd ed.) (pp. 1–12). Norwalk, CT: Appleton & Lange.

Watson, J. (1979). *Nursing: The philosophy and science of caring.* Boston: Little, Brown. [out of print]

Watson, J. (1985). *Nursing: Human science and human care.* Norwalk, CT: Appleton-Century-Crofts. (Reissued 1988, New York: National League for Nursing.)

Watson, J. (1989). Watson's philosophy and theory of human caring. In J. Riehl-Sisca (Ed.), *Conceptual models for nursing practice* (3rd ed.) (pp. 219–236). Norwalk, CT: Appleton & Lange.

*Webster's ninth new collegiate dictionary. (1991). Springfield, MA: Merriam.

Concept Development

$\mathcal{I}$ntroduction to Concept Development

Concept development is a critical but often neglected approach to theory development in nursing and indeed in many scientific disciplines. The very basis of any theory depends on the identification and explication of the concepts to be considered in it. Yet many attempts to describe, explain, or predict phenomena start without a clear understanding of what is to be described, explained, or predicted. The next three chapters will focus on ways to develop concepts systematically.

Concept development is needed when one of three situations occurs. The first situation requiring concept development is one in which few concepts or no concepts are available in the theorist's focal area of interest. In this case the theorist must somehow obtain or invent concepts that are relevant to the phenomenon of concern. Either concept derivation or concept synthesis would be useful strategies.

The second situation requiring concept development is one in which concepts are already available in the area of interest but they are unclear, outmoded, or unhelpful. In this situation the theorist might choose to do a concept analysis of one or more of the unclear concepts in an effort to refine and clarify the concept. If the concepts are outmoded, then concept derivation might provide new ones that could provide useful insights.

The third situation requiring concept development is one in which a lot of theoretical literature or a lot of research on a topic of interest exists, but somehow the literature and the research do not match. This does not occur often. However, on occasion theorists may be working at one level on an area of interest and researchers or practitioners are working at another level and there is no clear bridge between the two. This has in fact happened in some of the nursing diagnosis work. When this occurs, careful concept development on some of the bridge concepts can be very helpful. The most useful strategy for this kind of work is often concept derivation.

When you are trying to decide where to start with theory development, it might help to ask some questions before you begin. Such things as the level of theory development, the type of

---

Taken from: *Strategies for Theory Construction in Nursing*, Third Edition by Walker and Avant.

available literature, and the direction of the literature in the focal area of interest will all provide clues about where to begin. If any of the three situations above are predominant then one of the concept development strategies is the best place to begin.

Careful concept development is the basis of any attempt to describe or explain phenomena. It is also prerequisite to any adequate theory. By using one of the strategies discussed in the next three chapters, you will get off to a good start in your efforts at theory development.

Concept Analysis

Definition and Description

Concept analysis is a strategy that allows us to examine the attributes or characteristics of a concept. Concepts contain within them the defining characteristics or attributes that permit us to decide which phenomena are good examples of the concept and which are not. Concepts are mental constructions; they are our attempts to order our environmental stimuli. Concepts, therefore, represent categories of information that contain defining attributes. Concept analysis is a formal, linguistic exercise to determine those defining attributes. The analysis itself must be rigorous and precise but the end product is always tentative. The reasons for this tentativeness stem from the fact that two people will often come up with somewhat different attributes for the same concept in their analyses and from the fact that scientific and general knowledge changes so quickly that what is "true" today is "not true" tomorrow.

A further reason for the tentativeness of a concept analysis is that concepts change over time—often slowly, but occasionally very quickly. Therefore, anyone undertaking concept analysis should be aware of the dynamic quality of ideas and the words that express those ideas. Concepts are not carved in stone. Analysts change over time as well. Therefore their understanding of the concept may also change over time. This is one reason why concept analyses should never be viewed as a "finished product." The best one can hope for from a concept analysis is to capture the critical elements of it at the current moment in time. However, this is not to imply that trying to determine the defining attributes of a concept of interest is futile—far from it.

Concept analysis encourages communication. If we are precise about carefully defining the attributes of the concepts we use in theory development and in research, we will make it far easier to promote understanding among our colleagues about the phenomena being discussed.

Taken from: *Strategies for Theory Construction in Nursing*, Third Edition by Walker and Avant.

$\mathcal{P}$urpose and Uses

The basic purpose of concept analysis is to distinguish between the defining attributes of a concept and its irrelevant attributes. It is a process of determining the likeness and unlikeness between concepts. By breaking a concept into its simpler elements, it is easier to determine its internal structure. Since a concept is expressed by a word or a term in language (Reynolds, 1971), an analysis of a concept must, perforce, be an analysis of the descriptive word and its use. Concept analysis is ultimately only a careful examination and description of a word and its uses in the language coupled with an explanation of how it is "like" and "not like" other related words. We are concerned with both actual and possible uses of words that convey concept meanings.

Concept analysis is useful for several reasons. It can be useful in refining ambiguous concepts in a theory. It can help clarify those overused vague concepts that are prevalent in nursing practice so that everyone who subsequently uses the term will be speaking of the same thing. And concept analysis results in a precise operational definition that by its very nature has construct validity; that is, it will accurately reflect its theoretical base.

Concept analysis is an excellent way to begin examining information in preparation for research or theory construction. The results yield to the theorist or investigator a basic understanding of the underlying attributes of the concepts. This helps to clearly define the problem and to allow the investigator or theorist to construct hypotheses that accurately reflect the relationships between the concepts.

But perhaps the two most fruitful uses of concept analysis are in tool development and in developing nursing diagnoses. Nunnally (1978) has spoken to the need for careful conceptual development for research instruments. The results of concept analysis—the operational definition, list of defining attributes, and antecedents—can provide the scientist with an excellent beginning for a new tool or an excellent way to evaluate an old one. To begin a new tool, items could be constructed to reflect each of the defining attributes. Questions could be constructed to determine whether proposed antecedents occurred. With careful psychometric testing, the new tool could be useful for continuing research by interested scientists. The results of concept analysis are also useful in evaluating existing instruments. The instruments to be used in a research project could be examined in light of the results of the concept analysis to determine if the instruments accurately reflect the defining attributes of the relevant concepts.

The other primary use of concept analysis is in developing or evaluating nursing diagnoses. In many cases, nursing diagnoses have been developed consensually or in practice settings without thoroughly considering the theoretical or moral issues relating to assigning labels to clients or placing clients into diagnostic categories. It is not in the purview of this book to deal with the moral issues. However, it is within our purview to suggest that conducting a thorough concept analysis for any potential diagnosis would greatly facilitate taxonomic work and would thoroughly ground the nursing diagnosis in the pertinent theoretical and research literature. That is, each nursing diagnosis should be treated as a separate concept and should be analyzed independently. Most nursing diagnoses are written with three components—the health problem, the etiology, and the defining signs and symptoms (Gordon, 1982). These three components closely parallel the results of concept analysis—antecedents (etiology), defining characteristics (defining signs and symptoms), and operational definition (health problem). It seems reasonable to suggest using the two processes iteratively to improve our taxonomies and contribute to theory development simultaneously.

In the following pages we will discuss the steps in a classic concept analysis. The method we put forward here is only one of several methods available for concept analysis. We feel it is the easiest to understand and master, especially for beginners. For those who wish to examine other methods, Rodgers and Knafl's (1993) book on concept development is a good start.

Specific Procedures

According to Wilson (1963), there are eleven steps in concept analysis. We have modified and simplified his procedure so there are only eight steps. These are:

1. Select a concept.

2. Determine the aims or purposes of analysis.

3. Identify all uses of the concept that you can discover.

4. Determine the defining attributes.

5. Construct a model case.

6. Construct borderline, related, contrary, invented, and illegitimate cases.

7. Identify antecedents and consequences.

8. Define empirical referents.

The steps in conducting a concept analysis will be discussed as if they were sequential. In fact, however, many of these steps occur simultaneously. Often some revision must be made in an earlier step because of information or ideas arising from a later one. This is to be expected. The iterative nature of the process results in a much cleaner, more precise analysis.

Select a Concept

The first step is often the hardest. Concept selection should be done with care. It is best to choose a concept in which you are already interested, one that is associated with your work, or one that has always "bothered" you.

It is important to avoid primitive terms that can be defined only by giving examples. It is equally important to avoid "umbrella" terms that are so broad they may encompass several meanings and confuse the analysis. Generally, concept selection should reflect the topic or area of greatest interest to you. Unexplored concepts can be found in nursing practice, can be generated from nursing research studies, or can be drawn from a theory that is as yet incomplete or that has concepts that are unclear. However, the concept should be one that is important and useful to your research program or to further theoretical developments in your area of interest. Choosing a trivial concept or one that does not contribute significantly to knowledge development about your phenomenon of concern is an exercise in futility and a waste of your valuable time.

Aims of Analysis

The second step in a concept analysis is to determine the aims or purposes of the analysis. This second step helps focus attention on exactly what use you intend to make of the results of your effort. It essentially answers the question: "Why am I doing this analysis?"

Some aims of an analysis might be to clarify the meaning of an existing concept, to develop an operational definition, or to add to existing theory. Another aim might be to distinguish between the normal, ordinary language usage of the concept and the scientific usage of the same concept. There are other possible purposes. The important thing is to decide for your-self, in advance, why you are interested in conducting a concept analysis. This definition of pur-pose is useful if as you begin to determine the defining attributes you discover several very dissimilar uses of the concept. The selection you make regarding which specific use of the con-cept you will choose should reflect the aims of the analysis.

Identify Uses of the Concept

The next step is to identify as many uses of the concept as you can find. To accomplish this, you may use dictionaries, thesauruses, colleagues, and available literature. At this initial stage do not limit yourself to only one aspect of the concept. You must consider all uses of the term. Do not limit your search to just nursing or medical literature as this may bias your understand-ing of the true nature of the concept. Ignoring the physical aspects of a concept and focusing only on the psychosocial, for instance, may deprive you of a great deal of valuable informa-tion. Remember to include both implicit as well as explicit uses of the concept. Extensive read-ing in as many different sources as possible is invaluable. This review of literature helps you support or validate your ultimate choices of the defining attributes.

For instance, if you were examining the concept of "coping," you would discover that not only are there psychological uses for the term but there are copings on buildings, coping saws, a method of trimming a falcon's beak called coping, and a coping that is an ecclesiastical gar-ment similar to a cloak. All of these uses of the term must be included in your final analysis.

Failing to identify, or worse, ignoring some uses of a concept may result in an analysis which severely limits the usefulness of the outcome. A few years ago, one of our students was analyzing the concept "presence" as it relates to the care of hospitalized children. In the initial phase, the student reported many positive uses of the concept but none that were negative. When other students mentioned things such as "evil presence" or "presence of a hostile army on the border," the student was reluctant to consider those aspects of "presence." Yet, in the final analysis, one critical attribute of the nurse's "presence" with a hospitalized child turned out to be the potential for threat engendered in the presence.

Occasionally, once you have identified all the usages of the concept, both ordinary and scientific, you may have to decide whether to continue to consider all aspects of the concept or only those pertinent to the scientific use. We generally feel that when possible you should continue to consider all aspects of the concept usage since that is likely to yield richer mean-ings. However, at times that will clearly be impractical or unhelpful. In these cases, use the aims of your analysis to guide your decision making.

As you collect the instances of concept use, you will find other instances that are similar or related to the concept being analyzed but are not quite the "real thing." Keep a list of these related and borderline instances. They will be helpful to you when you begin to construct bor-derline or related cases.

Determine Defining Attributes

When you have examined as many of the different instances of a concept as you can find, read through them all at once. As you read, make notes of the characteristics of the concept that appear over and over again. This list of characteristics, called defining or critical attributes, functions very much like the criteria for making differential diagnoses in medicine. That is, they help you and others name the occurrence of a specific phenomenon as differentiated from another similar or related one.

The defining attributes are not immutable. They may change as your understanding of the concept improves. They may change slightly over time if the concept changes. Or they may change when used in a different context than the one under study. The effort is to try to show the cluster of attributes that are the most frequently associated with the concept and that allow the analyst the broadest insight into the concept.

Sometimes when you have gathered all the instances of a concept there will be a large number of possible meanings. A decision is clearly necessary regarding which will be the most useful and which will provide you the greatest help in relation to the aims of your analysis. You may decide to choose more than one meaning and continue analyzing using several meanings. For example, in the analysis of the concept of "attachment" at the end of this section we found that attachment can occur in both animate and inanimate forms. We chose to examine which attributes were common to both kinds and then to continue our analysis further to include the specific defining attributes for animate attachment since our area of interest was in mother-infant attachment (Avant, 1979). Consideration of the social or nursing care context in which the concept is to be used may be important in your decision as it was to us in the example. The final decision is up to you.

For instance, in our example of the concept "coping," the three characteristics that seemed to be most obvious among all those divergent uses of the term were (1) the attribute of covering something—an action, a cape, a window, a beak, (2) the attribute of protection—one's psyche, the garment under the cape, the flowers under the window, and (3) the attribute of adjusting or rebalancing. We decided that the idea of the coping saw was not relevant to the general concept since it does not reflect any of the three attributes that occur in all the other instances we have found. We will use this, in fact, as the example of an "illegitimate" case later in the analysis—one in which the term is used incorrectly in relation to its generally accepted meaning.

Develop Model Case(s)

At about the same time that you are developing the list of defining attributes, you should begin to develop a model case or cases. The model case can come first, may be developed simultaneously with the attributes, or may emerge after the attributes are tentatively determined. A model case is a "real life" example of the use of the concept that includes all the critical attributes of the concept. That is, the model case should be a pure case of the concept, a paradigmatic example. In fact, when a concept is reasonably new to you, a model case may come first in your analysis. At this stage it is often helpful and sometimes necessary to seek out a thoughtful colleague or two who can listen with a fresh ear as you talk through your examples. If there are flaws or errors you haven't seen, it is likely that someone else can spot them for you.

Basically, the model case is one that we are absolutely sure is an instance of the concept. Wilson (1963) suggests that the model case is one in which the analyst can say, "Well, if that isn't an example of it, then nothing is." Model cases may be constructed by you or may be actual case examples from real life. Some concepts lend themselves more easily than others to this effort. At times the best you will be able to do may be a little fuzzy at the edges, especially if the concept has a lot of synonyms or related concepts that overlap the concept of interest. Don't despair. The effort here is to try to keep the case as paradigmatic as possible.

In our coping example, for instance, the model case was stated as follows:

> A young woman is walking along a street wearing high heels and a silk dress. On her briefcase is a pouch with an umbrella in it. As she walks, it begins to rain heavily. She takes out her umbrella and raises it. She begins to run, but stumbles. She stops, removes her shoes quickly, and resumes running to the nearest shelter.

This model case includes all three of the critical attributes, covering, protection, and rebalancing. There are several other examples, or cases, of coping that could have been used instead. We tried to use one that was simple and commonplace for demonstration.

Develop Additional Cases

Often it is difficult to tease out the defining attributes that are the most representative of the concept of interest as they may overlap with some related concepts. Examining cases that are not exactly the same as the concept of interest but are similar to it or contrary to it in some ways will help you make better judgments about which defining characteristics have the best "fit" for the concept of interest. We will discuss several types of cases that have proved useful in the past. The basic purpose for the use of these cases is to help you come to a decision about what "counts" as a defining attribute for the concept of interest and what doesn't "count." The cases we will suggest here are borderline, related, invented, and contrary cases. These cases are constructed for the purpose of providing examples of "not the concept" and for promoting further understanding of the concept being discussed. Again, these cases maybe "real life" examples. We use the term "develop" since you must find the examples and set them up in such a way as to be useful to your analysis.

Borderline cases are those examples or instances that contain some of the critical attributes of the concept being examined but not all of them. They may even contain most or all of the criteria but differ substantially in one of them, such as length of time or intensity of occurrence. These cases are inconsistent in some way and as such they help us see why the model case is not. In this way we help clarify our thinking about the defining or critical attributes of the concept of interest. Again using the coping example, a borderline case might be that of a college student who was facing a big exam. He had not studied until the evening before the test, when he "crammed all night." Halfway through the examination, he fell fast asleep and thereby flunked the test. This meets both attributes of covering and protection but breaks down when it comes to rebalancing.

Perhaps another example of a borderline case will make things even clearer. Since concepts act as a way of helping us classify things, we gave students an exercise in class. We asked them to categorize the contents of their closet. One student classified her clothes as "things I wear above my waist" and "things I wear below my waist." She was puzzled as to how to classify the belts since they were worn at the waist. This is a classic, indeed a concrete, example of a borderline case since the belt may fit into either category and yet really belongs to neither.

Related cases are instances of concepts that are related to the concept being studied but that do not contain the critical attributes. They are similar to the concept being studied. They are in some way connected to the main concept. The related cases help us understand how the concept being studied fits into the network of concepts surrounding it. Concepts that could be developed into related cases in our coping example, for instance, might be "stress," "conflict," "achievement," and "adaptation." Related cases are those cases that demonstrate ideas that are very similar to the main concept but that differ from them when examined closely.

Contrary cases are those that are clear examples of "not the concept." Again, Wilson (1963) suggests that it can be said of the contrary case, "Well, whatever the concept is, that is certainly not an instance of it." In our coping example, for instance, the contrary case might describe a young woman who is preparing dinner for a group of people. The roast burns on one end. She becomes hysterical, throws out the whole roast, and sends her guests home unfed. We can see from this example that whatever "coping" is, that young woman's behavior is not an example of it. It meets none of the three critical attributes we have said must pertain to an instance of coping—covering, protection, and rebalancing. Contrary cases are often very helpful to the analyst, since we often find it easier to say what something is not than what

TABLE 1-7 Examples of Concept Analyses

Concept(s)	Author(s)	Journal	Year
Aggregate	Schultz	Adv in Nsg Sci	1987
Meaning in suffering	Steeves & Kahn	Image	1987
Health	Simmons	Int J of Nsg Stud	1989
Reassurance	Teasdale	J of Adv Nsg	1989
Feeling	Beyea	Nsg Diagnosis	1990
Family management style	Knafl & Deatrick	J of Ped Nsg	1990
Quality of life	Oleson	Image	1990
Therapeutic reciprocity	Marck	Adv in Nsg Sci	1990
Comfort	Kolcaba	Image	1991
Serenity	Roberts & Fitzgerald	Schol Inquiry for Nsg Prac	1991
Chronic sorrow	Teel	J of Adv Nsg	1991
Experience	Watson	J of Adv Nsg	1991
Hypothermia	Summers	Nsg Diagnosis	1992
Spiritual perspective, hope, acceptance self transcendence	Hasse, Britt, Coward, Leidy & Penn	Image	1992
Empathy	Morse, Anderson, Bottorff, Yonge, O'Brien, Solberg, McIlveen	Image	1992
Pain management	Davis	Adv in Nsg Sci	1992
Knowing the patient	Jenny & Logan	Image	1992
Preventive health behavior	Kulbok & Baldwin	Adv in Nsg Sci	1992
Fear	Whitley	Nsg Diagnosis	1992
Quality of life	Meeberg	J of Adv Nsg	1993

it is; and discovering what a concept is not helps us see in what ways the concept being analyzed is different from the contrary case. This, in turn, gives us information about what the concept should have as defining attributes if the ones from the contrary case are clearly excluded.

Invented cases are cases that are constructed using ideas outside our own experience. They often read like science fiction. Invented cases are useful when you are examining a very familiar concept such as "man," or "love," or one that is such a commonplace as to be taken for granted, such as "air." Often to get a true picture of the critical defining attributes, you must take the concept out of its ordinary context and put it into an invented one.

For example, suppose that a being from another planet visited earth. His physiology is such that when he becomes upset or frightened in our atmosphere, he floats straight up into the air, often bumping his head sharply on ceilings. He begins carrying a cement block in his backpack to keep him on the ground. In addition, he pads his helmet and wears it constantly. This is an example of coping in an invented case.

The last type of case is not always included in a concept analysis. It is the **illegitimate case**. These cases give an example of the concept term used improperly or out of context. In the case of the coping saw, the use of the term "coping" demonstrates neither the attribute of "covering" nor the one of "protection" and so is illegitimately used. These cases are helpful when you come across one meaning for a term that is completely different from all the others. It may have one or two of the critical attributes, but most of the attributes will not apply at all. In the "attachment" analysis at the end of this section, the term "attachment" as used to mean those pieces that fit onto a sewing machine contains only the attribute of "touch" and none of the other four.

Once the model cases are constructed, they must be compared to the critical or defining attributes one more time to ensure that all the critical attributes have been discovered. Sometimes, once the model case is constructed and compared with the other cases and the proposed critical attributes, some areas of overlap, vagueness, or contradiction will become apparent. It is at this point that further refinement becomes necessary. An analysis cannot be completed until there are no overlapping attributes and no contradictions between the defining attributes and the model case.

Identify Antecedents and Consequences

The next steps in a concept analysis are the identification of antecedents and consequences. Although these two steps are often ignored, they may shed considerable light on the social contexts in which the concept is generally used. They are also helpful in further refining the critical attributes. Something cannot be an antecedent and an attribute at the same time, for example. Antecedents are those events or incidents that must occur prior to the occurrence of the concept. For example, Ward (1986) gives a clear example of antecedents of role strain, identifying role conflict, role accumulation, rigidity of time and place, which role demands must be met, and the amount of activity prescribed by some roles as the antecedents. Consequences, on the other hand, are those events or incidents that occur as a result of the occurrence of the concept. For example, Rew (1986) indicates that one consequence of intuition is discovery. In our coping example, one antecedent was an intensely stressful stimulus (the burned roast); the consequence was the regaining of balance. Another clear example presents itself to us: If we examine the concept of "pregnancy," one of the antecedents is clearly ovulation, while a consequence is some kind of delivery experience whether or not the pregnancy goes to term or produces a viable baby.

Antecedents and consequences are often extremely useful theoretically. Blalock (1969) has spoken of constructing theoretical models of determinants and results around a focal variable or construct. His notion of determinants and results is very close to the notion of antecedents and consequences in concept analysis. Antecedents are also useful in helping the theorist identify underlying assumptions about the concept being studied. In our attachment example at the end of this section, you will see that one of the antecedents is the ability to distinguish between internal and external stimuli. This implies that an assumption of living, sentient beings has been made. Consequences are useful in determining often neglected ideas, variables, or relationships that may yield fruitful new research directions.

Define Empirical Referents

The final step is to determine the empirical referents for the critical attributes. In many cases the critical attributes and the empirical referents will be identical. However, there are times when the concept being analyzed is highly abstract and so are its critical attributes. In these cases, the question arises, "If we are to measure this concept or determine its existence in the real world, how do we do so?" Empirical referents are classes or categories of actual phenomena that by their existence or presence demonstrate the occurrence of the concept itself. As an example, "kissing" might be used as an empirical referent for the concept of "affection." In our "coping" example an empirical referent might be "ability to successfully solve a problem in a stressful situation."

Empirical referents, once identified, are extremely useful in instrument development because they are clearly linked to the theoretical base of the concept, thus contributing to both the content and construct validity of any new instrument. They are also very useful in practice since they provide the clinician with clear, observable phenomena by which to "diagnose" the existence of the concept in particular clients. The Boyd (1985), Rew (1986), Meize-Grochowski (1984), and Ward (1986) articles listed in the reference section of this section all have good examples of empirical referents.

*A*dvantages and Limitations

The main advantage of concept analysis is that it renders very precise theoretical as well as operational definitions for use in theory and research. Another advantage is that concept analysis could help clarify those terms in nursing that have become catchphrases and hence have lost their meanings. A third advantage is its utility for tool development and nursing diagnosis. Additionally, the rigorousness of this intellectual exercise is extremely good practice in thinking.

The limitations are that the theorist must be painstaking and is likely to encounter pitfalls that will hinder the analysis.

Concept analysis clarifies the symbols used in communication. There are few firm rules for concept analysis. Table 1–7 will provide you with several examples of concept analyses using several different sets of rules. But there are some pitfalls you should avoid. These pitfalls tend to obscure the meanings you want to convey (Wilson, 1963). They are:

1. The tendency to moralize when the concept being analyzed has some value implications. Many concepts hold some implicit if not explicit value to us. As we begin a concept analysis it is important to recognize that just choosing the concept demonstrates a bias on our part. We must be doubly careful, then, to treat the concept objectively as subject matter rather than subjectively as a persuasive weapon.

2. The feeling of being absolutely in over your head. Since there are no firm rules in concept analysis, this may make you very anxious. There is no way we can say to you, "First do this, then do that, and when you have done so, all will be wonderful." We have attempted to give you guidelines, but the actual intellectual work must be yours. Once you have begun, the anxiety subsides and the fun begins.

3. The feeling that concept analysis is too easy. Some people initially grow impatient with the process and tend to throw up their hands with the comment, "Well, everybody knows that term means so-and-so. Why do we need to keep on with this?" The point is that not everybody knows what it means. Concept analysis is not easy; it is a vigorous intellectual exercise, but it is fruitful and useful and even enjoyable.

4. The compulsion to analyze everything, or the "how-do-you-turn-it-off syndrome," as one of our students calls it. This occurs fairly often in students. The process of analysis somehow gets their creative juices flowing and they get very excited. The result is often that they don't want to stop. There are some concepts more worthy of analysis than others, but all analyses must finally come to an end. In addition, analysis is only one strategy in theory development. Some energy should be saved for the rest!

5. The need to protect oneself from others' criticism or debate during the process of analysis. Good concept analysis cannot occur in a vacuum. Only the insights and criticisms of others can fully expand the analyst's ideas. The willingness to look foolish is one of the criteria for creativity. If you restrain yourself in discussions or fail to seek criticism because you may look "silly" or "dumb," you are cutting yourself off from successful concept development. In dealing with concept analysis, it is vital to say something and then trust that it will lead somewhere.

6. The feeling that verbal facility equals thinking. There is sometimes a tendency to engage in superficial fluency instead of productive dialogue. Most of us know people who can talk or write easily but have little of real substance to say. There are times in concept analysis when the analyst must struggle with difficult and substantive problems. It is often tempting to go for the hasty solution or to beg the question by substituting verbiage for substance. But the results of hasty analysis are meager and unproductive. It is far more helpful to "hang in there" with the difficulties until you solve them in a way that provides the best results, not the easiest.

7. Another pitfall in concept analysis may occur if theorists attempt to add critical attributes because they see that their list is short. Doing so can confound the results of the analysis since many of the added attributes are not critical to the concept and may even overlap the antecedents and consequences. A rule of thumb is to "quit when you're done" with the original analysis.

Any or all of these pitfalls hinder analysis. A sense of proportion, a little risk taking, a sense of humor, and a low anxiety level are all helpful in the process of analysis. This is a new way of thinking for many people and as such requires a little getting used to in the beginning. It is a very important aspect to theory construction. Since concepts are the bricks of theory development, it is critical that they be structurally sound. If a theory contains careful concept analyses, all who read the theory or use it in practice will be able to clearly understand what is meant by the concepts within it and their relationships to each other.

Finally, concepts, even well-analyzed ones, can contribute only the basics of theory. Only when concepts are studied for relationships among them and relational statements are constructed can real forward progress be made in theory construction.

$\mathcal{U}$tilizing the Results of Concept Analysis

We have discussed several uses of the results of concept analysis. These are refining ambiguous terms in theory, education, research, and practice; providing operational definitions with a clear theoretical base; providing an understanding of the underlying attributes of a concept; facilitating instrument development in research; and providing assistance in the development of nursing diagnoses. However, once a concept has been analyzed, what is the next step for the theorist? This depends in part on the aims of the analysis. If one of the aims, for instance, was to develop an instrument, then the next step would be to construct items that would reflect the defining attributes of the concept. If the aim was to propose a nursing diagnosis, the next step would be to clinically validate the defining attributes. Using the empirical referents for the defining attributes and assessing clients for the presence or absence of the attributes would help substantiate the potential diagnosis. If the aim was to construct an operational definition, the next step would be to attempt to find a research instrument that accurately reflects the defining attributes of the concept.

It is clear that concept analysis alone will not provide useful theories for nursing education, research, or practice. It will only be when the concepts are linked to each other that useful theories will result. In the meantime, scientists, educators, and clinicians should continue to examine concepts critically in an effort to refine our knowledge and to discover what those linkages are.

$\mathcal{S}$ummary

This section has described the process of concept analysis. This strategy employs the processes of analysis to extract the defining, or critical, attributes of a concept. There are no rules for accomplishing the analysis. Selection of the concept and the theorist's familiarity with the literature will have some impact on where the theorist begins. The steps in concept analysis include selecting the concept, determining the aims of analysis, identifying all uses of the concept, determining the defining or critical attributes of the concept, constructing model cases, constructing additional cases, defining identifying antecedents and consequences, and defining empirical referents.

Concept analysis increases the richness of our vocabulary and provides precise and rigorously constructed theoretical and operational definitions for use in theory and research. It is limited by the level of theory that can be attained using only concepts.

There has been some criticism of the method we propose here as being positivistic, reductionistic, rigid, and requiring a correspondence theory of truth (Rodgers, 1988). It has never been our intent to subscribe to these tenets. Indeed, it is not the intent of most current philosophers of science to subscribe to such outmoded views (Schumacher & Gortner, 1992). However, there are some reasonable and logical methods which have served the development of science in many disciplines over time. Nursing science will be judged by whether it solves "significant disciplinary problems" (DeGroot, 1988), "offers defensible interpretations of multiple realities of interest to nurses" (Coward, 1990), or provides practitioners with an adequate and holistic knowledge base from which to practice (Avant, 1991). It is our belief that concept analysis, using the method proposed here, will be a useful tool in fulfilling these criteria. We leave it up to the reader to make the final judgment as to the usefulness and validity of the method.

$\mathcal{P}$ractice Exercise and One Additional Example

To aid you with the subsequent practice exercise, we have presented below a brief summary of a concept analysis of "attachment." This is by no means a complete, formal analysis. It is presented merely to show you how one looks as it is developed.

Concept: Attachment.

Aim of Analysis: Develop operational definition of theoretical concept.

Critical Attributes:

All cases of attachment:

1. Visual contact must have been made between the person and the object of attachment.

2. The object of attachment must have been touched by the person at some time during the process of attachment.

3. There must be some positive affect associated with the object of attachment.

Cases of animate attachment have in addition to the above:

4. There must be reciprocal interaction between the two parties in attachment.

5. Vocalization by at least one of the two parties is supportive of attachment process.

Model Cases

■ Person-to-Object Attachment

A woman explains to her friend that she simply can't throw out her old bathrobe because she has had it since she married and is just too "attached to it."

■ Person-to-Person Attachment

An eight-month-old boy is playing in the room where his mother is sewing. As he plays, he occasionally looks around at her, or comes over and touches her. When she leaves the room, he cries and begins to search for her. When she returns, he climbs into her lap. She hugs him close and talks to him until he is ready to continue playing.

■ Contrary Case

A 22-year-old woman delivers a baby under general anesthesia and cesarean section as a result of abruptio placenta. The infant is about 26 weeks' gestation and weighs 2 lbs. He is immediately transferred to the regional perinatal center 200 miles away. When the mother wakes from anesthesia, she is told she has a 2-lb. baby boy and also about his transfer. She is told the baby will stay in the hospital until he weighs about 5 lbs. Due to postpartum complications, the mother is not released from the hospital for three weeks. Even though her husband brings reports of the baby, she says "Do I really have a baby?"

■ Borderline Case

Jeffrey is being seen at the health clinic for possible child abuse. Jeffrey is blind due to retrolental fibroplasia. He also has spastic cerebral palsy. Jeffrey's mother says she gets angry because he won't look at her or cuddle when she picks him up. When he cries too long, she hits him. This is borderline attachment because two defining characteristics, touch and vocalization, are met. Visual contact, positive affect, and reciprocal interaction are absent or severely diminished. Attachment may still occur, but it will be difficult.

■ Related Cases

Love	Deprivation
Separation	Dependency
Detachment	Symbiosis

■ Illegitimate Case

A salesman demonstrating a new sewing machine makes a point of explaining "the most useful attachment—the buttonholer."

- Antecedents
    1. Ability to distinguish between internal and external stimuli.
    2. Ability to receive and respond to cues of the persons involved in attachment process.

- Consequences
    1. Proximity-maintaining behavior
    2. Separation anxiety

- Empirical Referents. Examples:
    1. Eye-to-eye contact
    2. Patting, stroking, holding hands, etc.
    3. Speaking positively about the person
    4. Speaking, singing, reading to the person

Practice Exercise

Analyze the concept of "play" using the foregoing analysis as a guide. Some of your critical attributes probably were similar to the ones below:

1. Movement or activity
2. One animate entity
3. Voluntariness or choice
4. Expectation of diversion or pleasure
5. Novelty or unpredictability
6. Creativity

Did you remember to include the ideas "play on words," "play in the steering wheel," "play" as in a drama, and so forth?

Using the critical attributes above, develop a model case that includes all of them.

What are some related concepts? How about "games," "work," "exercise," "performance," "imitate," "sport"?

Try developing a contrary case using "work" as "not play." Use the concept "exercise" as a borderline case.

Complete the analysis using the outline given.

References

Avant K: Nursing diagnosis: Maternal attachment. Adv Nurs Sci 2(1):45–56, 1979.

Avant KC: The theory-research dialectic: A different approach. *Nurs Sci Q* 4(1):2, 1991.

Beyea SC: Concept analysis of feeling: A human response pattern. *Nurs Diag* 1(3):97–101, 1990.

Blalock HM: *Theory Construction From Verbal to Mathematical Formulations.* Englewood Cliffs, NJ: Prentice-Hall, 1969.

Boyd C: Toward an understanding of mother–daughter identification using concept analysis. *Adv Nurs Sci* 7(3):78–86, 1985.

Coward DD: Critical multiplism: A research strategy for nursing science. *Image* 22(3):163–166, 1990.

Davis G: The meaning of pain management: A concept analysis. *Adv Nurs Sci* 15(1):77–86, 1992.

DeGroot HA: Scientific inquiry in nursing: A model for a new age. *Adv Nurs Sci* 10(3):1–21, 1988.

Gordon M: *Nursing Diagnosis: Process and Application*. New York: McGraw-Hill, 1982.

Haase JE, Britt T, Coward DD, Leidy NK, Penn PE: Simultaneous concept analysis of spiritual perspective, hope, acceptance, and self-transcendence. *Image* 24(2):141–147, 1992.

Jenny J, Logan J: Knowing the patient: One aspect of clinical knowledge. *Image* 24(4):254–258, 1992.

Knafl KA, Deatrick JA: Family management style: Concept analysis and development. *J Pediatr Nurs* 5(1):4–14, 1990.

Kolcaba KY: A taxonomic structure for the concept comfort. *Image* 23(4):237–240, 1991.

Kulbock PA, Baldwin JH: From preventive health behavior to health promotion: Advancing a positive construct of health. *Adv Nurs Sci* 14(4):5064, 1992.

Marck P: Therapeutic reciprocity: A caring phenomenon. *Adv Nurs Sci* 13(1):49–59, 1990.

Meeberg GA: Quality of life: A concept analysis. *J Adv Nurs* 18:3238, 1993.

Meize-Grochowski R: An analysis of the concept of trust. *J Adv Nurs* 9:563–572, 1984.

Morse JM, Anderson G, Bottorff JL, Yonge O, O'Brien B, Solberg SM, McIlveen KH: Exploring empathy: A conceptual fit for nursing practice. *Image* 24(4):273–280, 1992.

Nunnally J: *Psychometric Theory*. New York: McGraw-Hill, 1978.

Oleson M: Subjectively perceived quality of life. *Image* 22(3):187–190, 1990.

Rew L: Intuition: Concept analysis of a group phenomenon. *Adv Nurs Sci* 8(2):21–28, 1986.

Reynolds PD: *A Primer in Theory Construction*. Indianapolis: Bobbs-Merrill 1971.

Roberts KT, Fitzgerald L: Serenity: Caring with perspective. *Schol Inquiry Nurs Pract* 5(2):127–141, 1991.

Rodgers BL: Concepts, analysis and the development of nursing knowledge: The evolutionary cycle. *J Adv Nurs* 14:330335, 1989.

Rodgers BL, Kanfl KA: *Concept Development in Nursing: Foundations, Techniques, and Applications*. Philadelphia: WB Saunders, 1993.

Schultz PR: When the client means more than one: Extending the foundational concept of person. *Adv Nurs Sci* 10(1):71–86, 1987.

Schumacher KL, Gortner SR: (Mis)conceptions and reconceptions about traditional science. *Adv Nurs Sci* 14(4):1–11, 1992.

Simmons SJ: Health: A concept analysis. *Int J Nurs Studies* 26(2):155–161, 1989.

Steeves RH, Kahn DL: Experience of meaning in suffering. *Image* 19(3):114–116, 1987.

Summers S: Hypothermia: One nursing diagnosis or three? *Nurs Diag* 3(1):2–11, 1992.

Teel CS: Chronic sorrow: Analysis of the concept. *J Adv Nurs* 16:1311–1319, 1991.

Teasdale K: The concept of reassurance in nursing. *J Adv Nurs* 14:444–450, 1989.

Ward C: The meaning of role strain. *Adv Nurs Sci* 8(2):39–49, 1986.

Watson SJ: An analysis of the concept of experience. *J Adv Nurs* 16:1117–1121, 1991.

Whitley GG: Concept analysis of fear. *Nurs Diag* 3(4):155–161, 1992.

Wilson J: *Thinking with Concepts*. New York: Cambridge Univ Press, 1963.

*A*dditional Readings

Arakelian M: An assessment and nursing application of the concept of locus of control. *Adv Nurs Sci* 3(1):25–42, 1980.

Carnevali D: Conceptualizing, a nursing skill. In Mitchell PH, (ed): *Concepts Basic to Nursing.* 2nd ed. New York: McGraw-Hill, 1977.

Carper B: Fundamental patterns of knowing in nursing. *Adv Nurs Sci* 1(1):13–23, 1978.

Chinn PL, Jacobs K: A model for theory development in nursing. *Adv Nurs Sci* 1(1):1–12, 1978.

Englemann S: *Conceptual Learning.* San Rafael, CA: Dimensions, 1969.

Hempel CG: *Fundamentals of Concept Formation in Empirical Science.* Chicago: Univ of Chicago Press, 1952.

Klausmeier HJ, Ripple RE: *Learning and Human Abilities.* New York: Harper & Row, 1971.

Matthews C, Gaul A: Nursing diagnosis from the perspective of concept attainment and critical thinking. *Adv Nurs Sci* 2(1):17–26, 1979.

Norris CM: Restlessness: A nursing phenomenon in search of meaning. *Nurs Outlook* 23:103-107, 1975.

Popper KR: *Conjectures and Refutations.* 4th ed. London: Rutledge & Kegan Paul, 1972.

Rawnsley M: The concept of privacy. *Adv Nurs Sci* 2(2):25–32, 1980.

Smith J: The idea of health: A philosophical inquiry. *Adv Nurs Sci* 3(3):43–50, 1981.

Stern PN: Grounded theory methodology: Its uses and processes. *Image* 12(2):20–23, 1980.

SECTION 2

Conceptual Models and Theories

This section lays the groundwork for the remainder of the book. Here, conceptual models and theories are defined, described, and placed in a structural hierarchy of knowledge. Then, the argument is advanced that conceptual models and theories are clearly distinguished by their levels of abstraction and thus must be used in different ways. The section concludes with a discussion of the conceptual-theoretical systems of nursing knowledge required for scientific and professional activities.

The key terms used in this section are listed below. Each term is defined and described in the section.

Key Terms

Conceptual Model	Word Views
Conceptual Framework	Mechanism and Organicism
Conceptual System	Change and Persistence
Paradigm	Categories of Conceptual Models of Nursing
Disciplinary Matrix	Developmental
Concept	Systems
Proposition	Interaction
Metaparadigm	Needs
Nursing's Metaparadigm Concepts	Outcomes
Person, Environment, Health, Nursing	Humanistic

Continued

Key Terms *(continued)*

Categories of Conceptual Models
    of Nursing *Cont.*
    Energy Fields
    Intervention
    Substitution
    Conservation
    Sustenance
    Enhancement
Theory
Types of Theories
    Descriptive Theory
    Explanatory Theory
    Predictive Theory

Scope of Theories
    Grand Theory
    Middle Range Theory
    Partial Theory
Structural Hierarchy of Knowledge
Conceptual-Theoretical Systems of Nursing
    Knowledge for:
    Research
    Clinical Practice
    Education
    Administration

---

*C*onceptual Models

The term conceptual model, and synonymous terms such as conceptual framework, conceptual system, paradigm, and disciplinary matrix, refer to global ideas about the individuals, groups, situations, and events of interest to a discipline. Conceptual models are made up of concepts, which are words describing mental images of phenomena, and propositions, which are statements about the concepts. A conceptual model, therefore, is defined as a set of concepts and the propositions that integrate them into a meaningful configuration (Lippitt, 1973; Nye & Berardo, 1981).

The concepts of a conceptual model are highly abstract and general. Thus, they are not directly observed in the real world nor are they limited to any specific individual, group, situation, or event. Adaptation is an example of a conceptual model concept. It can refer to all types of individuals and groups, in a wide variety of situations.

The propositions of a conceptual model also are very abstract and general. Therefore, they are not amenable to direct empirical observation or test. Some propositions provide the foundation for further development of the model; these are the basic assumptions of the model. An example of this kind of proposition is: People are rational beings. Other propositions are broad definitions of the conceptual model concepts. Adaptation, for example, might be defined as the ability to adjust to changing situations. Because conceptual model concepts are so abstract, not all of them are defined, and those that are defined have rather loose definitions. Definitional propositions for conceptual model concepts, therefore, do not and cannot state how the concepts are observed or measured.

Still other propositions state the relationships between conceptual model concepts. This kind of proposition is exemplified by the following statement: Nursing intervention is directed toward management of environmental stressors.

The concepts and propositions of each conceptual model often are stated in a distinctive vocabulary. One model, for example, uses the terms adaptation and stress, and another uses the terms helicy and resonancy. Furthermore, the meaning of each term usually is connected to the particular focus of the model. Thus, the same or similar terms may have different meanings in different conceptual models. For example, stressor may be defined as a negative stimulus in one model and as a positive, growth-promoting force in another.

In summary, a conceptual model is composed of abstract and general concepts and propositions. These global ideas and statements are expressed in a distinctive manner in each model.

Uses of Conceptual Models

A conceptual model provides a distinctive frame of reference for its adherents, telling them what to look at and speculate about. Most importantly, a conceptual model determines how the world is viewed and what aspects of that world are to be taken into account (Redman, 1974; Rogers, 1973). Conceptual models thus have the "basic purpose of focusing, ruling some things in as relevant, and ruling others out due to their lesser importance" (Williams, 1979, p. 96). For example, one conceptual model may focus on interventions designed to help the person adapt to stressors, and another may emphasize the person's capacity for self-care.

The utility of conceptual models comes from the organization they provide for thinking, for observations, and for interpreting what is seen. Conceptual models also provide a systematic structure and a rationale for activities. Furthermore, they give direction to the search for relevant questions about phenomena and they point out solutions to practical problems. Conceptual models also provide general criteria for knowing when a problem has been solved. These features of conceptual models are illustrated in the following example: Suppose that a conceptual model focuses on adaption of the person to external stressors, and proposes that management of the stressor most obvious to the person leads to adaptation. Here, a relevant question might be: What is the most obvious stressor in a given situation? Anyone interested in solutions to problems in adaptation would focus on the various ways of managing stressors. And, one would be led to look for manifestations of adaptation when seeking to determine if the problem has been solved.

Development of Conceptual Models

Conceptual models have existed since people began to think about themselves and their surroundings. Lippitt (1973) identified examples of conceptual models in the early Egyptian and Chinese civilizations; in early sciences such as physics and medicine; in later sciences such as mathematics, chemistry, and biology; and in all modern sciences. He noted that many of the models were influential in shaping the world. For example,

> The thinking of Karl Marx, Albert Einstein and Sigmund Freud is paramount in the shaping of the 20th-century world. Each had a conceptual model. Marx's was a political, philosophic, social, and economic model forming the framework of communist ideology. Einstein's model of relativity paved the way to the atomic era. His model helped break an adherence to inflexible laws of physics and mathematics which hindered the development of science and technology. Freud's model was a tri-dimensional structure for the understanding of man which he called psychoanalysis. (Lippitt, 1973, p. 14)

In each instance, the conceptual model evolved from empirical observations and intuitive insights of scholars and/or from deductions that creatively combined ideas from several fields of inquiry. A conceptual model is inductively developed when generalizations about various observed events are formulated and is deductively developed when specific situations are seen as examples of other more general events. For example, Freud induced his concepts of the ego, id, and superego from observations of his patients' behavior. In contrast, much of Einstein's model of relativity was deduced from previous work dealing with the physical world.

Conceptual models present diverse views of certain phenomena in the world that have profound influences on our perceptions of that world. A model is, however, only an approximation or simplification of reality, a representation of the world that includes only those concepts that the model builder considers relevant and as aids to understanding (Lippitt, 1973; Reilly, 1975). Each conceptual model is a unique combination or a synthesis of many concepts, and, therefore, presents a distinctive perspective for the phenomena of interest to a discipline (Phillips, 1977; Reilly, 1975). Such a combination or synthesis, however, must adhere to the criterion of logical congruence of ideas. A detailed discussion of logically incompatible world views is presented later in this section. Suffice it to say now that a model would not be logically congruent if it combined an emphasis on the person as passively reacting to the environment with a focus on the person as actively interacting with the environment.

Metaparadigms and Conceptual Models

Now that conceptual models have been defined and their use and development have been described, they may be placed within the structural hierarchy of knowledge within disciplines. This will be done by introducing the idea of the metaparadigm. Later in the section, the relation of metaparadigms and conceptual models to theories will be explained.

Each discipline singles out certain phenomena with which it will deal in a unique manner. The concepts and propositions that identify and interrelate these phenomena are even more abstract and general than those of conceptual models, and comprise the metaparadigm of the discipline (Kuhn, 1977). The metaparadigm, therefore, is the most global perspective of a discipline and "acts as an encapsulating unit, or framework, within which the more restricted . . . structures develop" (Eckberg & Hill, 1979, p 927). The metaparadigm of sociology, for example, tells the sociologist to look at the social behavior of human beings.

Disciplines are differentiated from each other by virtue of the phenomena of concern to each. The metaparadigm of each discipline, therefore, is the first level of distinction between disciplines. It is not unusual, however, to find that more than one discipline is interested in the same or similar concepts. The unique perspective of each discipline with regard to the concepts is specified by its metaparadigm. For example, both sociology and psychology are concerned with behavior, but sociology focuses on social behavior and psychology focuses on psychological behavior.

Most disciplines have a single metaparadigm, but multiple conceptual models. These are derived from the metaparadigm and, therefore, incorporate the most global concepts and propositions in a more restrictive, yet still abstract manner. Each conceptual model, then, provides a different view of the metaparadigm concepts. As Kuhn (1970) explained, although adherents of different models are looking at the same phenomena, "in some areas they see different things, and they see them in different relations to one another" (p. 150). Nye and Berardo (1981), for example, identified 16 different conceptual models of the family derived from the metaparadigm of sociology.

The content of each conceptual model reflects the philosophical stance, cognitive orientation, research tradition, and practice modalities of a particular group of scholars within a discipline, rather than the beliefs, values, thoughts, research methods, and approaches to practice of all members of the discipline. The adherents of each conceptual model, then, comprise a subculture or community of scholars within a discipline (Eckberg & Hill, 1979). The conceptual model maps and categorizes the activities of its adherents and, therefore, distinguishes one group of researchers, clinicians, educators, and administrators from another group (Nye & Berardo, 1981). One conceptual model, for example, may lead its adherents to study stress and adaptation, and another conceptual model will lead its adherents to look at structure and function.

Furthermore, conceptual models move beyond metaparadigms to provide a second level of distinction between disciplines (Aggleton & Chalmers, 1986; Nye & Berardo, 1981). This is especially so when more than one discipline is interested in a particular concept. Stress is a prominent example of a concept that is of interest to many disciplines. Close examination of the focus of each discipline, however, reveals that ideas and statements about stress are quite different. Consider, for example, the meaning of stress to the engineers who build bridges versus its meaning to psychologists who study intrapsychic reactions to noxious stimuli.

Metaparadigm of Nursing

Considerable agreement now exists that the central concepts the discipline of nursing are: person, environment, health, and nursing. Person refers to the recipient of nursing actions, who may be an individual, a family, a community, or a particular group. Environment refers to the recipient's significant others and surroundings, as well as to the setting in which nursing actions occur. Health refers to the wellness and/or illness state of the recipient. And, nursing refers to the actions taken by nurses on behalf of or in conjunction with the recipient.

The connections among the four metaparadigm concepts are clearly made in the following statement: "Nursing studies the wholeness or health of humans, recognizing that humans are in continuous interaction with their environments" (Donaldson & Crowley, 1978, p. 119). This statement may be considered the major proposition of nursing's metaparadigm, reflecting as it does the overall focus of the discipline of nursing.

Three other propositions state relationships between and among the metaparadigm concepts. These statements, which reflect the major areas of interest to the discipline of nursing, are:

- The principles and laws that govern the life-process, well-being, and optimum function of human beings, sick or well

- The patterning of human behavior in interaction with the environment in normal life events and critical life situations

- The processes by which positive changes in health status are effected (Donaldson & Crowley, 1978; Gortner, 1980)

Nursing's metaparadigm has been evolving since Nightingale (1859) first wrote of nurses' actions in relation to environmental influences on the person's health. Explicit formalization of the metaparadigm, however, has occurred only recently (Fawcett, 1983, 1984).

Conway (1985) raised the question of whether nursing should be considered a concept within the metaparadigm of nursing. She regarded nursing as the discipline and did not accept the view of nursing as action or activity of discipline members as an appropriate metaparadigm concept. Contemporary works by Meleis (1985) and Kim (1987), however, do underscore the centrality of person, environment, health, and nursing (as activity or action), but present slight variations of the metaparadigm. Meleis's list includes nursing client, transitions, interaction, nursing process, environment, nursing therapeutics, and health. She proposed that

> The nurse interacts (interaction) with a human being in a health/illness situation (nursing client) who is in an integral part of his sociocultural context (environment) and who is in some sort of transition or is anticipating a transition (transition); the nurse/patient interactions are organized around some purpose (nursing process) and the nurse uses some actions (nursing therapeutics) to enhance, bring about, or facilitate health (health). (Meleis, 1985, p. 184)

Kim (1987) identified four domains of nursing knowledge. The client domain is concerned with the client's development, problems, and health care experiences. The client-nurse domain focuses on encounters between client and nurse and the interactions between the two in the process of providing nursing care. The practice domain emphasizes the cognitive, behavioral, and social aspects of nurses' professional actions. The domain of environment is concerned with time, space, and quality variations of the client's environment.

Hinshaw (1987) pointed out that Kim's work does not include the concept of health, and asked: "Is health a strand that permeates each of the . . . domains . . . rather than a major separate domain?" (p. 112). Kim (personal communication, October 31, 1986) has indicated that the client domain could encompass health.

Conceptual Models of Nursing

Peterson (1977) and Hall (1979) linked the proliferation of conceptual models of nursing with interest in conceptualizing nursing as a distinct discipline and to the concomitant introduction of ideas about nursing theory. Meleis (1985) reached the same conclusion in her historiography of nursing knowledge development. Readers who are especially interested in the progression of nursing knowledge are referred to her excellent work, for a comprehensive historic review is beyond the scope of this book.

The works of several nurse scholars currently are recognized as conceptual models. Among the best known are Johnson's (1980) Behavioral System Model, King's (1981) Interacting Systems Framework, Levine's (1973, in press) Conservation Model, Neuman's (in press) Systems Model, Orem's (1985) Self-Care Framework, Rogers's (1986) Science of Unitary Human Beings, and Roy's (1984) Adaptation Model.

As with conceptual models and metaparadigms of other disciplines, the conceptual models of nursing represent various paradigms derived from the metaparadigm of the discipline of nursing. Thus, it is not surprising that each defines the four metaparadigm concepts differently and links these concepts in diverse ways.

Examination of conceptual models of nursing reveals that person usually is identified as an integrated bio-psycho-social being, but is defined in diverse ways, such as an adaptive system, a behavioral system, a self-care agent, or an energy field. Environment frequently is identified as internal structures and external influences, including family members, the community, and society, as well as the person's physical surroundings. The environment is seen as a source of stressors in some models, but a source of resources in others. Health is presented in various ways, such as a continuum from adaptation to maladaptation, a dichotomy of behavioral stability or instability, or a value identified by each cultural group. The conceptual models also present descriptions of the concept of nursing, usually by defining nursing and then specifying goals of nursing actions and a nursing process. The goals of nursing action frequently are derived directly from the definition of health given by the model. For example, a nursing goal might be to assist people to attain, maintain, or regain the ability to care for themselves, with health equated with self-care ability. The nursing process described in each model emphasizes assessing the person's health status, setting goals for nursing action, implementing nursing actions, and evaluating the person's health status after nursing intervention. The steps of the process, however, frequently differ from model to model. Later sections in this book present detailed descriptions of several conceptual models of nursing and discuss the connections among the concepts of each model.

Conceptual models are not really new to nursing, as they have existed since Nightingale (1859) first advanced her ideas about nursing. Most early conceptualizations of nursing, however, were not presented in the formal manner of models. It remained for the Nursing Development Conference Group (1973, 1979), Johnson (1974), Riehl and Roy (1974, 1980), and Reilly (1975) to explicitly label various perspectives of nursing as conceptual models.

The development of conceptual models and labeling them as such is an important advance for the discipline of nursing. Reilly's (1975) comments help to underscore this point.

We all have a private image (concept) of nursing practice. In turn, this private image influences our interpretation of data, our decisions, and our actions. But can a discipline continue to develop when its members hold so many differing private images? The proponents of conceptual models of practice are seeking to make us aware of these private images, so that we can begin to identify commonalities in our perceptions of the nature of practice and move toward the evolution of a well-ordered concept. (p. 567)

Johnson (1987) also pointed out that nurses always use some frame of reference for their activities and explained the drawbacks of implicit frameworks. She stated,

It is important to note that some kind of implicit framework is used by every practicing nurse, for we cannot observe, see, or describe, nor can we prescribe anything for which we do not already have some kind of mental image or concept. Unfortunately, the mental images used by nurses in their practice, images developed through education and experience and continuously governed by the multitude of factors in the practice setting, have tended to be disconnected, diffused, incomplete and frequently heavily weighted by concepts drawn from the conceptual schema used by medicine to achieve its own social mission. (p. 195)

Conceptual models of nursing, then, are the formal presentations of some nurses' private images of nursing. The proponents of nursing models maintain that use of a conceptual model facilitates communication among nurses and provides a systematic approach to nursing practice, education, administration, and research.

The importance of conceptual models of nursing was highlighted by Johnson (1987), who commented,

Conceptual models are important for the . . . nurse as they provide philosophical and pragmatic orientations to the service nurses provide patients—a service which only nurses can provide— a service which provides a dimension to total care different from that provided by any other health professional. (p. 195)

Conceptual models of nursing provide explicit orientations not only for nurses but also for the general public. They identify the purpose and scope of nursing and provide frameworks for objective records of the effects of nursing. Johnson (1987) explained, "Conceptual models specify for nurses and society the mission and boundaries of the profession. They clarify the realm of nursing responsibility and accountability, and they allow the practitioner and/or the profession to document services and outcomes" (pp. 196–197).

World Views of Conceptual Models of Nursing

Conceptual models of nursing, like the conceptual models of other disciplines, reflect different and logically incompatible views of the world. As used here, world view refers to philosophical beliefs about the nature of person-environment relationships underlying each conceptual model. Watson (1981) pointed out that such beliefs clearly influence the focus of inquiry and the approach to development of nursing knowledge. The contrasting world views of mechanism and organicism and of change and persistence are appropriate when considering conceptual models of nursing.

Mechanism and Organicism

The metaphor for the mechanistic world view is the machine, and that for the organismic world view is the living organism. The elements of each of these contrasting world views are listed in Table 2–1.

The mechanistic world view proposes that the person, much like a machine, is inherently at rest, responding in a reactive manner to external forces. Behavior is then considered a linear chain of causes and effects, or stimuli and responses.

TABLE 2–1 Elements of Organicism and Mechanism

Organicism	Mechanism
Metaphor is the living organism	Metaphor is the machine
Human being is active	Human being is reactive
Behavior is probabilistic	Behavior is a predictable linear chain
Holism and expansionism assumed—focus on wholes	Elementarism and reductionism assumed—focus on parts
Change is qualitative and quantitative	Change is quantitative

Mechanism assumes elementarism, such that the whole of any phenomenon, living or non-living, is the sum of its discrete parts. This world view also assumes reductionism, "a doctrine that maintains that all objects and events, their properties, and our experience and knowledge of them are made up of ultimate elements, indivisible parts" (Ackoff, 1974, p. 8). Reductionism is associated with the notion that behavior is objective and predictable by reducing it to its component parts. This is a deterministic view, such that if enough is known about the parts, then behavior is completely predictable. Furthermore, changes in the person are described as quantitative, an adding or subtracting of a certain number of parts (Battista, 1977; Looft, 1973; Reese & Overton, 1970).

The organismic world view contrasts sharply with mechanism. This world view proposes that the person is inherently and spontaneously active, the source of acts. The person engages in interactions with the environment, rather than reacting to it. Here, cause and effect are denied and complete prediction is rejected. Rather, behavior is understood only in a probabilistic sense.

Organicism assumes holism, such that the living organism is postulated to be an integrated, organized entity who is not reducible to discrete parts. Although parts of the organism are acknowledged, they have meaning only within the context of the whole. Ackoff (1974) explained that this doctrine, which is called expansionism, "maintains that all objects, events, and experiences of them are parts of larger wholes. It does not deny that they have parts but focuses on the wholes of which they are part" (p. 12). Kahn (1988) has identified two interpretations of the phrase associated with holism, "the whole is more than the sum of its parts." One interpretation, which Kahn called emergent holism, maintains that the whole has a property not found in any of its parts; the new property emerged from the part. The other interpretation, called connected holism, maintains that the whole forms different relationships with other objects than do the separate parts. Thus, a simple sum of the relationships of each part with another object, such as the environment, does not yield an accurate understanding of the relationship of the whole with the other object.

Organicism also proposes that behavior is associated with structural changes in the organism. These changes are qualitative as well as quantitative, such that one stage of life is completely distinct from another (Battista, 1977; Looft, 1973; Reese & Overton, 1970).

Parse (1987) proposed two world views that are related to mechanism and organicism. The description of what she calls the simultaneity paradigm reflects the organismic world view. Simultaneity regards the person as "more than and different from the sum of the parts . . . an open being free to choose in mutual rhythmical interchange with the environment" (p. 136). Parse's totality paradigm, however, does not seem to reflect the mechanistic world view, as she claims, but rather has elements of both mechanism and organicism. Totality regards the person as the sum of bio-psycho-socio-spiritual parts. The person adapts to the environment, which in turn can be manipulated to maintain or promote balance. Furthermore, the person "interacts with the environment, establishes transactions, and plans toward goal attainment" (p. 32). Although the sum of parts and adaptation to environment notions reflect a mechanistic view, interaction, transaction, and planning to attain goals imply a much more active organism than the passively reacting person of mechanism. The totality world view, then, may be regarded as a bridge between the mechanistic and organismic views of the world.

In summary, from a mechanistic view of the world, the person, who is composed of discrete parts, is passive and reacts when external environmental forces provide the necessary stimulation. In contrast, from an organismic world view, the person, who is seen as an integrated whole, is active and interacts with the environment. These two world views, then, are not logically compatible.

Change and Persistence

The world view of change uses the growth metaphor, and the persistence world view focuses on stability. The elements of these contrasting world views are presented in Table 2–2.

Hall (1981) explained that the change world view holds that "change processes are an inherent and natural part of life" (p. 2). This view also maintains that change is continuous, such that the person always is in a site of transition. Change may be thought of as continual intraindividual variance (Thomae, 1979). Here, progress is valued, and realization of one's potential is emphasized.

In contrast, the persistence world view maintains that stability is natural and normal, "the certain, secure, and healthy condition" (Hall, 1983, p. 19). Persistence is endurance in time and is produced by a synthesis of growth and stability. The focus is on continuation and maintenance of patterns and routines in human behavior through socialization and the commitment of support systems. People are viewed as becoming more like themselves throughout their lifetimes. Furthermore, persistence assumes that people have the power to shape their own lives. Change occurs only when necessary for survival, and is regarded as creative invention of new routines to avoid the disaster of extinction.

Persistence may be thought of as intraindividual invariance (Thomae, 1979). Here, solidarity and stability are valued, and conservation and retrenchment are emphasized.

Thomae (1979) presented evidence for both change and persistence throughout the life cycle. He stated that research supports the proposition that behavior during all periods of life "can be ordered along a dimension running from low to high change or from high to low stability. It is a matter of convenience whether we prefer 'change' or 'stability' as the label" (p. 288).

TABLE 2–2 Elements of Change and Persistence

Change	Persistence
Metaphor is growth	Metaphor is stability
Change is inherent and natural	Stability is natural and normal
Change is continuous	Change occurs only for survival
Intraindividual variance	Intraindividual invariance
Progress valued	Conservation and retrenchment emphasized
Realization of potential emphasized	Solidarity valued

In summary, from the change view of the world, change and growth are desirable and continual throughout the person's life. From the persistence world view, to the contrary, stability is the natural state. These two world views, then, also are not logically compatible.

Categories of Conceptual Models of Nursing

Conceptual models of nursing reflect not only different world views, but also different broad classifications. Nursing models have been categorized according to the discipline or anthropology from which they were derived and most often are labeled developmental, systems, or interaction models (Johnson, 1974; Reilly, 1975; Riehl & Roy, 1980). Additional categories mentioned in the nursing literature are needs and outcomes (Meleis, 1985); humanistic and energy fields (Marriner, 1986); and intervention, substitution, conservation, sustenance, and enhancement (Stevens, 1984).

The various categories of nursing models are "different classes of approaches to understanding the person who is a patient, [so that they] not only call for differing forms of practice toward different objectives, but also point to different kinds of phenomena, suggest different kinds of questions, and lead eventually to dissimilar bodies of knowledge" (Johnson, 1974, p. 376).

Developmental Models

Developmental models emphasize processes of growth, development, and maturation. Emphasis also is placed on identification of actual and potential developmental problems and delineation of intervention strategies that foster maximum growth and development of people and their environments.

The major thrust of this type of model is change, with the assumption made "that there are noticeable differences between the states of a system at different times, that the succession of these states implies the system is heading somewhere, and that there are orderly processes that explain how the system gets from its present state to wherever it is going" (Chin, 1980, p. 30). Following from the assumption of change are the characteristics of direction, identifiable state form of progression, forces, and potentiality.

Developmental models postulate that changes are directional, that the individuals, groups, situations, and events of interest are headed in some direction. Chin (1980) outlined the direction of change as "(a) some goal or end state (developed, mature), (b) the process of becoming (developing, maturing), or (c) the degree of achievement toward some goal or end state (increased development, increase in maturity)" (p. 31).

The characteristic of identifiable state refers to the different states of the person seen over time. These states frequently are termed stages, levels, phases, or periods of development. Such states may be quantitatively or qualitatively differentiated from one another. And, as Chin (1980) pointed out, shifts in state may be either small, nondiscernible steps that eventually are recognized as change, or sudden, cataclysmic changes.

Developmental change, according to Chin (1980), is possible through four different forms of progression. First, unidirectional development may be postulated, such that "once a stage is worked through, the client system shows continued progression and normally never turns back" (p 31). Second, developmental change may take the form of a spiral, so that while return to a previous problem may occur, the problem is dealt with at a higher level. Third, development may be seen as "phases which occur and recur . . . where no chronological priority is assigned to each state; there are cycles" (p 32). And fourth, development may take the form of "a branching out into differentiated forms and processes, each part increasing in its specialization and at the same time acquiring its own autonomy and significances" (p. 32).

The developmental models postulate the existence of forces, defined by Chin (1980) as "causal factors producing development and growth" (p. 32). These forces may be viewed as a natural component of the person undergoing change, a coping response to new situations and environmental factors that leads to growth and development; or internal tensions within the person that at some time reach a peak and cause a disruption that leads to further growth and development.

Developmental models also postulate that people have the inherent potential for change. Potentiality may be overt or latent, triggered by internal states or by certain environmental conditions.

The characteristics of developmental models are listed in Table 2–3.

Systems Models

Systems models treat phenomena "as if there existed organization, interaction, interdependency, and integration of parts and elements" (Chin, 1980, p. 24). This type of model emphasizes identification of actual and potential problems in the function of systems and delineation of intervention strategies that maximize efficient and effective system operation. The focus of this category of models, then, is the examination of the system, its parts, and their relationships at a given time. In contrast to developmental models, change is of secondary importance in systems models.

The major features of systems models are the system and its environment. Hall and Fagen (1968) defined system as "a set of objects together with relationships between the objects and between their attributes" (p. 83). They defined environment as "the set of all objects a change in whose attributes affect the system and also those objects whose attributes are changed by the behavior of the system" (p 83). When viewing any particular phenomenon, the designation of what is system and what is environment depends on the situation. Thus, a system could be the person whose parts are body organs, and whose environment is the family. Or the system might be the community, whose parts are families and whose environment is the state in which the community is located.

Systems are open or closed. An open system "maintains itself in a continuous inflow and outflow, a building up and breaking down of components," but a closed system is "considered to be isolated from [its] environment" (Bertalanffy, 1968, p. 39). Moreover, open systems continuously import energy in a process called negative entropy or negentropy, so that the system may become more differentiated, more complex, and more ordered. Conversely, closed systems exhibit entropy, such that they move toward increasing disorder.

According to Bertalanffy (1968), all living organisms are open systems. Although closed systems therefore do not exist in nature, it sometimes is convenient to view a system as if it had no interaction with its environment (Chin, 1980). The artificiality of such a view, however, must be taken into account.

TABLE 2–3 Characteristics of Developmental Models

Growth, Development, and Maturation
Change
Direction of Change
Identifiable State
Form of Progression
Forces
Potentiality

Important characteristics of the systems models are boundary; tension, stress, strain, and conflict; equilibrium and steady state; and feedback. Boundary refers to the line of demarcation between a system and its environment. The placement of the boundary must take all relevant system parts into account. Thus, boundary is "the line forming a closed circle around selected variables, where there is less interchange of energy . . . across the line of the circle than within the delimiting circle" (Chin, 1980, p. 24). Boundaries may be thought of as more or less permeable. The greater the boundary permeability, the greater the interchange of energy between the system and its environment.

Tension, stress, strain, and conflict are terms that refer to the forces that alter system structure. Chin (1980) explained that the differences in system parts, as well as the need to adjust to outside disturbances, lead to different amounts of tension within the system. He further noted that internal tensions arising from the system's structural arrangements are called the stresses and strains of the system. Conflict occurs when tensions accumulate and become opposed along the lines of two or more components of the system. Change then occurs to resolve the conflict.

Systems are assumed to tend to move toward a balance between internal and external forces. Chin (1980) explained that "when the balance is thought of as a fixed point or level, it is called 'equilibrium.' 'Steady state,' on the other hand, is the term . . . used to describe the balanced relationship of parts that is not dependent upon any fixed equilibrium point or level" (p. 25). Bertalanffy (1968) maintained that steady state, which also is referred to as a dynamic equilibrium, is characteristic of living open systems. He further commented that the steady state is maintained by a continuous flow of energy within the system and between the system and its environment.

The flow of energy between a system and its environment is called feedback. Chin (1980) described feedback as a series of outputs and inputs across the system-environment boundary. He claimed that systems:

> are affected by and in turn affect the environment. While affecting, the environment, a process we call output, systems gather information about how they are doing. Such information is then fed back into the system as input to guide and steer its operations. (p. 27)

The feedback process works so that as open systems interact with their environments, any change in the system is associated with a change in the environment, and vice versa.

The characteristics of systems models are listed in Table 2–4.

TABLE 2–4   Characteristics of Systems Models

Integration of Parts
System
Environment
Open and Closed Systems
Boundary
Tension, Stress, Strain, Conflict
Equilibrium and Steady State
Feedback

Interaction Models

Interaction models emphasize social acts and relationships between people. The focus, therefore, is on identification of actual and potential problems in interpersonal relationships and delineation of intervention strategies that promote optimal socialization.

This type of model is derived from symbolic interactionism, which "sees human beings as creatures who define and classify situations, including themselves, and who choose ways of acting toward and within them" (Benoliel, 1977, p. 110). Symbolic interactionism "postulates that the importance of social life lies in providing the [person] with language, self-concept, role-taking ability, and other skills" (Heiss, 1976, p. 467). The major characteristics of this category of models are perception, communication, role, and self-concept.

The person's perceptions of other people, the environment, situations, and events—that is, the awareness and experience of phenomena—depend on meanings attached to these phenomena. These meanings, or definitions as they sometimes are called, determine how the person behaves in a given situation. Thus, the key data to be gathered when working in the context of interaction models are the person's perceptions, that is, his or her definition of the situation. Heiss (1981) explained,

> The fact that an other is, in fact, kindly or cruel may not be very significant. The fact that we define him or her as one or the other is important, because—regardless of the facts—we will act on that belief. (p. 3)

The person's perceptions are derived from social interactions with others. People may adopt fully, modify, or reject others' definitions of phenomena, but they always are influenced in some way by others. This is especially so when the other is significant to the person.

During social interactions, people communicate with one another. Communication is through language, "a system of significant symbols" (Heiss, 1981, p. 5). Communication, therefore, involves the transfer of arbitrary meanings of things from one person to another. Thus, people must communicate with one another to find out each other's perceptions of the particular situation.

Communication is important in learning roles, which are "prescriptions for behavior which are associated with particular actor-other combinations. They are the ways we think people of a particular kind ought to act toward various categories of others" (Heiss, 1981, p. 65). Each person has many different roles, each one providing a behavioral repertoire. We adopt the behaviors associated with a given role, when, through communication, we determine that a given role is called for in a particular situation.

The person's ability to perform roles, and to perform them according to self-imposed and societal standards, influences self-concept. "The self-concept is the individual's thoughts and feelings about himself" (Heiss, 1981, p. 83). An important aspect of self-concept is self-evaluation, which refers to "our view of how good we are at what we think we are" (Heiss, 1981, p. 83).

TABLE 2–5 Characteristics of Interaction Models

Social Acts and Relationships
Perception
Communication
Role
Self-Concept

An especially important feature of interaction models is their emphasis on the person as an active participant in interactions. People are thought to actively evaluate communication from others, rather than passively accept their ideas. Moreover, they actively set goals on the basis of their perceptions of the relevant factors in a given situation.

The characteristics of interaction models are listed in Table 2–5.

Other Categories of Conceptual Models

Other categories of conceptual models of nursing have been identified in recent years. The little that has been written about these categories is summarized below. The characteristics of these categories are listed in Table 2–6.

Needs and Outcomes Models

The needs and outcomes categories of conceptual models were developed by Meleis (1985), who also included an interaction category in her classification scheme. The needs category of conceptual models focuses on nurses' functions and consideration of the patient in terms of a hierarchy of needs. When patients cannot fulfill their own needs, nursing care is required. The function of the nurse if to provide the necessary action to help patients meet their needs. This category reduces the human being to a set of needs, and nursing, to a set of functions. Nurses are portrayed as the final decision makers for nursing care.

The outcomes category of conceptual models is not well described by Meleis (1985), who commented only that emphasis is placed on the outcomes of nursing care and comprehensive descriptions of the recipient of care. No one perspective of the care recipient was noted.

Humanistic and Energy Fields Models

Marriner (1986) identified two other categories of nursing models, the humanistic and energy fields. Her classification scheme also included an interpersonal relationships category, which is similar to the interaction category already discussed in this section. Marriner mentioned that humanistic models view nursing as an art and science, and she implied that energy field models incorporate the concept of energy. The bulk of her discussion, however, focused on an overview of various models within the categories, rather than on identification of specific characteristics of each category.

TABLE 2–6   Characteristics of Other Categories of Models

Category	Characteristics
Needs	Nursing as set of functions to help patients meet their needs
Outcomes	Outcomes of nursing care
Humanistic	Nursing as art and science
Energy fields	Energy
Intervention	Manipulation of patient or environmental variables to effect change
Substitution	Provision of substitutes for lost or impaired patient capabilities
Conservation	Preservation of beneficial aspects of patient's situation
Sustenance	Helping patient endure insults to health
Enhancement	Improvement of quality of patient's existence

Intervention, Substitution, Conservation, Sustenance, and Enhancement Models

Stevens (1984) developed a substantially different classification scheme for conceptual models of nursing. This scheme is based on "the character of the nursing act in relation to the patient" (p. 257). The intervention category emphasizes the nurse's professional actions and decisions and regards the patient as an object of nursing rather than a participant in nursing care. Agency rests with the nurse, who makes the care decision and manipulates selected patient or environmental variables to bring about change.

Substitution models focus on provision of substitutes for patient capabilities that cannot be enacted or have been lost. Agency rests with the patient, in that the patient exercises his or her will and physical control to the greatest possible extent. In contrast, conservation models emphasize preservation of beneficial aspects of the patient's situation that are threatened by illness or actual or potential problems. This category bridges the polarity of agency seen in the intervention and substitution categories in that agency rests with nurses, but they conserve the existing capabilities of the patient.

The sustenance category of models emphasizes helping the patient endure insults to health. The focus is on supporting the patient and building psychological and physiological coping mechanisms. The enhancement category regards nursing as a way to improve the quality of the patient's existence following a health insult.

In summary, each category of model emphasizes different phenomena and leads to different questions about the nurse-patient situation. It is anticipated that each category of nursing models will foster development of a different body of knowledge about the person, the environment, health, and nursing.

*T*heories

A theory may be defined as "a statement that purports to account for or characterize some phenomenon" (Stevens, 1984, p. 1). Theories, like conceptual models, are made up of concepts and propositions. Theories, however, address phenomena with much greater specificity than do conceptual models (Reese & Overton, 1970; Reilly, 1975).

The specificity of a theory requires that its concepts be more specific and concrete than those of a conceptual model. Therefore, they are tied more closely to particular individuals, groups, situations, or events. Examples of such concepts are temperature, pulse, blood pressure, distress, social support.

The propositions of a theory also are more specific than those of a conceptual model. Some statements, called nonrelational propositions, define or describe the concepts of a theory. One type of nonrelational proposition states the existence of a concept. An example is: There is a phenomenon known as social support. Another type of nonrelational proposition is the definition. Definitional propositions are required for all theory concepts. Indeed, though the concepts of a conceptual model may not be defined at all, or may be only loosely defined, the concepts of a theory must be constitutively defined. Such definitions, which also are called theoretical definitions, provide meaning for concepts by defining them in terms of other concepts; they are circular in nature. An example of a constitutive definition is: Social support is defined as supportive transactions that include expression of positive affect of one person toward another; affirmation of another's behavior, perceptions, or views; and provision of symbolic or material aid to another (Norbeck, Lindsey, & Carrieri, 1981). The concepts of a theory also must be operationally defined, so that the theory may be empirically tested. These definitions specify the way in which the concept is to be measured. An example of an operational definition is: In this study, social support was measured by the Norbeck Social Support Questionnaire. Operational definitions, then, connect constitutively defined concepts to the real world.

Other statements that may be part of a theory are called relational propositions. These propositions link two or more concepts; they express an association between concepts or identify the effect of one concept on another. An example of a relational proposition is: Social support is positively related to well-being. Another example is: Psychoeducational information given prior to surgery has a positive effect on postoperative recovery.

The hypothesis is a special type of proposition that states a conjecture about one or more concepts in empirically testable form. More specifically, a hypothesis is a prediction about the scores obtained from the measures of concepts. Suppose, for example, that social support was measured by the Norbeck Social Support Questionnaire (NSSQ) and well-being was measured by a Well-Being Inventory (WBI). Given the relational proposition about social support and well-being presented above, the hypothesis would state: As scores on the NSSQ increase, scores on the WBI will increase.

Types of Theories

A theory may be a description of a particular phenomenon, an explanation of the relations between phenomena, or a prediction of the effects of one phenomenon on another. Theories are developed by means of research, which may be defined as "a systematic, formal, rigorous, and precise process employed to gain solutions to problems and/or to discover and interpret new facts and relationships" (Waltz & Bausell, 1981, p. 1).

Descriptive theories describe or classify specific dimensions or characteristics of individuals, groups, situations, or events by summarizing the commonalities found in discrete observations. They are generated and tested by descriptive research. For example, Patterson, Freese, and Goldenberg (1986) conducted a descriptive study to generate a theory of self-diagnosis of pregnancy.

Explanatory theories specify relations among the dimensions or characteristic of individuals, groups, situations, or events. They are developed by correlational research. Rutledge (1987), for example, used correlational procedures to test a theory of the relationship of perceived susceptibility, perceived benefits, perceived barriers, self-concept, and age to frequency of breast self-examination.

Predictive theories move beyond explanation to the prediction of precise relationships between the dimensions or characteristics of a phenomenon or differences between groups. Experimental research is used to generate and test predictive theories. For example, an experimental study was designed by King and her associates (1987) to test a theory of the effects of a personal control intervention—self-administered versus nurse-administered medication—on patients' desire for control, pain intensity, disruption in daily activities, emotional responses, and use of pain medication over time.

Regardless of whether a theory is a description, an explanation, or a prediction, its strength "is its ability to bring a great deal of thought and information to bear on a specific problem or set of problems, and thereby go far beyond unsystematic thought" (Skidmore, 1975, p. 2). Inasmuch as each theory deals only with very specific problems, many theories are needed to deal with all phenomena of interest to a discipline. Mennell's (1974) comment helps to underscore this point: "Reality is so immense and complex that no theory, however well authenticated, ever represents more than a drop in the ocean. Some theories are broader in scope than others, but no theory can ever explain everything" (p 1).

Scope of Theories

Theories that are broadest in scope are called grand theories. These theories frequently lack operationally defined concepts, because the concepts are quite abstract. Thus, they are not amenable to direct empirical testing. Indeed, grand theories rarely are developed by means of empirical research, but rather through thoughtful and insightful appraisal of existing ideas or creative leaps beyond exists knowledge. Some nurse scholars consider conceptual models and grand theories to be synonymous (e.g., Kim, 1983; Stevens, 1984). Although it is recognized that the line between a conceptual model and a grand theory is sometimes difficult to discern, it seems more accurate to separate the two. Furthermore, grand theories are beginning to appear in the nursing literature, and clearly demonstrate the differences between conceptual models and theories. For example, Newman's (1979, 1986) theory of health as expanding consciousness was derived from Rogers's (1970) conceptual model of nursing. Rogers's conceptual model was developed to deal with all that is of interest to nursing, whereas Newman's grand theory focuses primarily on health, albeit in an abstract manner. This example illustrates the fact that although a grand theory is quite abstract, it still is more circumscribed than a conceptual model.

Theories of the middle range are narrower in scope than grand theories, encompassing a limited number of concepts and a limited aspect of the real world. Merton (1957) contended that middle range theories are the most useful, because they can be empirically tested in a direct manner. The examples of descriptive, explanatory, and predictive theories cited earlier in this section are middle range theories. In fact, most research reported in the contemporary nursing literature is directed toward the generation and testing of middle range theories.

Partial theories, which also are called micro theories or empirical generalizations, are the most limited in scope and utility. They are summary statements of isolated observations dealing with an extremely narrow range of phenomena. Though partial theories frequently are regarded as trivial due to their limited scope, they do have heuristic value, and some may be developed into middle range theories through further research. For example, case studies, such as Durand's (1975) description of the impact of nursing care on a child with Down's syndrome, may yield partial theories that can be developed into middle range theories with additional study.

These examples illustrate the fact that theories deal with a limited number of concepts and propositions, and that these components of theories are quite specific and concrete. The examples also show the relation of theory to research. Inasmuch as the purpose of this book is to examine conceptual models, the discussion of theory development is necessarily limited. Readers who are interested in a detailed discussion of theory construction strategies are referred to the seminal work by Walker and Avant (in press).

Nursing Theories

A nursing theory may be defined as a relatively specific and concrete set of concepts and propositions that purports to account for or characterize phenomena of interest to the discipline of nursing. Theories that may be considered unique to nursing are being developed at the present time. Many unique nursing theories have been derived from the conceptual models that are discussed in this book. These theories are presented in later sections.

Many other theories used by nurses have been borrowed from other disciplines. Theories of role, change, development, stress, and coping are just a few examples. Unfortunately, these theories sometimes are used with no consideration given to their credibility for the nursing situation. There is, however, increasing awareness of the need to test borrowed theories to determine if they are credible in nursing situations. The theory testing work by Lowery and her associates (1987) is an outstanding example of what can happen when a theory, borrowed in this case from psychology, is tested in the real world of acute and chronic illness. These investigators have determined that a basic proposition of attribution theory, stating that people search for causes to make sense of their lives, has not been fully supported in their research with patients with arthritis, diabetes, hypertension, or myocardial infarction. This result means that attribution theory cannot be considered a shared theory, that is, a theory that is borrowed from another discipline but found to be credible in the nursing milieu (Stevens, 1984). Further research should determine whether a modification of attribution theory is credible in nursing situations or if an entirely new theory is required.

An example of a borrowed theory that has become a shared theory is that of social support. This theory was developed initially in other disciplines, and many of its propositions have been supported in several nursing situations (Barnard, Brandt, Raff, & Carroll, 1984).

Many nurses continue to claim that there are few, if any, nursing theories. It is likely, however, that the apparent paucity of recognizable nursing theories is due to investigators' failure to explicit about the theoretical components of their studies. Thus, the ideas presented by nurses in books and articles should be closely examined for evidence of the specific concepts and propositions that comprise theories. Identification of the components of a theory is accomplished by the technique of theory formalization, also called theoretical substruction. Discussion of this technique is beyond the scope of this book. Readers who are interested in theory formalization are, therefore, referred to Hinshaw's (1979) pioneering work and Fawcett and Downs's (1986) more recent work.

Metaparadigms, Conceptual Models, and Theories

Earlier in this section, the discussion of the structural hierarchy of knowledge within disciplines was begun. It was explained that most disciplines have a single metaparadigm and multiple conceptual models. Theories will now be placed within the structural hierarchy.

It already has been noted that the multiple conceptual models of each discipline specify the metaparadigm phenomena in diverse ways. Theories provide still greater specification of these phenomena. Theories are derived from or linked with conceptual models, as Reese and Overton (1970) explained:

> Any theory presupposes a more general model according to which the theoretical concepts are formulated. At the more general levels, the concepts are generally less explicitly formulated, but they nonetheless necessarily determine the concepts at the lower levels. (p. 117)

The abstract nature of conceptual models requires many theories to fully describe, explain, and predict phenomena within the domain of the model. Thus, the structural hierarchy of knowledge progresses from a single metaparadigm to multiple conceptual models and multiple theories derived from each model. This progression is depicted in Figure 2–1.

Although all theories are derived from conceptual models, the parent model is not always identified in reports of the theory development work. This omission has created difficulties in classifying theory development efforts and evaluating the state of knowledge development in a discipline. Nurse authors, however, are beginning to be more explicit about the conceptual models upon which their works are based. Silva (1986, 1987), for example, was able to identify many published research reports and doctoral dissertations associated with Johnson's, Orem's, Rogers's and Roy's conceptual models, and Newman's grand theory. Many of these studies, as well as other work based on the conceptual models presented in this book, are discussed in later sections.

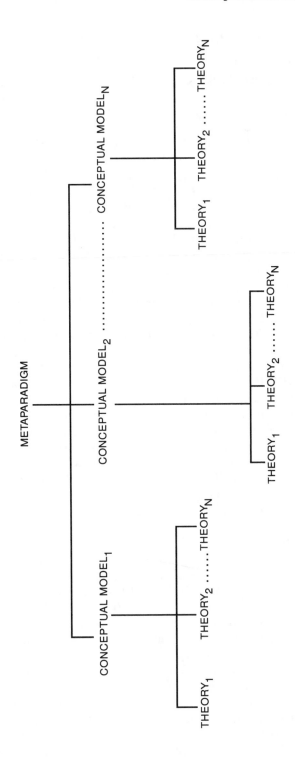

FIGURE 2–1

Structural Hierarchy of Knowledge.

Distinctions Between Conceptual Models and Theories

Throughout this section, emphasis has been placed on the point that a conceptual model is not a theory, nor is a theory a conceptual model. This point requires further discussion because there still is considerable confusion about these two levels of knowledge in the nursing literature. Although some writers consider distinctions between conceptual models and theories a semantic point (e.g., Flaskerud & Halloran, 1980; Meleis, 1985), this issue should not be dismissed so easily. The distinctions should be made because of the differences in the way that conceptual models and theories are used. Indeed, if one is to know what to do next, then one must know whether the starting point is a conceptual model or a theory.

The primary distinction between a conceptual model and a theory is the level of abstraction. A conceptual model is an abstract and general system of concepts and propositions. A theory, in contrast, deals with one or more relatively specific and concrete concepts and propositions. Conceptual models are only general guides that must be specified further by relevant and logically congruent theories before action can occur. Thus, all pragmatic activities of members of a discipline are finally directed by conceptual-theoretical systems of knowledge.

Distinguishing between conceptual models and theories on the basis of level of abstraction raises the question of how abstract is abstract enough for a work to be considered a conceptual model. Although the decision in a few cases may be somewhat arbitrary, the following rule serves as one guideline for classification of conceptual models and theories. This rule requires determination of the purpose of the work. If the purpose was to describe, explain, or predict specific phenomena, the work most likely is a theory. For example, works by Peplau (1952), Orlando (1961), and Travelbee (1966) focused on the interpersonal relationship between nurse and patient. There was no obvious intent on the part of these authors to address the entire domain of nursing. The specificity of these works, therefore, leads to their classification as theories. Conversely, if the purpose of the work was to articulate a body of distinctive knowledge for the discipline of nursing, the work most likely is a conceptual model. Given that this was the explicitly stated purpose of authors such as Johnson (1980), King (1981), Levine (1973, in press), Neuman (in press), Orem (1985), Rogers (1986), and Roy (1984), their works are classified as conceptual models. In summary, if a given work is an abstract, general, and comprehensive perspective of the metaparadigm of nursing, it is a conceptual model. If the work is more specific, concrete, and restricted to a more limited range of phenomena than that identified by the metaparadigm, it is a theory.

Another important distinction between conceptual models and theories is the number of steps required before the work can be used for pragmatic activities such as clinical practice or research. This distinction leads to another rule for classification of conceptual models and theories. This rule requires determination of how many levels of knowledge are needed before the work may be applied in particular nursing situations. If, for example, the work identifies physiologic needs as an assessment parameter, but does not explain the differences between normal and pathological functions of body systems, it most likely is a conceptual model. As such, the work is not directly applicable in clinical practice. A theory of normal and pathological functions must be linked with the conceptual model so that judgments about the functions of body systems may be made. Conversely, if the work includes a detailed description of behavior, or an explanation of how particular factors influence particular behaviors, it most likely is a theory. In this case, the work may be directly applied in clinical practice.

This rule also is exemplified by the number of steps required before empirical testing can occur (Reilly, 1975). A conceptual model cannot be tested directly, because its concepts are not operationally defined nor are the relationships between concepts observable. More specific concepts and propositions have to be derived from the conceptual model; that is, a theory must be formulated. These more specific concepts then must be defined in measurable ways, and hypotheses stating observable relationships must be derived from the propositions of the theory. Three steps, therefore, are required before a conceptual model can be tested, albeit indirectly. First, the conceptual model must be formulated; second, a theory must be derived from the conceptual model; and third, operational definitions must be given to the theory concepts, and hypotheses must be derived. In contrast, only two steps are required for empirical testing of a theory. First, the theory must be stated. Second, as above, the theory concepts must be operationally defined, and hypotheses must be formulated from the propositions.

Failure to distinguish between a conceptual model and a theory leads to considerable misunderstanding and inappropriate expectations about the work. When a conceptual model is labeled a theory, expectations regarding empirical testing immediately arise. When such expectations cannot be met, the work frequently is regarded as inadequate. Similarly, when a theory is labeled a conceptual model, expectations regarding comprehensiveness arise. When those expectations cannot be met, that work also may be regarded as inadequate.

The distinctions between conceptual models and theories described here are in keeping with Johnson's (1974) and Reilly's (1975) statements about these two levels of knowledge. The meaning given to conceptual models in this book should not be confused with the meaning of model found in the philosophy of science literature and some nursing literature. The latter refers to representations of testable theories. Rudner (1966), for example, defined a model for a theory as "an alternative interpretation of the same calculus of which the theory itself is an interpretation" (p. 24). This kind of a model is made up of ideas or diagrams that are more familiar to the novice than are the concepts and propositions of the theory. Thus, the model is a heuristic device that facilitates understanding of the theory. Rudner illustrated this by the analogy of the flow of water through pipes as a model for a theory of electric current wires.

In summary, a conceptual model cannot be used directly, whether in research, clinical practice, education, or administration. Rather, a conceptual model must be linked with one or more theories to form the conceptual-theoretical systems of knowledge needed for action.

*C*onceptual-Theoretical Systems of Nursing Knowledge

In nursing, conceptual models now are used as general guides for the organization of nursing knowledge and the design and implementation of research projects, clinical nursing practice, educational programs, and administrative systems. Currently, many theories used to amplify the concepts and propositions of any nursing model are borrowed from other disciplines, including psychology, sociology, biology, physics, and chemistry. When borrowed theories are linked with conceptual models, care must be taken to ensure logical congruence. Whall (1980) presented the first substantial discussion in the nursing literature of elements to consider when assessing congruence between conceptual models of nursing and borrowed theories. She proposed that conceptual models and theories must be examined for their stands on holism and linearity. Holism is the major focus of the organismic world view, and linearity is encompassed by the mechanistic world view. Both world views were discussed earlier in this section. Whall's discussion suggested that if conceptual model and theory are not congruent with regard to mechanism or organicism, the theory should be discarded and another more congruent one chosen, or the theory should be reformulated so that it is congruent with the model. Inasmuch as the conceptual model is the more abstract starting point, the theory—not the model—is reformulated to ensure congruence. Examples of construction of logically congruent conceptual-theoretical systems of nursing knowledge using borrowed theories are given in Fitzpatrick, Whall, Johnston, and Floyd (1982), and in Whall (1986). The same care to ensure logical congruence must be taken if a shared nursing theory is to be linked with a conceptual model of nursing, or if a unique nursing theory not derived from all explicit conceptual model is to be linked with a model.

The following discussion focuses on general considerations in constructing conceptual-theoretical systems of nursing knowledge in the areas of research, clinical practice, education, and administration. Later sections will document the use of conceptual models of nursing and related theories in various situations.

Nursing Research

The function of nursing research is to generate or test nursing theories. A fully developed conceptual model reflects a particular research tradition that includes the following six rules that guide theory generation and testing through all phases of a study:

- The first rule identifies the distinctive nature of the problems to be studied and the purposes to be fulfilled by the research.

- The second rule identifies the phenomena that are to be studied.

- The third rule identifies the research techniques that are to be employed and the research tools that are to be used.

- The fourth rule identifies the settings in which data are to be gathered and the subjects who are to provide the data.

- The fifth rule identifies the methods to be employed in reducing and analyzing the data.

- The sixth rule identifies the nature of contributions that the research will make to the advancement of knowledge. (Laudan, 1981; Schlotfeldt, 1975)

Thus, a conceptual model identifies the concepts from which specific variables are derived for the research. The model also presents the general propositions from which testable hypotheses eventually are derived. The subject matter of the study might be one concept or the relations between two or more concepts. Theories borrowed from other disciplines may be linked with the conceptual model in order to test the credibility of such knowledge in nursing situations. Or a study may involve generation or testing of a unique nursing theory.

The findings of research based on explicit conceptual-theoretical systems of nursing knowledge are, of course, used to evaluate the credibility of the theory. These findings, which constitute indirect evidence regarding the conceptual model, also should be used to evaluate its credibility (Fawcett & Downs, 1986; Silva, 1986). Thus, the credibility of the conceptual model should be considered as well as that of the theory whenever research is conducted. The empirical data, therefore, serve as a direct test of the theory and an indirect test of the conceptual model.

Clinical Nursing Practice

Conceptual models of nursing provide general guidelines for nursing practice. More specifically, a fully developed conceptual model represents a particular view of and approach to nursing practice. The domain of nursing practice and nursing processes are specified in the following four rules that are inherent in the conceptual model:

- The first rule identifies the general nature of the clinical problems to be considered and the purposes to be fulfilled by nursing practice.

- The second rule identifies the settings in which nursing practice occurs and the characteristics of legitimate recipients of nursing care.

- The third rule identifies the nursing process to be employed and the technologies to be used, including assessment format, diagnostic taxonomy, intervention typology, and evaluation methods.

- The fourth rule identifies the nature of contributions that nursing practice makes to the well-being of recipients of nursing care.

Thus, a conceptual model guides all aspects of clinical practice. The model tells the clinician what to look at when interacting with clients and how to interpret observations. It also tells the clinician how to plan interventions in a general manner, and provides beginning criteria for evaluation of intervention outcomes.

The specifics of nursing assessment, diagnosis, intervention, and evaluation, however, must come from theories. Although the conceptual model may, for example, direct the clinician to look for certain categories of problems in adaptation, theories of adaptation are needed to describe, to explain, and to predict manifestations of actual or potential patient problems in particular situations. Similarly, theories are needed to direct the particular nursing interventions required in such situations.

Nursing Education

In nursing education, the conceptual model, or conceptual framework as it usually is called, provides the general outline for curriculum content and teaching-learning activities. More specifically, a fully developed conceptual model represents a particular view of and approach to nursing education. The curricular structure and educational processes are specified in the following four rules inherent in each conceptual model:

- The first rule identifies the distinctive focus of the curriculum and the purposes to be fulfilled by nursing education.

- The second rule identifies the general nature and sequence of the content to be presented.

- The third rule identifies the settings in which nursing education occurs and the characteristics of the students.

- The fourth rule identifies the teaching-learning strategies to be employed.

When a conceptual model is used for curriculum construction, it must be linked with theories about education and the teaching-learning process, as well as with substantive theoretical content from nursing and other disciplines (Fawcett, 1985). The resulting conceptual-theoretical system then applies to the patient, the student, and the educator.

Nursing Administration

When a conceptual model is used in nursing administration, it provides a systematic structure for thinking about administrative matters, for observations of the administrative situation, and for interpreting what is seen in administrative settings. Each fully developed conceptual model, then, represents a particular view of and approach to administration of nursing services. The administrative structure and management practices are specified in the following three rules that are inherent in each conceptual model:

- The first rule identifies the distinctive focus of nursing in the clinical agency and the purpose to be fulfilled by nursing services.

- The second rule identifies the characteristics of nursing personnel and the settings in which nursing services are delivered.

- The third rule identifies the management strategies to be employed.

When a conceptual model is used to guide administrative practices, it must be linked with theories of organization and management developed in nursing and other disciplines. The resulting conceptual theoretical structure then is applicable to the patient, the nursing staff, and the nurse administrator.

Conclusion

This section discussed the definitions and distinctions between conceptual models and theories, as well as the formation of conceptual-theoretical systems of nursing knowledge. The distinctions between conceptual models and theories mandate separate criteria for analysis and evaluation of each of these levels of knowledge. Analysis and evaluation of theories have been discussed by many authors, including Chinn and Jacobs (1987), Fawcett and Downs (1986), and Walker and Avant (in press).

References

Ackoff, R. L. (1974). *Redesigning the future. A systems approach to societal problems.* New York: John Wiley & Sons.

Aggleton, P., & Chalmers, H. (1986). Nursing research, nursing theory and the nursing process. *Journal of Advanced Nursing,* 11, 197–202.

Barnard, K. E., Brandt, P. A., Raff, B. S., & Carroll, P. (Eds.) (1984). *Social support and families of vulnerable infants* (Birth Defects: Original Article Series, Vol. 20, No. 5). White Plains, NY: March of Dimes Birth Defects Foundation.

Battista, J. R. (1977). The holistic paradigm and general system theory. *General Systems,* 22, 65–71.

Benoliel, J. Q. (1977). The interaction between theory and research. *Nursing Outlook,* 25, 108–113.

Bertalanffy, L. von (1966). *General system theory.* New York: George Braziller.

Chin, R. (1980). The utility of systems models and developmental models for practitioners. In J.P. Riehl and C. Roy, *Conceptual models for nursing practice* (2nd ed., pp. 21–37). New York: Appleton-Century-Crofts.

Conway, M. E. (1985). Toward greater specificity in defining nursing's metaparadigm. *Advances in Nursing Science,* 7(4), 73–81.

Donaldson, S. K. & Crowley, D.M. (1978). The discipline of nursing. *Nursing Outlook,* 26, 113–120.

Durand, B. (1975). Failure to thrive in a child with Down's syndrome. *Nursing Research,* 24, 272–286.

Eckberg, D.L., & Hill, L., Jr. (1979). The paradigm concept and sociology: A critical review. *American Sociology Review,* 44, 925–937.

Fawcett, J. (1985). Theory: Basis for the study and practice of nursing education. *Journal of Nursing Education,* 24, 226–229.

Fawcett, J., & Downs, F. S. (1986). *The relationship of theory and research.* Norwalk, CT: Appleton-Century-Crofts.

Flaskerud, J. H., & Halloran, E. J. (1980). Areas of agreement in nursing theory development. *Advances in Nursing Science, 3*(1), 1–7.

Hall, B. A. (1981). The change paradigm in nursing: Growth versus persistence. *Advances in Nursing Science. 3*(4), 1–6.

Hall, B. A. (1983). Toward an understanding of stability in nursing phenomena. *Advances in Nursing Science, 5*(3). 15–20.

Hall, K. V. (1979). Current trends in the use of conceptual frameworks in nursing education. *Journal of Nursing Education, 18*(4), 26–29.

Hall, A. D., & Fagen, R. E. (1968). Definition of system. In W. Buckley (Ed.), *Modern systems research for the behavioral scientist* (pp. 81–92). Chicago Aldine.

Heiss, J. (1981). *The social psychology of interaction.* Englewood Cliffs, NJ: Prentice-Hall.

Hinshaw, A. S. (1967). Response to "Structuring the nursing knowledge system: A typology of four domains." *Scholarly Inquiry for Nursing Practice, 1,* 111–114.

Johnson, D. E. (1974) Development of theory: A requisite for nursing as a primary health profession. *Nursing Research, 23,* 372–377.

Johnson, D. E. (1980). The behavioral system model for nursing. In J.P. Riehl and C. Roy, *Conceptual models for nursing practice* (2nd ed., pp. 207–216). New York: Appleton-Century-Crofts.

Kim, H. S. (1987). Structuring the nursing knowledge system: A typology of four domains. *Scholarly Inquiry for Nursing Practice, 1,* 99–110.

Kuhn, T. S. (1970). *The structure of scientific revolutions* (2nd ed.). Chicago University of Chicago Press.

Kuhn, T. S. (1977). Second thoughts on paradigms. In F. Suppe (Ed.), *The structure of scientific theories* (2nd ed., pp. 459–517). Chicago: University of Illinois Press.

Laudan, L. (1981). A problem-solving approach to scientific progress. In I. Hacking (Ed.), *Scientific revolutions* (pp. 144–155). Fair Lawn, NJ: Oxford University Press.

Lippitt, G. L. (1973). *Visualizing change. Model building and the change process.* Fairfax, VA: NTL Learning Resources.

Looft, W. R. (1973). Socialization and personality throughout the life span: An examination of contemporary psychological approaches. In P. B. Baltes & K. W. Schaie (Eds.), *Life span developmental psychology. Personality and socialization* (pp. 25–52). New York: Academic Press.

Lowery, B. J., Jacobsen, B. S., & McCauley, K. (1987). On the prevalence of causal search in illness situations. *Nursing Research, 36,* 88–93.

Marriner, A. (1986). *Nursing theorists and their work.* St. Louis: CV Mosby.

Meleis, A. I. (1985). *Theoretical nursing: Development and progress.* Philadelphia: JB Lippincott.

Merton, R. K. (1957). *Social theory and social structure* (rev. ed.). New York: Free Press.

Neuman, B. (in press). The Neuman systems model: A holistic approach to client care. In B. Neuman, *The Neuman systems model. Application to nursing education and practice* (2nd ed.). Norwalk, CT: Appleton and Lange.

Norbeck, J. S., Lindsey, A. M., & Carrieri, V. L. (1981). The development of an instrument to measure social support. *Nursing Research, 30,* 264–269.

Nursing Development Conference Group. (1973). *Concept formalization in nursing. Process. and product.* Boston: Little, Brown & Co.

Nye, F. I., & Berardo, F. N. (Eds.). (1981). *Emerging conceptual frameworks in family analysis.* New York: Macmillan.

Orem, D. E. (1985). *Nursing: Concepts of practice* (3rd ed.). New York: McGraw-Hill.

Patterson, E. T., Freese, M. P. & Goldenberg, R. L. (1986). Reducing uncertainty: Self-diagnosis of pregnancy. Image. *The Journal of Nursing Scholarship, 18*, 105–109.

Peterson, C. J. (1977). Questions frequently asked about the development of a conceptual framework. *Journal of Nursing Education, 16*(4), 22–32.

Phillips, J. R. (1977). Nursing systems and nursing models. *Image, 9*, 4–7.

Redman, B. K. (1974). Why develop a conceptual framework? *Journal of Nursing Education, 13*(3), 2–10.

Reese, H. W., & Overton, W. F. (1970). Models of development and theories of development. In L.R. Goulet & P.B. Baltes (Eds.), *Life span developmental psychology. Research and theory* (pp. 115–145). New York: Academic Press.

Reilly, D. E. (1975). Why a conceptual framework? *Nursing Outlook, 23*, 566–569.

Riehl, J. P., & Roy, C. (1980). *Conceptual models for nursing practice* (2nd ed.). New York: Appleton-Century-Crofts.

Rogers, C. G. (1973). Conceptual models as guides to clinical nursing specialization. *Journal of Nursing Education, 12*(4), 2–6.

Roy, C. (1984). *Introduction to nursing: An adaption model* (2nd ed.). Englewood Cliffs, NJ: Prentice-Hall.

Rudner, R. S. (1966). *Philosophy of social science.* Englewood Cliffs, NJ: Prentice-Hall.

Schlotfeldt, R. M. (1975). The need for a conceptual framework. In P. J. Verhonick (Ed.), *Nursing Research I* (pp. 3–24). Boston: Little, Brown & Co.

Stevens, B. J. (1984). *Nursing theory. Analysis, application, evaluation* (2nd ed.). Boston: Little, Brown & Co.

Thomae, H. (1979). The concept of development and life-span developmental psychology. In P. B. Baltes & O. G. Brim, Jr. (Eds.). *Life-span development and behavior* (Vol. 2. pp. 281–312). New York: Academic Press.

Waltz, C., & Bausell, R. B. (1981). *Nursing research: Design, statistics and computer analysis.* Philadelphia: FA Davis.

Whall, A. L. (1980). Congruence between existing theories of family functioning and nursing theories. *Advances in Nursing Science, 3*(1), 59–67.

Whall, A. L. (1986). *Family therapy theory for nursing. Four approaches.* Norwalk, CT: Appleton-Century-Crofts.

The Empirical Approach to the Development of Nursing Science

Joyce J. Fitzpatrick

Nursing is witnessing a scientific revolution that will change not only how we label things but also our view of reality. The revolution must not be in structure and form, but in content. We must reconceptualize what we study, not how we know. Empiricism, as a stable scientific method, as a force that is known, can provide the structure to this revolution in nursing science.

This section will first address the following significant questions: What is science? What is empiricism? What research methods flow from the empirical approach to science and, importantly, what implications do they have for developing our nursing science? I will then share some of the research that I undertook from an empirical mode. Finally, I will challenge all of us to understand and support multiple modes of inquiry so that we might conserve our energy for the critical task at hand, that is, defining the content of our discipline.

It is my belief that, philosophically and practically, form follows substance. Our preoccupation with the forms, the structure, and the processes of science and knowledge development should have prepared us well to advance the discipline through an aggressive approach to the delineation of our content, the phenomena of concern to nursing as a science and to nurses as scientists and professionals.

Science represents means of understanding ourselves and our world. One of the ways in which we develop knowledge in nursing, a field of inquiry, as a discipline, is through science. Although our focus here is on the development of scientific nursing knowledge, we should be

Taken from: *Conceptual Models of Nursing: Analysis and Application*, Third Edition by Fitzpatrick and Whall.

equally compelled to develop other types of nursing knowledge, and to combine them masterfully. Before returning to this synthesis, let us first attend to the subject at hand.

Empiricism continues to dominate contemporary science. Even the popular "person in the street" image of the scientist—mad or otherwise—as the cold, impersonal, white-lab-coated individual in a laboratory accompanied by a wide array of strange equipment supports the concept of the scientist as objective and distant from the environment. Further, the scientist is often understood or characterized as having difficulty with human interactions. Think about the portrayals of scientists in science fiction movies, for example. Most often they work alone. Their efforts are directed at controlling the environment, and they are emotionally distant. One does not often see scientists portrayed as warm, caring individuals.

Feyerabend challenged the general perception of all science as empiricism. In fact, he proposed that a "good empiricist" must be a critical metaphysician who considers alternative explanations of the phenomena of concern (Nadditch, 1968). We shall return to this idea later.

Historical Development of Empiricism

Often, when we discuss the development of knowledge in general and of science in particular, we begin with Aristotle's attempts to develop a link between the ideas of the mind and the objects of the physical world. In fact, our relationship to the external world has provided content for philosophers from the beginning of time. In the prepositivist scientific era (from approximately 350 B.C. to 100 A.D.) there was an emphasis on a natural approach to knowledge development, whereby the scientist was primarily a passive observer of what was.

Many great thinkers paved the way for positivism and the positivist era. The beginnings of empiricism are often traced to the sixteenth century philosopher Francis Bacon, who stressed the importance of induction in data collection and of forming generalizations as a corresponding method of data interpretation. Bacon's approach was to perform experiments to obtain reliable information, to classify results so that all instances of the phenomenon studied could be compared, to develop theorems or generalizations that would give rise to laws, and to use the laws to point out confirming evidence.

It is important to note that Bacon's empiricist approach was not without challenge and controversy. In fact, his ideas were debated for centuries, and in some circles the debate continues. Other predominant views contemporary to baconian logic were those of Galileo and Descartes. Galileo developed his mechanistic arguments from a deductive approach and launched many astronomical experiments. Descartes, a rationalist, is credited with the ultimate rational approach to science, *Cogito, ergo sum:* "I think, therefore I am."

Although at the time there was a great debate between the empiricists and the rationalists, there was also some merging and overlap of ideas, and some intellectual movement from an emphasis on purely sensory observations to an emphasis on a combined approach wherein the observations were interpreted.

In the seventeenth century, John Locke gave structure to empiricism with the publication of his "Essay on Human Understanding," in which he asserted that all knowledge was developed by observation in the course of experience. Further, Locke proposed that meaning could not be inferred by the rational processes of the mind, and that skepticism and uncertainty should prevail.

Kant imposed additional structure on science, allowing that sensory experience was necessary, but supporting a rational organizing approach of the mind. Kant's approach to empiricism represented the merging of scientific approaches.

Basic to empiricism is the understanding that scientists employ research procedures that lead them to take cause for granted. Four of these procedures are (1) isolation of the phenomenon under investigation from external sources of influence, which is achieved by conducting laboratory research in enclosed settings that exclude extraneous sounds, chemicals in the air, and the like; (2) the identification of dependent variables that are often inert and would not be expected to change over time for reasons other than the cause under investigation; (3) the development of explicit and precise theories specifying the exact size of an expected effect, whether it be the expansion of a metal or the change in a moon's orbit; and (4) the use of measurement instruments whose calibrations are so fine relative to the size of the predicted effect that repeated tests can be made of how closely the observed data fit the expected pattern.

In Vienna in the early twentieth century a group known as the logical positivists saw an opportunity to reform the acquisition of knowledge by use of the scientific method.

Although the positivists were originally concerned with reform of ethics, religion, and politics, the principal focus of their efforts came to be the reform of science. In fact, positivism is characterized by an extremely positive view of science and the scientific method. The efforts of the positivists led to paradigm revolution in science and scientific methods.

The understandings basic to the positivists' view are (1) that there is an external reality that can be observed and described objectively in scientific language, that is, artificial constructions or models, yielding explanation in the sense of a logic of hypotheses and deduction; (2) science is a linguistic system in which true propositions are in one-to-one correspondence with facts; (3) theories can be inferred from observations, but correspond to external reality; and (4) scientists stand apart from the world and theorize about it objectively and dispassionately.

Hume is often credited with positing the approach to scientific analysis that reflects classic positivist analysis. This included (1) contiguity between the presumed cause and effect; (2) temporal precedence, in that the cause has to precede the effect in time; and (3) constant conjunction, in that the cause has to be present whenever the effect is obtained. Hume further proposed that no cause can be directly observed; one can only note coincidence in space and time. Accordingly, all cause is attributed to past correlations between variables, an understanding that leads to powerful predictions.

The empiricist view is characterized by the principle of correspondence, that is, the correspondence of external reality to the laws and principles of science. Scientific truth must be verified by experimentation, or, according to a classic modification of this approach proposed by Popper (1959), our scientific methods should be focused on falsification.

Following the era of positivism, there occurred a period of thought and scientific growth based on retrospective analysis. For example, in Kuhn's (1977) revolutionary view of science, the development of disciplines is based on the convergence of scientific thought.

In a recently completed analysis of scientific thought in relation to nursing, Gortner (1987) proposed a distinction between the analytic form of empiricism reflected in classic logical positivism and the alternative form, referred to as integrative or synthetic empiricism, which she considers acceptable for nursing.

In summary, the classic empiricist is one who demands that science start from observable facts and proceed by generalization, and who refuses to entertain metaphysical ideas at any point in the scientific process. Although this extreme view is no longer the predominant one, we often hear reference to this scientific philosophy as the ideal or orthodox mode, particularly in times of uncertainty. One could interpret the present state of nursing science as one of uncertainty. Such uncertainty exists because of the absence of predominance of any one paradigm, the preparadigm state described by Kuhn.

$\mathscr{I}$mplications of Research Methods for Nursing Science

There exists a strong need to focus nursing science on the delineation of the substance, the content, of nursing rather than the form. The classic structured scientific approach has come to mean slow, cautious, deliberate development of knowledge through a process of gradual accumulation. We must, however, find ways to return the excitement to science, and to empiricism in particular, to advance our discipline and further our mission to participate in providing health care to people. I believe that it is more important to energize empiricism, to temper it with metatheoretical issues, than abandon it for other philosophical forms.

In his treatise on personal knowledge, Polanyi (1958) proposed the more extreme view that scientists must engage in intellectual passions, that as scientists we must be passionately preoccupied with problems, committed to our beliefs, and prepared to make leaps or guesses that advance our work. The various challenges to extreme empiricism or positivism have been summarized by Lincoln and Guba (1985) in their proposal for naturalistic inquiry. They list the following assumptions:

1. An ontological assumption of a single, tangible reality "out there" that can be broken apart into pieces capable of being studied independently; that is, the whole is simply the sum of the parts.

2. An epistemological assumption about the possibility of separation of the observer from the observed, the knower from the known.

3. An assumption of the temporal and contextual independence of observations, so that what is true at one time and place may, under appropriate circumstances (such as sampling), also be true at another time and place.

4. An assumption of linear causality: there are no effects without causes and no causes without effects.

5. An axiological assumption of value freedom, that is, that the methodology guarantees that the results of an inquiry are essentially free from the influence or any value system (bias). (p. 28)

We should continue to challenge these assumptions as we further develop our empirical method.

Thus, postpositivist empiricism is a reaction to the shortcomings of the approaches of the logical positivists. As such, the basic tenets of positivism have been reversed. Hesse (1980) has summarized the postpositivist understanding as including the following assumptions:

1. Theory and data are not detachable, for what count as data are determined according to some theoretical interpretation; facts must be restructured in light of interpretation.

2. Theories and laws are not exclusively external; what we count as facts are constructed into laws or propositions by what the theory says about the interrelationships.

3. The language of science is metaphorical and inexact; its formal nature distorts the richness and creativity of the scientific experience.

4. Meanings are significant and are determined by theory; they are understood by theoretical coherence rather than by correspondence with facts.

$\mathcal{R}$esearch Models

It is my belief that my own research represents postpositivist empiricism or the integrative empiricism described by Gortner (1987), in which the lived experience determines not only the observations but also the theoretical meanings. The examples of my research described below illustrate the theory–method links and, importantly, the use of the empirical method.

I developed my initial research inductively, then proceeded to examine theoretical understandings that existed in the literature, and finally delineated a new conceptualization that integrated the first two phases. Although this work proceeded from an inductive through a deductive approach in an effort to extract meanings, I will first present the basic theoretical approaches of Rogers (1970) that served to integrate my research.

Rogers proposed that the object of nursing science should be the unitary person, described as a four-dimensional negentropic energy field identified by pattern and organization and manifesting characteristics and behaviors that are different from those of its parts and that cannot be predicted from knowledge of its parts. Basic to Rogers' science of unitary persons are the conceptualizations of person–environment interaction, the movement of holistic persons toward increasing complexity and diversity, and the changes in field pattern and organization evidenced by changes in the associated wave patterns and rhythmic activity identifying the whole. The process of human development is viewed as consistent with environmental changes, and variations in rhythmic patterns of person–environment interaction can be identified.

Empirical evidence relevant to both phylogenetic and ontogenetic evolution supports the postulated developmental correlate related to time experiences, the primary focus of my research. For example, in childhood, the individual experiences time as slow and dragging; in adulthood time is perceived as flying or racing; and among the aged, there are reports of movement toward timelessness. Elsewhere, I have used the picket fence to illustrate the conceptualization of rhythmic developmental progres-sion. The fence pickets represent an identifiable short-amplitude, high-frequency rhythm of peaks and troughs. If viewed in rapid motion, the pickets (i.e., the peaks and troughs, the waves and rhythms) blur and suggest a straight line or nonpicket fence (Fitzpatrick, 1980).

To support the theoretical propositions in this conceptual model, I have cited a wide range of empirical investigations related to rhythmic phenomena. In addition, my extensive review and evaluation of the theory has led to the identification of movement patterns, nonlinear temporal experiences, patterns of consciousness, and perceptual experiences related to wave patterns of stimuli, for example, auditory and visual, as possible indices of holistic persons (Fitzpatrick, 1983).

In summary, the basic theory that is proposed has a unifying concept, rhythmic phenomena. Although the research related to rhythms, particularly biologic and circadian rhythms, is extensive, the conceptualizations underlying these investigations are contiguous rather than comparable and exact in reference to a theory of unitary persons. The rhythm research relevant to my conceptualization and research has been focused primarily on the rhythmic phenomena of temporal experiences.

My initial interest in the theoretical relationships identified stems from extensive clinical observations of death-involved individuals, specifically, those who were suicidal. I began from an inductive approach based on my observations of the day-to-day life experience of such persons. More particularly, I was interested in how suicidal persons understood their present experience.

I had worked for several years with persons in crisis who were considering suicide. One of my most consistent clinical observations was that these persons had a great deal of difficulty integrating their present experiences with their lives. They were so intensely focused on their crisis that they believed the only way for them to change the here and now was to suicide.

Before addressing any of the specific research questions in any substantive manner, a more basic conceptual issue required attention. In order to clarify the concept of time within the understandings inherent in the conceptual system, I began a series of empirical investigations directed at refining the conceptualization and the measurement of temporality.

The purpose of my initial research study was to describe the interrelationships between the subjective experience of time (i.e., temporal perspective) and the perception of the passage of external time. The study was conducted among a relatively homogeneous, healthy, adult population. It was anticipated that the descriptions of the relationships among the temporal dimensions within a normal adult population would provide a broader theoretical framework for interpreting human experience (Fitzpatrick, 1975).

In retrospect, the major contribution of the study seems to be that it generated questions regarding the experience and measurement of time. The study itself represented a linear view of reality. Only after its completion was it possible to begin questioning the basic conceptualizations and measurement instruments utilized.

The second in my series of studies was an attempt to identify differences among aged individuals on the basis of their residential situation (Fitzpatrick & Donovan, 1978). It was argued that, theoretically, the environment situation would be directly related to older persons' understandings of their life experiences. The same temporal variables used in the preceding study were used to evelute the conceptualizations and the methodology.

Perhaps most significant in this research were anecdotal findings from the study. Many of the noninstitutionalized older persons presented themselves in a constant state of vigilance, primarily owing to their uncertainty regarding their circumstances. They seemed to be very focused on the here and now and described their lives in terms of the present and immediate future. At the completion of this study, I developed a conceptual interest in the relationship of crisis theory to my clinical data, research observations, and theoretical framework. I began to reconceptualize my work as related to the crisis perspective and systematically presented arguments in the literature proposing this link (Fitzpatrick, 1983).

The third in my series of studies was an exploration of temporal experiences among four groups of hospitalized individuals: medical, surgical, psychiatric nonsuicidal, and psychiatric suicidal patients. As in the previous study, it was thought that the temporal experience might be related to the environmental situation, namely, hospitalization. At this stage of the research, however, the crisis perspective was integrated from the onset. The study was described as focused on the crisis of hospitalization.

This particular study is important for several reasons. It clearly emphasized clinical groups, and particularly included a group of suicidal individuals. It was a first attempt in a plan to study individuals experiencing crisis situations, in this case the crisis of hospitalization, and thus was the precursor of a study of the crisis of dying.

Findings of related studies, that is, of temporality among terminally ill cancer patients, among individuals experiencing a suicidal crisis, and among an aged group, will be discussed. The same temporal variables were assessed with each of these groups and comparable control groups.

The underlying theoretical proposition was that among these clinical groups—terminally ill, suicidal, and aged—more similarities than differences would be identified in the various temporal dimensions because (1) they were all experiencing a crisis; and (2) they were all intimately involved with death. Similarities have been determined with respect to some of the temporal dimensions. For example, all death-involved individuals have a limited future perspective and are focused more directly on the near past, the present, and the immediate future; and all of them report a heightened sense of time pressure. There was no clear indication from the data of whether time passes slowly or rapidly for them. The extent to which this reflects the timelessness proposed by Rogers as characteristic of developmental progression has yet to be evaluated. There does exist some support for the basic temporal components of crisis theory. For example, the time-limited nature of the crisis was reflected in their focus on the immediate future. The tendency to focus on the present situation was clearly evident in these groups. Tentative support for the rogerian conceptual model may be inferred, although continued refinement of the conceptualization and measurement of temporality is necessary.

In summary, it may be helpful to refer back to some statements regarding temporality and motion patterns. Extensive evaluation of the rogerian model has led to the postulation that these dimensions may be indices of holistic persons. It would seem that the logical development of programmatic research would lead one to the refinement of each of these indices and, subsequently, to the assessment of the interrelationships among the indices. Because such a project would necessarily extend over a long period of time, it would be more expeditious to encourage collaboration among several investigators exploring any one of these manifestations.

The particular developmental periods to be studied would be selected arbitrarily by the investigators. If one accepts the basic assumptions of rhythm theory, differences in behavioral manifestations would be identified more easily during the peaks of wave patterns. In the investigations described in this presentation, these peak rhythm periods are assumed to be crisis experiences, that is, turning points in the developmental process. The crisis of dying has been given particular attention in that it has been assumed to represent the most complex and differentiated phase of human growth, that period characterized by the highest degree of non-linear temporality, or timelessness.

While developing conceptualizations about the human experience of life and thus of health, my empirical investigations have focused primarily on the descriptions of temporal patterns. More recently, however, my research has directly addressed the meanings of death and thus the meanings of life. This recent research on life and death stems not only from the basic concern but also from the empirical investigations on temporal patterns. I think that the more general problem of the meaning of life has been rediscovered through the specific research on time.

Based on my empirical observations and subsequent conceptualizations, I have proposed a life perspective rhythm model to guide our research and practice in nursing (Fitzpatrick, 1983). My development of this conceptualization was inspired by a professional interest in how nurses can help people live through and move through life's experiences. I have been concerned with the meanings that individuals attach to life. Based on my extensive clinical and research-based observations of people involved in death-related experiences, I would propose that the meaningfulness of life is essential to its maintenance and enhancement. Furthermore, it seems that the meaning attached to life is linked intimately to health, regardless of whether health is defined as absence of disease, quality of life, or maximum wellness. As I have recently suggested, perhaps we should seek an alternative term for "health" (Chinn, 1987). Whether or not we change our terminology, our efforts must be channeled directly into the clarification of definitions and concomitant research, based on a wide range of philosophies and methods of conducting research.

The life perspective rhythm paradigm proposed here could provide a variety of avenues for significant research related to health. Simultaneously, it offers an organizing and integrating framework for research on human rhythms. For example, differences identified in rhythmic patterns of healthy and ill persons would be most relevant to this conceptualization.

In reference to specific patterns inherent in the crisis situation, there is a continued need for clarification of the conceptual, methodologic, and clinical concerns related to temporal patterns. Toward the advancement of science, specific efforts should be focused on the refutation of theoretical postulations. For example, an alternative hypothesis methodology can be used to examine the data.

Predictive principles underlying professional nursing practice and specific strategies for intervention can be derived from these conceptualizations and empirical investigations, hence the questionnaires used for assessment of temporal perspective have been useful in clinical interventions with elderly persons when the focus has been reminiscence therapy. Additionally, elderly persons experiencing the crisis of retirement might find therapeutic attempts at temporal integration particularly helpful as they derive meaning from their life experiences. Suicidal individuals who cannot move from their present crisis are especially assisted by a focus on movement toward future planning. More generally, individuals may be assisted through the use of variety of rhythmic intervention strategies, including mediation, relaxation, and biofeedback. The range of potential applications is extensive, although some intervention paths seem to lead more directly to the desired destination of maximum health.

The research presented here represents for me the clearest example of the application of integrated empiricism. More recently, I have embarked on two new phases of research: an analysis of the development of our profession and discipline over time, and a set of decision analysis studies that will directly address the ways of knowing that are basic to our discipline. In the first study of this set we are approaching the research questions from the expert clinicians' viewpoint, asking how they make the clinical judgments that guide their practice. I expect sometime to share the results of this current study. To me it represents a new combination of methods, a new synthesis of our understandings, and, importantly, a new interlinkage of clinical scientific knowledge.

In conclusion, then, the question can be raised, as it is frequently, about why empiricism is necessary for nursing science. More generally, why should we advocate a classic or traditional scientific approach for nursing?

I have argued elsewhere that quality research is rather simple to identify from a general scientific standard (Fitzpatrick & Abraham, 1987). Our scientific peers across disciplines judge our research as acceptable based on the logic and structure of our scientific approaches and the outcomes of our science. It does matter whether our research is published in referred research journals and funded through the sanctioned scientific bodies in our society (e.g., the National Institutes of Health and the National Science Foundation). We must be careful to work within the system to influence change, and to acknowledge the prevailing scientific paradigm. At the same time, we must take risks to create new conceptualizations within our scientific pursuits. I cannot advocate strongly enough this two-pronged approach to creating change.

References

Chinn, P. (1987). Policy for health? *Advances in Nursing Science, 9,* xxi–xiii.

Fitzpatrick, J. J. (1975). An investigation of the relationship between temporal orientation, temporal extension, and time perception. Unpublished doctoral dissertation, New York University, New York.

Fitzpatrick, J. J. (1980). Patients' perceptions of time: Current research. *International Nursing Review, 27*(5), 148–153, 160.

Fitzpatrick, J. J. (1983). Integration of the domains. In *Proceedings of the 1982 Forum on Doctoral Education in Nursing.* Cleveland: Case Western Reserve University.

Fitzpatrick, J. J., & Donovan, M. J. (1978). Temporal experience and motor behavior among the aging. *Research in Nursing and Health, 1,* 60–68.

Fitzpatrick, J. J., & Abraham, I. L. (1987). Toward the socialization of scholars and scientists. *Nurse Educator, 12*(3), 23–25.

Gortner, S. R. (1987). *Nursing science methods: A reader.* San Francisco: University of California, San Francisco Press.

Hesse, M. (1980). *Revolutions and reconstructions in the philosophy of science.* Bloomington: Indiana University Press.

Kuhn, T. S. (1977). *The essential tension: Selected studies in scientific tradition and change.* Chicago: University of Chicago Press.

Lincoln, Y. S., & Guba, E. G. (1985). *Naturalistic inquiry.* Beverly Hills, CA: Sage.

Nadditch, P. H. (Ed.). (1986). *The philosophy of science.* London: Oxford University Press.

Polanyi, M. (1958). *Personal knowledge.* Chicago: University of Chicago Press.

Popper, K. (1959). *The logic of scientific discovery.* New York: Basic Books.

Rogers, M. E. (1970). *An introduction to the theoretical basis of nursing.* Philadelphia: F.A. Davis.

Nursing's Fundamental Patterns of Knowing

It is the general conception of any field of inquiry that ultimately determines the kind of knowledge that field aims to develop as well as the manner in which that knowledge is to be organized, tested and applied. . . . Such an understanding . . . involves critical attention to the question of what it means to know and what kinds of knowledge are held to be of most value in the discipline of nursing.

Barbara A. Carper (1978, p. 13)

Knowing and knowledge are reflections of four patterns: empirics, aesthetics, ethical, and personal. Together they form an essential whole. Praxis—thoughtful reflection and action that occur in synchrony—comes from the whole of knowing and knowledge in nursing practice. This section presents a conception of the whole of knowing and knowledge in nursing.

*K*nowing and Knowledge

In this text, we use the term *knowing* to refer to ways of perceiving and understanding the self and the world. Knowing is an ontologic, dynamic, changing process. We use the term *knowledge* to refer to knowing that is in a form that can be shared or communicated with others. Additionally, knowledge represents what is collectively taken to be a reasonably accurate accounting of the world as it is known by the members of the discipline. Knowledge, then, is a representation of knowing that is collectively judged by standards and criteria shared within the nursing community. The ways in which knowledge and knowing are developed

Taken from: *Knowledge and Nursing: Integrated Approach*, Fifth Edition by Chinn and Kramer
Copyright © 1999 by Mosby, Inc.; St. Louis, Missouri 63146.

are epistemologic concerns that reveal how we come to know and how we acquire shared knowledge in the discipline.

As nurses practice, they know more than they can communicate symbolically or justify as knowledge. Much of what is known is expressed through actions, movements, or sounds. These are the everyday actions or nondiscursive expressions of knowing that always reflect the whole of knowing. Each of the patterns of knowing has nondiscursive forms of expression that give nursing its distinctive character as a healing practice and that can be recognized as arising from a particular pattern of knowing. At the same time, what is expressed in a nurse's actions always conveys a simultaneous wholeness. Actions also convey a fuller expression of what is known than the formal, discursive expressions of knowledge. Others can observe and comprehend action as a whole, but direct observation is accessible only to those who observe a particular scenario and is therefore limited in serving as a means for communicating what is known to the broader audience of the discipline.

We believe that much of what nurses know has potential to become formally expressed. Although language and other symbols will only partially reflect the whole of knowing, it is important to begin the challenge of formal expression of knowledge in order to communicate what is known within the discipline as a whole. This makes it possible to focus, shape, question, and influence what is collectively accepted as sound, useful, and valued. It is the formal expressions that have potential to become the knowledge of the discipline. Sharing knowledge is important because it creates a disciplinary community, beyond the isolation of individual experience. Once this happens, social purposes form, and knowledge development and shared purposes form a cyclic interrelationship that moves us toward prospective, value-grounded change or praxis.

We have organized this text to focus on processes for development of discursive disciplinary knowledge for nursing praxis, drawing on each of four patterns of knowing within nursing. The methods for developing knowledge are unique to each of the patterns of knowing. The methods that are required for one pattern cannot be used to develop knowledge within another pattern. The scientific methods of empirics, for example, cannot be used to develop personal, ethical, or aesthetic knowledge. This is a challenging ontologic-epistemologic paradox, for the experience of knowing always draws the knower into the whole, where one aspect cannot be comprehended without immediate grasp of the whole of knowing. For example, the methods of science can be described and applied uniquely to the development of empiric knowledge. In the actual experience of scientific inquiry, however, the scientist's personal, ethical, and aesthetic knowing shapes and influences how the inquiry unfolds.

While we discuss the unique features of developing the knowledge of each fundamental pattern, we return again and again to the complementarity of each process and to the aspects of the whole of knowing that influence the unfolding knowledge development process. In the next section we present a conceptualization of the fundamental patterns of knowing that serves as an organizing framework for the entire text. This section includes an overview of (1) the essential nature of each pattern in relation to the whole, (2) knowledge development processes within each pattern, and (3) the importance of developing knowledge within all of the fundamental patterns of knowing.

*O*verview of Nursing's Fundamental Patterns of Knowing

Since Nightingale first established formal education for nurses, nursing has depended on formal knowledge as a basis for practice. The nature of knowledge seen as valuable for nursing changes with time, yet overall the whole of knowledge and knowing that guides and constitutes practice has remained remarkably stable.

Carper (1978) examined early nursing literature and named four fundamental and enduring patterns of knowing that nurses have valued and used in practice. One of the patterns is the familiar and respected pattern of empirics, the science of nursing. In addition, she identified ethics, the component of moral knowledge in nursing; aesthetics, the art of nursing; and personal knowing in nursing.

Other authors have proposed viable additions or adaptations to Carper's conception (Munhall, 1993; Silva, Sorrell, & Sorrell, 1995; White, 1995; Wolfer, 1993). Each of the proposed adaptations to Carper's conception makes a valuable contribution to understanding knowledge and knowing in nursing, and each can be embraced. The patterns that Carper identified remain the fundamental patterns that were reflected in nursing's early literature and have endured as essential aspects of nursing knowledge for more than a century. The fundamental patterns do not exclude other conceptualizations of knowing, and with time certain adaptations to nursing's fundamental knowledge will emerge in new directions.

The fundamental patterns of knowing remain valuable in that they conceptualize a broad scope of knowing that accounts for a holistic practice. We retain our focus on these fundamental patterns in this text because until very recently the development of empiric knowledge has been the prevailing approach to knowledge development, and the other fundamental patterns have not been formally developed within the discipline. In part, neglect of the personal, ethical, and aesthetic patterns of knowing reflects an overvaluing of empirics as the knowledge of the discipline. In addition, methods for developing knowledge within the other patterns, particularly personal and aesthetic knowledge, are only beginning to be systematically described and developed.

In the following sections we describe each of the fundamental patterns and provide an overview of the methods we propose for developing each of the patterns.

Empirics: The Science of Nursing

Empirics is based on the assumption that what is known is accessible through the senses: seeing, touching, hearing, and so forth. Empirics can be traced to Nightingale's precepts concerning the importance of accurate observation and record keeping. The science of nursing emerged during the late 1950s (Carper, 1978). Empirics as a pattern of knowing draws on traditional ideas of science in which reality is viewed as something that can be known by observation and verified by other observers.

Empiric knowing is expressed in practice through the nurse's scientific competence—embodied knowing that makes possible competent action grounded in scientific theory. There is a cognitive component of empiric competence that involves problem solving and logical reasoning, but much of the underlying empiric knowing that informs competent reasoning remains in the background of conscious awareness. It is also accessible to conscious reasoning when attention turns to the reasoning process itself.

Empiric knowledge is formally expressed in the form of empiric theories, statements of fact, or descriptions of empiric events or objects. The development of empiric knowledge has traditionally been accomplished by the methods of science. Usually this has involved testing hypotheses derived from a theory that offers a tentative explanation of empiric phenomena. Although many conceptualizations of empiric knowledge in nursing are linked to this traditional view of science, ideas about what is legitimate for developing the science of nursing have broadened to include activities that are not strictly within the realm of hypothesis testing, such as phenomenologic or ethnographic descriptions or inductive means of generating theory.

Ethics: The Moral Component of Knowledge in Nursing

Ethics in nursing is focused on matters of obligation or what ought to be done. The moral component of knowing in nursing goes beyond knowledge of the norms or ethical codes of nursing, other related disciplines, and society; it involves making moment-to-moment judgments about what ought to be done, what is good and right, and what is responsible. Ethical knowing guides and directs how nurses conduct their practice, what they select as important, where loyalties are placed, and what priorities demand advocacy.

Ethical knowing also involves confronting and resolving conflicting values, norms, interests, or principles. There may be no satisfactory answer to an ethical dilemma or moral distress—only alternatives, some of which are more or less satisfactory. Ethical knowing in nursing requires both an experiential knowledge, from which ethical reasoning arises, and knowledge of the formal principles, ethical codes, and theories of the discipline and society (Carper, 1978). Like empiric knowing, ethical knowing is expressed in nursing actions—what we call moral-ethical comportment. Nursing actions based on ethical knowing can be observed by others, and the underlying ethical principles can be discerned and examined.

The discipline's ethical principles, codes, and theories are set forth in the philosophic ideals on which ethical decisions rest. Ethical knowledge does not describe or prescribe what a decision or action should be; rather, it provides insight about which choices are possible and why, and it provides direction toward choices that are sound, good, responsible, or just.

Ethical theories are like empiric theories in that they describe some dimensions of reality and express relationships between phenomena. However, empiric theory relies on observable reality that can be confirmed by others. Ethical theory cannot be tested in this sense because the relationships of the theory rest on underlying philosophic reasoning that leads to conclusions concerning what is right, good, responsible, or just. The reasoning can include description of experience to substantiate an argument, but the conclusions are value statements that cannot be perceived or confirmed empirically.

Personal Knowing in Nursing

Personal knowing in nursing concerns the inner experience of becoming a whole, aware, genuine self. Personal knowing encompasses knowing one's own self and the self of others. As Carper (1978, p. 18) stated, "One does not know about the self, one strives simply to know the self." It is through knowing one's own self that one is able to know the other. Full awareness of the self, the moment, and the context of interaction makes possible meaningful, shared human experience. Without this component of knowing, the idea of therapeutic use of self in nursing would not be possible (Carper, 1978).

Personal knowing is most fully communicated as an authentic, aware, genuine self. What is perceived by others is the existence of a person, an embodied self. As personal knowing emerges more fully throughout life, the unique or genuine self can be more fully expressed and becomes accessible as a means by which deliberate action and interaction take form. It is possible to describe certain things about the self in personal stories and autobiographies. These descriptions provide sources for deep reflection and a shared understanding of how personal knowledge can be developed and used in a deliberative way. Descriptions about the self are limited in that they never fully reflect personal knowing, and they are retrospective in that they can describe only the self that was. However, publicly expressed descriptions can be a tool for developing self-awareness and self-intimacy and for communicating to others valuable possibilities for developing personal knowing (Hagan, 1990; Nelson, 1994).

In a sense, all knowing is personal; each individual can know only through their personal senses and sensibilities. Empiric theories can be learned, but their meaning for the individual comes from personal reflection and experience with the phenomena of the theory. Aesthetic sensibilities, ethical precepts, and moral beliefs are likewise highly personal in nature. We recognize this broad meaning of personal knowing, but our focus is the aspect of personal knowing that delves into the processes of knowing the self and of developing self-knowing through healing encounters with others.

Aesthetics: The Art of Nursing

Aesthetic knowing in nursing involves deep appreciation of the meaning of a situation, calling forth inner creative resources that transform experience into what is not yet real but possible. Aesthetic knowing makes it possible to move beyond the surface—beyond the limits and circumstances of a particular moment—to sense the meaning of the moment and connect with depths of human experience that are common but unique in each experience (sickness, suffering, recovery, birth, death). Aesthetic knowing in nursing is made visible through the actions, bearing, conduct, attitudes, narrative, and interactions of the nurse in relation to others. It is also expressed in art forms such as poetry, drawings, stories, and music that reflect and communicate symbolic meanings embedded in nursing practice.

Aesthetic knowing is what makes possible knowing what to do with—and how to be in—the moment, instantly, without conscious deliberation. It arises from a direct perception of what is significant in the moment—that is, grasping meaning in the encounter. Perception of meaning in an encounter creates artful nursing action, and the nurse's perception of meaning is reflected in the action taken (Carper, 1978). The meaning is often a shared meaning that is perceived without conscious exchange of words and may not be consciously or cognitively formed. Sometimes meaning is brought to the situation from the nurse's own creative sensibilities, opening possibilities that would not otherwise enter into the encounter. The actions—movements and verbal expressions—of the nurse serve to transform and shape the experience into what would not otherwise exist, creating new possibilities in the encounter. The nurse's actions take on an element of artistry, creating unique, meaningful, deeply moving interactions with others that touch common chords of human experience. We refer to this aspect of nursing practice as the transformative art-act.

Aesthetic knowing is expressed in the moment of experience-action (Benner, 1984; Benner and Wrubel, 1989), in the transformative art-act. Aesthetic knowledge is formally expressed in aesthetic criticism and in works of art that symbolize experience. Aesthetic criticism is the discursive expression of aesthetic knowledge that conveys the artful aspects of the art, the technical skill required to perform the art-act, knowledge that informs the development of the art-act, the historical and cultural significance of specific aspects of nursing as an art, and the potential for the future development of the art.

Processes for Developing Nursing Knowledge

Nursing's patterns of knowing are interrelated and arise from the whole of experience. Nurses learn a portion of the knowledge of the discipline in their basic education and continue to build on their acquired knowledge as they practice (Benner, 1984). In addition to the knowledge that is acquired through formal and informal education, the experience of practice forms dimensions of knowing. What is known through the experience of practice is reflected in the practice and contributes to the development of formally expressed nursing knowledge. Formally expressed nursing knowledge is developed by using methods of inquiry that are grounded in both practice and formal scholarly methods specifically designed for each pattern.

Figure 2–2 is a representation of how the unique processes and expressions of each pattern contribute to the whole of knowing. In the figure, each of the fundamental patterns is represented in a quadrant. At the periphery of each quadrant are critical questions that each pattern addresses. In the center of each quadrant, a large arrow represents the forms of expression of knowledge within each pattern. The arrow points to the inner sphere, showing the practice or action expression of knowing that is associated with the pattern. The inner sphere is shown as a whole, without quadrant boundaries, representing our view that in nursing practice knowing is experienced as a whole and cannot be experienced as discrete patterns. Along the vertical axis, represented by vertical broken arrows, are the processes for developing the formal knowledge expressions. Along the horizontal axis, represented by horizontal broken arrows, are the collective processes used within the discipline for validating or authenticating what is known.

The outer area, where the critical questions appear, and the inner sphere, showing the action expressions of knowing, represent the ontologic dimensions of knowing. The processes shown along the vertical and horizontal arrows represent the epistemologic dimensions of processes for developing and authenticating knowledge.

Another way of conceptualizing these processes is shown in Table 2–7. The dimensions of the critical questions, the creative processes for developing knowledge, the formal expression of knowledge, the processes for authenticating knowledge, and the nondiscursive expressions of knowing in practice are shown for each pattern. Each of the dimensions are unique to each pattern of knowing; you cannot create empiric theory, for example, by using the creative

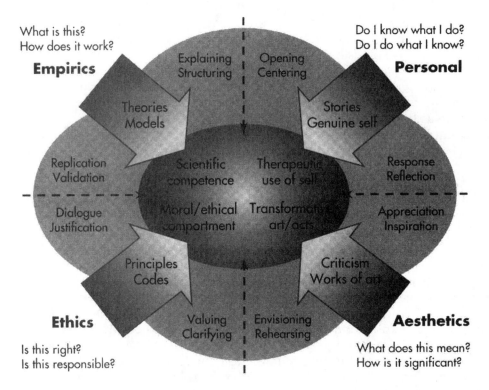

FIGURE 2–2

The processes for developing nursing knowledge.

TABLE 2–7	Dimensions Associated with Each of the Fundamental Patterns of Knowing			
Dimension	**Empirics**	**Ethics**	**Personal**	**Aesthetics**
Critical questions	What is this? How does it work?	Is this right? Is this responsible?	Do I know what I do? Do I do what I know?	What does this mean? How is it significant?
Creative processes	Explaining, structuring	Valuing, clarifying	Opening, centering	Envisioning, rehearsing
Formal expression of knowledge	Facts, models, theories, descriptions	Principles, codes, ethical theories	Autobiographical stories, the genuine self	Aesthetic criticism, works of art
Authentication processes	Replication, validation	Dialogue, justification	Response, reflection	Appreciation, inspiration
Nondiscurssive expression of knowing in practice	Scientific competence	Moral-ethical comportment	Therapeutic use of self	Transformative art/acts

processes of ethics, personal, or aesthetic knowing. However, in the realm of nondiscursive expression of knowing in practice, knowing is experienced as a whole, even though you can discern those aspects of practice that are possible because of each fundamental pattern of knowing.

Critical questions represent the kind of understanding that emerges within the individual patterns. Empirics, the science of nursing, poses the critical questions "What is this?" and "How does it work?" Personal knowing poses the critical questions "Do I know what I do?" and "Do I do what I know?" Ethics poses the critical questions "Is this right?" and "Is this responsible?" Aesthetics poses the critical questions "What does this mean?" and "How is this significant?"

The creative inquiry processes lead toward formal expression of knowledge. Empiric knowledge development uses the reasoning processes of explaining and structuring empirical phenomena. Personal knowledge is developed by opening and centering the self. Development of ethical knowledge uses processes of clarifying and valuing issues of rights and responsibilities in practice. Aesthetic knowledge is developed by envisioning possibilities and rehearsing art-acts that can be called upon to transform experience.

From these processes, formal discursive forms of expression are created that can be presented to members of the discipline. In Figure 2–2, these are shown in the large arrows leading to the center sphere. Empiric inquiry leads to the development of theories, models, and other formal expressions, such as statements of fact and conceptual frameworks. Personal inquiry leads to the creation of autobiographic stories and the lived expression of the nurse's being in nursing care situations. This lived experience of being who we are is what we call the genuine self. Ethical inquiry leads to ethical principles and codes and to other expressions such as theories and precepts that guide ethical conduct in practice. Aesthetic inquiry leads to aesthetic criticism that reveals deep meaning embedded in nursing art-acts and works of art that symbolize nursing experience.

The formal expressions of each pattern, once they are available to the members of the discipline, make possible certain kinds of formal inquiry processes that depend on the community or on the collective efforts of several members of the discipline. These are the processes for authenticating knowledge, represented in Figure 2–2 along the horizontal axis. In the empiric pattern, statements representing empiric reality are translated into inquiry statements that can be replicated in similar but different situations, and the adequacy of the statement can be validated in these similar but different situations. Autobiographic stories and the expression of the genuine self lead to reflection and response from others in the discipline with the intent of discerning the value and adequacy of personal insights. Ethical principles and codes lead to collective dialogue and justification of the soundness of the principles in addressing nursing's ethical and moral dilemmas. Aesthetic criticism and works of art lead to formation of collective appreciation of aesthetic meanings in practice and becomes a source of inspiration for development of the art of nursing.

The innermost sphere in Figure 2–2 represents the nondiscursive forms of expression of knowing that are enacted in the practice of nursing. The nondiscursive expressions represent nursing praxis—the synchrony of thoughtful reflection and action that constitutes nursing as a human caring practice. Praxis assures, through reflections, the continual asking of critical questions associated with each fundamental pattern of knowing, as well as ongoing knowledge development.

All of these processes are interactive and nonlinear, and there is no one starting point. Nurses in practice and nurses who primarily engage in the formal inquiry processes all contribute to the activities that are involved in creating nursing knowledge. Each nurse engages in activities that make possible scientific competence, moral-ethical comportment, therapeutic use of self, and transformative art-acts.

To illustrate how these processes interact, suppose you have an empiric problem concerning what nursing approaches to relieving pain are effective in practice, and why. You might begin by planning a research program to systematically study two different approaches to pain relief. You would identify the theoretical explanations associated with each approach and plan research studies that test selected hypothetical relationships. Whereas the empiric questions are the starting point and remain the focus of your method, your approaches and methods are influenced by aesthetic meanings of experiences of relieving pain and suffering, personal meanings concerning the experience of pain, and ethical values that influence how and when pain relief is given and received.

Personal knowing is frequently the avenue through which awareness of possibilities that are not yet fully understood first emerges. For example, suppose a nurse comes to realize and appreciate the perspective of a family who is receiving care in the clinic. Something has not seemed to fit, has not felt right, and a growing appreciation of the family's perspective gradually brings a new perspective. The nurse shares her awareness with the family, and the relationship shifts to bring the family's perspective to the center. Personal knowing is the starting point to bring a situation to awareness, but as you explore your awareness, your knowledge of empiric theories also is used as a tool, within a frame of ethical and aesthetic sensibilities.

Suppose you want to address an ethical question concerning what is right. You might begin with the focused creative activities of making explicit the personal and group values (valuing) that should guide your actions, clarifying the positions you find in ethical theories and principles that inform the issue, and setting forth how the application of these principles would function with the people with whom you work. These processes would lead you to a dialogue and justification of your ideas based primarily in ethical reasoning. When you begin to share your ideas with your colleagues, the questioning and discussion that result will bring to awareness the personal insights of others engaged in the dialogue, empiric evidence about similar situations, and the range of aesthetic meanings that are possible in this and similar situations.

Aesthetics as a starting point, like personal knowing, often begins with a nurse's own awareness, but the expression often takes an art form that shows what the nurse envisions about the situation. The art can be in the form of the nurse's action in a situation. Suppose a nurse feels a connection to a person's experience of chronic pain. In a moment of caring for the person, the nurse acts from a deeply developed knowing of the meaning of chronic pain in a way that connects with the person's own experience, bringing together empiric, personal, and ethical knowing and creating a possibility that was not previously present.

*P*atterns Gone Wild

When knowledge within any one pattern is not critically examined and integrated with the whole of knowing, distortion instead of understanding is produced. Failure to develop knowledge integrated within all of the patterns of knowing leads to uncritical acceptance, narrow interpretation, and partial utilization of knowledge. We call this "the patterns gone wild." When this occurs, the patterns are used in isolation from one another, and the potential for synthesis of the whole is lost.

Empirics removed from the context of the whole of knowing produces control and manipulation. Ironically, these have been explicit traditional goals of the empiric sciences. When the validity of empiric knowledge is not questioned, one danger is its potential use in contexts where it does not belong. When you recognize how all the patterns contribute to the validity of empirics, you begin to see the unquestioned goals of control and manipulation as a distortion or misuse of empiric knowledge.

Ethics removed from the context of the whole of knowing produces rigid doctrine and insensitivity to the rights of others. This happens when someone simply sets forth personal ideas concerning what is right or good and advocates a position on reasoning derived from personal perspectives. The person may present a justification for a perspective to others but not take seriously the processes of dialogue that the justification invites. In the absence of this integrating process, the person's position remains isolated, with little or no opportunity for empiric, personal, or aesthetic insights to give meaning and social relevance to the ideas.

Personal knowing removed from the context of the whole of knowing produces isolation and self-distortion. When this happens, the self remains isolated, and knowledge of self comes only from what is known internally. Self-distortions can take a wide range of forms, from aggrandizement and overestimation of self to destruction and underestimation of self.

Aesthetics removed from the context of the whole of knowing produces indulgence in self-serving expressions and lack of appreciation for the fullness of meaning in a context. Human actions emerge from and are represented by the tastes and desires of the individual alone, without taking into account the deep cultural meanings inherent in the art-act. Art-acts become self-serving, shallow, arrogant, and empty. Self-serving preferences grow out of a failure to comprehend the deeper cultural, historical, and political significance of the art-act itself. Inauthentic meanings are assigned to another's experience, or a self-serving posture is assumed with respect to another person.

To illustrate "patterns gone wild," imagine an elderly woman admitted to a nursing home. She has lived a life rich in experience and activities and loves to verbally explore her past, making sense of what it means and how it relates to her present life. Having always been physically active, she takes a nightly stroll before going to bed. In the nursing home, she climbs over the bed rails after the lights are out and, with her walker, walks the halls, unsteady but determined, smiling and peering into other rooms. Hearing other residents talking or moaning, she sometimes goes into their rooms and tells them stories or talks with them to ease their troubled nights.

Consider what you might see if any one of the patterns of knowing were isolated from the context of the whole of knowing. Empirics isolated from the other patterns of knowing might require giving a drug that would be effective in bringing sleep to the woman soon after the lights go out, thereby controlling the situation and manipulating her into compliance, regardless of any other concerns. Ethics taken alone might impose the nurse's view of what is right or good for the woman and lead to a rule that would confine the woman to her bed after the lights are out and create a rigid, rule-oriented atmosphere that is insensitive to what the woman and others see as right or good. Personal knowing in isolation would impose the nurse's perspective, with the nurse isolated in the view that the old woman is a nuisance who is interfering with the time needed to complete the charting for the night. Aesthetics alone would impose the nurse's own tastes, preferences, and meanings on the situation. The nurse might restrain the woman in her bed and use a tape recorder to play the nurse's favorite new age music without considering whether the woman can hear the music or whether she finds the music soothing or appealing.

When ethics, aesthetics, personal knowing, and empirics come together as a whole, the purposes of developing knowledge and the actions based on that knowledge become more responsible and humane and create liberating choices. A whole understanding of the woman in the nursing home would take into account the woman's own safety and the needs of other residents; her personal life history and that which gives her pleasure; the ethical dimensions of personal empowerment, moral development, and caring for others; the aesthetic meaning of her actions in the cultural context of aging; and the personal perspective of the nurses who care for her. Many choices remain open in addressing this situation, but all of these considerations together would lead to nursing approaches that would differ from any of the approaches taken from one knowing perspective alone.

*W*hy Develop Nursing's Patterns of Knowing?

As is shown in Figure 2–2 and our discussion of it, the fundamental reason for developing a body of knowledge in nursing is for the purpose of creating expert nursing practice. Nursing's unique perspective and the particular contributions nurses bring to care come from the whole of knowing, a wholeness that has survived despite a cultural and contextual dominance of empiric knowing (Fry, 1992). In a sense the discipline of nursing can be viewed as the empiric pattern of knowing gone wild in that the majority of formal knowledge development efforts have focused on empiric knowledge development methods. Moreover, knowledge has been equated with empiric forms to the exclusion of any other forms of expression.

The idea that knowledge development is separate from the realities of practice can be seen as deriving from the dominance of empirics. Empiric theory is inadequate to represent the complexity of the practice world, and the methods of science traditionally have considered the uncontrolled and unpredictable contingencies in the practice realm unacceptable for the purposes of developing empiric knowledge. The practice implications of empiric theory are often not direct or immediately obvious, and empiric theory often uses a different language from that used in practice.

A shift to a balance in knowledge development to reflect each of the patterns of knowing in nursing holds potential to bring the realm of knowledge development and the realm of practice together. Methods for developing aesthetic, personal, and ethical knowing compel immersion within the realm of practice. Giving attention to these aspects of knowledge development shifts how empirics itself is viewed; empirics becomes part of a larger whole, and its value takes on different meaning in this context. In addition, as greater attention is given to methods other than empirics, many of the traditions and assumptions that underlie empiric methods are challenged, opening the way for creating empiric methods that better accommodate the contingencies of practice.

Formally expressed nursing knowledge provides professional and disciplinary identity, which in turn conveys to others what nursing contributes to the health care process. Professional identity that evolves from distinct disciplinary knowledge provides a basis from which nurses can create certain aspects of their practice. Nursing practice has traditionally been controlled by others, and what nurses do is often invisible. The knowledge that forms nursing practice provides a language for talking about the nature of nursing practice and for demonstrating its effectiveness. Once nursing practice is described, it is made visible. Moving to a conceptualization of knowledge that more fully embraces the whole of practice will serve to impart value to what has been intangible. Also, when nursing's effectiveness can be shown, it can be deliberately shaped or controlled by those who practice it.

On an individual level, nursing knowledge can provide self-identity and esteem as a nurse because you will have a firmer base when your ideas are questioned. As you become familiar with the language and processes of knowledge development, you can begin to think about how assumptions, definitions, and relationships within each of the patterns of knowing can be challenged. The study and understanding of knowledge development will provide a basis on which to take risks, to act deliberately, and to improve practice.

Imagine yourself as a nurse who is using massage to ease chronic pain for a hospitalized person. A physician notices that you are using this method of care. Because this is an unfamiliar approach to the physician, she asks you about it. You explain your reasoning, which is based on nursing knowledge. You can provide research evidence of the effectiveness of massage and information about the positive results that this particular person is experiencing. You can explain the ethical dimensions of providing relief from suffering, the aesthetic components of meaning in the situation, and what you have learned about the therapeutic use of self in giving a massage. Your explanation leads to an informed discussion about various approaches to caring for people with pain and why your approach seems to be effective for this person. As other practitioners learn of your knowledge in this area, they seek your consultation in caring for people with pain. Your knowledge of empiric pain theory and what is effective in caring for people with pain, as well as your ethical, aesthetic, and personal knowledge, provides a valuable resource for developing and improving practice.

Nursing's formally expressed body of knowledge also provides the discipline with a coherence of purpose. Coherence of professional purpose is closely linked to professional identity. Coherence of purpose contributes to a collective identity when nurses agree on the general practice domain. The processes of developing nursing's body of knowledge serve as a means for resolving significant disagreements among practitioners about what is to be accomplished. Varying points of view concerning the general purpose of nursing are reflected in the following questions:

■ Should nurses address prevention of illness?

■ Should nurses treat human responses to illness?

■ Should educational programs be structured around nursing process? Nursing diagnosis? Patterns of knowing? Critical thinking?

■ Should nurses view health and illness as opposites?

■ Can ill or diseased people also be healthy?

As nurses develop individual and collective responses to these questions, our directions for developing knowledge will be clearer, and in turn our knowledge development efforts will contribute to clarifying responses to questions such as these. Nursing knowledge facilitates coherence by examining such questions as a basis for deliberate choices. When nurses examine and agree about professional purposes and develop knowledge related to those purposes, the public and other practitioners will recognize nursing's expertise in relation to that arena. The fact that nurses are responsible for certain situations will be directly and indirectly communicated to society, and professional identity and coherence of purpose will continue to evolve. By shifting to a balance in the development of all the fundamental knowledge patterns, a sense of purpose can develop that is grounded in the whole of knowing that shapes and directs nursing practice.

Conclusion

In this section we considered nursing's patterns of knowing and introduced ideas about how the whole of knowing emerges. We have described traits of each pattern: empiric, ethical, aesthetic, and personal knowing. We introduced ideas about how the inquiry processes for each pattern form the knowledge of the discipline. The next section provides a description of the history of nursing knowledge development. In the sections that follow, each of the patterns of knowing and its distinct methods are addressed more fully.

References

Benner P. *From novice to expert: excellence and power in clinical nursing practice,* Menlo Park, Calif, 1984, Addison-Wesley.

Benner P., Wrubel J. *The primacy of caring: stress and coping in health and illness,* Menlo Park, Calif, 1989, Addison-Wesley.

Carper B. A. Fundamental patterns of knowing in nursing, *Adv Nurs Sci* 1:13, 1978.

Fry S. T. Neglect of philosophical inquiry in nursing: cause and effect. In Kikuchi JF, Simmons H., editors: *Philosophic inquiry in nursing,* Newbury Park, Calif, 1992, Sage.

Hagan K. L. *Internal affairs: a journalkeeping workbook for intimacy,* New York, 1990, Harper & Row.

Munhall P. L. "Unknowing": toward another pattern of knowing in nursing. *Nurs Outlook* 41:125, 1993.

Nelson G. L. *Writing and being: taking back our lives through the power of language,* San Diego, 1994, LuraMedia.

Silva M. C., Sorrell J. M., Sorrell C. D. From Carper's patterns of knowing to ways of being: an ontological philosophical shift in nursing, *Adv Nurs Sci* 18:1, 1995.

White J. Patterns of knowing: review, critique, and update, *Adv Nurs Sci* 17:73, 1995.

Wolfer J. Aspects of reality and ways of knowing in nursing: in search of an integrating paradigm, *Image J Nurs Sch* 25:141, 1993.

Integrative Healing

It is part of the cure to wish to be cured.

Seneca

Not everything that can be counted counts,
and not everything that counts can be counted.

Albert Einstein

Most of nursing education in the United States, Canada, the United Kingdom, Europe, and Australia, often referred to as Western countries, has been under the umbrella of biomedicine, and thus Western nurses are familiar and comfortable with its beliefs, theories, practices, strengths, and limitations. Fewer nurses have studied alternative medical theories and practices and as a result may lack information or even harbor misinformation about these healing practices. Unlike the medical profession in general, the profession of nursing has traditionally embraced the concepts of holism and humanism, commonly embodied in alternative therapies, in its approach with clients. Nurses have long believed that healing and caring must be approached holistically and that biological, psychological, emotional, and spiritual aspects of health and illness are equally important. Our humanistic perspective includes propositions such as the mind and body are indivisible, people have the power to solve their own problems, people are responsible for the patterns of their lives, and well-being is a combination of personal satisfaction and contributions to the larger community. This theoretical basis gives us a solid foot in each camp and places us, as nurses, in the unique position to help create a bridge between biomedicine and alternative medicine (Lamont, 1967; Leininger, 1997; Peplau, 1952; Rogers, 1970; Roy, 1976).

Taken from: *Healing Practices: Alternative Therapies for Nursing* by Fontaine.

$\mathcal{B}$ ackground

Many interesting exchanges around the world have debated the appropriate terminology of various healing practices. Some people become vested in the use of particular terms and have difficulty getting past the language limitations. For example, many people view the term *alternative medicine* as being too narrow or misleading and are concerned that the term lacks a full understanding of traditional healing practices. It would be more helpful for a common language to be developed without people being captive to it. As language evolves, the terms used today may be quite different from those used 20 years from now. For consistency purposes, the terms chosen for this text are *conventional medicine* or *biomedicine* to describe Western medical practices and the terms *alternative medicine* or *complementary medicine* to describe other healing practices. There are no universally accepted terms. For example, the term *alternative medicine* is used more in the United States while *complementary medicine* is used in Europe. The following list presents commonly used words and their counterparts:

Mainstream	Complementary/alternative
Modern	Ancient
Western	Eastern
Allopathic	Homeopathic
Conventional	Unconventional
Orthodox	Traditional
Biomedicine	Natural medicine
Scientific	Indigenous healing methods

The line between conventional and alternative medicine is imprecise and frequently changing. For example, is the use of megavitamins or diet regimes to treat disease considered medicine, a lifestyle change, or both? Can having one's pain lessened by massage be considered a medical therapy? How should spiritual healing and prayer—some of the oldest, most widely used, and least studied traditional approaches—be classified (*Alternative Medicine,* 1994)? Although the terms *alternative* or *complementary* are frequently used, in some instances they represent the primary treatment modality for an individual. Thus, conventional medicine sometimes assumes a secondary role and actually becomes a complement to the primary treatment modality.

Conventional Medicine

Biomedical or Western medicine is only about 200 years old. It is founded on the philosophical beliefs of René Descartes (1596–1650), that the mind and body are separate, and on Sir Isaac Newton's (1642–1727) principles of physics, that the universe is like a large mechanical clock where everything operates in a linear, sequential form. This mechanistic perspective of medicine views the human body as a series of body parts. It is a reductionistic approach in which the person is converted into increasingly smaller components: systems, organs, cells, and biochemicals. People are reduced to patients, patients are reduced to bodies, and bodies are reduced to machines. Health is viewed as the absence of disease or in other words, nothing being broken at the present time. The focus of sick care is on the symptoms of dysfunction. Doctors are trained to fix or repair broken parts through the use of drugs, radiation, surgery, or replacement of body parts. The approach is aggressive and militant with physicians being in a war against disease, with a take-no-prisoners attitude. Both consumers and practitioners of biomedicine believe it is better to:

- do something rather than wait and see whether the body's natural processes resolve the problem.

- attack the disease directly by medication or surgery rather than try to build up the person's resistance and ability to overcome the disease.

Biomedicine views the person primarily as a physical body, with the mind and spirit being separate and secondary, or at times, even irrelevant. It is powerful medicine in that it has virtually eliminated some infectious diseases such as small pox and polio. As a "rescue" medicine, the biomedical approach is wonderful. It is highly effective in emergencies, traumatic injuries, bacterial infections, and some highly sophisticated surgeries. In these cases, treatment is fast, aggressive, and goal-oriented, with the responsibility for cure falling on the practitioner. The priority of intervention is on opposing and suppressing the symptoms of illness. This approach is evidenced in many medications with prefixes such as "an" or "anti" as in analgesics, anesthetics, anti-inflamatories, and antipyretics. Because conventional medicine is preoccupied with parts and symptoms and not with whole working systems of matter, energy, thoughts, and feelings, it does not do well with long-term systemic illnesses such as arthritis, heart disease, and hypertension (Cantor and Rosenzweig, 1997; Fries, 1993; Seaward, 1994).

Alternative Medicine

Alternative medicine is an umbrella term for hundreds of therapies drawn from all over the world. Many forms have been handed down over thousands of years, both orally and as written records. They are based on the medical systems of ancient peoples, including Egyptians, Chinese, Asian Indians, Greeks, and Native Americans. Others, such as osteopathy and naturopathy, evolved in the United States over the past two centuries. Still others, such as some of the mind-body and bioelectromagnetic approaches, are on the frontier of scientific knowledge and understanding.

Although they represent diverse approaches, alternative therapies share certain attributes. They are based on the paradigm of whole systems and the belief that people are more than physical bodies with fixable and replaceable parts. Mental, emotional, and spiritual components of well-being are considered to play a crucial and equal role in a person's state of health. Since body, mind, and spirit are one unified reality, all illness is considered to be somatopsychic or psychosomatic, "somatic" meaning physiologic and "psychic" meaning psychologic. Even Hippocrates, the father of Western medicine, espoused a holistic orientation when he taught doctors to observe their patients' life circumstances and emotional states. Socrates agreed, declaring, "Curing the soul; that is the first thing." In alternative medicine, symptoms are believed to be an expression of the body's wisdom as it reacts to cure its own imbalance or disease. Other threads or concepts common to most forms of alternative medicine include the following:

- An internal self-healing process exists within each person.

- People are responsible for making their own decisions regarding their health care.

- Nature, time, and patience are the great healers.

When Albert Einstein (1879–1955) introduced his theory of relativity in 1905, the way of viewing the universe changed dramatically. Einstein said that all matter is energy, energy and matter are interchangeable, and all matter is connected at the subatomic level. No single entity could be affected without all connecting parts being affected. In this view, the universe is not a giant clock, but a living web. The human body is animated by an integrated energy called the *life force*. The life force sustains the physical body but is also a spiritual entity that is linked to a higher being or infinite source of energy. When the life force flows freely throughout the body, a person experiences optimal health and vitality. When the life force is blocked or weakened, organs, tissues, and cells are deprived of the energy they need to function at their full potential, and illness or disease results.

The value of alternative medicine is especially effective for people with chronic, debilitating illnesses for which conventional medicine has few, if any, answers. It has much to offer in the arena of health promotion and disease prevention. As costs of conventional medicine grow and people continue to suffer from chronic illnesses and degenerative diseases, the place of alternative medicine is moving closer to the mainstream. Box 2-1 provides an overview of the paradigms of conventional and alternative medicine.

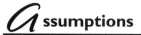ssumptions

In understanding conventional and alternative medicine, it is helpful to study the assumptions basic to their theories, practices, and research. These assumptions include the origin of disease, the meaning of health, the curative process, and health promotion.

Origin of Disease

Biomedicine and alternative medicine have widely divergent assumptions regarding the origin of disease. Biomedicine was shaped by the observations that bacteria were responsible for producing disease and pathologic damage and that antitoxins and vaccines could improve a person's ability to ward off the effects of pathogens. Armed with this knowledge, physicians began to conquer a large number of devastating infectious diseases. As the science developed, physicians came to believe that germs and genes caused disease and once the offending pathogen, metabolic error, or chemical imbalance was found all diseases would eventually yield to the appropriate vaccine, antibiotic, or chemical compound. Conventional medicine has also been influenced by Darwin's concept of survival of the fittest, which says that all life

---

BOX 2-1 Paradigms of Medicine

View	Conventional Medicine	Alternative Medicine
Mind/body/spirit	are separate	are one
The body is	a machine	a living microcosm of universe
Disease results when	parts break	energy/life force becomes unbalanced
Role of medicine	to combat disease	to restore mind/body/spirit harmony
Approach	treat and suppress symptoms	search for patterns of disharmony or imbalance
Focuses on	parts/matter	whole/energy
Treatments	attempt to "fix" broken parts	support self-healing
Primary interventions	drugs, surgery, radiation	diet, exercise, herbs, stress, management social support
System	sick care	health care

is a constant struggle and that only the most successful competitors survive. When this concept is applied to medicine it is translated that we live under constant attack by the thousands of microorganisms that, in the Western view, cause most diseases. People must defend themselves and counterattack with treatments that kill the enemy (*Alternative Medicine,* 1994; Castleman, 1996). Based on this assumption, symptoms are regarded as harmful manifestations and should be suppressed. For example, a headache is an annoyance that should be eliminated and a fever should be reduced with the use of medications.

Alternative medicine is based on the belief of a life force or energy that flows through each person and sustains life. Balance refers to harmony among organs in the body and among body systems, and in relationships to other individuals, society, and the environment. A balanced organism presents a strong defense against external insults such as bacteria, viruses, and trauma. When the life force or energy is blocked or weakened, the vitality of organs and tissues is reduced, oxygen is diminished, waste products accumulate, and organs and tissues degenerate. Symptoms are the body's way of communicating that the life force has been blocked or weakened resulting in a compromised immune system. Disease is not necessarily a surprise encounter with a bacteria or virus, since these surround us constantly, but rather the end result of a series of events that began with a disruption of the life force (Monte, 1997). Based on this assumption, symptoms are not suppressed unless they endanger life such as a headache from an aneurysm or a fever above 105°F. Rather, symptoms are cooperated with because they express the body's wisdom as it reacts to cure its own disease. For example, a headache is a signal that one's whole system needs realignment, and a fever may be the result of the breakdown of bacterial proteins or toxins. When symptoms are suppressed, they are not resolved but merely held off, gathering energy for renewed expression as soon as the outside, counteractive force is removed.

Meaning of Health

If you were to ask a healer from the Chinese, Indian, or Native American traditions about the meaning of health, you would hear answers very different from those that would be given by a Western physician. The biomedical view of health, in the past, was often described as the absence of disease or other abnormal conditions. That definition expanded to include the view that health is not a static condition; the body undergoes constant change and adaptation to both internal and external environmental challenges. The majority of conventional medical practitioners would define health as a state of well-being. They may disagree, however, about who determines well-being—the health professional or the individual.

Those practicing alternative medicine describe health as a condition of wholeness, balance, and harmony of the body, mind, emotions, and spirit. Health is not a concrete goal to be achieved; rather, it is a lifelong process that represents growth toward potential, an inner feeling of aliveness. Physical aspects include optimal functioning of all body systems. Emotional aspects include the ability to feel and express the entire range of human emotions. Mental aspects include feelings of self-worth, a positive identity, a sense of accomplishment, and the ability to appreciate and create. Spiritual aspects involve self, others, and society. Self components are the development of moral values and finding a meaningful purpose in life. Spiritual factors relating to others include the search for meaning through relationships and the feeling of connectedness with others and with an external power often identified as God or the divine source. Societal aspects of spiritual health can be understood as a common humanity and a belief in the fundamental sacredness and unity of all life. These beliefs motivate people toward truth and a sense of fairness and justice to all members of society. The World Health Organization (WHO) states that "the existing definition of health should include the spiritual aspect and that health care should be in the hands of those who are fully aware of and sympathetic to the spiritual dimension."

Curative Process

The curative process is another example of divergent viewpoints. Conventional medicine promotes the view that external treatments—drugs, surgery, radiation—cure people, and practitioners are trained to fix or repair broken parts. The focus is on the disease process or abnormal condition. Alternative practitioners look at conditions that block the life force and keep it from flowing freely through the body. Healing occurs when balance and harmony are restored. The focus is on the health potential of the person rather than the disease problem.

Health Promotion

Conventional and alternative medical systems have somewhat different foci on promotion of health. The thrust by conventional medicine is toward disease prevention. Consumers are taught how to decrease their risk of cancer, cardiac disorders, and other life-threatening diseases that kill most people prematurely in Western society. As important as these behaviors are, however, disease prevention is only one piece of health promotion. Health promotion, from the alternative perspective, is a lifelong process that focuses on optimal development of our physical, emotional, mental, and spiritual selves. An individual's world views, values, lifestyles, and health beliefs are considered to be of critical importance. Consumers are encouraged to adopt healthier lifestyles, to accept increased responsibility for their own well-being, and through greater self-reliance, to learn how to handle common health problems on their own.

esearch

Scientific beliefs rest not just on facts but on paradigms (broad views of how these facts are related and organized). Differences in views among groups of nursing and medical researchers are a reflection of the different scientific paradigms in which each group believes. This understanding may provide some insight into the ongoing conflict between quantitative and qualitative researchers, nursing and medical researchers, Western and Eastern researchers, and conventional and alternative medical researchers. A common yet seemingly almost invisible presumption is that "experts" of conventional medicine are entitled and qualified to pass judgment on the scientific and therapeutic merits of alternative therapies. Since the paradigm is quite different, they are not qualified (*Alternative Medicine,* 1994).

Particulate-deterministic, or quantitative, research represents the principles of Western scientific method, which include formulating and testing hypotheses and then rejecting or not rejecting the hypotheses. Every question is reduced to the smallest possible part. Results can be replicated and generalized. Outcomes can be predicted and controlled. Particulate-deterministic research is said to be objective in that the observer is separate from that which is being observed. Another part of this objective paradigm is that all information can be derived from physically measurable data. This type of research has been extremely effective for isolating causative factors of disease and developing cures. On the other hand, it cannot explain the whole person as an integrated unit (Guzzetta, 1989; Micozzi, 1996; Newman et al., 1991).

Interactive-integrative research studies the context and meaning of interactive variables as these variables form patterns reflective of the whole. Researchers observe, document, analyze, and qualify the interactive relationship of variables. In the science of physics, it is believed that objectivity is ultimately not possible. The Heisenberg uncertainty principle states that the act of observing phenomena necessarily influences the behavior of the phenomena being observed. Another part of the paradigm relates to the belief that interactions between living organisms and environments are transactional, multidirectional, and synergistic in ways that cannot be reduced. This holistic approach (the whole is greater than the parts) is basic to the interactive-integrative paradigm (Guzzetta, 1989; Micozzi, 1996; Newman et al., 1991).

The unitary-transformative approach to research represents a significant paradigm shift. A phenomenon is viewed as an integral, self-organizing unit embedded in a larger, self-organizing unit. Change is nonlinear and unpredictable as systems move through organization and disorganization. Knowledge is a function of both the observer and the phenomenon being studied and involves pattern recognition. Knowledge is personal in that it includes thoughts, values, feelings, choices, and purpose (Newman et al., 1991).

Just as conventional and alternative medicine complement one another, so do multiple perspectives of research. Some research explores patterns about which little is known (inter-active-interpretative) while other research validates new knowledge and predicts outcomes of interventions (particulate-deterministic). Yet other research may help us understand such aspects as the mutuality of nurse-client encounters (unitary-transformative). All paradigms are needed to further scientific knowledge.

Jean Watson's article on caring knowledge (1990) included a wonderful metaphor from Margaret Mead's book, *Blackberry Winter* (pp. 289–290), which Watson believes is relevant to nursing science. Mead is discussing the theoretical physicist Oppenheimer (1904–1967) and his well-chosen metaphor of science as a house:

> I would like to see us build a NEW room in that vast and rambling structure [of a house called "science"]. This room, like the others, would have no door and over the entrance would be the words, THOUGHT, REFLECTION, CONTEMPLATION. It would have no tables with instruments, no whirring machinery. There would be no sound except the soft murmur of words carrying the thought of men [and women] in the room. It would be a Commons Room to which men [and women] would drift in from those rooms marked geology, anthropology, taxonomy, technology, biology, paleontology, logic, mathematics, psychology, linguistics, and many others. Indeed, from without the walls of the House would come poets and artists. All these would drop in and linger. This room would have great windows; the vistas our studies have opened. Men [and women] singly or together would from time to time walk to those windows to gaze out on the landscape beyond. This landscape in all its beauty, sometimes gentle, sometimes terrible, cannot be seen fully by any one of the occupants of the room. Indeed, it cannot be known fully by a whole generation of men [and women]. Explorers of each generation travel into its unknown recesses and, with luck, return to share their discoveries with us. So the life of the NEW room would go on—thought, reflection, contemplation—as the explorers bring back their discoveries to share with the room's occupants. This landscape that we gaze on and try to understand is an epic portion of the human experience.

Those who limit themselves to Western scientific research have virtually ignored anything that cannot be perceived by the five senses and repeatedly measured or quantified. It is dismissed as superstitious and invalid if it cannot be scientifically explained by cause and effect. Many continue to cling with an almost religious fervor to this cultural paradigm about the power of science. Nonwestern, scientific paradigms are considered to be inferior at best and inaccurate at worst. And yet, biomedical research cannot explain many of the phenomena that concern alternative practitioners regarding caring-healing processes. When therapies such as acupuncture or homeopathy are observed to result in a physiologic or clinical response that cannot be explained by the biomedical model, many have tried to deny the results rather than modify the scientific model (Micozzi, 1996; Watson, 1995). In contrast to the biomedical perspective, Buckminster Fuller, an American architect and inventor, said, "Eighty percent of reality cannot be perceived or detected through the five senses." If people limit themselves to the five senses, they will never come to understand human energy fields, electromagnetic fields, thoughts as a form of energy, or the healing power of prayer.

Conventional medicine believes that procedures and substances must pass the double-blind study to be proven effective. As a testing method, the double-blind study examines a single procedure or substance in isolated, controlled conditions and measures results against an inactive procedure or substance (called a placebo). This approach is based on the assumption that single factors cause and reverse illness, and that these factors can be studied alone and out of context. Alternative medicine, however, believes that no single factor causes anything nor can a magic substance single-handedly reverse illness. Multiple factors contribute to illness, and multiple interventions work together to promote healing. The double-blind method is incapable of reconciling this degree of complexity and variation.

Although major alternative medical systems may not have a great deal of quantitative research, they are generally *not* experimental. They rely on well-developed clinical observational skills and experience that is guided by their explanatory models. Likewise, 70 to 85 percent of biomedical practices are guided by observation and experience and have *not* been tested quantitatively. New medicines must have rigorous proof of efficacy and safety before clinical use. The use of tests, procedures, and treatments, however, are not similarly constrained (Grimes, 1993). A tiny fraction of new devices undergoes formal review by the Food and Drug Administration before marketing approval. Western physicians, like alternative practitioners, use the same well-developed clinical observational skills and experience guided by their explanatory biomedical model. Thus, the argument really becomes one of cultural turf rather than scientific method (Cassidy, 1996).

This text does not offer meticulous documentation for all claims which are made by the various therapies. The Office of Alternative Medicine (OAM) at the National Institutes of Health has been mandated to facilitate the evaluation of alternative medical treatments and to provide the public with this information. There may be a wait for new knowledge from quantum physics and psychoneuroimmunology before alternative medicine can be understood in terms of the biomedical model. Successful alternative therapies, however, should not be withheld from the public while research is being debated. Box 2-2 lists the institution-affiliated centers for research on alternative medicine.

*C*onsumers

Many Americans are looking outside of conventional medicine for relief of illness and improvement of health. According to a random survey in 1997, 32–54 percent of adults (83 million people) in the United States used one or more types of alternative medicine in the past year, often to treat a chronic medical condition as listed in Box 2-3. Sixty percent of these consumers did not discuss the use of alternative therapies with their primary conventional practitioner, even though the vast majority used both approaches simultaneously. In total, they made 629 million visits to alternative healers, which was nearly 243 million more visits than to all U.S. primary care physicians. They spent approximately $27 billion out-of-pocket on alternative therapies (Eisenberg et al., 1998). Another study of consumers of family practice medicine found that 50 percent had used at least one form of alternative medicine and 53 percent of these did not discuss the use with their primary practitioner (Elder et al., 1997). Studies thus far have demonstrated that consumers of alternative medicine tend to be better educated and have a higher socioeconomic status than the general population. The use of alternative medicine is most likely underestimated since the studies have focused on English-speaking individuals, often in

---

BOX 2-2 Institution-Affiliated Centers of Research on Alternative Medicine

Institution	Specialty of Center
Bastyr University Bethel, WA	HIV/AIDS
Columbia University New York, NY	Women's health issues
Harvard Medical School Boston	General medical conditions
Kessler Institute for Rehabilitation West Orange, NJ	Stroke and neurological conditions
Palmer Center for Chiropractic Research Davenport, IA	Chiropractic
Stanford University Palo Alto, CA	Aging
University of Arizona Health Science Center Tucson	Pediatric conditions
University of California Davis	Asthma, allergy, and immunology
University of Maryland School of Medicine Baltimore	Pain
University of Michigan Ann Arbor	Cardiovascular diseases
University of Minnesota Medical School Minneapolis	Addictions
University of Texas Health Science Center Houston	Cancer
University of Virginia Charlottesville	Pain

Source: Medical News & Perspective, November 11, 1998. *JAMA.* 280(18): 1553.

---

small numbers, and have omitted prayer and other religious/spiritual resources from the studies (Eisenberg et al., 1998).

Burg (1998) and associates surveyed the use of alternative therapies by conventional health care professionals. In this study more than half of the respondents reported that they had used one or more types of alternative therapies, the most frequent being massage, relaxation techniques, dietary supplements, and chiropractic. The highest overall use was reported by allied health professionals followed by nursing, dentistry, pharmacy, veterinary medicine, and medicine. Alternative medicine use appears to be similar to rates of use in the general population.

The mainstream medical community can no longer ignore alternative therapies. The public interest is extensive and growing. One has only to look at the proliferation of popular health books, health food stores, and clinics offering healing therapies to realize that this interest cannot be dismissed. Americans spent an estimated $32.7 billion on alternative therapies in 1997, of which more than $19 billion was out-of-pocket. In other words, Americans want something more than biomedicine, and they are willing to pay for it (Eisenberg et al., 1998).

BOX 2-3 Thirteen Most Frequently Reported Conditions of Those Seeking Alternative Therapies

Problem	Percentage of Sufferers
Neck problems	57
Back problems	48
Anxiety	43
Depression	41
Headaches	32
Arthritis	27
GI problems	27
Fatigue	27
Insomnia	26
Sprain/strains	24
Allergies	17
Lung problems	13
Hypertension	12

Source: Eisenberg et al., 1998. Trends in Alternative Medicine Use in the United States, 1990–1997. *JAMA.* 280(18): 1569–1576.

What are consumers seeking from alternative medicine? Some have the same goal for both types of medicine, such as the use of pain medications and acupuncture to control chronic pain. Other consumers may have a different expectation for each approach, such as seeing a conventional practitioner for antibiotics to eradicate an infection and using an alternative practitioner to improve natural immunity through a healthy lifestyle. A person receiving chemotherapy may use meditation and visualization to control the side effects of the chemotherapeutic agents. People who combine conventional and alternative therapies are making therapeutic choices on their own and assuming responsibility for their own health (Lazar, and O'Connor, 1997).

It is important for nurses to understand the reasons consumers choose alternative practitioners. Some utilize alternative healers because of financial, geographic, and cultural barriers to biomedical care. Many turn to alternative healers for a sense of hope, control, personal attention, physical contact, and regard for the whole person that seems to be overlooked in conventional medicine. Some of the common reasons for seeking alternative practitioners are listed in Box 2-4.

Because alternative therapists are rushing to meet the demand, it is increasingly difficult for consumers to figure out how and where to get the best health care. It may be problematic to find reliable information to help separate the healers from those who pretend to have medical knowledge. Consumers should beware of healers who (Tiedje, 1998):

■ say they have all the answers

■ maintain that theirs is the only effective therapy

■ promise overnight success

BOX 2-4 Reasons for Choosing Alternative Therapies

Pursue therapeutic benefit

Seek a degree of wellness not supported in biomedicine

Attend to quality of life issues

Prefer high personal involvement in decision making

Believe conventional medicine treats symptoms not underlying cause

Find conventional medical treatments to be lacking or ineffective

Avoid toxicities and/or invasiveness of conventional interventions

Decrease use of prescribed or OTC medications

Identify with a particular healing system as a part of cultural background

---

Sources: Dunn and Perry, 1997. Primary Care: Clinics in Office Practice, 24(4): 715–721; Lazar and O'Connor, 1997. Primary Care: Clinics in Office Practice, 24(4): 699–714.

- refuse to include other practitioners as part of the healing team

- seem more interested in money than in people's well-being

Some alternative specialties are more regulated and licensed than others, but none come with guarantees any more than conventional medicine comes with guarantees. Most consumers locate alternative therapists through friends, family, an exercise instructor, health food stores, and referral lines at local hospitals. Nurses must initiate discussion with clients regarding alternative medicine. The most frequent reason clients give for not discussing their use of alternative medicine is the fear of ridicule or censure on the part of the conventional health care provider. In light of this fear, nurses must create a safe climate in which clients can openly discuss these issues. Nurses must remain nonjudgmental and supportive if they are to help people achieve their health care goals.

*I*ntegrated Nursing Practice

In the past 20 years, nursing has been moving away from a biomedical orientation that has largely defined and directed it toward a nursing-caring-healing model. Watson (1997) describes it as a shift from *nursing qua medicine* paradigm (nurses helping doctors practice medicine) to a *nursing qua nursing* paradigm (practicing the distinct art and science of nursing). This movement has reconnected us with the finest tradition of Florence Nightingale in using our hands, heart, and head in creating healing environments. The modern nurse-healer draws upon biomedical and caring/healing models by utilizing technology and focusing on caring relationships and healing processes. Dossey, Keegan, Lolkmeier, and Guzzetta (1989) have described the modern nurse-healer as a hybrid of scientific skills and spiritual commitment. We need scientific principles, methods, and skills, but we also need to teach people ways to become more self-reliant as we shift in the role from caregiver to healer.

In 1979, Watson published her text *Nursing: The Philosophy and Science of Caring,* which evolved from her experiences of nursing within the limitations of traditional biomedical models. She sought to bring new meaning to the nursing paradigm of caring-healing and health. Her ten carative factors, listed in Box 2-5, became a philosophical and conceptual guide toward

---

BOX 2-5 Watson's Ten Carative Factors

1. Forming a humanistic-altruistic system of values.
2. Enabling and sustaining faith-hope.
3. Being sensitive to self and others.
4. Developing a helping-trusting, caring relationship (seeking transpersonal connection).
5. Promoting and accepting the expression of positive and negative feelings and emotions.
6. Engaging in creative, individualized, problem-solving, caring processes.
7. Promoting transpersonal teaching-learning.
8. Attending to supportive, protective, and/or corrective mental, physical, societal, and spiritual environments.
9. Assisting with gratification of basic human needs while preserving human dignity and wholeness.
10. Allowing for, and being open to, existential-phenomenological, and spiritual dimensions of caring and healing that cannot be fully explained scientifically through modern Western medicine.

Source: Watson, in *Blueprint for Use of Nursing Models* (New York: NLN Press, 1996), 141–184.

---

a model of nursing that is well known throughout the world. Reading this list, it becomes obvious how nursing as a caring profession embraces philosophical perspectives similar to those of many alternative healing systems and therapies.

The art of nursing is in being there, with another person or persons, in a context of caring. It is the capacity of the nurse "to receive another human being's expression of feelings and to experience those feelings for oneself" (Chinn and Watson, 1994, p. xvi). Caring involves compassion and sensitivity to each person within the context of her or his entire life. In the past, the biomedical model urged us not to care too much or get too involved. Caring, successful nurses, however, do get involved with clients as they practice nursing as an art instead of nursing as just a day-to-day job. Caring is a philosophy or context wherein we practice nursing. What makes our practice caring are not the tools we use but the attitude or perspective we bring. It is possible, of course, to use the tools of alternative therapies in the same reductionistic way of biomedicine. For example, if one knows the pressure point for headaches and simply uses this pressure point for pain relief without any further assessment, it could hardly be considered holistic or healing. The symptom of headache has been addressed, but the meaning of the headache and the person's experience of the pain has been totally ignored.

Before nurses can care for clients, they must first learn to value and care for themselves. One of your goals in reading this text might be discovering how to care for yourself more effectively because it is only when we can care first for ourselves that we have the energy to care for our patients. Caring for yourself means reducing unnecessary stress, managing conflict more effectively, communicating with family and friends more clearly, and taking time out for yourself. Caring for yourself includes developing a daily routine in practices such as relaxation, meditation, prayer, yoga, communion with nature, and other such forms of contemplation. In Watson's words, "If one is to work from a caring-healing paradigm, one must live it out in daily life" (1997, p. 51). The following guidelines will help you maintain your self-care practices (Jahnke, 1997):

■ Choose self-care activities that appeal to you and fit into your lifestyle.

■ Do one or more of these practices every day. Consider them as important as you do rest and daily hygiene activities.

- Seek guidance and support from teachers/practitioners if appropriate.

- Find a good spot for your practice that is physically and mentally comfortable.

- Build up your practice slowly. Success is not gained by aggressive or compulsive practice.

- Look for opportunities to practice with others.

- Focus on relaxing. The foundation of all self-healing, health enhancement, stress mastery, and personal empowerment is deep relaxation.

Much data is currently being gathered relating to the concept of the nurse as healer. The principles that have thus far been identified are listed in Box 2-6. Read these principles closely. You will see the same precepts appearing again and again in the various healing practices described in this text.

The plurality of the sick-care, health-care systems may be one of its greatest strengths. It enables us to meet the diverse needs of diverse populations. The question is, how can we combine the best ideas of conventional nursing practice and alternative healing practices? First, we must have education. At the basic level, our nursing curricula must include courses in caring and alternative medicine. All nurses could learn Therapeutic Touch, healthy dietary plans, the use of basic herbs, as well as the use of visualization and prayer in the healing process. We must also participate in continuing education courses to expand our knowledge beyond the

---

BOX 2-6 Principles of Nurse Healers' Practice

1. There is a unity and interdependence within the mind, body, and spirit.
2. Health is a process that may include disease.
3. One's attitudes and beliefs toward life (mental-emotional energy fields or consciousness) is a major etiological factor in health and disease.
4. One's health and disease are manifested in one's lifestyle, habits, and conscious awareness, as well as the body's physical being and energy.
5. The self is empowered with the ability to create or maintain health/disease.
6. Changes in health can occur through experiential learning, which is defined as a change in behavior that occurs as a result of living through an activity, event, or situation.
7. Experiential learning is essential to changing one's lifestyle for high-level wellness.
8. Human beings are energy fields.
9. Healing involves a transformational change that encompasses the whole person; it requires the involvement of the spiritual, emotional, and intellectual domains, as well as the physical body.
10. Energy fields can become unbalanced as a response to stress in any one of the three domains of body, mind, and spirit.
11. The client-practitioner relationship is one of partnership—equal with differing responsibilities.
12. Any modality or health system that supports healing should be valued.
13. Each health system should be respected for the resources and the tools that it offers while being challenged to prove its credibility.
14. Each person is an open system with the environment without separating boundaries.
15. Energy fields are constantly interacting.

Source: Keegan, *The Nurse as Healer* (Albany, NY: Delmar, 1994).

basic level. With additional education, we can learn such things as basic massage and reflex-ology, meditation, and yoga. Some nurses will choose to continue their education by com-pleting formal programs in alternative medicine such as naturopathy, ayurveda, homeopathy, chiropractic medicine, or hypnotherapy. Nurses should also participate in research on the effectiveness of alternative therapies.

Next, we must provide community education. We must provide people with information, tools, skills, and support to enable them to make healthy decisions about life and negotiate their way through the health care systems. We must also attempt to keep ourselves healthy most of the time. We should exemplify good health, since teaching by example is a powerful influ-ence. We can teach wherever our practice is located: acute care, long-term care, community nurse-managed centers, and in areas of advanced practice nursing. And, finally, we must doc-ument our findings, utilize and participate in nursing research, and design new studies to mea-sure the effectiveness of various healing practices.

References

Alternative Medicine: Expanding Medical Horizons. 1994. A report to the National Institutes of Health on Alternative Medical Systems and Practices in the United States. U.S. Govern-ment Printing Office. Washington, DC.

Burg, M. A. et al. 1998. Personal use of alternative medicine therapies by health science cen-ter faculty. *JAMA.* 280(18): 1563.

Cantor, I.S., and S. Rosenzweig. 1997. Anthroposophic perspectives in primary care. Com-plementary and Alternative Therapies in Primary Care. *Primary Care: Clinics in Office Prac-tice.* 24(4): 867–885.

Cassidy, C. M. 1996. Cultural context of complementary and alternative medical systems. In M.S. Micozzi, ed. *Fundamentals of Complementary and Alternative Medicine.* New York: Churchill Livingstone, 9–34.

Castleman, M. 1996. *Nature's Cures.* Emmaus, PA: Rodale Press.

Chinn, P. and J. Watson, eds. 1994. *Art and Aesthetics in Nursing.* New York: NLN Press.

Department of Health and Human Services (DHHS). 1991. *Healthy People 200.* Washington, DC; Publication number (PHS) 91-50213.

Dossey, B. M., L. Keegan, L.G., Lolkmeier, and C.E. Guzzetta, eds. 1989. *Holistic Health Pro-motion: A Guide for Practice.* Rockville, MD: Aspen.

Dunn, L. and B. L. Perry. 1997. Where your patients are. Complementary and Alternative Ther-apies in Primary Care. *Primary Care: Clinics in Office Practice.* 24(4): 715–721.

Eisenberg, D. M. et al. 1998. Trends in alternative medicine use in the United States, 1990–1997. *JAMA.* 280(18): 1569–1576.

Elder, N. C., A. Gillcrist, and R. Minz. 1997. Use of alternative health care by family practice patients. *Arch Fam Med.* 6: 181–184.

Fries, J. F., et al. July 29, 1993. Reducing health care costs by reducing the need and demand for medical services. *N Eng J Med.* 329(5): 321–325.

Grimes, D. A. June 16, 1993. Technology follies. The uncritical acceptance of medical innova-tion. *JAMA.* 269(23): 3030–3033.

Guzzetta, C. E. Research and holistic implications. 1989. In B. M. Dossey, L. Keegan, L. G. Lolk-meier, and C. E. Guzzetta, eds. *Holistic Health Promotion: A Guide for Practice.* Rockville, MD: Aspen, 85–92.

Jahnke, R. 1997. *The Healer Within.* San Francisco: Harper.

Keegan, L. 1994. *The Nurse as Healer.* Albany, NY: Delmar.

Lamont, C. 1967. *The Philsosophy of Humanism.* New York: Frederick Ungar Pub.

Lazar, J. S. and B. B. O'Connor. 1997. Talking with patients about their use of alternative therapies. Complementary and Alternative Therapies in Primary Care. *Primary Care: Clinics in Office Practice.* 24(4): 699–714.

Leininger, M. 1997. Alternative to what? Generic vs. professional caring, treatments, and healing modes. *J Transcultural Nrsg.* 9(1): 37.

Mead, M. 1972. *Blackberry Winter.* New York: William Morrow.

Micozzi, M. S. 1996. Characteristics of complementary and alternative medicine. In M. S. Micozzi, ed. *Fundamentals of Complementary and Alternative Medicine.* New York: Churchill Livingstone, 3–8.

Monte, T. 1997. *The Complete Guide to Natural Healing.* New York: Perigee.

Newman, M. A., A. M. Sime, S. A. Corcoran-Perry. 1991. The focus of the discipline of nursing. *Adv Nurs Sci.* 14(1): 1–6.

Peplau, H. E. 1952. *Interpersonal Relations in Nursing.* New York: Putnam.

Rogers, M. E. 1970. *The Theoretical Basis of Nursing.* Philadelphia: F. A. Davis.

Roy, C. 1976. *Introduction to Nursing: An Adaptation Model.* Englewood Cliffs, NJ: Prentice-Hall.

Seaward, B. L. 1994. Alternative medicine complements standard. *Health Progress.* 15(9): 52–57.

Tiedje, L. B. 1998. Alternative health care: An overview. *JOGNN.* 27(5): 557–562.

Watson, J. 1997. The theory of human caring: Retrospective and Prospective. *Nurs Sci Quart.* 10(1): 49–52.

Watson, J. 1996. Watson's theory of transpersonal caring. In P. H. Walker, and B. Newman, eds. *Blueprint for Use of Nursing Models: Education, Research, Practice, and Administration.* New York: NLN Press, 141–184.

Watson, J. 1995. Nursing's caring-healing paradigm as exemplar for alternative medicine? *Alternative Therapies.* 1(3): 64–69.

Watson, J. 1990. Caring knowledge and informed moral passion. *Adv Nurs Sci.* 13(1): 15–24.

Statement Analysis

Definition and Description

Statement analysis is a process of examining relational statements to determine in what form they are presented and what relationship the concepts within those statements have to one another. As in all analyses, statement analysis includes the examination of each part and its relationship to each other part and to the whole. Statement analysis focuses on each concept within a statement, the relationship of each concept with each other concept, and the role the statement plays as a whole.

As we have said, there are two types of nonrelational statements used in theory. One is what Reynolds (1971) has called an *existence* statement. This type of statement simply identifies a concept or an object and claims its existence. For example, we might say "the phenomenon of a person's subjective feelings is termed the affect." The label "affect" is claimed to exist and is identified by a brief summary statement. Existence statements occur in theories to provide background and explanation prior to positing relationships.

The second type of nonrelational statement in theory is called a *definition*. A definition describes the characteristics of a concept. It may be a theoretical definition—one that is abstract and useful to the theory but with no empirical referents named—or it may be an operational definition, in which the method of measurement is clearly spelled out. Leaving rods and cones out of it for now, let us assume that the concept of "color blindness" has a theoretical definition that implies visual inability to distinguish accurately between colors. The operational definition of color blindness, then, might include criteria such as which colors would be included in testing, how many times the test must be run, and how many "wrong" answers constitute failure before "color blindness" can be said to be present. Definitions are useful in theory because they provide the basis for clear communication between the theorist and the reader/user.

In theory building, statements are usually thought of as relational statements. Each statement describes some type of relationship among the concepts within it. Relational statements

---

Taken from: *Strategies for Theory Construction in Nursing*, Third Edition by Walker and Avant.

are a bit more complex than either existence statements or definitions. Basically they come in several forms that will be discussed individually in the analysis section. Suffice it to say at this point that relational statements may be associational, causal, deterministic, probabilistic, or theoretical (Reynolds, 1971). Relational statements are the skeleton of theory. They are the means by which everything appears to hang together. When they occur singly, they form the basis for research or at least further reflection on the phenomenon in question. When they occur in groups and are not interrelated, they are the stimulus for thinking and exploration to find their linkages. If they occur in groups and are interrelated, they are called "theory."

Purposes and Uses

Statement analysis is a way of examining statements in an orderly way in an effort to determine if the statements are useful, informative, and logically correct. It is a rigorous process.

The purposes of statement analysis are (1) to classify statements as to form and (2) to examine the relationship between the concepts. Statement analysis is suited to situations in which one or more statements about a phenomenon exist but have not yet been organized into a theoretical system. The strategy is useful in that it provides the theorist with information about the structure and function of the statements being considered. In addition, it is particularly useful because once the statement has been analyzed, any deficiencies in it are obvious and may be corrected or modified.

Statement analysis provides a way of looking at and formalizing theoretical constructions that are already available in the literature or through research. It is also useful when a theorist is building a "new" theory to carefully analyze the proposed relational statements before subjecting them to the criticism and scrutiny that such a "new" theory invariably generates from the scholarly community.

Steps in Statement Analysis

There are seven steps in statement analysis: (1) select the statement(s) to be analyzed; (2) simplify the statement; (3) classify the statement; (4) examine concepts within the statement for definition and validity; (5) specify relationships between concepts by type, sign, and symmetry; (6) examine the logic; and (7) determine testability.

Selecting the Statement

Although the first step appears to be the easiest, it may, in fact, prove very difficult. Selecting a statement to be analyzed involves some commitment to the idea behind the statement. One does not usually choose to do statement analysis without some underlying purpose. Anyone attempting statement analysis should have clearly in mind what reason he or she has for doing so. Perhaps you have some doubt about the statement, or perhaps the idea excites you and you wish to examine the structure for soundness before you refute it or act upon it in some way. In any case, the theorist should have the rationale for analysis clearly in mind before beginning.

The second reason for the difficulty in selecting a statement is the problem that arises in some verbal or written theories: a lack of specificity of relational statements. Theories, especially in the social and behavioral sciences, may be elaborately verbal (Blalock, 1969). On close inspection, however, one may find it very difficult to isolate one single relational statement. It then becomes the task of the analyst to extract or construct simple relational statements from all the verbiage. This exercise requires a great deal of careful reading to be sure one has actually reflected the meaning in the way the original theorist intended. Cross-checking with colleagues or even the original theorist is often a big help when you are confronted by such a problem.

The third consideration in selecting a statement for analysis is that it be relevant. That is, it is far better to select a prominent or major statement in a theory than to select an insignificant one. To tell the difference in major and minor statements, examine the statement's breadth. A major statement will yield more information to the analyst than a minor one will. In addition, if the major statement has validity, the likelihood increases that the minor one does too.

Simplify the Statement if Necessary

This step is necessary only if one of two things occurs. The first is the problem of the elaborate verbal model that must be reduced to manageable statements. The second problem is complexity, which may occur in theories in which one concept may be linked to several others at the same time. When this happens, it simplifies analysis to break the concept linkages into several shorter, more manageable statements. Assume a statement could be diagrammed as the one in Figure 2–3. It is clear that the analyst might find his or her job much easier to handle if the formulation looked more like the one in Figure 2–4. The analyst now has four simple discrete relationships to examine instead of one set of complex relationships. It is also clear, however, that great care must be exercised when doing this or relationships may be overlooked or misconstrued.

Classify the Statement

When we speak of the classification of a statement, we are examining the use of the statement within the theory. There are three basic classifications of statements: (1) existence statements, (2) definitions, and (3) relational statements.

Existence statements claim existence for concepts (Reynolds, 1971). The statement "That object is called a refrigerator" is an existence statement. Existence statements are not definitions and thus do not describe characteristics of the concept. They simply assert that something is so. Existence statements can be accurate or inaccurate. If the object in our example is really a dishwasher then the statement is inaccurate. If the object in the statement corresponds to reality (it *is* a refrigerator) then the statement is accurate.

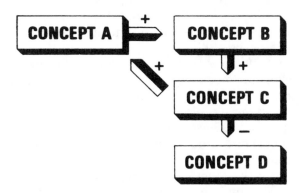

FIGURE 2–3

A complicated statement. See Figure 2–4 for simplification.

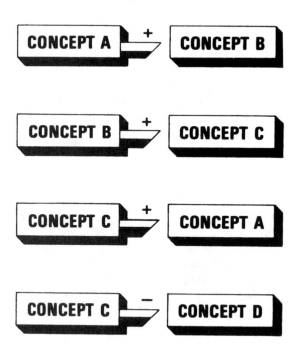

FIGURE 2–4

The statement in Figure 2–3 broken down into several shorter, more manageable statements.

Definitions have three subforms—descriptive, stipulative, and operational (Hempel, 1966). A descriptive definition describes the accepted meaning for a term already in use. It describes the term in other terms that are already understood by the reader. It generally can be considered accurate.

A stipulative definition, on the other hand, describes the term in such a way that it has a very specific use within the theory; a use that is not always the same as the general meaning of the term. These definitions cannot be considered either accurate or inaccurate because they are specifically formulated *only* for use in the way the author of the theory has decreed.

For example, a descriptive definition of "kitten" might read "A kitten is the biological offspring of an adult female cat." A stipulative definition of "kitten," however, might read "For the purpose of this study, a kitten shall be defined as any healthy female offspring of a healthy female cat that is less than eight weeks old."

A stipulative definition is not the same as an operational definition. An operational definition includes the specific means for measuring or testing each scientific term within it. An operational definition must be so precise that it can be used repetitively by different scientists and still obtain objective results. In our definition of "kitten," for instance, the operational definition might be "For the purposes of this study, a kitten shall be any healthy offspring of a healthy female cat weighing between 4 and 12 ounces and no less than 3 days or more than 12 days old."

A *relational* statement is one that specifies relationships between concepts. It may be so well supported empirically and logically that it functions as a law or an axiom within the theory. It may be less well supported by data or logic than a law and serve as a proposition or empirical generalization. Or it may be any hypothesis that is as yet unsupported by data even if it may appear reasonable logically. Identifying the relational statements is very important when you get to Step 5 in the statement analysis. It is that step in which you will specify exactly which *type* of relationship the statement exemplifies.

Examine the Concepts Within the Statement

Identifying the concepts within the statement to be analyzed is perhaps the easiest part of statement analysis. It is the examination of them that requires a certain rigor. Identifying the concepts simply involves scanning the statement for the major ideas expressed in it. The labels for these ideas are the concepts that must be examined.

After the concepts in a statement are identified, examining them involves two actions. The first is to determine the definitions of the terms that reflect the concepts. The definition should reflect all the critical defining attributes or characteristics of the concept so that everyone who reads the theory will know precisely how the theorist intends the term to be used. If the concept is not adequately defined, can its meaning be determined from the context of the theoretical formulation? If so, the analyst should use this material to help formulate additions to the definition that will aid the analysis and even perhaps help refine the theory. If not, then the analyst must simply state that the concepts are inadequately defined for the purpose of analysis.

The second step in the examination of concepts in a statement is to determine if the concepts *as they are defined* are theoretically valid. This process is a bit like determining construct validity in research. That is, the analyst attempts to determine whether the concepts as they are defined accurately reflect the general semantic usage for that concept. This process involves a brief overview of the relevant literature that concerns the concept being considered. If the concept is being used in the same ways as it has previously been used in the literature and the definition reflects it, the concept may be considered valid. In addition, if the theorist has conducted a careful concept analysis, the concept is considered valid even if it does not reflect the relevant literature but goes beyond traditional usage. The concept may be more valid, in fact, than a concept defined by tradition alone.

Specify Relationships by Type, Sign, and Symmetry

Type. The assessment of a relational statement for type, sign, and symmetry is for the purpose of determining its function. Several types of relational statements may occur. These are causal, probabilistic, concurrent, conditional, time-order, necessary, and sufficient types of statements (Hardy, 1974). We shall consider each type briefly and give an example of each. For the purposes of clarity and simplicity, we are assuming that all relational statements are linear until proven otherwise. (Statement analysis can often provide the clue to curvilinear relationships. If you can't classify a statement or determine its sign, it may express a nonlinear relationship.)

The causal statement is one in which the first concept is said to be the "cause" of the other. Causal statements are generally deduced from laws. There are few causal statements in the social and behavioral sciences primarily because there are so many intervening variables that influence causation. There are more in the physical sciences. For example, the statement "Raising the temperature of a gas held under constant pressure will increase its volume" is a causal statement. It asserts that some event (raising the temperature of a gas under pressure) causes another event (increased gas volume). This is the simplest form of causal statement although there are more complex ones involving several causal events for one phenomenon. Causal statements are difficult to find, especially in beginning attempts at theory construction, because the caused event must *always* happen if the causal event or events occur.

It is often helpful to use symbols for the concepts in statements so that you don't become confused by the content of the concepts during analysis. Using the symbols G_p for gas under pressure, T for temperature, and GV for gas volume, you can diagram the statement thus:

$$\text{If } \uparrow T \rightarrow G_p \text{ then always } \uparrow GV.$$

If the event (GV) always occurs, it can be labeled a causal statement.

If the event only occurs some of the time or even most of the time, but not *all* of the time, the statement is called probabilistic. Probabilistic statements are usually derived from statistical data. They assert that if one event occurs, the second event probably will also. An excellent example of a probabilistic statement is that cigarette smoking (CS) is highly likely to lead to lung cancer (LC). There is no direct causality in this statement since everyone who smokes does not develop lung cancer. But the *probability* of developing lung cancer is increased significantly in the presence of cigarette smoking. Probabilistic relationships, if diagrammed, might look like this:

$$\text{If } CS \rightarrow \text{ then probably } LC.$$

Concurrent relationships demonstrate that if event A occurs, event B also occurs. There may or may not be any correlation or causation between the two events—they simply exist together. An example of this kind of statement might be "A low level of educational preparation and a low income often occur together." The statement does not infer that little education *causes* poverty or even that the two are correlated. Another example can be found in Muhlenkamp and Parsons' study of nurses (1972) and is confirmed in Kaiser and Bickle's study (1980). These authors found that nurses have personality characteristics that are highly feminine rather than masculine. This is a good example of a concurrent statement. It simply asserts that nurses (N) and feminine personality (FP) characteristics occur together. It makes no other claim. A diagram of this statement would be:

$$\text{If } N, \text{ also } FP.$$

A conditional statement is one that demonstrates a relationship between two concepts or events but that requires the presence of a third concept or event before the relationship can come about. A good example of a conditional statement is one found in a study by Reichert and Fuller on the effects of sodium bicarbonate on intraventricular hemorrhage in premature infants (1980). Their statement indicates that sodium bicarbonate ($NaHCO_3$) can be given to correct acidosis in premature infants with respiratory distress without the occurrence of intraventricular hemorrhage (IVH) but only if given in conservative doses (CD) and over a 15- to 30-minute time period (TTP). This can be simplistically diagrammed as:

$$\text{If } NaHCO_3, \text{ then no } IVH, \text{ but only if } CD \text{ and } TTP.$$

Time-ordered statements are those that indicate that some amount of time intervenes between the first concept or event and the second. An example of a time-ordered statement might be one that indicates that if a person experiences numerous stressful life events (SLE) within a year the likelihood of that person becoming ill (I) is quite high (Holmes & Rahe, 1968; Rahe, 1972). This relationship is time-ordered because time passes between the first episodes of stress and the resultant illness. This statement can be diagrammed like this:

$$\text{If } SLE, \text{ then later } I.$$

A necessary relationship is shown by a statement that indicates that one and only one concept or event can lead to the second concept or event. These necessary relationships function very much as differential diagnoses do in medicine. That is, a patient can be positively said to have cancer, for instance, if and only if there is a pathologist's report of malignant cells on biopsy. In the same way, relationships among concepts may occur only under certain conditions. An example from nursing might be a statement relating to stress and adaptation. Both Roy's (1976) and Neuman's (1980) models of nursing have stated that adaptation (*A*) occurs as a response to stressors (*S*). Stressors then become *necessary* before adaptation can occur. The diagram would look like this:

If and only if S, then A.

Sufficient relationships are reflected in statements in which the first concept or event and the second concept or event are related regardless of anything else. Using the stressor/adaptation idea above, we can see that if stressors occur then adaptation will begin in the person whether or not she or he wills it and whether or not someone intervenes to help. In other words, the presence of the first concept guarantees the presence of the second concept. A sufficient relationship could be diagrammed like this:

If *S*, then *A* regardless of anything else.

Some students, when first introduced to statement analysis, mistakenly believe that a statement can only be one type at a time. This is clearly not the case. Most relational statements are probabilistic *in addition to* being conditional or concurrent or time ordered, etc.

Sign. Determining the sign of relationships is reasonably easy. Signs generally fall into one of three categories: positive, negative, or unknown (Mullins, 1971; Reynolds, 1971). The rule of thumb is that if the concepts vary in the same direction, that is, as one increases or decreases so does the other, then the relationship is positive. If one concept increases while the other decreases, the relationship is said to be negative. If you have no information about the way the concepts vary, the relationship is unknown. Below are three probabilistic statements and one inferred statement from the first three with their relationships drawn to help you see how this is done.

When members of a group become anxious (*A*), hostility (*H*) increases.

$$A \underset{\rightarrow}{+} H$$

Hostility is related to a decrease in group cohesiveness (*GC*).

$$H \underset{\rightarrow}{-} GC$$

Creativity (*C*) decreases as anxiety increases in groups.

$$A \underset{\rightarrow}{-} C$$

Inferred: Anxiety has a negative impact on group cohesiveness.

$$A \underset{\rightarrow}{-} GC$$

This inferred statement was derived logically from the first two statements. Since both *A* and *GC* are related to *H*, they are therefore related to each other.

What we cannot tell from these four statements is what effect creativity and group cohesiveness have on each other. So that might look like this:

$$C \underline{\quad} \underline{?} \underline{\quad} GC$$

Symmetry. Relationships can be symmetrical or asymmetrical (Blalock, 1969). So far, all our examples have been asymmetrical, that is, one-direction relationships. In asymmetrical statements, the relationship only goes from one concept to the next but is never reciprocated.

There are many examples of asymmetrical relationships in our discussions. One example is the statement above that anxiety is negatively related to group cohesiveness. If the relationship is a two-way relationship in which each concept affects the other, it is considered symmetrical. An example of a symmetrical statement might be one from research done by one of us on maternal attachment behaviors (Avant, 1981). High attachment scores (*At*) were associated with low anxiety (*Ax*) scores and high anxiety scores were associated with low attachment scores in primiparous women. This relationship can be diagrammed like this:

$$At \underset{\leftrightarrow}{-} Ax$$

Examine the Logic

The logic of a single statement can be examined for origin, reasonableness, and adequacy. When examining the origin of a statement, ask yourself whether the statement is constructed deductively, that is, from a more general law, or inductively, from observation or available data. If the statement is deductive in origin, its logic should be adequate since a conclusion in a deductive argument cannot be false if the premises are true. If the statement is inductive, its logic cannot be judged except by the amount of empirical support it has and by comparison to existing knowledge (Hempel, 1966). If it has strong support in both empirical testing and in agreement with existing literature, its logic is probably adequate. The logic can also be determined by examining the relationships of the concepts to each other. If the relationship cannot be classified by type, sign, or symmetry, there may be a logical flaw.

Comparison to existing knowledge is also used in determining the reasonableness of a statement. One simply asks if this statement seems reasonable given what we already know on the subject. If it makes sense in the light of existing knowledge, it is reasonable.

Determining adequacy of a single statement is more difficult than determining adequacy of a theory since we cannot construct matrices or models to demonstrate where logical gaps may occur. It is possible, however, to draw a simple diagram as we have done in the previous section labeling the concepts by letters or numbers and determining types and signs that are relevant. If you are unable to do any one of the three, there is some fault in the statement.

Determine Testability

The final step in a statement analysis is to determine if the statement is empirically testable. In this step of the analysis you must determine whether or not there are operational measures that can be used in the "real world" to obtain data that will support or refute the statement. It is at this point that the analyst will run up against the situation Hempel calls "testability-in-principle." Basically, this is a statement that *could* be tested empirically if the tools were available to measure the concepts; but they are not available (Hempel, 1966). He considers these statements equally useful in theory construction as the actually empirically testable statements. Since so many of our concepts in nursing may lack the instruments to measure them, we feel that the criterion of testability can be met if a statement is either testable-in-principle or actually testable.

This is not to imply, however, that all statements are therefore testable. In order for a statement to meet the criterion of testability it must render some test implications. That is, one should be able to say "If I tested this under the specified conditions, then the outcome hypothesized should actually happen." A relatively "new" statement might render fewer testable ideas than one that has more age and support, but if it is testable at all, it meets the criterion. Any statement that cannot produce one testable idea or that is constructed in such a way that the concepts have vague meanings cannot meet the criterion of testability until modified.

*A*dvantages and Limitations

Statement analysis has several advantages. The primary advantage is that it provides a systematic way of examining the relationships between concepts. In addition, it assists the theorist in examining the structure and function of statements. But perhaps the most important function of statement analysis is that when you are thinking carefully and systematically about the linkages between concepts, you may discover other linkages or relationships that are important to the final theoretical formulations. In just such analysis situations have many scientists "happened on to" important theoretical ideas as if by accident.

The limitations of statement analysis are that it is often difficult to analyze just one statement if it is part of a theoretical whole. Removing the statement from its context can often result in loss of valuable information, and the analysis is hindered. In addition, determining the logic of a statement is often more difficult when it is removed from the theory. The final limitation of the statement analysis process is that it does take a little time and it is rigorous. This is only a limitation as it applies to the theorist, however, since it is this very rigorousness and time taking that are ultimately so valuable in assessing statements.

*U*tilizing the Results of Statement Analysis

Statement analysis formalizes statements so that their underlying structures and functions are made explicit. But what does one do with the resulting information? It can be used in a variety of different ways in education, practice, research, and theory development.

In education, analyzed statements can be used as springboards for discussion. Discussions can include ideas about which concepts were clear, which ones were related to each other, and how, or what, inconsistencies were discovered. The amount of empirical evidence for or against the statement can be examined and used as the basis for designing classroom activities such as proposing research studies that would produce either more evidence for the statement or more evidence against the statement. The amount of empirical evidence could also be used to launch a discussion about the efficacy of the statement to guide clinical practice. Another use for statement analysis in education might be to have a faculty interest group discuss the issues raised from analyzing several similar statements or several statements about the same topic of interest. This discussion could lead to curriculum changes or to faculty research projects.

In practice, statement analysis can guide clinicians in the judicious use of research findings. Knowing whether or not a statement is associational, causal, or time ordered can help in decisions about when to use the statement and under what conditions. Certain nursing diagnoses may be considered or certain nursing interventions chosen as a result of the statement analysis that might not have been considered previously by the nurse. In addition, faced with the choice of two potential interventions, statement analysis would provide the nurse with knowledge of which has the most empirical support, thus leading to a more educated decision on her part.

In research, statement analysis provides fruitful information about what the next steps in a research program are. Inconsistencies, unclear definitions, and gaps in knowledge become apparent. These provide direction for planning concept analyses, reformulating ideas, or proposing new hypotheses to test.

In theory development, statement analysis allows the theorist to see where the problems in a statement are and to take the appropriate next step. Do concepts need clarifying? Are there inconsistencies? If so, the theorist can plan strategies for dealing with these issues. If the analysis has demonstrated that the statement is sound, the theorist can begin to look for additional concepts and linkages to add to what is already known. This is how theories are built—one step at a time.

Summary

We have said that statement analysis is a process of systematically examining the relationships between concepts. There are seven steps involved: selecting the statement; simplifying it if necessary; classifying it; examining the concepts for definition and validity; specifying relationships by type, sign, and symmetry; examining the logic; and determining the testability.

The process of statement analysis provides useful information for the theorist in that once the statement has been analyzed, any deficiencies in the statement are clear and may be corrected. Furthermore, the process of thinking aloud (or in writing) about two or more concepts often generates additional statements either by deduction or by serendipity that are valuable additions to future theoretical formulations.

Practice Exercises

Below are several statements from a study of faculty attitudes (Ruiz, 1981).

A. Classify each statement as either
   a. Relational statement
   b. Descriptive definition
   c. Stipulative definition
   d. Operational definition

   1. Ethnocentrism means ethnic narrow-mindedness.
   2. Dogmatism shall be defined as close-mindedness.
   3. Intolerance of ambiguity and dogmatism are the two factors underlying ethnocentrism for this study.
   4. Faculty who are highly dogmatic view patients with different ethnocultural backgrounds as annoying and superstitious.
   5. Faculty who have high ethnocentrism scores have negative attitudes toward culturally different patients.

B. Using statement 4, simplify it into two statements and diagram them.

C. Using statements 4 and 5, examine the concepts and specify the relationships by type, sign, and symmetry. Determine the logic and testability of each.

Answers

A. 1. b, 2. c, 3. d, 4. a, 5. a

B. 1. Dogmatic faculty (*DF*) view patients with differing ethnocultural (*DEB*) backgrounds as annoying (*A*):

If *DF*, then *A*, but only if *DEB*.

2. Dogmatic faculty (*DF*) view patients with differing ethnocultural backgrounds (*DEB*) as superstitious (*S*):

If DF, then S, but only if DEB.

C. Statement 4 can be diagrammed as $DF \xrightarrow{} DEB$

statement 5 as ethnocentric faculty (*EF*) $\xrightarrow{}$ attitudes toward

culturally different patients (*ACDB*) or $EF \xrightarrow{} ACDB$.

Both statements are probabilistic since they are drawn from statistical data and statement 4 as it is diagrammed in Practice Exercise B is conditional. Both statements are asymmetrical. The signs are negative since less dogmatic faculty had higher views of ethnocentric patients.

Some of the concepts from statements 4 and 5, such as "patient," "faculty," "ethnocultural background," "annoying," and "superstitious," are undefined. If these concepts were intended to be used in their common language meanings, the author should state that clearly. Otherwise each should be defined. The two concepts that were defined, "ethnocentrism" and "dogmatism," are given only in vague, equally undefined terms in this exercise. (They were operationally defined in the actual study.) The concept of "intolerance of ambiguity" is not defined but is used as part of an operational definition. This is clearly to be avoided. None of the concept definitions is unambiguous.

The statements are logical. They are testable only if better concept definitions are constructed so that operational measures can be found for them. Only when there are careful operational definitions that reflect the theoretical definitions can it be said that the concepts are measurable or the statement testable.

$\mathcal{R}$eferences

Avant K: Anxiety as a potential factor affecting maternal attachment. *JOGN* 10(6):416–420, 1981.

Blalock H, Jr: *Theory Construction: From Verbal to Mathematical Formulations.* Englewood Cliffs, NJ: Prentice-Hall, 1969.

Hardy M: Theories: Components, development, and evaluation. *Nurs Res* 23:100-126, 1974.

Hardy M (ed): *Theoretical Foundations for Nursing.* New York: MSS Information Corporation, 1973.

Hempel C: *Philosophy of Natural Science.* Englewood Cliffs, NJ: Prentice-Hall, 1966.

Holmes R, Rahe R: The social readjustment rating scale. *J Psychosom Res* 11:213, 1968.

Kaiser J, Bickle I: Attitude change as a motivational factor in producing behavior change related to implementing primary nursing. *Nurs Res* 19(5):290–300, 1980.

Muhlenkamp A, Parsons J: Characteristics of nurses: An overview of recent research published in a nursing research periodical. *J Vocational Behav* 2:261–273, 1972.

Mullins N: *The Art of Theory: Construction and Use.* New York: Harper & Row, 1971.

Neuman B: The Betty Neuman health-care systems model. In: Riehl JP, Roy C, (eds). *Conceptual Models for Nursing Practice.* 2nd ed. New York: Appleton-Century-Crofts, 1980.

Rahe R: Subject's recent life changes and their near future illness susceptibility. *Adv Psychosom* Med 8:2–19, 1972.

Reichert E, Fuller P: Relationship of sodium bicarbonate to intraventricular hemorrhage in premature infants with respiratory distress syndrome. *Nurs Res* 29(6):357-361, 1980.

Reynolds P: *A Primer in Theory Construction.* Indianapolis: Bobbs-Merrill, 1971.

Roy C: *Introduction to Nursing: An Adaptation Model.* Englewood Cliffs, NJ: Prentice-Hall, 1976.

Ruiz M: Open-closed mindedness, intolerance of ambiguity and nursing faculty attitudes toward culturally different patients. *Nurs Res* 30(3):177–181, 1981.

$\mathcal{A}$dditional Readings

Greenwood D: *The Nature of Science and Other Essays.* New York: Philosophical Library, 1959.

Hage J: *Techniques and Problems of Theory Construction in Sociology.* New York: John Wiley & Sons, 1972.

Lerner D (ed): *Parts and Wholes.* New York: Free Press of Glencoe, 1963.

Pasch A: *Experience and the Analytic: A Reconsideration of Empiricism.* Chicago: Univ of Chicago Press, 1958.

Zetterberg HL: *On Theory and Verification in Sociology.* 3rd ed. New York: Bedminster Press, 1965.

Theory Derivation

$\mathcal{D}$efinition and Description

Theory derivation is the process of using analogy to obtain explanations or predictions about a phenomenon in one field from the explanations or predictions in another field (Maccia, Maccia, & Jewett, 1963). Thus, a theory (T_1) from one field of interest (F_1) offers some new insights to a theorist who then moves certain content or structural features into his or her own field of interest (F_2) to form a new theory (T_2). Theory derivation is an easy way to develop theory rapidly in a new field since all that is required is (1) the ability to see analogous dimensions of phenomena in two distinct fields of interest and (2) the ability to redefine and transpose the content and/or structure from Field 1 to Field 2 in a manner that adds significant insights about some phenomenon in Field 2 (Figure 2–5).

Theory derivation is not a mechanical exercise. Seeing the analogy requires imagination and creativity. Theory derivation also requires the theorist to be able to redefine the concepts and statements so that they are meaningful in the new field. Since the two fields are obviously different, certain modifications will have to be made when transposing a theory from one to the other field.

Two distinctions must be made here: the distinction between theory derivation and statement derivation, and the distinction between "borrowing" or sharing theory and theory derivation. Theory derivation is a process whereby a whole set of interrelated concepts or a whole

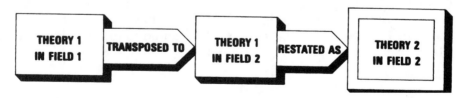

FIGURE 2–5

Process of theory derivation.

Taken from: *Strategies for Theory Construction in Nursing,* Third Edition by Walker and Avant.

structure is moved from one field to another and modified to fit the new field, whereas in statement derivation one moves only *individual* isolated statements from one field to another and modifies them. Statement derivation is on a smaller scale than theory derivation although the actual steps in the process are similar.

Borrowing or sharing theory is a practice that nurses have used frequently. When one borrows or shares a theory, the theory is moved *unchanged* from one discipline to another. For example, we have used chemical, biological, and psychologic theories in nursing for many years without any changes needing to be made in the original theories when they are applied in nursing. However, if we wished to *derive* a new theory to use in nursing from any of these fields, we would need to modify the concepts and/or the structure in those theories to fit our particular needs in nursing. Theories cannot be moved unchanged from one field to another as an example of theory derivation. True theory derivation requires that at least some modifications in content or structure be made.

*P*urpose and Uses

The purposes of theory derivation are to acquire a means of explanation and prediction about some phenomenon that is currently poorly understood, or for which there is no present means to study it, or for which there is no theory at all. Theory derivation is particularly useful where no data are available or where new insights about a phenomenon are needed to inspire research and testing. Theory derivation is useful when a theorist has a set of concepts that are somehow related to each other, but has no structural way to represent those relationships. In this case, the theorist might find that some other field of interest has a structure in one of its theories that is analogous to the relationships of the concepts in which he or she is interested. The theorist may use the derivation strategy appropriately by adopting and adapting the structure to fit the concepts being considered. This adds to the body of knowledge in the theorist's field in a significant and rapid way that might not have happened for some time without the derivation strategy. An example of this is Nierenberg's use of Maslow's hierarchical structure of needs to derive a theory of negotiation (1968; 1973).

Theory derivation is also very useful when a theorist has some ideas about the basic structure of a phenomenon but has no concepts to describe it. Another theory in a different field may provide the theorist with a set of analogous concepts that can help describe the phenomenon, if modified slightly. Again, this procedure rapidly adds to the body of knowledge in the theorist's own field. One example of this strategy is Roy & Roberts (1981) developing the concepts of focal, contextual, and residual stimuli in patient assessment from a psychophysics theory by Helson.

Several examples of theory derivation come quickly to mind when we consider systems theory. Many of our nursing models in their original form have been direct derivations from systems theory—Roy & Roberts (1981), Neuman (1980) and others have significant aspects of theory derivation strategies in them.

*P*rocedures for Theory Derivation

Theory derivation can be discussed as a series of sequential steps, although the actual process may not occur sequentially. Many times theory derivation becomes an iterative process. That is, the theorist repeats some or all of the steps until the level of sophistication of the theory is acceptable.

There are several basic steps in theory derivation:

1. Become thoroughly familiar with the literature on the topic of interest. This implies that the theorist is cognizant of the level of theory development in his or her own field of interest and has evaluated the scientific usefulness of any such developments. If none of the current theories are suitable for the purpose of the theorist, then theory derivation can proceed.

2. Read widely in other fields for ideas. Reading widely enables a theorist to understand ways of putting theory together in other disciplines. But reading widely is not enough. The theorist must read while allowing imagination and creativity free reign. Discovering analogies is often done accidentally or as a creative intuitive leap rather than systematically.

3. Select a parent theory to use for derivation. The parent theory should be chosen because it offers a new and insightful way of explaining or predicting about a phenomenon in the theorist's field of interest. Just any theory won't do. Many theories will shed no light at all on the concepts of interest or will provide no useful structure for the concepts and are therefore worthless to the theorist. Keep in mind here that the whole parent theory may not be needed to form the new theory. Only those portions that are analogous and therefore relevant need be used.

4. Identify what content and/or structure from the parent theory is to be used. Perhaps only the concepts or only the statements are analogous, but not the structure. Or perhaps the structure is perfect but the parent concepts and statements are not. Perhaps the theorist needs both concepts and statements as well as structure. In the derivation strategy, the theorist is free to choose what best fits the needs of the situation.

5. Develop or redefine any new concepts or statements from the content or structure of the parent theory in terms of the phenomenon of interest to the theorist. This is the hardest part of theory derivation, but also the most fun. It requires creativity and thoughtfulness on the part of the theorist. Basically, the concepts or structure that is borrowed from the parent field is modified in such a way that it becomes meaningful in the theorist's field. Often the modifications are small, but occasionally they will need to be substantial before the theory makes sense in the new setting.

We are giving you several brief examples of theory derivation. Often, an example is clearer than an explanation alone can be. Let us begin with Wewers and Lenz's (1987) theory of relapse among ex-smokers that they derived from Cronkite and Moos's theory of post-treatment functioning of alcoholics (1980). Wewers and Lenz primarily used content derivation but also derived a simplified structure. Listed on above are three propositions from Cronkite and Moos with the derivations made by Wewers and Lenz. In some cases we have adapted the wording of the propositions to show the derivations more clearly.

Because there was a rich literature already available on smoking, Wewers and Lenz adopted propositions in their derivation that fit knowledge specifically about smoking. This is an excellent example of how to use the strategy flexibly in theory-building efforts.

Another example is the reconceptualization of the uncertainty of illness theory undertaken by Mishel (1990). Mishel used the content and structure of chaos theory to help her describe the outcome portion of her model more clearly. We have selected three statements to illustrate how the derivation was made. In an effort to be as clear and succinct as possible, we have at times restated the propositions to make the analogies more obvious.

Cronkite and Moos (1980) Propositions	Wewers and Lenz (1987) Derivations
1. Pretreatment symptoms such as alcohol consumption, type of drinker, depression, and occupational functioning are related to alcohol treatment outcomes (p 48).	1. Pretreatment symptoms such as cigarette consumption and type of smoker are related to smoking relapse (p 48).
2. "Stressful life events were negatively associated with some aspects of recovery" (p 49).	2. "Both the social contextual stressor of major life events and the internal stressor of craving" are associated with smoking relapse (p 49).
3. Family environment is "weakly related to alcohol recovery" (p 49).	3. "Long term smoking cessation is associated with having family members who are nonsmokers or who had previously been able to quit smoking" (p 49).

A third example in which theorists used a derivation strategy is one in which Maccia and Maccia used both concepts and structure of a theory of eye blinks to derive a theory of education. Listed below are a few of the principles and their derivations from Maccia and Maccia's work (Maccia & Maccia, 1963).

As you can see, theory derivation can happen using two widely disparate fields. It is the theorist's creativity and intuition that provide the insight into the analogy.

Now that we have seen three examples in which both concepts and structure were used in theory derivation, let us examine one example in which only concepts were used and another example in which only structure was used.

Parent Theory Statements	Mishel's Derivation
1. "In a far-from equilibrium (sic) system, the sensitivity of the initial condition is such that small changes yield huge effects, and the system reorganizes itself in multiple ways" (p 259).	1. "Abiding uncertainty can dismantle the existing cognitive structures that give meaning to everyday events. This loss of meaning throws the person into a state of confusion and disorganization" (p 260).
2. "Fluctuations in the system can become so powerful . . . that they shatter the preexisting organization" (p 259).	2. "If the uncertainty factors of disease or illness multiply rapidly past a critical value, the stability of the personal system can no longer be taken for granted" (p 260).
3. ". . . Auto-catalytic processes result in a product whose presence encourages further production of itself . . . producing disorder" (p 259).	3. "The existence of uncertainty in one area of illness often feeds back on itself and generates further uncertainty in other illness-related events" (p 260).

Parent Theory	Maccia et al
1. Either the eyes are or are not covered by lids.	1. The student is either distracted or attentive.
2. Blinking functions to protect the eyes from contact and to rest the retina and the ocular muscles.	2. Distraction functions to protect the student from mental stress and to rest from mental effort.
3. Blinking may be either reflexive or nonreflexive.	3. Distraction may be either voluntary or nonvoluntary.
4. Reflex blinking may be inhibited by a fixation object or by drugs.	4. Nonvoluntary distraction may be inhibited by attention cues or by drugs.
5. Nonreflexive blinking may occur if seeing is unwanted.	5. Voluntary distraction may occur if learning is unwanted.

The example we would like to use of a theory derivation where the concepts from the parent theory were used, but not the structure, is one by Suchman on predicting health behavior. Using the traditional epidemiological concepts of "host," "agent," and "environment," Suchman modified these concepts to become "personal readiness," "situational factors," and "social control factors," respectively. In his studies to test his new concepts, personal readiness factors were found to be the most predictive of the adoption of a health protection measure. Social control and situational factors were much less predictive of adoption of a health protection measure (Suchman, 1967).

An example in which the structure, but not the concepts, was derived into a new theory is Lawrence Kohlberg's theory of moral development, which he based on the structure of Piaget's theory of cognitive development. Both theories speak to the relationship of the child's age to its cognitive or moral development. Below we have listed both Piaget's structure and the derivation from it made by Kohlberg (Piaget, 1950; Piaget & Inhelder, 1958; Kohlberg, 1964).

Kohlberg used the phase/stage structure of Piaget's levels of cognitive development and modified it to organize his concepts of the levels of moral reasoning. This strategy helped him to make clear the orderliness of moral development and, in addition, saved him a considerable amount of development time. In this case, the parent field was not so disparate from Kohlberg's

Piaget	Kohlberg
Level I: Preoperational Phase	Level I: Premoral Level
1. Sensorimotor stage	Type 1: Punishment and obedience orientation
2. Preconceptual stage	Type 2: Naive instrumental hedonism
Level II: Concrete Operations Phase	Level II: Morality of Conventional Role-Conformity
1. Intuitive state	Type 3: Good boy morality
2. Concrete operation state	Type 4: Authority maintaining morality
Level III: Formal Operations Phase	Level III: Morality of Self-Accepted Moral Principles
1. Formal operations state	Type 5: Morality of control, individual rights, an democratically accepted law
	Type 6: Morality of individual principles of conscience

as was the eye blink theory from that of Maccia (et al). But in both cases, the discovery of the analogous relationships between the parent theory and the new theory was extremely helpful to the theorist by facilitating the construction efforts.

Derived theories, it must be remembered, are constructed in the context of discovery. The theories thus developed have no validity until they are subjected to empirical testing in the context of justification. Even if the theory is extremely relevant to practice or research, it must first be validated before it can be used.

Another way to test theory is to subject it to examination in light of the existing literature on the topic. Is there any support in the literature that makes it more plausible or likely? Finally, if the theory is reliable in predicting outcomes, this reliability provides an additional measure of support. None of these methods can substitute for a full-scale empirical test, but they can provide a general estimate of the theory's plausibility.

Advantages and Limitations

The major advantage of theory derivation is that it is a reasonably easy and quick way to obtain formal theory in new areas of interest. It is an exciting exercise in that it requires the theorist to use creativity and imagination in seeing analogies from one field and modifying them for use in a new field. In addition, theory derivation provides a way of arriving at explanation and prediction about a phenomenon where there may be little or no information, literature, or formal studies.

The major disadvantage of theory derivation is that novice theorists become so excited about their new generalizations that they fail to take into account any dissimilarities, or disanalogies, present in the parent theory. These disanalogies should at least be considered for any valuable information that they might provide in the "new" theory.

A second disadvantage is that the theorist must be familiar with a number of fields of interest other than his or her own. This implies reading widely and being constantly on the alert for new and profitable analogies. In addition, the theorist must be thoroughly familiar with the literature and current thinking about his or her particular area of interest. Otherwise, when the time comes to draw an analogy, the theorist will have difficulty choosing appropriate boundaries for the new theory.

Utilizing the Results of Theory Derivation

We have said the uses of theory derivation are to provide structure when only concepts are available, to provide concepts when only structure is available, or to provide both concepts and structure as an efficient way to begin theory development. The results of theory derivation are easily used in nursing education, practice, research, and theory development.

In education, theory derivation is an excellent way to obtain a theoretical framework for curriculum building. In addition, it can be used as a teaching tool with graduate students as a way to introduce them to theorizing in general.

Theory derivation can provide significant new insights for clinical practice. Clinicians can provide themselves with a useful theoretical framework to guide their practice by using the results of theory derivation.

In research and theory development, theory derivation is a simple way to design a research program. Moving concepts and/or structure from the parent field with appropriate changes yields a rich source of potential hypotheses for study, as Wewers and Lenz demonstrated. It is a very efficient strategy for achieving a body of knowledge about a phenomenon.

$\mathcal{S}$ummary

Theory derivation is the process of using analogy to obtain explanations or predictions about a phenomenon in one field from explanations or predictions in another field. Theory derivation is an excellent way of obtaining rapid theory development in the new field. Both concepts and structure can be moved from the parent field to the new one undergoing modifications along the way.

There are five steps to theory derivation: (1) become thoroughly familiar with the topic of interest; (2) read widely in other fields, allowing your imagination to help you find useful analogies; (3) select a parent theory to use for derivation; (4) identify what content and/or structure from the parent theory is to be used; (5) modify or redefine new concepts and/or statements in terms of the phenomenon of interest. Once the new theory has been formulated, it must be tested empirically to validate that the new concepts and structure actually reflect reality in the new field.

The advantages of theory derivation are the ease and rapidity with which new constructions can be made. One disadvantage is that the theorist must be widely read in several fields as well as his or her own field. In addition, the theorist must remember to consider the dissimilarities as well as the similarities between the parent field and the new field.

Theory derivation is a highly workable strategy for nursing at this point in our development of a knowledge base. It provides a means of rapid acquisition of theory with meaningful content. If carefully done and carefully tested, derived theories could play an immediate role in the development of scientific knowledge in nursing.

$\mathcal{P}$ractice Exercises

Below is a list of 17 relational statements from a general systems theory for behavioral science (Miller, 1955). Using the derivation strategy in this section, construct a new theory for nursing in your own particular area of clinical interest. You don't have to include all 17 statements. Choose the ones most relevant to your area of interest. Remember that an open system is one that is bounded in space and time and that exchanges energy and information with its subsystems and with its environment (suprasystem).

- A. Greater energy is required for transmission across a boundary than for transmission within the environment or within a subsystem.

- B. Spread of energy or information throughout systems is quantitatively comparable.

- C. There is a constant systematic distortion—or alteration—between inputs of energy or information into the system and outputs from the system.

- D. The distortion of a system is the sum of the effects of processes that subtract from the input to reduce the strains in subsystems or add to the output to reduce the strains.

- E. When variables in a system return to equilibrium after stress, the rate of return and the strength of the restorative forces are stronger than a linear function of the amount of displacement from the equilibrium point.

- F. Living systems respond to continuously increasing stress first by a lag in response, then by overcompensation, then by collapse of the system.

G. Systems that survive employ the least expensive defenses against stress first and increasingly more expensive ones later.

H. Systems that survive perform at an optimum efficiency for maximum power output, which is always less than maximum efficiency.

I. When a system's negative feedback discontinues, its steady state vanishes, its boundaries disappear, and the system ends.

J. The output of a system is always less than its input.

K. Decentralization of the maintenance of variables in equilibrium is always more expensive of energy than centralization although it may increase utility.

L. As decentralization increases, subsystems increasingly act without the benefit of information available elsewhere in the system.

M. The more subsystems there are in efficient systems, the more variables they can maintain in equilibrium.

N. The more subsystems there are in efficient systems, the more subsystems whose destruction will cause the system to collapse.

O. When reduction of several strains is not possible simultaneously, the order in which they are reduced in systems that survive is from strongest to weakest, if the effort required for reduction is the same.

P. Up to a maximum, the more energy in a system devoted to information processing, the more likely the system is to survive.

Q. When one living species feeds on another in a given suprasystem, and both species continue to survive, an oscillation of numbers of predators and prey occurs around an equilibrium point.[1]

Just for fun, we derived a theory about graduate students in nursing. You may wish to compare your theory with ours below. We chose to use only a few statements to give you an example of how derivation might work. We have used the same alphabetical notation as the parent theory statements to help you identify where our statements come from.

A. Graduate students in nursing communicate with each other more efficiently than with their professors.

C. When graduate students are told the course requirements at the beginning of a course, they will ask for clarification of those requirements before mid-term.

F. 1. The nearer exams or deadlines approach, the more study groups are formed.

2. As exams or deadlines approach, the illness rate in students increases.

O. When several projects are due at once, graduate students will complete the most difficult project first.

[1]From Miller JG: Toward a general theory for behavioral science. Amer Psychol 10:(9):513–531, 1955. Copyright (1955) by the American Psychological Association. Reprinted by permission of the publisher and the author.

P. The more reading and thinking done by the student, the more likely he or she is to complete the degree.

J. Graduate students must complete a full curriculum in order to have enough skills to complete a thesis or dissertation.

I. When the final thesis or dissertation defense is completed, the student graduates.

*R*eferences

Cronkite RC, Moos RH: Determinants of the post-treatment functioning of alcoholic patients: A conceptual *framework J Consult Clin Psychol* 48:305–316, 1980.

Kohlberg L: Development of moral character and moral ideology. In: Hoffman M, Hoffman L, (eds). *Review of Child Development Research*. New York: Russell Sage Foundation, 1964, 383–431.

Maccia ES, Maccia GS, Jewett RE: Construction of Educational Theory Models. Cooperative Research Project #1632. Columbus, OH: Ohio State Univ Research Foundation, 1963.

Miller JG: Toward a general theory for behavioral science. *Amer Psychol* 10(9):513–531, 1955.

Mishel, M.H.: Reconceptualization of the uncertainty of illness theory. *Image.* 22(4):256–262, 1990.

Nierenberg GI: *The Art of Negotiating.* New York: Hawthorne, 1968.

Nierenberg GI: *Fundamentals of Negotiating.* New York: Hawthorne, 1973.

Neuman B: The Betty Neuman health care systems model: A total person approach to patient problems. In: Riehl JP, Roy C (eds). *Conceptual Models for Nursing Practice.* 2nd ed. New York: Appleton-Century-Crofts, 1980.

Piaget J: *The Psychology of Intelligence.* London: Routledge and Kegan Paul, 1950.

Piaget J, Inhelder B: *The Growth of Logical Thinking from Childhood to Adolescence.* New York: Basic Books, 1958.

Roy C, Roberts SL: *Theory Construction in Nursing: An Adaptation Model.* Englewood Cliffs, NJ: Prentice-Hall, 1981.

Suchman EA: Preventive health behavior: A model for research on community health campaigns. *J Health Social Behav* 8:197, 1967.

Wewers ME, Lenz E: Relapse among ex-smokers: An example of theory derivation. *Adv Nurs Sci* 9(2):44–53, 1987.

*A*dditional Readings

Burr JW: *Theory Construction in Sociology of the Family.* New York: John Wiley, 1973.

Ghiselin B (ed): *The Creative Process: A Symposium.* New York: New American Library, 1952.

Kaplan A: *The Conduct of Inquiry.* New York: Chandler, 1964.

Miller JG: *Living Systems.* New York: McGraw-Hill, 1978.

Olson RW: *The Art of Creative Thinking: A Practical Guide.* New York: Barnes and Noble, 1980.

SECTION 3

Dorothea E. Orem

Peggy Coldwell Foster

Agnes M. Bennett*

Dorothea E. Orem, MSNEd, DSc, RN was born in 1914 in Baltimore, Maryland. She began her nursing education at Providence Hospital School of Nursing in Washington, DC. After receiving her diploma in the early 1930s, she earned her Bachelor of Science in nursing education in 1939 and her Master of Science in nursing education in 1945 from the Catholic University of America.

She has received several honorary degrees including a Doctor of Science from Georgetown University in 1976; Doctor of Science from the Incarnate Word College, San Antonio, Texas, in]980; and Doctor of Humane Letters from Illinois Western University, Bloomington, Illinois, in 1988. Orem is a member of Sigma Theta Tau and Pi Gamma Mu. She has received several national awards, including the Catholic University of America's Alumni Achievement Award for Nursing Theory in 1980, and the Linda Richards Award from the National League for Nursing in 1991. Orem was named an Honorary Fellow of the American Academy of Nursing in 1992.

During her professional nursing career, she has worked as a staff nurse, private duty nurse, nurse educator, nurse administrator, and consultant. Orem continues to work as a nurse consultant and to develop her nursing theory.

> *If you give a man a fish he will have a single meal; If you teach him how to fish he will eat all his life.*—Kuan Tzer

Taken from: *Nursing Theories: The Base for Professional Nursing Practice*, Fourth Edition by George.

*Gratitude is expressed to Nancy Janssens for her contributions to this section in previous editions.

During 1958–1959, as a consultant to the Office of Education, Department of Health, Education, and Welfare, Dorothea E. Orem participated in a project to improve practical (vocational) nurse training. This work stimulated her to consider the question, "What condition exists in a person when that person or others determine that that person should be wider nursing care?" Her answer encompassed the idea that a nurse is "another self." This idea evolved into her nursing concept of "self-care" (Orem, 1991, p. 3). That is, when they are able, individuals care for themselves. When the person is unable to provide self-care, then the nurse provides the assistance needed. For children, nursing care is needed when the parents or guardians are unable to provide the amount and quality of care needed.

In 1959, Orem's concept of nursing as the provision of self-care was first published. In 1965, she joined with several faculty members from the Catholic University of America to form a Nursing Model Committee. In 1968, a portion of the Nursing Model Committee, including Orem, continued their work through the Nursing Development Conference Group (NDCG). This group was formed to produce a conceptual framework for nursing and to establish the discipline of nursing. The NDCG published *Concept formalization in nursing: Process and product* in 1973 and 1979.

Orem further developed her nursing concepts of self-care and in 1971 published *Nursing: Concepts of practice*. The second, third and fourth editions of this book were published in 1980, 1985, and 1991. The first edition focused on the individual. The second edition was expanded to include multiperson units (families, groups, and communities). The third edition presented Orem's general theory of nursing as it is constituted from three related theoretical constructs: self-care, self-care deficits, and nursing systems. In the fourth edition (1991) her writing incorporates a greater emphasis on the child, groups, and society.

rem's General Theory of Nursing

Orem (1991) states her general theory as follows:

> The condition that validates the existence of a requirement for nursing in an adult is *the absence of the ability to maintain continuously that amount and quality of self-care which is therapeutic in sustaining life and health, in recovering from disease or injury, or in coping with their effects.* With children, the condition is the *inability of the parent (or guardian) to maintain continuously for the child the amount and quality of care that is therapeutic* (p. 41).

Orem developed the Self-Care Deficit Theory of Nursing (her general theory), which is composed of three interrelated theories: (1) the theory of self-care, (2) the self-care deficit theory, and (3) the theory of nursing systems. Incorporated within these three theories are six central concepts and one peripheral concept. Understanding these central concepts of self-care, self-care agency, therapeutic self-care demand, self-care deficit, nursing agency, and nursing system, as well as the peripheral concept of basic conditioning factors, is essential to understanding her general theory.

The Theory of Self-Care

To understand the theory of self-care it is important to understand the concepts of self-care, self-care agency, basic conditioning factors, and therapeutic self-care demand. *Self-care* is the performance or practice of activities that individuals initiate and perform on their own behalf to maintain life, health, and well-being. When self-care is effectively performed, it helps to maintain structural integrity and human functioning, and it contributes to human development (Orem, 1991).

Self-care agency is the human's ability or power to engage in self-care. The individual's ability to engage in self-care is affected by basic conditioning factors. These *basic conditioning factors* are age, gender, developmental state, health state, sociocultural orientation, health care system factors (i.e., diagnostic and treatment modalities), family system factors, patterns of living (eg, activities regularly engaged in), environmental factors, and resource adequacy and availability. "Normally, adults voluntarily care for themselves. Infants, children, the aged, the ill, and the disabled require complete care or assistance with self-care activities" (Orem, 1991, p. 117). The *therapeutic self-care demand* is the totality of "self-care actions to be performed for some duration in order to meet known self-care requisites by using valid methods and related sets of operations and actions" (p. 123). The therapeutic self-care demand is modeled on deliberate action—that is, "action deliberately performed by some members of a social group to bring about events and results that benefit others in specified ways" (p. 79).

An additional concept incorporated within the theory of self-care is self-care requisites. Orem (1991) presents three categories of *self-care requisites,* or requirements, as: (1) universal, (2) developmental, and (3) health deviation. Self-care requisites can be defined as actions directed toward the provision of self-care. *Universal self-care requisites* are associated with life processes and the maintenance of the integrity of human structure and functioning. They are common to all human beings during all stages of the life cycle and should be viewed as interrelated factors, each affecting the others. A common term for these requisites is the activities of daily living. Orem (1991) identifies self-care requisites as follows:

1. The maintenance of a sufficient intake of air.

2. The maintenance of a sufficient intake of water.

3. The maintenance of a sufficient intake of food . . .

4. The provision of care associated with elimination processes and excrements.

5. The maintenance of a balance between activity and rest.

6. The maintenance of a balance between solitude and social interaction.

7. The prevention of hazards to human life, human functioning, and human well-being.

8. The promotion of human functioning and development within social groups in accord with human potential, known human limitations, and the human desire to be normal. *Normalcy* is used in the sense of that which is essentially human and that which is in accord with the genetic and constitutional characteristics and the talents of individuals (p. 126).

Developmental self-care requisites are "either specialized expressions of universal self-care requisites that have been particularized for developmental processes or they are new requisites derived from a condition . . . or associated with an event" (Orem, 1991, p. 130). Examples are adjusting to a new job or adjusting to body changes such as facial lines or hair loss.

Health deviation self-care is required in conditions of illness, injury, or disease or may result from medical measures required to diagnose and correct the condition (eg, right upper quadrant abdominal pain when foods with a high fat content are eaten, or learning to walk using crutches following the casting of a fractured leg.) The health deviation self-care requisites are as follows:

1. Seeking and securing appropriate medical assistance . . .

2. Being aware of and attending to the effects and results of pathologic conditions and states . . .

3. Effectively carrying out medically prescribed diagnostic, therapeutic, and rehabilitative measures . . .

4. Being aware of and attending to or regulating the discomforting or deleterious effects of prescribed medical care measures . . .

5. Modifying the self-concept (and self-image) in accepting oneself as being in a particular state of health and in need of specific forms of health care

6. Learning to live with the effects of pathologic conditions and states and the effects of medical diagnostic and treatment measures in a life-style that promotes continued personal development (Orem, 1991, p. 134).

In the theory of self-care, Orem explains *what* is meant by self-care and lists the various factors that affect its provision. In the self-care deficit theory, she specifies *when* nursing is needed to assist the individual in the provision of self-care.

The Theory of Self-Care Deficit

The theory of self-care deficit is the core of Orem's (1991) general theory of nursing because it delineates when nursing is needed. Nursing is required when an adult (or in the case of a dependent, the parent or guardian) is incapable of or limited in the provision of continuous effective self-care. Nursing may be provided if the "care abilities are less than those required for meeting a known self-care demand . . . [or] self-care or dependent-care abilities exceed or are equal to those required for meeting the current self-care demand, but a future deficit relationship can be foreseen because of predictable decreases in care abilities, qualitative or quantitative increases in the care demand, or both" (p. 71); when individuals need "to incorporate newly prescribed, complex self-care measures into their self-care systems, the performance of which requires specialized knowledge and skills to be acquired through training and experience" (p. 174); or the individual needs help "in recovering from disease or injury, or in coping with their effects" (p. 41). It is important to note that the first category includes universal, developmental, and health-deviation self-care needs whereas the other categories focus on health-deviation self-care.

Orem (1991) identifies the following five methods of helping:

1. Acting for or doing for another

2. Guiding and directing

3. Providing physical or psychological support

4. Providing and maintaining an environment that supports personal development

5. Teaching (p. 9).

The nurse may help the individual by using any or all of these methods to provide assistance with self-care.

Orem presents a model to show the relationship between her concepts (Fig. 3–1). From this model it can be seen that at any given time an individual has specific self-care abilities as well as therapeutic self-care demands. If there are more demands than abilities, nursing is needed. The activities in which nurses engage when they provide nursing care can be used to describe the domain of nursing. Orem (1991) has identified five areas of activity for nursing practice:

- Entering into and maintaining nurse-patient relationships with individuals, families, or groups until patients can legitimately be discharged from nursing

- Determining if and how patients can be helped through nursing

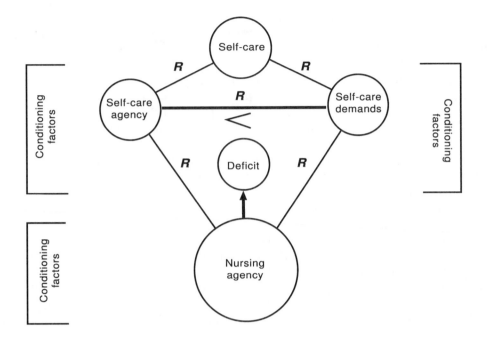

FIGURE 3–1

A Conceptual Framework for Nursing. (R = relationship; < = deficit relationship, current or projected.) (*Used with permission from Orem, D. E. (1991). Nursing: Concepts of practice (4th ed.). St. Louis: Mosby, p. 64.*)

- Responding to patients' requests, desires, and needs for nurse contacts and assistance

- Prescribing, providing, and regulating direct help to patients (and their significant others) in the form of nursing

- Coordinating and integrating nursing with the patient's daily living, other health care needed or being received, and social and educational services needed or being received (p. 340).

Self-care has been defined and the need for nursing explained in the first and second theories. In Orem's third theory of nursing systems, she outlines *how* the patient's self-care needs will be met by the nurse, the patient, or both.

The Theory of Nursing Systems

The nursing system, designed by the nurse, is based on the self-care needs *and* abilities of the patient to perform self-care activities. If there is a self-care deficit, that is, if there is a deficit between what the individual can do (self-care agency) and what needs to be done to maintain optimum functioning (self-care demand), then nursing is required.

Nursing agency is a complex property or attribute of people educated and trained as nurses that enables them to act, to know, and to help others meet their therapeutic self-care demands by exercising or developing their own self-care agency (Orem, 1991). Nursing agency is analogous to self-care agency in that both symbolize characteristics and abilities for specific types of deliberate action. They differ in that nursing agency is exercised for the benefit and well-being of others, and self-care agency is developed and exercised for the benefit of oneself.

Orem (1991) has identified three classifications of nursing systems to meet the self-care requisites of the patient (see Fig. 3–2). These systems are the wholly compensatory system, the partly compensatory system, and the supportive-educative system.

The design and elements of the nursing system define "(1) the scope of the nursing responsibility in health care situations; (2) the general and specific roles of nurses, patients, and others; (3) reasons for nurses' relationships with patients; and (4) the kinds of actions to be performed and the performance patterns and nurses' and patients' actions in regulating patients' self-care agency and in meeting their therapeutic self-care demand" (Orem, 1991, pp. 285, 287).

The *wholly compensatory nursing system* is represented by a situation in which the individual is unable "to engage in those self-care actions requiring self-directed and controlled ambulation and manipulative movement or the medical prescription to refrain from such activity. . . . Persons with these limitations are socially dependent on others for their continued existence and well-being" (Orem, 1991, p. 289). Subtypes of the wholly compensatory system are nursing systems for people who are: "[1] unable to engage in any form of deliberate action, for example, persons in a coma, . . . [2] aware and who may be able to make observations, judgments, and decisions about self-care and other matters but cannot or should not perform actions requiring ambulation and manipulative movements, . . . [3] unable to attend to themselves and make reasoned judgments and decisions about self-care and other matters but who can be ambulatory and may be able to perform some measures of self-care with continuous

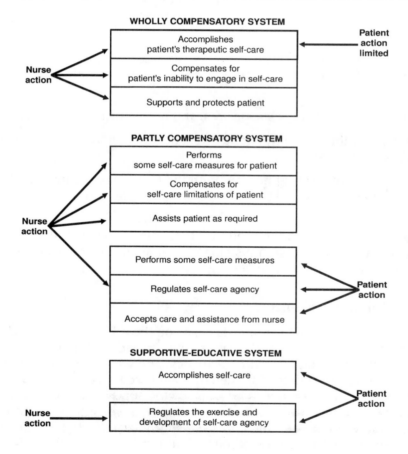

FIGURE 3–2

Basic Nursing Systems. *(Adapted with permission from Orem, D. E. (1991). Nursing: Concepts of practice (4th ed.), St. Louis: Mosby, p. 288).*

guidance and supervision (p. 289). Examples of persons in the second subtype could include those with C3–C4 vertebral fractures, and those in the third subtype, persons who are severely mentally retarded.

The *partly compensatory nursing system* is represented by a situation in which "both nurse and patient perform care measures or other actions involving manipulative tasks or ambulation. . . . [Either] the patient or the nurse may have the major role in the performance of care measures" (Orem, 1991, p. 291). An example of a person needing nursing care in the partly compensatory system would be an individual who has had recent abdominal surgery. This patient might be able to wash his or her face and brush his or her teeth but needs the nurse for help in ambulating and in changing the surgical dressing.

The third nursing system is the *supportive-educative system*. In this system, the person "is able to perform or can and should learn to perform required measures of externally or internally oriented therapeutic self-care but cannot do so without assistance" (Orem, 1991, p. 291). This is also known as a supportive-developmental system. In this system the patient is doing all of the self-care. The "patient's requirements for help are confined to decision making, behavior control, and acquiring knowledge and skills" (p. 291). The nurse's role, then, is to promote the patient as a self-care agent. An example of a person in this system would be a 16-year-old who is requesting birth control information. The nurse's role in this system is primarily that of a teacher or consultant.

One or more of the three types of systems may be used with a single patient. For example, a woman in labor may move from a supportive-educative system while she is in early labor to a partly compensatory system as her labor advances. If she requires a cesarean delivery, her care might require her to be in a wholly compensatory system. She would then progress to a partly compensatory system as she recovers from the anesthetic. Later, as she prepares to go home, a supportive-educative system would again be appropriate.

rem's Theory and Nursing's Metaparadigm

Orem discusses each of the four major concepts of human beings, health, society, and nursing in her work. "*Human beings* are distinguished from other living things by their capacity (1) to reflect upon themselves and their environment, (2) to symbolize what they experience, and (3) to use symbolic creations (ideas, words) in thinking, in communicating, and in guiding efforts to do and to make things that are beneficial for themselves or others" (Orem, 1991, p. 180). Integrated human functioning includes physical, psychological, interpersonal, and social aspects. Orem believes that individuals have the potential for learning and developing. The way an individual meets self-care needs is not instinctual but is a learned behavior. Factors that affect learning include age, mental capacity, culture, society, and the emotional state of the individual. If the individual cannot learn self-care measures, others must learn the care and provide it.

In the fourth edition of *Nursing: Concepts of practice*, Orem (1991) considers human beings from two different perspectives. The first is as persons viewed as moving "toward maturation and achievement of the individual's human potential. . . . *Self-realization* and *personality development* are terms used at times to refer to the process of personalization" (p. 185). The second perspective "focuses on structural and functional differentiations within the unity that is a human being . . . developed by various human and life sciences . . . [including] biochemistry, biophysics, human anatomy, and human physiology, . . . psychology, psychophysiology and social psychology" (p. 186). Orem emphasizes, however, that both perspectives need to be integrated for effective nursing.

Orem (1991) supports the World Health Organization's definition of *health* as the state of physical, mental, and social well-being and not merely the absence of disease or infirmity. She states that "the physical, psychological, interpersonal and social aspects of health are inseparable in the individual" (p. 180). Orem also presents health based on the concept of preventive health care. This health care includes the promotion and maintenance of health (primary prevention), the treatment of disease or injury (secondary prevention), and the prevention of complications (tertiary prevention).

About *nursing*, Orem (1991) states:

> In modern society, adults are expected to be self-reliant and responsible for themselves and for the well-being of their dependents. Most social groups further accept that persons who are helpless, sick, aged, handicapped, or otherwise deprived should be helped in their immediate distress and helped to attain or regain responsibility within their existing capacities. Thus, both self-help and help to others are valued by society as desirable activities. Nursing as a specific type of human service is based on both values. In most communities people see nursing as a desirable and necessary service (p. 41).

Orem speaks to several factors related to the concept of nursing. These are the art and prudence of nursing, nursing as a service, role theory related to nursing, and technologies in nursing. The art of nursing is "the quality of individual nurses that allows them to make creative investigations and analyses and syntheses of the variables and conditioning factors within nursing situations in order to work toward the goal of the production of effective systems of nursing assistance for individual or multiperson units" (p. 256). These decisions require a theoretical base in the discipline of nursing and in the sciences, arts, and humanities. This base directs decisions when designing nursing systems within the nursing process. "*Nursing prudence* is the quality of nurses that enables them (1) to seek and take counsel in new or difficult nursing situations, (2) to make correct judgments . . . , (3) to decide to act in a particular way, and (4) to take action" (p. 256). The development of the individual nurse's art and prudence is affected by unique life and nursing experiences.

Orem (1991) further defines nursing as a human service. Nursing is distinguished from other human services by its focus on persons with inabilities to maintain the continuous provision of health care (pp. 4–5). Nursing is needed when the adult is unable "to maintain continuously that amount and quality of self-care which is therapeutic in sustaining life and health, in recovering from disease or injury, or in coping with their effects" (p. 41). With children, nursing is needed when the parent or guardian is unable to "maintain continuously for the child the amount and quality of care that is therapeutic" (p. 41). For children, nursing may be needed to assist with development or maturation.

The nurse's and the patient's roles define the expected behaviors for each in the specific nursing situation. Various factors that influence the expected role behaviors are culture, environment, age, sex, the health setting, and finances. The roles of nurse and patient are complementary. That is, a certain behavior of the patient elicits a certain response in the nurse, and vice versa. Both work together to accomplish the goal of self-care.

In the nurse-patient relationship, the nurse or patient may experience role conflict because each is performing concurrent roles; for example, the patient also has expected behaviors from his roles as father, husband, Cub Scout leader, soccer coach, and librarian. Thus, the conflict in the behaviors required for the various roles may affect the performance of self-care.

It is important to note that although Orem (1991) recognizes that specialized technologies are usually developed by members of the health professions, she emphasizes the need for social and interpersonal dimensions in nursing. The effective integration of social and interpersonal technologies with regulatory technologies promotes quality professional nursing. She states, "Treatment or regulatory operations are the practical activities through which what is prescribed is executed and through which the diagnosed condition or problem is treated in order to remove it[,] to control it or to keep it within boundaries compatible with human life, health, and well-being" (p. 266).

*O*rem's Theory and the Nursing Process

According to Orem (1991), "Nursing process is a term used by nurses to refer to the professional-technologic operations of nursing practice and to associated planning and evaluative operations" (p. 269). Process is a continuous and regular action or succession of actions taking place or carried out in a definite manner.

Orem (1991) discusses a three-step nursing process which she labels the technologic process operations of nursing practice. These steps are shown in Table 3–1 as:

- Step 1. Nursing diagnosis and prescription—that is, determining why nursing is needed; analysis and interpretation—making judgments regarding care, also labeled case management operations.

- Step 2. Designing the nursing system and planning for delivery of care.

- Step 3. The production and management of nursing systems, also labeled planning and controlling.

Nursing Diagnosis and Prescription (Step 1)

"Nursing diagnosis necessitates investigation and the accumulation of facts about patients' self-care agency and their therapeutic self-care demand and the existent or projected relationships between them" (Orem, 1991, p. 270). The goal defines the direction and nature of the actions. Prescriptive operations specify the means (course of actions, care measures) to be used to meet particular self-care requisites, or to meet all components of the therapeutic self-care demand. Orem emphasizes that, in nursing diagnostic and prescriptive operations and in the regulatory or treatment operations, patients' and families' abilities and interests in collaboration affect what nurses can do.

Designs for Regulatory Operation (Step 2)

Designing an effective and efficient system of nursing involves selecting valid ways of assisting the patient. This design includes nurse and patient roles in relation to which self-care tasks will be performed when adjusting the therapeutic self-care demands, regulating the exercise of self-care agency, protecting the already developed powers of self-care agency, and assisting with the new developments in self-care agency (Orem, 1991).

TABLE 3–1   Comparison of Orem's Nursing Process and the Nursing Process

Nursing Process	Orem's Nursing Process
1. Assessment 2. Nursing diagnosis	Step 1. Diagnosis and prescription; Determine why nursing is needed. Analyze and interpret—make judgments regarding care.
3. Plans with scientific rationale	Step 2. Design of a nursing system and plan for delivery of care.
4. Implementation	Step 3. Production and management of nursing systems.
5. Evaluation	

Planning is the movement from the design of nursing systems to ways and means of their production. A plan sets forth the organization of essential tasks to be performed in accordance with role responsibilities (Orem, 1991). The planning for implementation of the design and related procurement activities determines when nurses should be with patients and when essential materials and equipment will be available and ready for use.

Production and Management of Nursing Systems (Step 3)

Regulatory nursing systems are produced when nurses interact with patients and take consistent action to meet their prescribed therapeutic self-care demands and regulate the exercise or development of their capabilities for self-care. In this, the third step of the technologic nursing process, nurses act to produce and manage nursing systems (Orem, 1991).

During the interactions of nurses and patients, nurses do the following:

1. Perform and regulate the self-care tasks for patients or assist patients with their performance of self-care tasks

2. Coordinate self-care task performance so that a unified system of care is produced and coordinated with other components of health care

3. Help patients, their families, and others bring about systems of daily living for patients that support the accomplishment of self-care and are, at the same time, satisfying in relation to patients' interests, talents, and goals

4. Guide, direct, and support patients in their exercise of, or in withholding the exercise of, their self-care agency

5. Stimulate patients' interest in self-care by raising questions and promoting discussions of care problems and issues when conditions permit

6. Support and guide patients in learning activities and provide cues for learning as well as instructional sessions

7. Support and guide patients as they experience illness or disability and the effects of medical care measures and as they experience the need to engage in new measures of self-care or change their ways of meeting ongoing self-care requisites

8. Monitor patients and assist patients to monitor themselves to determine if self-care measures were performed and to determine the effects of self-care, the results of efforts to regulate the exercise or development of self-care agency, and the sufficiency and efficiency of nursing action direction to these ends

9. Make characterizing judgments about the sufficiency and efficiency of self-care, the regulation of the exercise or development of self-care agency, and nursing assistance

10. Make judgments about the meaning of the results derived from nurses' performance of the preceding two operations for the well-being of patients and make or recommend adjustments in the nursing care system through changes in nurse and patient roles (Orem, 1991, pp. 280–281).

The first seven operations constitute direct nursing care. The last three are for the purpose of deciding if the care provided should be continued in the present form or changed. This comprises the evaluation component of the nursing process.

The following example demonstrates the use of Orem's theory and the nursing process (see Tables 3–2 and 3–3):

TABLE 3–2 Application of Orem's Theory to Nursing Process

ASSESSMENT

Personal Factors	Universal Self-Care	Developmental Self-Care	Health Deviations	Medical Problem and Plan	Self-Care Deficits
Age	Air, water, food	Specialized needs for developmental process	Conditions of illness or injury	Physician's perspective of condition	Difference between self-care needs and self-care capabilities
Sex	Excrements	New requisites from a condition	Treatments to correct the condition	Medical diagnosis	
Height	Activity and rest	Requisites associated with an event		Medical treatment	
Weight	Solitude and social interaction				
Culture	Hazards to life and well-being				
Race	Promotion of human functioning and development				
Marital Status					
Religion					
Occupation					

Nursing Diagnosis	Plan	Implementation	Evaluation
Based on self-care deficits	Nursing goals and objectives: a. Congruent with nursing diagnosis b. Based on self-care demands c. Promote patient as self-care agent Designing the Nursing System: a. Wholly compensatory b. Partly compensatory c. Supportive-educative Appropriate methods of helping: a. Guidance b. Support c. Teaching d. Acting or doing for e. Providing developmental environment	Nurse-patient actions to: a. Promote patient as self-care agent b. Meet self-care needs c. Decrease self-care deficits	Effectiveness of nurse-patient actions to: a. Promote patient as self-care agent b. Meet self-care needs c. Decrease self-care deficits

Adapted from Pinnell, N. N. & de Meneses, M. (1986). *The nursing process—Theory, application and related processes*, Norwalk, Conn.:Appleton-Century-Crofts, p. 66. Used with permission.

TABLE 3–3   Application Of Orem's Theory Using Ms. M.'s Case Study Within The Nursing Process

Personal Factors	Universal Self-Care	Developmental Self-Care	Health Deviaitons	Medical Problem and Plan	Self-Care Deficits
48 yr	Smokes 1.5 ppd	Loss of husband	Potential for cardiac disease related to obesity, smoking, cholesterol, lack of exercise, family history	Diagnoses of obesity with potential for cardiac disease and low motivation for weight loss	Difference between Ms. M.'s knowledge base and life style which increases risk for heart attack or stroke
Female	Fast foods	Loss of social activity			
5'2"	Late pm meal			Prescription to:	
175 lb	No data			Monitor cholesterol levels and vital signs	
Italian	No exercise				
White	Decreased social interaction x 6 mo			Decrease cholesterol and fat intake	
Widowed	Family history:			Increase exercise	
Catholic	F—heart attack age 50				
University faculty	M—stroke				
	Cholesterol 280 mg				
	High-fat diet				
	Lacks knowledge of risk factors and cardiovascular functioning				
	T = 98.4				
	138/96				
	P = 92				
	R = 30				
	Works 12 hour days				
	Well groomed				

Nursing Diagnosis	Plan	Implementation	Evaluation
Potential for impaired cardiovascular functioning related to her lack of knowledge about relationship between current life style and risk of heart attack or stroke	Nursing goals and objectives: *Goal:* To decrease risk for cardiac impairment *Objective:* Ms. M. will state that high cholesterol levels increase her risk for cardiac impairment Design of Nursing System: Supportive-educative Methods of helping: Guidance, support, teaching, and provision of a developmental environment	Jointly develop contract related to goal of cholesterol reduction Ms. M. will keep a 3-day food diary Ms. M will learn about cholesterol and its effects on cardiovascular functioning Ms. M. will request or obtain cholesterol and fat content of fast foods Ms. M. will learn about low cholesterol and fat foods, foods which decrease cholesterol, and restaurants which serve low cholesterol and fat foods Jointly analyze food diary and decide how to decrease cholesterol and fat intake Jointly determine Italian foods which are low in cholesterol and fat, or recipes which may be adapted Ms. M's accomplishments will be reinforced	Does Ms. M. understand that with her present life style her risk of heart attack or stroke is high? Did Ms. M. select low-cholesterol foods? Is Ms. M's cholesterol level lower? Did Ms. M.'s self-care deficit decrease? Was the supportive-educative system effective in promoting Ms. M. as a self-care agent?

Situation. Ms. M., a well-groomed university faculty member of Italian Catholic descent, is 48 years old, 5 feet 2 inches, and weighs 175 pounds. She smokes one and a half packs of cigarettes per day. She was very happily married for 25 years and has been widowed for six months. She and her husband enjoyed social activities, including playing bridge, gourmet cooking, and collecting antiques. She has not participated in any of these activities since her husband's death because of lack of interest and energy. Currently, she engages in no regular exercise, eats mainly fast foods during her 12-hour working day, and eats a late evening meal before retiring.

Ms. M.'s mother died of a stroke and her father had a heart attack at age 50. During her annual physical two weeks ago, her vital signs were 138/86, P 92, R 30, T 98.4 (F). Her laboratory values were all within normal limits except a blood cholesterol of 280 mg. Her physician advised her to lose 40 pounds but recognized that Ms. M. has inadequate knowledge of basic nutrition and has not been motivated to lose weight. He foresees potential problems related to cardiovascular disease.

Step 1. Orem defines Step 1 as the diagnosis and prescription phase, determining if nursing is needed. In this assessment phase, the nurse collects data in six areas:

1. The person's health status

2. The physician's perspective of the person's health

3. The person's perspective of his or her health

4. The health goals within the context of life history, life style, and health status

5. The person's requirements for self-care

6. The person's capacity to perform self-care

Specific data are gathered in the areas of the individual's universal, developmental, and health-deviation self-care needs and their interrelationship. Data are also collected about the individual's knowledge, skills, motivation, and orientation.

Within Step 1, the nurse seeks answers to the following questions:

1. What is the patient's therapeutic care demand? Now? At a future time?

2. Does the patient have a deficit for engaging in self-care to meet the therapeutic self-care demand?

3. If so, what is its nature and the reasons for its existence?

4. Should the patient be helped to refrain from engagement in self-care or to protect already developed self-care capabilities for therapeutic purposes?

5. What is the patient's potential for engaging in self-care at a future time period? Increasing or deepening self-care knowledge? Learning techniques of self-care? Fostering willingness to engage in self-care? Effectively and consistently incorporating essential self-care measures (including new ones) into the systems of self-care and daily living? (Orem, 1985, pp. 225–226).

Once the assessment data have been gathered, they must be analyzed. In the category of universal self-care needs, Ms. M. demonstrates a deficit in adequate air, water, and food intake because she is 5 feet 2 inches, weighs 175 pounds, and consumes excessive calories, fat, and cholesterol from fast food and late-night meals. Ms. M. shows an imbalance between activity and rest because she has minimal exercise. There is also an imbalance between her solitude and social interaction since her husband's death, which is a significant loss for her in the mid-life developmental needs category. Ms. M.'s elevated cholesterol levels, when interrelated with her family history of stroke and heart attack, present a hazard to her life, functioning, and well-being. The physician's perspective is that Ms. M. needs to lose 40 pounds because of her family history and elevated blood cholesterol but that she has limited nutritional knowledge. However, Ms. M. has a motivational deficit to lose weight because her Italian cultural tradition associates food with family and love.

Based on the analysis of Ms. M.'s data, she has potential hazards to her health related to obesity, high cholesterol, smoking, social isolation, and decreased exercise. The analysis of the collected data leads to the nursing diagnosis, enabling the nurse to prioritize self-care deficits. The nursing diagnosis must include the response and etiology pattern. Within Orem's framework, the nursing diagnosis would be stated as an inability to meet the self-care demand (the response) related to the self-care deficit (etiology) (Ziegler, Vaughn-Wrobel, & Erlen, 1986). For Ms. M. the response pattern would be "potential for impaired cardiovascular functioning," and the etiology would be "lack of knowledge about how her current life style increases her risk for heart attack and stroke." Therefore, for Ms. M. the nursing diagnosis could be stated: "Potential for impaired cardiovascular functioning related to lack of knowledge about how her current life style increases her risk for heart attack and stroke."

Step 2. Orem defines Step 2 as designing the nursing systems and planning for the delivery of nursing. The nurse designs a system that is wholly compensatory, partly compensatory, or supportive-educative. "The actual design of a concrete nursing system emerges as nurses and patients interact and take action in order to calculate and meet patient's therapeutic self-care demands, to compensate for or overcome the identified action limitations of patients, and to regulate the development and exercise of patients' self-care abilities" (Orem, 1991, p. 285).

Using Orem's model, the goals are congruent with the nursing diagnosis to enable the patient to become an effective self-care agent. Goals are directed by the response statement of the nursing diagnosis and are focused on health. The goal for Ms. M. would be: Decrease her risk of cardiovascular impairment.

Once the goals have been determined, the objectives can be stated. An example of an objective for Ms. M. would be: Ms. M. will state that high cholesterol levels increase her risk for cardiac impairment. Other objectives might relate to the risk factors of obesity, lack of exercise, smoking, and family history. The designed nursing system for Ms. M. would be the supportive-educative nursing system.

Step 3. Within Orem's (1991) nursing process, Step 3 includes the production and management of the nursing system. In this step, the nurse performs and regulates the patient's self-care tasks, or assists the patient in doing so; coordinates the performance of self-care with other components of health care; helps patients, families and others create and use systems of daily living that meet self-care needs in a satisfying way; guides, directs, and supports patients in exercising, or not exercising, self-care agency; stimulates patient's interest in care problems; supports learning activities; supports and guides the patient in adapting the needs arising from medical measures; monitors and assists in self-monitoring the performance and effects of self-care measures; judges the sufficiency and efficiency of self-care, self-care agency, and nursing agency; adjusts the nursing care system as needed.

The nurse and patient actions are directed by the etiology component of the nursing diagnosis. "Lack of knowledge about how her current life style increases her risk for heart attack and stroke" is the etiology component of Ms. M.'s nursing diagnosis. When the nurse and patient implement this supportive-educative system, each has specific roles. Examples of these roles might be: Together they would develop a contract relating to the goal of blood cholesterol reduction. Ms. M. would keep a three-day food diary. The nurse would provide information about cholesterol and its effects on cardiovascular function. Ms. M. would request and obtain the fat and cholesterol content of the fast-food menu items from the restaurants she frequents. The nurse would provide information about specific foods that are low in fat and cholesterol, those food items that help reduce cholesterol, and a list of fast-food restaurants that offer low-fat and low-cholesterol food items. Together they would analyze the three-day food diary and decide how Ms. M. might modify her diet to reduce her fat and cholesterol intake. They would determine which Italian dishes are low in fat and cholesterol or how these recipes can be adapted. As her blood cholesterol levels decrease, Ms. M. would be praised for her accomplishments. During this implementation, the nurse would teach, guide, and support Ms. M. while providing a developmental environment.

Step 3 includes evaluation. The nurse and patient together do the evaluation. Questions they might ask are: When evaluating some of Ms. M.'s plans, does she understand that her present life style may increase her risk of developing a heart attack or stroke? Did she select low-fat and low-cholesterol fast foods? Did she attain her goal of reducing her blood cholesterol levels? Were the plans effective in decreasing the self-care deficit? Was the nursing system effective in promoting the patient as a self-care agent?

Evaluation is an ongoing process. It is essential that the nurse and patient continually evaluate any changes in the data that would affect the self-care deficit, the self-care agent, and the nursing system.

rem's Work and the Characteristics of a Theory

Orem presented a conceptual framework in 1959. Since then her work has continued to evolve. Orem's general theory of nursing was formulated and expressed in 1979–1980. This Self-Care Deficit Theory of Nursing is comprised of three interrelated theories: the theory of self-care, the theory of self-care deficit, and the theory of nursing systems.

1. **Theories can interrelate concepts in such a way as to create a different way of looking at a particular phenomenon.** Orem's theoretical constructs of self-care, self-care deficits, and nursing systems are interrelated in her general comprehensive theory of nursing. This interrelationship provides a view of the practice of nursing (a particular phenomenon) that is unique.

2. **Theories must be logical in nature.** Orem's theory follows a logical thought process. She states her general theory, then presents the central idea of each of the three interrelated theories. In her discussion of each interrelated theory, she presents presuppositions that express larger contexts within which the theory or its parts can be understood. She also presents propositions or statements that describe a concept or explain and predict the relationship between concepts.

3. **Theories should be relatively simple yet generalizable.** Orem's theory has been used in both nursing education and practice. The theory is used by several schools of nursing as a theoretical foundation for a student's basic preparation for practice. Orem's concept of self-care with its proposition of universal self-care needs is easily understood by beginning and advanced nursing practitioners as the activities of daily living. The theories of self-care deficits and nursing systems can be comprehended and applied to all individual patients and, with further adaptation, to multiperson units.

4. **Theories are the bases for hypotheses that can be tested or for theory to be expanded.** Orem's theory of self-care has been used to generate testable hypotheses in a variety of settings. Several researchers have tested Orem's theory in the area of

self-care agency, including studies focused on the development of tools to measure aspects of self-care (see Bibliography at end of section).

5. **Theories contribute to and assist in increasing the general body of knowledge within the discipline through the research implemented to validate them.** Orem focuses on nursing as a helping art that assists an individual to meet self-care needs and that is the foundation for nursing practice. Research on self-care needs and the assistance to meet them adds to nursing's body of knowledge. Orem's theory is being tested by several nursing researchers.

6. **Theories can be used by the practitioners to guide and improve their practice.** Orem's theory is used by nurses in a variety of settings. These settings include that of an independent practitioner of nursing, rehabilitation, hemodialysis, bone marrow transplant, psychiatric care, and public and community health. Others have documented self-care in relation to children in pain and with leukemia, women with gestational diabetes, persons receiving enterostomal therapy, adult diabetics, the elderly, and the terminally ill (see Bibliography at end of section).

7. **Theories must be consistent with other validated theories, laws, and principles but will leave open unanswered questions that need to be investigated.** Orem's theory is consistent with role theory, need theory, field theory, and health promotion concepts. For example, she discusses the importance of an understanding of the roles of nurse and patient while determining the patient's need for nursing care.

Strengths and Limitations

In the preface to the fourth edition of *Nursing: Concepts of practice*, Orem (1991) outlines the following five broad divisions: contextual and process features of nursing practice, the self-care deficit theory of nursing, the characteristics of nursing as a practical science, nursing administration, and nursing education. In the text she describes her general theory, which is supported by three interrelated theories. Within these theories, six central concepts and one peripheral concept are identified. These provide the reader with a blueprint for the structure of Orem's Self-Care Deficit Theory of Nursing.

Orem's theory is derived from a clinical base. She states that, "in working on the components of [her] theory [she] needs to work with other people—utilizing data from clinicians" (Trench, Wallace, & Coberg, 1988). She cites Susan Taylor's work, which includes the position of family involvement within the self-care deficit nursing theory (Orem, 1991). Also, the Self-Care Deficit Theory of Nursing has been supported by clinical case-study data (Orem & Taylor, 1986).

Orem's theory of nursing provides a comprehensive base for nursing practice. It has utility for professional nursing in the areas of education, clinical practice, administration, research, and nursing information systems. A major strength of Orem's theory is that it is applicable for nursing by the beginning practitioner as well as the advanced clinician. The terms *self-care, nursing systems*, and *self-care deficit* are easily understood by the beginning nursing student and can be explored in greater depth as the nurse gains more knowledge and experience.

A major strength of Orem's (1991) theory is that she specifically defines when nursing is needed: Nursing is needed when the individual cannot maintain continuously that amount and quality of self-care necessary to sustain life and health, recover from disease or injury, or cope with their effects.

Orem (1991) promotes the concepts of professional nursing. She defines the roles of vocational, technical, and professional nurses, and recognizes the importance of each. She indicates that thinking nursing and conceptualizing the dynamics and structure of nursing situations is distinct from viewing nursing as skilled performance of tasks.

Her self-care premise is contemporary with the concepts of health promotion and health maintenance. Self-care in Orem's theory is comparable to holistic health in that both promote the individual's responsibility for health care. This is especially relevant with today's emphasis on early hospital discharge, home care, and outpatient services. Orem (1991) recognizes the term *client* as a regular seeker of services but prefers the term *patient* for one who is "under the care of nurses, physicians, or other direct health care providers" (p. 30).

According to Orem (1991), "nursing should select the type of nursing system or sequential combination of nursing systems that will have an optimum effect in achieving the desired regulation of patients' self-care agency and the meeting of their self-care requisites" (p. 292). Some practitioners have found Orem's theory to be more clinically applicable when more than one system is used concurrently (Knust & Quarn, 1983).

Another strength is Orem's delineation of three identifiable nursing systems. These are easily understood by the beginning nursing student. However, Orem's use of the term *system* is different from that used in general system theory. She defines a system as a "single, whole thing" (Orem, 1991, p. 269). In general system theory, a system is viewed as a dynamic, flowing process.

Orem (1991) has expanded her initial focus of individual self-care to include multiperson units (families, groups, and communities). She notes that when multiperson units are served by nurses, the resulting nursing systems combine the features of partly compensatory and supportive-educative nursing systems. However, an incongruence is present because she suggests that "it is advisable at this stage of the development of nursing knowledge to confine the use of the three nursing systems to situations where individuals are the units of care or service" (p. 289).

Orem's elaboration on self-care requisites seem to be essential to her theory and emerge as a core concept. Her theory would be more readily understood if the term *peripheral concept* were eliminated when she defines basic conditioning factors.

Orem's theory is simple yet complex. However, the essence is clouded by ancillary descriptions. The term *self-care* is used with numerous configurations. This multitude of terms, such as self-care agency, self-care demand, self-care premise, self-care deficit, self-care requisites, and universal self-care, can be very confusing to the reader.

Other limitations include her discussion of health. Health is often viewed as dynamic and ever changing. Orem's model of the boxed nursing systems (see Fig. 3–2) implies three static conditions of health. She refers to a "concrete nursing system," which connotes rigidity. Another impression from the model of nursing systems is that a major determining factor for placement of a patient in a system is the individual's capacity for physical movement. Throughout her work there is limited acknowledgment of the individual's emotional needs.

*S*ummary

Orem presents her general theory of nursing, The Self-Care Deficit Theory of Nursing, which is composed of the three interrelated theories of self-care, self-care deficit, and nursing systems. Incorporated within and supportive of these theories are the six central concepts of self-care, self-care agency, therapeutic self-care demand, self-care deficit, nursing agency, and nursing system, as well as the peripheral concept of basic conditioning factors.

Nursing is needed when the self-care demands are greater than the self-care abilities. Nursing systems are designed by the nurse when it has been determined that nursing care is needed. The systems of wholly compensatory, partly compensatory, and supportive-educative specify the roles of the nurse and the patient.

Throughout Orem's work, she interprets nursing's metaparadigm of human beings, health, nursing, and society. She defines three steps of nursing process as (1) diagnosis and prescription, (2) design of a nursing system and planning for the delivery of care, and (3) production and management of nursing systems. This process parallels the nursing process of assessment, diagnosis, planning, implementation, and evaluation.

Orem's theory of self-care has pragmatic application to nursing practice. It has been applied by nursing clinicians in a variety of settings. The theory has been used as the basis for nursing school curricula and the base for a nursing information system.

Orem's Self-Care Deficit Theory of Nursing continues to evolve; its impact is international. Its widespread use reflects its utility for professional nursing. This theory offers a unique way of looking at the phenomenon of nursing. Orem's work contributes significantly to the development of nursing theories.

References

Knust, S. J., & Quarn, J. M. (1983). Integration of self-care theory with rehabilitation nursing. *Rehabilitation Nursing, 26*–28.

Nursing Development Conference Group. (1973). *Concept formalization in nursing: Process and product.* Boston: Little, Brown.

Nursing Development Conference Group. (1979). *Concept formalization in nursing: Process and product* (2nd ed.). Boston: Little, Brown.

Orem, D. E. (1959). *Guides for developing curricula for the education of practical nurses.* Washington, DC: Government Printing Office.

Orem, D. E. (1971). *Nursing: Concepts of practice.* New York: McGraw-Hill. [out of print]

Orem, D. E. (1980). *Nursing: Concepts of practice* (2nd ed.). New York: McGraw-Hill. [out of print]

Orem, D. E. (1985). *Nursing: Concepts of practice* (3rd ed.). New York: McGraw-Hill. [out of print]

Orem, D. E. (1991). *Nursing: Concepts of practice* (4th ed.). St. Louis: Mosby.

Orem, D. E., & Taylor, S. G. (1986). Orem's General Theory of Nursing. In P. Winstead-Fry (Ed.), *Case studies in nursing theory* (pp. 37–71). New York: National League for Nursing.

Trench, A. S. (Executive producer), Wallace, D. (Producer), & Coberg, T. (Director). (1988). *Dorothea E. Orem—The nurse theorists: Portraits of excellence.* Oakland, CA: Studio Three Production, Samuel Merritt College of Nursing.

Ziegler, S. M., Vaughn-Wrobel, B. C., & Erlen, J. A. (1986). *Nursing process, nursing diagnosis, nursing knowledge—Avenues to autonomy.* Norwalk, CT: Appleton-Century-Crofts.

Bibliography

Allan, J. D. (1990). Focusing on living, not dying: A naturalistic study of self-care among seropositive gay men. *Holistic Nursing Practice, 4*(2), 56–63.

Brock, A. M., & O'Sullivan, P. (1985). A study to determine what variables predict institutionalization of the elderly. *Journal of Advanced Nursing, 10,* 533–537.

Bromley, B. (1980). Applying Orem's Self-Care Theory in enterostomal therapy. *American Journal of Nursing, 80,* 245–249.

Chang, B. L., Cuman, G., Linn, L. S., Ware, J. E., & Kane, R. L. (1985). Adherence to health care regimens among elderly women. *Nursing Research, 34,* 27–31.

Denyes, M. J. (1982). Measurement of self-care agency in adolescents. *Nursing Research, 31,* 63.

Fitzgerald, S. (1980). Utilizing Orem's Self-Care Model in designing an educational program for the diabetic. *Topics in Clinical Nursing, 2,* 57–65.

Foote, A., Holcombe, J., Piazza, D., & Wright, P. (1993). Orem's theory used as a guide for the nursing care of an eight-year-old child with leukemia. *Journal of Pediatric Oncology Nursing, 10*(1), 26–32.

Frey, M. A., & Denyes, M. J. (1989). Health and illness self-care in adolescents with IDDM: A test of Orem's theory. *Advances in Nursing Science, 12*(1), 67–75.

Gulick, E. E. (1987). Parsimony and model confirmation of the ADL Self-Care Scale for Multiple Sclerosis persons. *Nursing Research, 36,* 278–283.

Jirovec, M. M., & Kasno, J. (1993). Predictors of self-care abilities among the institutionalized elderly. *Western Journal of Nursing Research, 15,* 314–326.

Kearney, B. Y., & Fleischer, B. J. (1979). Development of an instrument to measure the exercise of self-care agency. *Research in Nursing and Health, 2,* 25–34.

Keohane, N. S., & Lacey, L. A. (1991). Preparing the woman with gestational diabetes for self-care. *Journal of Obstetric, Gynecologic and Neonatal Nursing, 20,* 189–193.

Kinlein, M. L. (1977). *Independent nursing practice with clients,* Philadelphia: Lippincott.

Kubricht, D. W. (1984). Therapeutic self-care demands expressed by outpatients receiving external radiation therapy. *Cancer Nursing, 7,* 43–52.

Mack, C. J. (1992). Assessment of the autologous bone marrow transplant patient according to Orem's self-care model. *Cancer Nursing, 15,* 429–436.

McDermott, M. A. N. (1993). Learned helplessness as an interacting variable with self-care agency: Testing a theoretical model. *Nursing Science Quarterly, 6,* 28–38.

Murphy, P. (1981). A hospice model and self-care theory. *Oncology Nursing Forum, 8,* 19–21.

Patterson, E. T., & Hale, E. S. (1985). Making sure: Integrating menstrual care practices into activities of daily living. *Advances in Nursing Science, 7*(3), 18–31.

Reed, P. G. (1986). Developmental resources and depression in the elderly. *Nursing Research, 35,* 368–374.

Scrak, B. M., Zimmerman, J., Wilson, M., & Greenstein, R. (1987). Moving from the gas station to a nurse-managed psych clinic. *American Journal of Nursing, 87,* 188–190.

Stollenwerk, R. (1985). An emphysema client: Self-care. *Home Healthcare Nurse, 3*(2), 36–40.

Taylor, S. G., & McLaughlin, K. (1991). Orem's General Theory of Nursing and community nursing. *Nursing Science Quarterly, 4,* 153–160.

Villarruel, A. M., & Denyes, M. J. (1991). Pain assessment in children: Theoretical and empirical validity. *Advances in Nursing Science, 14,* 32–41.

Weaver, M. T. (1983). Perceived self-care agency: A LISREL factor analysis of Bickel and Hanson's questionnaire. *Nursing Research, 36,* 381–387.

Woods, N. F. (1985). Self-care practices among young adult married women. *Research in Nursing and Health, 8,* 21–31.

Wyatt, G. K., & Omar, M. A. (1985). Interventions useful to the public health nurse: Improving health behaviors. *Journal of Nursing Education, 24,* 168–170.

Zinn, A. (1986). A self-care program for hemodialysis patients based on Dorothea Orem's concepts. *Journal of Nephrology Nursing, 3*(2), 65–77.

External Analysis

$\mathcal{N}$ursing Research on the Model

A review of the research literature on the self-care theory is beyond the scope of this section as over 175 articles and more than 80 doctoral dissertations are cited (Fawcett, 1995, pp. 355–366). It should be said that such reviews definitely are needed to support the ongoing development of this theory. All the same, several observations can be made about this body of research. First, studies coming from this theory can be described using all three categories of theory testing research proposed by Silva (1986). In one group are studies, such as those proposed by Allan (1988) and Hamera et al. (1992), where the theory is acknowledged but used only minimally, if at all, in guiding the research. In a second group are studies like those by Chang et al. (1984) and Sandman et al. (1986) where the theory is assumed to be correct and is used primarily to organize the research. In a third group are studies that are put forth as explicit tests of the theory, or operationalize and test theory concepts and relationships; among them are studies by Denyes (1988), Villaruel and Denyes (1991), Hanucharurnkul (1989), and Humphreys (1991). A fourth group, which could be added to Silva's, are studies of midrange theories derived from the self-care theory (Campbell, 1989).

A second observation about self-care research to date is that both qualitative and quantitative methodologies have been used. While most of the research is quantitative, examples of qualitative studies include Hungelmann's (1984) study of self-care abilities of older persons with chronic disease; Harris' (1990; Harris & Williams, 1991) studies of universal requisites of elderly homeless men and persons with persistent mental illnesses; Hartweg's (1993) study of health promotion self-care in middle-age women; and Dowd's (1991) study of self-care needs of women with urinary incontinence.

A third observation is that the research to date has addressed all concepts and relationships in the theory but certain concepts and relationships have received more attention than others; the section above on empirical adequacy supports this observation. Considerable research attention has been given to relationships between various basic conditioning factors and self-care agency or self-care; to exploring foundational aspects of self-care agency; to operationalizing self-care agency and examining predictors of, or consequence of, self-care

Taken from: *Conceptual Models of Nursing: Analysis and Application*, Third Edition by Fitzpatrick and Whall.

agency; and to identifying self-care requisites particular to certain health conditions, and age or developmental groups. There also are many studies of nursing interventions, most of which would be classified as supportive–educative nursing systems. The concept of nursing agency and the subconcepts of fully or partially compensatory nursing systems have received the least attention.

A fourth observation is that the research literature demonstrates applications of the self-care theory to a wide range of populations. With regard to age groups, while studies of adults predominate, there are numerous studies of children, including studies of preschoolers (Arneson & Triplett, 1990; Villaruel & Denyes (1991), school-age children (Alexander et al., 1988; Blazek & McClelland, 1983; Carlisle et al., 1993; Dashiff, 1992; Humphreys, 1991; Moore, 1987a, 1987b, 1993; Rew, 1987a, 1987b; Saucier, 1984; Wanich et al., 1992), and adolescents (Degenhart-Leskosky, 1989; Denyes, 1982; Denyes et al., 1991; Frey & Fox, 1990; Gaut & Kieckhefer, 1988; Monsen, 1992). Studies of elderly persons also are numerous (Biggs, 1990; Brock & O'Sullivan, 1985; Chang et al., 1984, 1985; Conn et al., 1991; Harper, 1984; Harris, 1990; Harris & Williams, 1991; Jirovec & Kasno, 1993; Jopp et al., 1993; Karl, 1982; Kerkstra et al., 1991; Sandman et al., 1986; Smits & Key, 1992; Wanich et al., 1992; Weinrich, 1990).

In addition to research applications across age groups are studies that span the spectrum of health promotion, illness prevention, and illness care. The categories of health promotion and illness prevention include studies of (1) general health promotion (Hartweg, 1993; Moore, 1993); (2) health promotion related to specific issues such as weight control (Allen, 1988) and breast self-examination (Baulch et al., 1992; Edgar et al., 1984; Malik, 1992); and (3) developmental issues such as menarche and menstruation (Dashiff, 1991; Kirkpatrick et al., 1990; Patterson & Hale, 1985; Seideman, 1990; Woods et al., 1992), pregnancy and childbirth (Bliss-Holtz, 1988, 1991), and menopause (McElmurry & Huddleston, 1991; Rothbert et al., 1990).

Studies of self-care for specific health deviations pertain to (1) asthma (Alexander et al., 1986; Huss et al., 1991; Rew, 1987a, 1987b); (2) cardiac conditions (Toth, 1980; Utz et al., 1990; Utz & Ramos, 1993); (3) cystic fibrosis (Kruger et al., 1980); (4) diabetes (Frey & Fox, 1990; Miller, 1982; Saucier, 1984); (5) cancer (Dodd, 1982, 1983, 1984a, 1984b, 1987, 1988a, 1988b; Dodd & Dibble, 1993; Gammon, 1991; Hagopian, 1990; 1991; Hagopian & Rubenstein, 1990; Hanucharurnkul, 1989; Hiromoto & Dugan, 1991; Kubricht, 1984; MacVicar et al., 1989; Oberst et al., 1991; Palmer & Meyers, 1990; Richardson, 1992; Weintraub & Hagopian, 1990; Williams et al., 1988); (6) multiple sclerosis (Gulick, 1987, 1988, 1989a, 1989b); (7) mental illness (Crockett, 1982; Hamera et al., 1992; Harris, 1990; Whetstone, 1986; Youssef, 1987); (8) physical abuse (Campbell, 1986, 1989; Humphreys, 1991); (9) respiratory illnesses (Hautman, 1987); (10) suicide (Palikkathayil & Morgan, 1988); (11) renal transplant (Hayward et al., 1989); (12) spinal cord injury (McFarland et al., 1992); (13) spina bifida (Monsen, 1992); (14) pain (Denyes et al., 1991; Villaruel & Denyes, 1991); (15) fatigue (Rhodes et al., 1988; Robinson & Posner, 1992); and (16) urinary incontinence (Dowd, 1991; Klem & Creason, 1991).

*N*ursing Education Based on the Theory

Orem developed the self-care theory of nursing, at least in part, in response to questions prevalent in the late 1950s and 1960s about the character and organization of essential content in nursing curricula. Thus, like many of the theories of its time, the self-care theory has had a strong association with nursing education from the outset. Over time it has become one of the more ubiquitous theories in nursing education; it is widely recognized and taught to some extent in many nursing curricula. One of the most consistent and well-developed applications is at the University of Missouri, where much of the curriculum development work has been done in consultation with Orem and the theory has been used over a number of years to inform both undergraduate and graduate programs. There are other noteworthy educational applications of the self-care theory that have stood the test of time, for example, at the Medical College of Ohio and Illinois Wesleyan University, and many schools that adopted the self-care theory during the years when the National League for Nursing viewed nursing conceptualization as criteria for accreditation.

The literature on educational applications of the self-care theory, although relatively small, has some particularly noteworthy entries. Among them is the anthology edited by Riehl-Sisca (1985a), which has a number of chapters that describe curricular applications: for preservice students (Taylor, 1985a); RN-BSN students (Farnham & Fowler, 1985); and undergraduate and graduate students (Riehl-Sisca, 1985b; Taylor, 1985b). Aids to teaching the self-care theory have been proposed; for example, model assessment and care plan forms designed to help students learn to apply the theory in practice were described by Lashinger (1990). The literature also reports a few studies of the impact of the theory on educational parameters. Hartweg and Metcalfe (1986) found significantly greater improvements in attitudes toward self-care in baccalaureate nursing students who completed a self-care nursing curriculum as compared to nonnursing undergraduate students. Berbiglia (1991) examined implementation of the self-care theory among administrators, faculty, and students in a small baccalaureate program using an "ideal perspective" as the criterion measure. Findings were that the perspectives of students and faculty were similar, and were closer to the ideal than those of administrators. Satisfaction with the theory was associated with faculty-related difficulties (e.g., turnover) for faculty, and familiarity with the theory for administrators; student dissatisfaction was associated with difficult terminology in the theory.

The literature also describes applications of the theory to staff and continuing education. Examples are two articles (Harman et al., 1989; Reid et al., 1989) that describe various educational strategies used to prepare staff to implement the self-care model at the Toronto General Hospital; one strategy was a very innovative multimedia exhibit based on the theory. Another example is an 8-day course in gerontological nursing based on self-care theory described by Langland and Farrah (1990), which at a 6 to 9 months post-test had a significant impact on participants' ability to maintain a strong nursing perspective.

Nursing Practice Based on the Theory

There is a large and varied literature on the self-care theory in practice. Fawcett (1995) identified over 140 articles or chapters on practice applications and another 85 on administration. Among these are applications to children, adolescents, adults, the elderly, parents, and families; a wide variety of health conditions across the health–illness continuum; diverse practice settings; and different ethnic groups. As a way to demonstrate practice relevance, the theory has been placed in the context of the nursing process. An example is the article by Taylor (1988) cited previously, which describes how the theory can be applied to all steps of the nursing process using a case vignette. A good example of how the theory informs assessment was provided by Underwood (1980) and her followers (Morrison et al., 1985), who established protocols for assessing universal self-care of psychiatric patients, or for determining acuity ratings (Ringerman & Luz, 1990). Some of the excellent literature on nursing diagnosis and the self-care theory will be reviewed in the next part of this section.

Compelling evidence for the applicability of this theory in practice is found in the fact that it serves as the model of practice in a number of health care institutions. As documented in a number of articles (Allison et al., 1991; Del Togno-Armanasco et al., 1989; Fernandez et al., 1990; Holzmer, 1992; Stella & MacLead, 1991; Titus & Porter, 1989), the processes used to accomplish this often extend over a period of a year or more and typically include efforts to gain sufficient administrative support, extensive initial and on-going staff education, revision of assessment instruments and documentation forms to reflect the theory, and evaluation. By way of evaluation is a study reported by Faucett (1990) that demonstrated that nurses in a nursing home setting who were taught to use the self-care theory, when compared to nurses who were not, engaged in more comprehensive assessments about personal capabilities of patients and articulated more specific and varied roles for patients' participation in care. A study reported by Rossow-Sebring et al. (1992) showed that nurses on three medical–surgical units of an acute care hospital where the self-care theory had been introduced over a period of a year expressed greater satisfaction with the nursing role and greater value for patient teaching.

Impressively, the self-care theory is being used to develop a computerized nursing information system. This work is being done in three hospitals in New Jersey (Bliss-Holtz et al., 1990; McLaughlin et al., 1990). An initial system reportedly is in place and has been validated using postpartum patients (Bliss-Holtz et al., 1992).

References

Alexander, F. S., Younger, R. E., Cohen, R. M., & Crawford, L. V. (1988). Effectiveness of a nurse-managed program for children with chronic asthma. *Journal of Pediatric Nursing, 3,* 312–317.

Allan, J. D. (1988) Knowing what to weigh: Women's self-care activities related to weight. *Advances in Nursing Science, 11*(1), 47–60.

Allison, S. E., McLaughlin, K., & Walker, D. (1991). Nursing theory: A tool to put nursing back into nursing administration. *Nursing Administration Quarterly, 15*(3), 72–78.

Anna, D. J., Christensen, D. G., Hohon, S. A., Ord, L., & Wells, S. R. (1978). Implementing Orem's conceptual framework. *Journal of Nursing Administration, 8*(11), 8–11.

Arneson, S. W., & Triplett, J. O. (1990). Riding with Bucklebear: An automobile safety program for preschoolers. *Journal of Pediatric Nursing, 5,* 115–122.

Arnold, M. B. (1960). Deliberate action. *In Emotion and personality.* Vol. 11. *Neurological and physiological aspects* (pp. 193–204). New York: Columbia University Press.

Avery, P. (1992). Self-care in the hospital setting: The Prince Henry Hospital experience. *Lamp, 492,* 26–28.

Baker, L. K. (1992). Predictors of self-care in adolescents with cystic fibrosis: A test and explication of Orem's theories of self-care and self-care deficit. *Dissertation Abstracts International, 53,* 1290B.

Baulch, Y. S., Larson, P. J., Dodd, M. J., & Dietrich, C. (1992). The relationship of visual acuity, tactile sensitivity and mobility of the upper extremities to proficient breast selfexamination in women 65 and older. *Oncology Nursing Forum, 19* 1367–1372.

Beckman, C. A. (1987). Maternal-child health in Brazil. *Journal of Obstetric, Gynecologic, and Neonatal Nursing, 16,* 238–241.

Berbiglia, V. A. (1991). A case study: Perspectives on a self-care deficit nursing theory-based curriculum. *Journal of Advanced Nursing, 16,* 1158–1163.

Biggs, A. J. (1990). Family care-giver versus nursing assessments of elderly self-care abilities. *Journal of Gerontological Nursing, 16*(8), 11–16.

Blazek, B., & McClellan, M. (1983). The effects of self-care instruction on locus of control in children. *Journal of School Health, 53,* 554–556.

Bliss-Holtz, V. J. (1988). Primiparas' prenatal concern for learning infant care. *Nursing Research, 37,* 20–24.

Bliss-Holtz, V. J. (1991). Developmental tasks of pregnancy and parental education. *International Journal of Childbirth Education, 6*(1), 29–31.

Bliss-Holtz, J., McLaughlin, K., & Taylor, S. G. (1990). Validating nursing theory for use within a computerized nursing information system. *Advances in Nursing Science, 13*(2), 46–52.

Bliss-Holtz, J., Taylor, S. G., & McLaughlin, K., (1992). Nursing theory as a base for a computerized nursing information system. *Nursing Science Quarterly, 5,* 124–128.

Brock, A. M., & O'Sullivan, P. (1985). A study to determine what variables predict institutionalization of elderly people. *Journal of Advanced Nursing, 10,* 533–537.

Campbell, J. C. (1986). Nursing assessment for risk of homicide with battered women. *Advances in Nursing Science, 8*(4), 36–51.

Campbell, J. C. (1989). A test of two explanatory models of women's responses to battering. *Nursing Research, 38,* 18–24.

Carlisle, J. B., Corser, N., Cull, V., Dimicco, W., Luther, L., McCaleb, A., Robuch, F., & Powell, K. (1993). Cardiovascular risk factors in young children. *Journal of Community Health Nursing, 10,* 1–9.

Chamorro, L. C. (1985). Self-care in the Puerto Rican Community. In J. Riehl-Sisca (Ed.), *The science and art of self-care* (pp. 189–195), Norwalk, CT: Appleton-Century-Crofts.

Chang, B., Uman, G., Linn, L., Ware, J., & Kane, R. (1984). The effect of systematically varying components of nursing care on satisfaction in elderly ambulatory women. *Western Journal of Nursing Research, 6,* 367–386.

Chang, B., Uman, G., Linn, L., Ware, J., & Kane, R. (1985). Adherence to health care regimens among elderly women. *Nursing Research, 34,* 27–31.

Clark, J., & Bishop, J. (1988). Model-making. *Nursing Times, 84*(27), 37–40.

Cleveland, S. A. (1989). Re: Perceived self-care agency: A LISREL factor analysis of Bickel and Hanson's questionnaire [Letter to the editor]. *Nursing Research, 38,* 59.

Conn, V. (1991). Self-care actions taken by older adults for influenza and colds. *Nursing Research, 40,* 176–181.

Conn, V. S., Taylor, S. G., & Kelley, S. (1991). Medication regimen complexity and adherence among older adults. *IMAGE: Journal of Nursing Scholarship, 23* 231–235.

Cretain, G. K. (1989). Motivational factors in breast self-examination: Implications for nurses. *Cancer Nursing, 12,* 250–256.

Crockett, M. S. (1982). Self-reported coping histories of adult psychiatric and nonpsychiatric subjects and controls. (Abstract). *Nursing Research, 31,* 122.

Dashiff, C. J. (1992). Self-care capabilities in black girls in anticipation of menarche. *Health Care for Women International, 13,* 67–76.

Del Togno-Armanasco, V. Olivas, G. S., & Harter, S. (1989). Developing an integrated nursing care management model. *Nursing Management, 20*(10), 26–29.

Degenhart-Leskosky, S. M. (1989). Health education needs of adolescent and nonadolescent mothers. *Journal of Obstetric, Gynecologic and Neonatal Nursing, 18,* 238–244.

Denyes, M. J. (1982). Development of an instrument to measure self-care agency in adolescents. *Dissertation Abstracts International, 49,* 3102B.

Denyes, M. J. (1988). Orem's model used for health promotion: Directions from research. *Advances in Nursing Science, 11*(1), 13–21.

Denyes, M. J., Neuman, B. M., & Villarruel, A. M. (1991). Nursing actions to prevent and alleviate pain in hospitalized children. *Issues in Comprehensive Pediatric Nursing, 14,* 31–48.

Dier, K. A. (1987). A model for collaboration in nursing practice: Thailand and Canada. In K. F. Hannah, M. Reimer, W. C. Mills, & S. Letourneau (Eds.), *Clinical judgment and decision making: The future with nursing diagnosis* (pp. 323–327). New York: John Wiley & Sons.

Dickoff, J., James, P., & Wiedenbach, E. (1968). Theory in a practice disciplines Part I: Practice oriented theory. *Nursing Research, 17*(5), 415–435.

Dodd, M. J. (1982). Assessing patient self-care for side effects of cancer chemotherapy—Part 1. *Cancer Nursing, 5,* 447–451.

Dodd, M. J. (1983). Self-care for side effects in cancer chemotherapy: An Assessment of nursing interventions—Part 2. *Cancer Nursing, 6,* 63–67.

Dodd, M. J. (1984a). Patterns of self-care in cancer patients receiving radiation therapy. *Oncology Nursing Forum, 11,* 23–27.

Dodd, M. J. (1984b). Measuring informational intervention for chemotherapy knowledge and self-care behaviors. *Research in Nursing and Health, 7,* 43–50.

Dodd, M. J. (1987). Efficacy of proactive information on self-care in radiation therapy patients. *Heart and Lung, 16,* 538–544.

Dodd, M. J. (1988a). Efficacy of proactive information on self-care in chemotherapy patients. *Patient Education and Counseling, 11,* 215–225.

Dodd, M. J. (1988b). Patterns of self-care in patients with breast cancer. *Western Journal of Nursing Research, 10,* 7–24.

Dodd, M. J., & Dibble, S. L. (1993). Predictors of self-care: A test of Orem's model. *Oncology Nursing Forum, 20,* 895–901.

Dowd, T. (1991). Discovering older women's experience of urinary incontinence. *Research in Nursing and Health, 14,* 179–186.

Dyer, S. (1990). Team work for personal patient care. *Nursing the Elderly, 3*(7), 28–30.

Edgar, l., Shamian, J., & Patterson, C. (1984). Factor affecting the nurse as a teacher and practicer of breast self-examination. *International Journal of Nursing Studies, 21,* 255–265.

Ewing, G. (1989). The nursing preparation of stoma patients for self-care. *Journal of Advanced Nursing, 14,* 411–420.

Farnham, S., & Fowler, M. (1985). Demedicalization, bilingualization, and reconceptualization: Teaching Orem's self-care model to the RN-BSN student. In J. Riehl-Sisca, *The science and art of self-care* (pp. 35–40). Norwalk, CT: Appleton-Century-Crofts.

Faucett, J., Ellis, V., Underwood, P., Naqvi, A., & Wilson, D. (1990). The effect of Orem's self-care model on nursing care in a nursing home setting. *Journal of Advanced Nursing, 15,* 659–666.

Fawcett, J. (1995). *Analysis and evaluation of conceptual models of nursing* (3rd ed.). Philadelphia: F. A. Davis.

Fernandez, R., Brennan, M. L., Alvarez, A., R., & Duffy, M. A. (1990). Theory-based practice: A model for nurse retention. *Nursing Administration Quarterly, 14*(4), 47–53.

Finnegan, T. (1986). Self-care and the elderly. *New Zealand Nursing Journal, 79*(4), 10–13.

Frey, M. A., & Denyes, M. J. (1989). Health and illness self-care in adolescents with IDDM: A test of Orem's theory. *Advances in Nursing Science, 12*(1), 67–75.

Frey, M. A., & Fox, M. A. (1990). Assessing and teaching self-care to youths with diabetes mellitus. *Pediatric Nursing, 16,* 597–800.

Gammon, J. (1991). Coping with cancer: The role of self-care. *Nursing Practice, 4*(3), 11–15.

Gast, H. L. (1984). The relationship between stages of ego development and developmental stages of health self-care operations. *Dissertations Abstracts International, 44,* 3039B.

Gast, H. L., Denyes, M. J., Campbell, J. C., Hartweg, D. L., Schott-Baer, D., & Isenberg, M. (1989). Self-care agency: Conceptualizations and operationalizations. *Advances in Nursing Science, 12*(1), 26–38.

Gaut, D. A., & Kieckhefer, G. M. (1988). Assessment of self-care agency in chronically ill adolescents. *Journal of Adolescent Health Care, 9,* 55–60.

Geden, E., & Taylor, S. (1991). Construct and empirical validity of the Self-As-Carer Inventory. *Nursing Research, 40*(1), 47–50.

Germaine, C. P., & Nemchik, R. M. (1989). Diabetes self-management and hospitalization. *IMAGE: Journal of Nursing Scholarship, 20,* 74–78.

Goodwin, J. O. (1979). Programmed instruction for self-care following pulmonary surgery. *International Journal of Nursing Studies, 16,* 29–40.

Gulick, E. E. (1987). Parsimony and model confirmation of the ADL self-care scale for multiple sclerosis persons. *Nursing Research, 36,* 278–283.

Gulick, E. E. (1988). The self-administered ADL scale for persons with multiple sclerosis. In C. F. Waltz & O. L. Strickland (Eds.), *Measurement of nursing outcomes. Vol. 1. Measuring client outcomes* (pp. 128–159). New York: Springer.

Gulick, E. E. (1989a). Model confirmation of the MS-related symptom checklist. *Nursing Research, 38,* 147–153.

Gulick, E. E. (1989b). Work performance by persons with multiple sclerosis: Conditions that impede or enable the performance of work. *International Journal of Nursing Studies, 26,* 301–311.

Haas, D. (1990). *The relationship between coping dispositions and power components of dependent-care agency in parents of children with special health care needs.* Unpublished doctoral dissertation, Wayne State University, Detroit, Michigan.

Hagopian, G. (1990). The measurement of self-care strategies of patients in radiation therapy, In O. L. Strickland & C. F. Waltz (Eds.), *Measurement of nursing outcomes. Vol 4 Measuring client self-care and coping skills* (pp. 475–570). New York: Springer.

Hagopian, G. A. (1991). The effects of a weekly radiation therapy newsletter on patients. *Oncology Nursing Forum, 18,* 1199–1203.

Hagopian, G. A., & Rubenstein, J. H. (1990). Effects of telephone call interventions on patients' well-being in a radiation therapy department. *Cancer Nursing, 13,* 339–344.

Hamera, E. K., Peterson, K. A., Young, L. M., & Schammloffel, M. M. (1992). Symptom monitoring in schizophrenia: Potential for enhancing self-care. *Archives of Psychiatric Nursing, 6,* 324–330.

Hamilton, L. W., & Creason, N. S. (1992). Mental status and functional abilities: Change in institutionalized elderly women. *Nursing Diagnosis, 3,* 81–86.

Hammons, T. A. (1985). Self-care practices of Navajo Indians. In J. Riehl-Sisca (Ed.), *The science and art of self-care* (pp. 171–180). Norwalk, CT: Appleton-Century-Crofts.

Hanson, B. R., & Bickel, L. (1985). Development and testing of the questionnaire on perception of self-care agency. In J. Riehl-Sisca (Ed.), *The science and art of self-care* (pp. 271–278). Norwalk, CT: Appleton-Century-Crofts.

Hanucharurnkul, S. (1989). Predictors of self-care in cancer patients receiving radiotherapy. *Cancer Nursing, 12* 21–27.

Hanucharurnkul, S., & Vinya-nguag, P. (1991). Effects of promoting patients' participation in self-care on postoperative recovery and satisfaction with care. *Nursing Science Quarterly, 4,* 14–20.

Harman, L., Wabin, D., MacInnis, L., Baird, D., Mattiuzzi, D., & Savage, P. (1989). Developing clinical decision-making skills in staff nurses: An educational program. *Journal of Continuing Education In Nursing, 20,* 102–106.

Harmer, B. (1955). *Textbook of the principles and practice of nursing* (4th ed.) New York: McMillan.

Harper, D. (1984). Application of Orem's theoretical constructs to self-care medication behaviors in the elderly. *Advances in Nursing Science, 6*(3), 39–43.

Harris, J. L. (1990). Self-care of chronic schizophrenics associated with meeting solitude and social interaction requisites. *Archives of Psychiatric Nursing, 4*(5), 293–307.

Harris, J. L., & Williams, L. K. (1991). Universal self-care requisites as identified by homelss elderly men. *Journal of Gerontological Nursing, 19*(6), 39–43.

Hartweg, D. L. (1993). Self-care actions of healthy middle-aged women to promote well-being. *Nursing Research, 42*(4), 221–227.

Hartweg, D. L., & Metcalfe, S. A. (1986). Self-care attitude changes of nursing students enrolled in a self-care curriculum: A longitudinal study. *Research in Nursing and Health, 9,* 347–353.

Hautman, M. A. (1987). Self-care responses to respiratory illnesses among Vietnamese. *Western Journal of Nursing Research, 9,* 223–243.

Hayward, M. B., Kish, J. P., Jr., Frey, G. M., Kirchner, J. M. Carr, L. S., & Wolfe, C. M. (1989). An instrument to identify stressors in renal transplant recipients. *Journal of the American Nephrology Nurses Association, 16,* 81–84.

Holzmer, W. L. (1992). Linking primary health care and self-care through case management. *International Nursing Review, 39,* 83–89.

Hiromoto, B. M., & Duncan, J. (1991). Contract learning for self-care activities: A protocol study among chemotherapy outpatients. *Cancer Nursing 14,* 148–154.

Humphreys, J. (1991). Children of battered women: Worries about their mothers. *Pediatric Nursing, 17,* 342–345, 354.

Hungelmann, J. A. (1984). Components of self-care ability of older persons with chronic disease. Doctoral Dissertation, Rush University, Chicago, Illinois.

Hunter, L. (1992). Applying Orem to skin. *Nursing (London),5*(4), 16–18.

Huss, K., Salerno, M., & Huss, R. W. (1991). Computer-assisted reinforcement of instruction: Effects on adherence in adult atopic asthmatics. *Research in Nursing and Health, 13,* 259–267.

Illich, I. (1976). *Medical nemesis: The expropriation of health.* New York: Pantheon Books.

Jenny, J. (1989). Classifying nursing diagnoses: A self-care approach. *Nursing and Health Care, 10*(2), 83–89.

Jenny, J. (1991). Self-care deficit theory and nursing diagnoses: A test of conceptual fit. *Journal of Nursing Education, 30,* 227–232.

Jirovec, M. M., & Kasno, F. (1990). Self-care agency as a function of patient-environmental factors among nursing home residents. *Research in Nursing and Health. 13,* 303–309.

Jopp, M., Carroll, M. C., & Waters, L. (1993). Using self-care theory to guide nursing management of the older adult after hospitalization. *Rehabilitation Nursing, 18,* 91–94.

Karl, C. (1982). The effect of an exercise program on self-care activities for the institutionalized elderly. *Journal of Gerontological Nursing, 8,* 282–285.

Kearney, B. Y., & Fleischer, B. J. (1979). Development of an instrument to measure exercise of self-care agency. *Research in Nursing and Health, 2,* 35–24.

Kerkstra, A., Castelein, E., & Phillipsen, H. (1991). Preventive home visits to elderly people by community nurses in the Netherlands. *Journal of Advanced Nursing, 16,* 631–637.

Kirkpatrick, M. K., Brewer, J. A., & Stocks, B. (1990). Efficacy of self-care measures for perimenstrual syndrome (PMS). *Journal of Advanced Nursing, 15,* 281–285.

Klemm, L. W., & Creason, N. S. (1991). Self-care practices of women with urinary incontinence—A preliminary study. *Health Care for Women International, 12,* 199–209

Kotarbinski, T. (1965). *Praxiology: An introduction to the sciences of efficient action* (Trans. O. Wojtasiewicz). New York: Pergamon Press.

Kruger, S. Shawver, M., & Jones, L. (1980). Reactions of families to the child with cystic fibrosis. *IMAGE: Journal of Nursing Scholarship, 12,* 67a–72.

Krouse, H. J., & Roberts, S. J. (1989). Nurse-patient interactive styles: Power, control and satisfaction. *Western Journal of Nursing Research, 11,* 717–725.

Kubricht, D. (1984). Therapeutic self-care demands expressed by outpatients receiving external radiation therapy. *Cancer Nursing, 7,* 43–52.

Lakin, J. A. (1988). Self-care, health locus of control, and health value among faculty women. *Public Health Nursing, 5,* 37–44.

Langland, R. M. & Farrah, S. J. (1990). Using a self-care framework for continuing education in gerontological nursing. *Journal of Continuing Education in Nursing, 21,* 267–270.

Lashinger, H. S. (1990). Helping students apply a nursing conceptual framework in the clinical setting. *Nurse Educator, 15*(3), 20–24.

Leininger, M. M. (1988). Leininger's theory of nursing: Cultural care diversity and universality. *Nursing Science Quarterly, 1*(4), 152–160.

Leininger, M. M. (1993). Self-care ideology and cultural incongruities: Some critical issues. *Journal of Transcultural Nursing, 4*(1), 2–4.

Lonergan, B. J. F. (1972). *Method in theology*. Minneapolis: Seabury Press.

Lorenson, M., Holter, I. M., Evers, G. C., Isenberg, M. A., & van Acterberg, T. (1993). Cross-cultural testing of the appraisal of self-care agency: ASA scale in Norway. *International Journal of Nursing Studies, 30,* 15–23.

Leininger, M. (1992). Self-care ideology and cultural incongruities: Some critical issues. *Journal of Transcultural Nursing, 4*(1), 2–4.

Macmurray, J. (1957). *The self as agent*. London: Faber and Faber.

MacVicar, M. G., Winningham, M. L., & Nickel, J. L. (1989). Effects of aerobic interval training on cancer patients' functional capacity. *Nursing Research, 38,* 348–351.

Malik, U. (1992). Women's knowledge beliefs and health practices about breast cancer and breast self-examination. *Nursing Journal of India, 83,* 186–190.

Maritain, J. (1959). *The degrees of knowledge* (G. B. Phelan, Trans.). New York: Schribners.

McBride, S. H. (1987). Validation of an instrument to measure exercise of self-care agency. *Research in Nursing and Health, 10,* 311–316.

McBride, S. H. (1991). Comparative analysis of three instruments designed to measure self-care agency. *Nursing Research, 40,* 12–16.

McCord, A. S., (1990). Teaching for tonsillectomies: Details mean better compliance. *Today's OR Nurse. 126,* 11–14.

McDermott, M. A. N. (1993). Learned helplessness as an interacting variable with self-care agency: Testing a theoretical model. *Nursing Science Quarterly, 6,* 28–38.

McElmurry, B. J., & Huddleston, D. L. (1991). Self-care and menopause: Critical review of research. *Health Care for Women International, 12,* 15–26.

McFarland, S. M., Sasser, L., Boss, B. J., Dickerson, J. L., & Stelling, F. D. (1992). Self-Care Assessment Tool for spinal cord injured person. *SCI Nursing, 9,* 111–116.

McLaughlin, K., Taylor, S. G., Bliss-Holtz, J., Sayers, P., & Nickle, L. (1990). Shaping the future: The marriage of nursing theory and informatics. *Computers in Nursing, 8,* 174–179.

Meleis, A. (1991). *Theoretical nursing: Development and progress* (2nd ed.). San Francisco: J. B. Lippincott.

Melnyk, K. A. M. (1983). The process of theory analysis: An examination of the nursing theory of Dorothea E. Orem. *Nursing Research, 32*(3), 170–178.

Miller, J. F. (1982). Categories of self-care needs of ambulatory patients with diabetes. *Journal of Advanced Nursing, 7,* 25–31.

Monsen, R. B. (1992). Autonomy, coping and self-care agency in healthy adolescents and in adolescents with spina bifida. *Journal of Pediatric Nursing, 7,* 9–13.

Moore, J. B. (1987a). Determining the relationship of autonomy to self-care agency or locus of control in school-aged children. *Maternal Child Nursing Journal, 16*(1) 47–60.

Moore, J. B. (1987b). Effects of assertion training and first aid instruction on children's autonomy and self-care agency. *Research in Nursing and Health, 10,* 101–109.

Moore, J. B. (1993). Predictors of children's self-care performance: Testing the theory of self-care deficit. *Scholarly Inquiry for Nursing Practice, 7,* 199–212.

Morrison, E., Fisber, L., Wilson, H. & Underwood, P. (1985). NSGAE: Nursing adaptation evaluation. *Journal of Psychosocial Nursing, 23,* 10–13.

Northrup, D. T. (1993). Self-care myth reconsidered. *Advances in Nursing Science, 15*(3), 59–66.

Nursing Development Conference Group. (1973). *Concept formalization in nursing: Process and product.* Boston: Little, Brown.

Nursing Development Conference Group. (1979). *Concept formalization in nursing: Process and product* (2nd ed.). Boston: Little, Brown.

Oakley, D., Denyes, M. J., & O'Connor, N. (1989). Expanded nursing care for contraceptive use. *Applied Nursing Research, 3,* 121–127.

Oberst, M. T., Hugest, S. H., Chang, A. S., & McCubbin, M. A. (1991). Self-care burden, stress appraisal and mood among persons receiving radiotherapy. *Cancer Nursing, 14,* 7–78.

Orem, D. E. (1971). *Nursing: Concepts of practice.* New York: McGraw Hill.

Orem, D. E. (1980). *Nursing: Concepts of practice* (2nd ed.). New York: McGraw Hill.

Orem, D. E. (1985). *Nursing: Concepts of practice* (3rd ed.). New York: McGraw Hill.

Orem, D. E. (1988). The form of nursing science. *Nursing Science Quarterly, 1*(2), 75–79.

Orem, D. E. (1991). *Nursing: Concepts of practice* (4th ed.) St. Louis: Mosby Year Book.

Palikkathayil, L., & Morgan, S. A. (1988). Emergency department nurses' encounters with suicide attempters: A qualitative investigation. *Scholarly Inquiry for Nursing Practice, 2,* 237–253.

Palmer, P., & Meyers, F. J. (1990). An outpatient approach to the delivery of intensive consolidation chemotherapy to adults with acute lymphoblastic leukemia. *Oncology Nursing Forum, 17,* 553–558.

Parsons, T. (1937). *The structure of social action.* New York: McGraw-Hill.

Parsons, T. (1951). *The social system.* New York: The Free Press.

Patterson, E., & Hale, E. (1985). Making sure: Integrating menstrual care practices into activities of daily living. *Advances in Nursing Science, 7*(3), 18–31.

Reid, B., Allen, A. F., Gauthier, T., & Campbell, H. (1989). Solving the Orem mystery: An educational strategy. *Journal of Continuing Education in Nursing, 20,* 108–110.

Reisch, S. K., & Hauck, M. R. (1988). The Exercise of Self-Care Agency: An analysis of construct and discriminant validity. *Research in Nursing and Health, 11,* 245–255.

Rew, L. (1987a). Children with asthma: The relationship between illness behaviors and health locus of control. *Western Journal of Nursing Research, 9,* 465–483.

Rew, L. (1987b). The relationship between self-care behaviors and selected psychosocial variables in children with asthma. *Journal of Pediatric Nursing, 2,* 333–341.

Rhodes, V. A., Watson, P. M., & Hanson, B. M. (1988). Patients' descriptions of the influence of tiredness and weakness on self-care abilities. *Cancer Nursing, 11,* 186–194.

Richardson, A. (1992). Studies exploring self-care for the person coping with cancer treatment: A review. *International Journal of Nursing Studies, 29,* 191–204.

Riehl-Sisca, J. (1985a). *The science and art of self-care.* Norwalk, CT: Appleton-Century-Crofts.

Riehl-Sisca, J (1985b). Determining criteria for graduate and undergraduate self-care curriculums. In J. Riehl-Sisca (Ed)., *The science and art of self-care* (pp 307–309). Norwalk, CT: Appleton-Century-Crofts.

Ringerman, E., & Luz, S. (1990). A psychiatric patient classification system. *Nursing Management, 21*(10), 66–71.

Robinson, K. D., & Posner, J. D. (1992). Patterns of self-care needs and interventions related to biologic response modifier therapy: Fatigue as a model. *Seminars in Oncology Nursing, 8*(4, Suppl. 1), 17–22.

Rossow-Sebring, J. Carrieri, V., & Seward, H. (1992). Effect of Orem's model on nurse attitudes and charting behavior. *Journal of Staff Development, 8,* 207–212.

Rothert, M., Rovner, D., Holmes, M., et al. (1990). Women's use of information regarding hormone replacement therapy. *Research in Nursing and Health, 13,* 355–366.

Sandman, P. O., Norberg, A., Adolfsson, R., Axelsson, K., & Hedley, V. (1986). Morning care of patients with Alzheimer-type dementia: A theoretical model based on direct observation. *Journal of Advanced Nursing, 11,* 369–378.

Saucier, C. (1984). Self concept and self-care management in school-age children with diabetes. *Pediatric Nursing, 10,* 135–138.

Seideman, R. Y. (1990). Effects of a premenstrual syndrome education program on premenstrual symptomatology. *Health Care for Women International, 11,* 491–501.

Sella, S., & MacLeod, J. A. (1991). One year later: Evaluating a changing delivery system. *Nursing Forum, 26*(2), 5–11.

Silva, M. C. (1986). Research testing nursing theory: State of the art. *Advances in Nursing Science, 9*(1), 1–11.

Smith, M. J. (1987). Critique of Orem's theory. In R. Parse (Ed.), *Nursing science: Major paradigms, theories and critiques* (pp. 91–105). Philadelphia: W. B. Saunders.

Smits, J., & Kee, C. C. (1992). Correlates of self-care among the independent elderly: Self-concept affects well-being. *Journal of Gerontological Nursing, 18*(9), 13–18.

Taylor, S. G. (1985a). Curriculum development for preservice programs using Orem's theory of nursing. In J. Riehl-Sisca (Ed.), *The science and art of self-care* (pp. 25–32). Norwalk, CT: Appleton-Century-Crofts.

Taylor, S. G. (1985b). Teaching self-care deficit theory to generic students. In J. Riehl-Sisca (Ed.), *The science and art of self-care* (pp. 41–46). Norwalk, CT: Appleton-Century-Crofts.

Taylor, S. G. (1988). Nursing theory and nursing process: Orem's theory in practice. *Nursing Science Quarterly, 1,* 111–119.

Taylor, S. G. (1989). An interpretation of family within Orem's general theory of nursing. *Nursing Science Quarterly, 2,* 131–137.

Taylor, S. G. (1991). The structure of nursing diagnosis from Orem's theory. *Nursing Science Quarterly, 4,* 24–32.

Titus, S., & Porter, P. (1989). Orem's theory applied to pediatric residential treatment. *Pediatric Nursing, 15,* 465–468, 556.

Toth, J. C. (1980). Effect of structured preparation for transfer on patient anxiety leaving coronary care unit. *Nursing Research, 29,* 28–34.

Underwood, P. (1979). Nursing care as a determinant in the development of self-care behavior by hospitalized adult schizophrenics. *Dissertation Abstracts International, 40,* 679B.

Underwood, P. (1980). Facilitating self-care. In P. C. Pothier (Ed), *Psychiatric nursing: A basic text* (pp. 115–135). Boston: Little Brown.

Urbanic, J (1992). Incest trauma resolution in adult female survivors. Unpubished doctoral dissertations. Wayne State University, Detroit, Michigan.

Utz, S. W., Hammer, J., Whitmire, V. M., & Grass, S. (1990). Perceptions of body image and health status in persons with mitral valve prolapse. *IMAGE: Journal of Nursing Scholarship, 22,* 18–22.

Utz, S. W., & Ramos, M. C. (1993). Mitral valve prolapse and its effects: A programme of inquiry within Orem's self-care deficit theory of nursing. *Journal of Advanced Nursing, 18,* 742–751.

van Acterberg, T., Lorensen, M., Isenberg, M. A., Evers, G. C. M., Levin E., & Phillipsen, H. (1991). The Norwegian, Danish and Dutch versions of the Appraisal of Self-Care Agency Scale: Comparing reliability aspects. *Scandinavian Journal of Caring Sciences, 5,* 101–108.

Villarreul, A. M., & Denyes, (1991). Pain assessment in children: Theoretical and empirical validity. *Advances in Nursing Science, 14*(2), 32–41.

Wallace, W. A. (1983). Being scientific in a practice discipline. In *From a realist point of view: Essays on the philosophy of science* (pp. 273–293). Washington, DC: University Press of America.

Wanich, C. K., Sullivan-Marx, E. M., Gottlieb, G. L., & Johnson, J. C. (1992). Functional status outcomes of nursing intervention in hospitalized elderly. *IMAGE: Journal of Nursing Scholarship, 24,* 201–207.

Weaver, M. T. (1987). Perceived self-care agency: A LISREL factor analysis of Bickel and Hanson's questionnaire. *Nursing Research, 36,* 381–387.

West, P. (1993). *The relationship between depression and self-care agency in young adult women.* Unpublished doctoral dissertation, Wayne State University, Detroit, Michigan.

Whetstone, W. R. (1987). Perceptions of self-care in East Germany: A cross-cultural empirical investigation. *Journal of Advanced Nursing, 12,* 167–176.

Whetstone, W. R. (1986). Social dramatics: Social skills development for the chronically mentally ill. *Journal of Advanced Nursing, 11,* 67–74.

Whetstone, W. R., & Hansson, A. M. O. (1989). Perceptions of self-care in Sweden: a cross-cultural empirical investigation. *Journal of Advanced Nursing, 14,* 962–969.

Weinrich, S. P. (1990). Predictors of older adults, participation in fecal occult blood screening. *Oncology Nursing Forum, 17,* 715–720.

Weintraub, F. N., & Hagopian, G. A. (1990). The effect of nursing consultation on anxiety, side effects and self-care of patient receiving radiation therapy. *Oncology Nursing Forum, 17*(3,Suppl), 31–36.

Williams, P. D., Valderrama, D. M., Gloria, M. D., Pascoguin, L. G., Saavedra, L. D., De La Rama, D. T., Ferry, T. C., Abaguin, C. M., & Zaldivar, S. B. (1988). Effects of preparation for mastectomy/hysterectomy on women's post-operative self-care behaviors. *International Journal of Nursing Studies, 25,* 191–206.

Woods, N. F., Taylor, D., Mitchell, E. S., & Lentz, M. J. (1992). Perimenstrual symptoms and health-seeking behavior. *Western Journal of Nursing Research, 14,* 418–443.

Youssef, F. A. (1987). Discharge planning for psychiatric patients: The effects of a family-patient teaching programme. *Journal of Advanced Nursing, 12,* 611–616.

Imogene M. King

Julia B. George

Imogene M. King was born in 1923, the youngest of three children. She received her basic nursing education from St. John's Hospital School of Nursing in St. Louis, Missouri, graduating in 1946. Her BS in nursing education (1948) and MS in nursing (1957) are from St. Louis University and her EdD (1961) is from Teachers College, Columbia University, New York. She has done postdoctoral study in research design, statistics, and computers (King, 1986b).

King has had experience in nursing as an administrator, an educator, and a practitioner. Her area of clinical practice is adult medical-surgical nursing. She has been a faculty member at St. John's Hospital School of Nursing, St. Louis; Loyola University, Chicago; and the University of South Florida. She served as director of the School of Nursing at The Ohio State University, Columbus. She was an Assistant Chief of the Research Grants Branch, Division of Nursing, Department of Health, Education and Welfare in the mid-1960s and on the Defense Advisory Committee on Women in the Services for the Department of Defense in the early 1970s. She is retired from the University of South Florida and continues to consult and work on the further application of her theory.

From the early 1960s the rapidity of scientific and technologic advances has had as great an impact on the profession of nursing as on other components of society. In the 1960s, as emerging professionals, nurses were identifying the knowledge base specific to nursing practice

Taken from: *Nursing Theories: The Base for Professional Nursing Practice*, Fourth Edition by George.

and to an expanding role for nurses. In this environment, Imogene M. King (1971) sought to answer several questions:

1. What are some of the social and educational changes in the United States that have influenced changes in nursing?

2. What basic elements are continuous throughout these changes in nursing?

3. What is the scope of the practice of nursing, and in what kind of settings do nurses perform their functions?

4. Are the current goals of nursing similar to those of the past half century?

5. What are the dimensions of practice that have given the field of nursing unifying focus over time? (p. 19).

In exploring the literature on systems analysis and general system theory, King (1971) developed additional questions:

1. What kind of decisions are nurses required to make in the course of their roles and responsibilities?

2. What kind of information is essential for them to make decisions?

3. What are the alternatives in nursing situations?

4. What alternative courses of action do nurses have in making critical decisions about another individual's care, recovery, and health?

5. What skills do nurses now perform and what knowledge is essential for nurses to make decisions about alternatives? (pp. 19–20)

King's *Toward a theory for nursing: General concepts of human behavior* was published in 1971 and *A theory for nursing: Systems, concepts, process* in 1981 (reprinted in 1990). These publications grew from King's thoughts about the vast amount of knowledge available to nurses and the difficulty this presents to the individual nurse in choosing the facts and concepts relevant to a given situation.

In the preface to *Toward a theory for nursing* (1971), King clearly states she was proposing a conceptual framework for nursing and not a nursing theory. As she denoted in the title, her purpose was to help move toward a theory for nursing. In contrast, in the preface to *A theory for nursing* (1981/1990a), she indicates that she has expanded and built upon the original framework. In this second publication, she

> presents a conceptual framework by linking concepts essential to understanding nursing as a major system within health care systems . . . offers one approach to developing concepts and applying knowledge in nursing . . . [and] demonstrates one strategy for theory construction by presenting a theory of goal attainment derived from the conceptual framework (p. vii).

King identifies the conceptual framework as an open systems framework and the theory as one of goal attainment. As her extensive documentation indicates, she has drawn from a wide variety of sources in developing the framework and deriving the theory from that framework.

Because the theory of goal attainment is derived from the open systems framework, the framework and its assumptions and concepts are presented first, and then the goal attainment theory is discussed.

*K*ing's Open Systems Framework

The purposes of the conceptual framework are to organize concepts that represent essential knowledge that might be used by many disciplines and to construct theories from the framework and test them from the perspective of nursing as a discipline (King, 1990c). The concepts and knowledge may be similar across disciplines, but the way each profession uses them will differ (King, 1989). The framework represents knowledge essential for nursing and has an additional purpose of allowing the construction and testing of theories from the perspective of nursing. The conceptual framework includes goal, structure, function, resources, and decision making, which King says are essential elements. The framework has health as the *goal* for nursing. *Structure* is represented by the three open systems. *Function* is demonstrated in reciprocal relations of individuals in interaction. *Resources* include both people (health professionals and their clients) and money, goods, and services for items needed to carry out specific activities. *Decision making* occurs when choices are made in resource allocation to support attaining system goals.

King (1989) presents several assumptions that are basic to her conceptual framework. These include the assumptions that human beings are open systems in constant interaction with their environment, that nursing's focus is human beings interacting with their environment, and that nursing's goal is to help individuals and groups maintain health.

The conceptual framework is composed of three interacting systems: the personal systems, the interpersonal systems, and the social systems. Figure 3–3 presents a schematic diagram of these interacting systems. King (1989) summarizes the conceptual framework as follows:

> Nursing phenomena are organized within three dynamic interacting systems: (1) personal systems (individuals); (2) interpersonal systems (dyads, triads, and small and large groups); and (3) social systems (family, school, industry, social organizations, and health care delivery systems) (p. 151).

King identifies several concepts as relevant for each of these systems. However, she also states that the placement of concepts with each system is arbitrary because all the concepts are interrelated in the human-environment interaction. For each system a comprehensive or major concept with additional subconcepts is identified.

Personal Systems

Each individual is a personal system. For a personal system the relevant concepts are perception, self, growth and development, body image, space, learning, and time (King, 1986a). *Perception* is presented as the major concept of a personal system, the concept that influences all behaviors or to which all other concepts are related. The characteristics of perception are that it is universal, or experienced by all; subjective or personal; and selective for each person, meaning that any given situation will be experienced in a unique manner by each individual involved. Perception is action oriented in the present and based on the information that is available. Perception is transactions; that is, individuals are active participants in situations and their identities are affected by their participation (King, 1981/1990a). King further discusses perception as a process in which data obtained through the senses and from memory are organized, interpreted, and transformed. This process of human interaction with the environment influences behavior, provides meaning to experience, and represents the individual's image of reality.

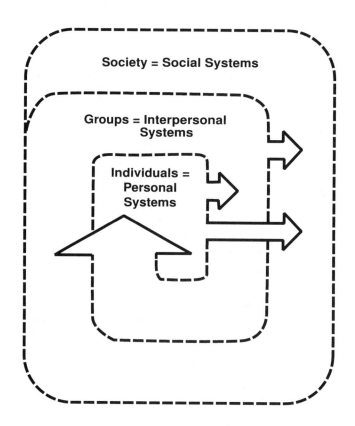

FIGURE 3–3

Dynamic Interacting Systems. *(Adapted from King, I. M. (1971).* Toward a theory for nursing, *New York: Wiley, p. 20. Copyright © 1971, by John Wiley & Sons, Inc., Used with permission.)*

The characteristics of *self* are a dynamic individual, an open system, and goal orientation. King (1981/1990a) accepts Jersild's (1952) definition of self:

> The self is a composite of thoughts and feelings which constitute a person's awareness of his individual existence, his conception of who and what he is. A person's self is the sum total of all he can call his. The self includes, among other things, a system of ideas, attitudes, values and commitments. The self is a person's total subjective environment. It is a distinctive center of experience and significance. The self constitutes a person's inner world as distinguished from the outer world consisting of all other people and things. The self is the individual as known to the individual. It is that to which we refer when we say "I" (pp. 9–10).

The characteristics of *growth and development* include cellular, molecular, and behavioral changes in human beings. These changes usually occur in an orderly manner, one that is predictable but has individual variations and is a function of genetic endowment, of meaningful and satisfying experiences, and of an environment conducive to helping individuals move toward maturity (King, 1981/1990a). Growth and development can be defined as the processes in people's lives through which they move from a potential for achievement to actualization of self. Theorists mentioned are Freud (1966), Erikson (1950), Piaget (Inhelder & Piaget, 1964), Gesell (1952), and Havinghurst (1953), but no particular model, theory, or framework of growth and development is specifically selected.

Body image is characterized as very personal and subjective, acquired or learned, dynamic and changing as the person redefines self. Body image is part of each stage of growth and development. King (1981/1990a) defines body image as the way one perceives both one's body and others' reactions to one's appearance.

Space is characterized as universal because all people have some concept of it. It may be personal or subjective; individual; situational and dependent on the relationships in the situation; dimensional as a function of volume, area, distance, and time; and transactional or based on the individual's perception of the situation. King's (1981/1990a) operational definition of space includes that space exists in all directions, is the same everywhere, and is defined by the physical area known as "territory" and by the behaviors of those who occupy it.

Time is characterized as universal or inherent in life processes; relational or dependent on distance and the amount of information occurring; unidirectional or irreversible as it moves from past to future with a continuous flow of events; measurable; and subjective because it is based on perception. King (1981/1990a) defines time as "a duration between one event and another as uniquely experienced by each human being; it is the relation of one event to another event" (p. 45).

In 1986, King (1986a) added *learning* as a subconcept in the personal system. She did not further define learning as a concept.

Perception, self, growth and development, body image, space, and time are the concepts of the personal system. The focus of nursing in the personal system is the person (King, 1986a). When personal systems come in contact with one another, they form interpersonal systems.

Interpersonal Systems

Interpersonal systems are formed by human beings interacting. Two interacting individuals form a dyad, three form a triad, and four or more form small or large groups. As the number of interacting individuals increases, so does the complexity of the interactions. The relevant concepts for interpersonal systems are interaction, communication, transaction, role, and stress (King, 1981/1990a). The concepts from the personal system are also used in understanding interactions (King, 1989).

The comprehensive or major concept, *interaction*, is characterized by values; mechanisms for establishing human relationships; being universally experienced; being influenced by perceptions; reciprocity; being mutual or interdependent; containing verbal and nonverbal communication; learning occurring when communication is effective; unidirectionality; irreversibility; dynamism; and having a temporal-spatial dimension (King, 1981/1990a). Interactions are defined as the observable behaviors of two or more persons in mutual presence.

Characteristics of *communication* are that it is verbal; nonverbal; situational; perceptual; transactional; irreversible, or moving forward in time; personal; and dynamic (King, 1981/1990a). Symbols for verbal communications are provided by language, for such communication includes the spoken and written language that transmits ideas from one person to another. An important aspect of nonverbal behavior is touch. Other aspects of nonverbal behavior are distance, posture, facial expression, physical appearance, and body movements. King defines communication as "a process whereby information is given from one person to another either directly in face-to-face meeting or indirectly through telephone, television, or the written word" (p. 146). Communication as a fundamental social process develops and maintains human relations and facilitates the ordered functioning of human groups and societies. As the information component of human interactions, communication occurs in all behaviors.

Transactions, for this conceptual framework, are derived from cognition and perceptions and not from transactional analysis. The characteristics of transactions are that they are unique because each individual has a personal world of reality based on that individual's perceptions; they have temporal and spatial dimensions; and they are experience—a series of events in time. King (1981/1990a) defines transactions as "a process of interactions in which human beings communicate with the environment to achieve goals that are valued . . . goal-directed human behaviors" (p. 82).

The characteristics of *role* include reciprocity in that a person may be a giver at one time and a taker at another time, with a relationship between two or more individuals who are functioning in two or more roles that are learned, social, complex, and situational (King, 1981/1990a). There are three major elements of role. The first is that role consists of a set of expected behaviors of those who occupy a position in a social system. The second is a set of procedures or rules that define the obligations and rights associated with a position in an organization. The third is a relationship of two or more persons who are interacting for a purpose in a particular situation. The nurse's role can be defined as interacting with one or more others in a nursing situation in which the nurse as a professional uses those skills, knowledge, and values identified as belonging to nursing to identify goals and help others achieve the goals.

The characteristics of *stress* are that it is dynamic as a result of open systems being in continuous exchange with the environment; the intensity varies; there is a temporal-spatial dimension that is influenced by past experiences; it is individual, personal, and subjective—a response to life events that is uniquely personal. King (1981/1990a) derives a definition of stress to be "a dynamic state whereby a human being interacts with the environment to maintain balance for growth, development, and performance, which involves an exchange of energy and information between the person and the environment for regulation and control of stressors" (p. 96). In addition, stress involves objects, persons, and events as stressors that evoke an energy response from the person. Stress may be positive or negative, and may simultaneously help an individual to a peak of achievement and wear the individual down.

The concepts of interpersonal systems are interaction, communication, transaction, role, and stress. The focus of nursing in the interpersonal system is the environment (King, 1986a). Interpersonal systems join together to form larger systems known as social systems.

Social Systems

A social system is defined as an organized boundary system of social roles, behaviors, and practices developed to maintain values and the mechanisms to regulate the practices and rules (King, 1981/1990a, p. 115).

Examples of social systems include families, religious groups, educational systems, work systems, and peer groups. The concepts relevant to social systems are organization, authority, power, status, decision making, and control plus all the concepts from the personal and interpersonal systems (King, 1989).

King (1981/1990a) proposes four parameters for *organization*:

(1) human values, behavior patterns, needs, goals and expectations; (2) a natural environment in which material and human resources are essential for achieving goals; (3) employers and employees, or parents and children, who form the groups that collectively interact to achieve goals; (4) technology that facilitates goal attainment (p. 116).

The major concept, organization, is characterized by structure that orders positions and activities and relates formal and informal arrangements of individuals and groups to achieve personal and organizational goals; functions that describe the roles, positions, and activities to be performed; goals or outcomes to be achieved; and resources. King defines organization as being made up of human beings who have prescribed roles and positions and who make use of resources to meet both personal and organizational goals.

The characteristics of *authority* include that it is observable through provisions of order, guidance, and responsibility for actions; universal; essential in formal organizations; reciprocal because it requires cooperation; resides in a holder who must be perceived as legitimate; situational; essential to goal achievement; and associated with power (King, 1981/1990a). Assumptions about authority include that it can be perceived by individuals and be legitimate; it can be associated with a position in which the position holder distributes rewards and sanctions; it can be held by professionals through their competence in using special knowledge and skills; and it can be exercised through group leadership by those with human relations skills. King defines authority as an active, reciprocal process of transaction in which the actors' backgrounds, perceptions, and values influence the definition, validation, and acceptance of those in organizational positions associated with authority.

Power is characterized as universal, situational (i.e., not a personal attribute), essential in the organization, limited by resources in a situation, dynamic, and goal directed (King, 1981/1990a). Premises about power are that it is potential energy, is essential for order in society, enhances group cohesiveness, resides in positions in an organization, is directly related to authority, is a function of human interactions, and is a function of decision making. King defines power in a variety of ways:

> Power is the capacity to use resources in organizations to achieve goals . . . is the process whereby one or more persons influence other persons in a situation . . . is the capacity or ability of a person or a group to achieve goals . . . occurs in all aspects of life and each person has potential power determined by individual resources and the environmental forces encountered. Power is social force that organizes and maintains society. Power is the ability to use and to mobilize resources to achieve goals (pp. 127–128).

Status is characterized as situational, position dependent, and reversible. King (1981/1990a) defines status as "the position of an individual in a group or a group in relation to other groups in an organization" and identifies that status is accompanied by "privileges, duties and obligations" (pp. 129–130).

Decision making is characterized as necessary to regulate each person's life and work, universal. Individual, personal, subjective, situational, a continuous process, and goal directed. Decision making in organizations is defined as "a dynamic and systematic process by which goal-directed choice of perceived alternatives is made and acted upon by individuals or groups to answer a question and attain a goal" (King, 1981/1990a, p. 132).

In 1986, King (1986a) added *control* as a subconcept in the social system. She did not further define control as a concept.

As with the other two systems. King (1986a) has identified a focus for nursing in the social system. In this system, nursing's focus in health.

The major theses of King's (1981/1990a) conceptual framework are (1) that "each human being perceives the world as a total person in making transactions with individuals and things in the environment" (p. 141), and (2) that "transactions represent a life situation in which perceiver and thing perceived are encountered and in which each person enters the situation as an active participant and each is changed in the process of these experiences" (p. 142). Theories may be derived from conceptual frameworks. King has derived a theory of goal attainment from the concepts and systems of her conceptual framework.

$\mathcal{K}$ing's Theory of Goal Attainment

The major elements of the theory of goal attainment are seen "in the interpersonal systems in which two people, who are usually strangers, come together in a health care organization to help and be helped to maintain a state of health that permits functioning in roles" (King, 1981/1990a, p. 142). The theory's focus on interpersonal systems reflects King's belief that the practice of nursing is differentiated from that of other health professions by what nurses do with and for individuals. The concepts of the theory are interaction, perception, communication, transaction, self, role, stress, growth and development, time, and personal space (King, 1990c).

These concepts are interrelated in every nursing situation (King, 1989). Although these terms have already been defined as concepts in the conceptual framework, they are defined again here as part of the theory of goal attainment. King (1989) states that although all have been conceptually defined, only transaction has been operationally defined. However, the operational definition given for transaction is also used for interaction in another publication (King, 1990c).

Interaction is defined as "a process of perception and communication between person and environment and between person and person, represented by verbal and nonverbal behaviors that are goal directed" (King, 1981/1990a, pp. 141, 142). King diagrams interaction as seen in Figure 3–4. Each of the individuals involved in an interaction brings different ideas, attitudes, and perceptions to the exchange. The individuals come together for a purpose and perceive each other; each makes a judgment and takes mental action or decides to act. Then each reacts to the other and the situation (perception, judgment, action, reaction). King indicates that only the interaction and transaction are directly observable.

Perception is "each person's representation of reality" (King, 1981/1990a, p. 145). The elements of perception are the importing of energy from the environment and organizing it by

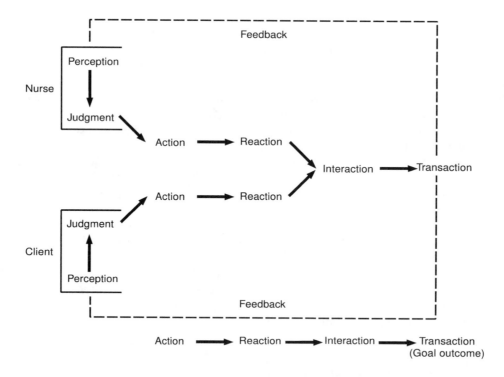

FIGURE 3–4

Interaction. *(Adapted from King, I. M. (1971). Toward a theory of nursing: General concepts of human behavior, New York: Wiley, pp. 26, 92. Copyright © 1971 by John Wiley & Sons, Inc. Used with permission.)*

information, transforming energy, processing information, storing information, and exporting information in the form of overt behaviors.

Communication is defined as "a process whereby information is given from one person to another either directly in face-to-face meetings or indirectly through telephone, television, or the written word" (King, 1981/1990a, p. 145). Communication represents, and is involved in, the information component of interaction.

Transaction is defined as "observable behaviors of human beings interacting with their environment" (King, 1981/1990a, pp. 145–146). Transactions represent the valuation component of human interactions and involve bargaining, negotiating, and social exchange. When transactions occur between nurses and clients, goals are attained.

Role is defined as "a set of behaviors expected of persons occupying a position in a social system; rules that define rights and obligations in a position; a relationship with one or more individuals interacting in specific situations for a purpose" (King, 1981/1990a, pp. 145-146). It is important that roles be understood and interpreted clearly to avoid conflict and confusion.

Stress is "a dynamic state whereby a human being interacts with the environment to maintain balance for growth, development, and performance . . . an energy response of an individual to persons, objects, and events called stressors" (King, 1981/1990a, p. 146). Although stress may be positive or negative, too high a level of stress may decrease an individual's ability to interact and to attain goals.

Growth and development can be defined as the "continuous changes in individuals at the cellular, molecular, and behavioral levels of activities . . . the processes that take place in the life of individuals that help them move from potential capacity for achievement to self-actualization" (King, 1981/1990a, p. 147).

Time is "a sequence of events moving onward to the future . . . a continuous flow of events in successive order that implies a change, a past and a future . . . a duration between one event and another as uniquely experienced by each human being . . . the relation of one event to another" (King, 1981/1990a, p. 147).

Space exists in every direction and is the same in all directions. Space includes that physical area named territory. Space is defined by the behaviors of those individuals who occupy it (King, 1981/1990a).

Health is not stated as a concept in the theory but is identified as an outcome variable. King (1986a) indicates the outcome is an individual's state of health or ability to function in social roles.

King's (1981/1990a, 1989, 1990c) operational definition of transaction has been used to identify the elements in interactions, at other times called a model of transactions. These elements are *action, reaction, disturbance (problem), mutual goal setting, exploration of means to achieve the goal, agreement on means to achieve the goal, transaction,* and *goal attainment.* The model essentially describes an interpersonal dyad (nurse and client) in interactions, using mutual goal setting or decision making as a process that leads to goal attainment.

From the theory of goal attainment. King (1990c) has developed predictive propositions:

- Perceptual accuracy, role congruence, and communication in a nurse-client interaction leads to transactions.

- Transactions lead to goal attainment and growth and development.

- Goal attainment leads to satisfaction and to effective nursing care (pp. 80–81).

She suggests that additional propositions may be generated.

In addition. King (1981/1990a) specifies internal and external boundary-determining criteria. Internal boundary criteria are derived from the characteristics of the concepts of the theory and speak to the theory itself. External boundary criteria speak to the area in which the theory is applicable. The internal boundary criteria for King's theory of goal attainment are the following:

1. Nurse and client do not know each other.

2. Nurse is licensed to practice professional nursing.

3. Client is in need of the services provided by the nurse.

4. Nurse and client are in a reciprocal relationship in that the nurse has special knowledge and skills to communicate appropriate information to help client set goals; client has information about self and perceptions of problems or concerns that when communicated to nurse will help in mutual goal setting.

5. Nurse and client are in mutual presence, purposefully interacting to achieve goals (p. 150).

The external boundary criteria for King's (1981/1990a) theory of goal attainment are the following:

1. Interactions in a two-person group

2. Interactions limited to licensed professional nurse and to client in need of nursing care

3. Interactions taking place in natural environments (p. 150).

In 1987, King added the boundary of client locus of control and states that it is difficult to achieve mutual goal setting with a client who has an external locus of control.

Thus, King is saying that a professional nurse, with special knowledge and skills, and a client in need of nursing, with knowledge of self and perceptions of personal problems, meet as strangers in a natural environment. They interact mutually to identify problems and to establish and achieve goals. The personal system of the nurse and the personal system of the client meet in interaction with the interpersonal system of their dyad. Their interpersonal system is influenced by the social systems that surround them as well as by each of their personal systems.

King's Theory and Nursing's Metaparadigm

In discussing her conceptual framework as an introduction to the presentation of her theory of goal attainment, King (1981/1990a) indicates that the abstract concepts of the framework are human beings, health, environment, and society. Because the theory is presented as a theory for nursing, King also defines nursing. Thus, the four major concepts of human beings, health, environment/society, and nursing are defined and discussed by King.

King (1981/1990a) identifies several assumptions about *human beings*. She describes human beings as social, sentient, rational, reacting, perceiving, controlling, purposeful, action-oriented, and time-oriented. From these beliefs about human beings, she has derived the following assumptions that are specific to nurse-client interaction:

■ Perceptions of nurse and of client influence the interaction process.

■ Goals, needs, and values of nurse and client influence the interaction process.

■ Individuals have a right to knowledge about themselves.

■ Individuals have a right to participate in decisions that influence their life, their health, and community services.

■ Health professionals have a responsibility to share information that helps individuals make informed decisions about their health care.

■ Individuals have a right to accept or to reject health care.

■ Goals of health professionals and goals of recipients of health care may be incongruent (pp. 143–144).

King (1981/1990a) further states that "nurses are concerned with human beings interacting with their environment in ways that lead to self-fulfillment and to maintenance of health" (p. 3). Human beings have three fundamental health needs: (1) the need for health information that is usable at the time when it is needed and can be used, (2) the need for care that seeks to prevent illness, and (3) the need for care when human beings are unable to help themselves. She states, "nurses are in a position to assess what people know about their health, what they think about their health, how they feel about it, and how they act to maintain it" (p. 8).

King defines *health* as "dynamic life experiences of a human being, which implies continuous adjustment to stressors in the internal and external environment through optimum use of one's resources to achieve maximum potential for daily living" (King, 1989, p. 152) and as "a dynamic state of an individual in which change is constant and ongoing and may be viewed as the individual's ability to function in his or her usual roles" (King, 1990b, p. 76). King (1990b) affirms that health is not a continuum but a holistic state. The characteristics of health are "genetic, subjective, relative, dynamic, environmental, functional, cultural, and perceptual" (p. 124). She discusses health as a functional state and illness as an interference with that functional state. She then defines illness as "a deviation from normal, that is, an imbalance in a person's biological structure or in his psychological make-up, or a conflict in a person's social relationships" (King, 1981/1990a, p. 5).

Environment and *society* are indicated as major concepts in King's framework but are not specifically defined in her work. Society may be viewed as the social systems portion of her open systems framework. In 1983, King extended the ability to interact in goal setting and selection of means to achieve the goal to include mutual goal setting with family members in relation to clients and families. Although her definition of health mentions both internal and external environment, and she has stated, "environment is a function of balance between internal and external interactions" (1990b, p. 127), the usual implication of the use of environment in *A theory for nursing* is that of external environment. Because she presents her material as based on open systems, it is assumed that a definition of external environment may be drawn from general system theory. Systems are considered to have boundaries that separate their internal components from the rest of the world. The external environment for a system is the portion of the world that exists outside of that boundary. Of particular interest as a system's external environment is the part of the world that is in direct exchange of energy and information with the system. King (1981/1990a) does say that the three systems form the environments that influence individuals.

Nursing is defined as "a process of action, reaction, and interaction whereby nurse and client share information about their perceptions in the nursing situation," and as "a process of human interactions between nurse and client whereby each perceives the other and the situation; and through communication, they set goals, explore means, and agree on means to achieve goals" (King, 1981/1990a, pp. 2, 144). *Action* is defined as a sequence of behaviors involving mental and physical action. The sequence is first mental action to recognize the presenting conditions; then physical action to begin activities related to those conditions; and finally, mental action in an effort to exert control over the situation, combined with physical action seeking to achieve goals. *Reaction* is not specifically defined but might be considered to be included in the sequence of behaviors described in action. *Interaction* has been discussed previously. Although King has altered her definition of nursing from that published in 1971, she has continued to refer to nursing as that which is done by nurses. "Lawyer" and "legal situation," "physical therapist," and "therapy situation," or any other practitioner who interacts with clientele could be substituted for "nurse" and "nursing situation" in her definitions of nursing. Such substitution would create definitions that could be applied to these other practices. This weakens her definition.

In addition to the foregoing definition of nursing, King (1981/1990a) discusses the goal, domain, and function of the professional nurse. The goal of the nurse is "to help individuals maintain their health so they can function in their roles" (pp. 3–4). Nursing's domain includes promoting, maintaining, and restoring health, and caring for the sick, injured, and dying. The function of the professional nurse is to interpret information in what is known as the nursing process to plan, implement, and evaluate nursing care.

Theory of Goal Attainment and the Nursing Process

The basic assumption of the theory of goal attainment—that nurses and clients communicate information, set goals mutually, and then act to attain those goals—is also the basic assumption of the nursing process. King (1990c) describes the steps of the nursing process as a system of interrelated actions and identifies concepts from her work that provide the theoretical basis for the nursing process as method.

According to King (1981/1990a), *assessment* occurs during the interaction of the nurse and client, who are likely to meet as strangers. Assessment may be viewed as paralleling action and reaction. The concepts King identifies are the perception, communication, and interaction of nurse and client. The nurse brings to this meeting special knowledge and skills, whereas the client brings knowledge of self and perceptions of the problems that are of concern. Assessment, interviewing, and communication skills are needed by the nurse as is the ability to integrate knowledge of natural and behavioral sciences for application to a concrete situation.

All concepts of the theory apply to assessment. Growth and development, knowledge of self and role, and the amount of stress influence perception and in turn influence communication, interaction, and transaction. In assessment, the nurse needs to collect data about the client's level of growth and development, view of self, perception of current health status, communication patterns, and role socialization, among other things. Factors influencing the client's perception include the functioning of the client's sensory system, age, development, sex, education, drug and diet history, and understanding of why contact with the health care system is occurring. The perceptions of the nurse are influenced by the cultural and socioeconomic background and age of the nurse and the diagnosis of the client (King, 1981/1990a). Perception is the basis for gathering and interpreting data, thus the basis for assessment. Communication is necessary to verify the accuracy of perceptions. Without communication, interaction and transaction cannot occur.

The information shared during assessment is used to derive a *nursing diagnosis*, defined by King (1981/1990a) as a statement that "identifies the disturbances, problems, or concerns about which patients seek help" (p. 177). The implication is that the nurse makes the nursing diagnosis as a result of the mutual sharing with the client during assessment. Stress may be a particularly important concept in relation to nursing diagnosis because stress, disturbance, and problem or concern may be closely connected.

After the nursing diagnosis is made, *planning* occurs. King (1981/1990a) says that the concepts involved are *decision making* about goals and *exploring means* and *identifying means* to attain goals. King describes planning as setting goals and making decisions about how to achieve these goals. This is part of transaction and again involves mutual exchange with the client. She specifies that clients are requested to participate in decision making about how the goals are to be met. Although King assumes that in nurse-client interactions clients have the right to participate in decisions about their care, she does not say they have the responsibility. Thus, clients are requested to participate, not expected to do so.

Implementation occurs in the activities that seek to meet the goals. Implementation is a continuation of transaction in King's theory. She states that the concept involved is the making of *transactions*.

Evaluation involves descriptions of how the outcomes identified as goals are attained. In King's (1981/1990a) description, evaluation not only speaks to the attainment of the client's goals but also to the effectiveness of nursing care. She also indicates that the involved concept is goal attainment or, if not, why not.

Although all the theory concepts apply throughout the nursing process, communication with perception, interaction, and transaction are vital for goal attainment and need to be apparent in each phase. King emphasizes the importance of mutual participation in interaction that focuses on the needs and welfare of the client and of verifying perceptions while planning and activities to achieve goals are carried out together. Although King emphasizes mutuality, she does not limit it to verbal communication, nor does she require the client's active physical participation in actions to achieve goal attainment.

In *A theory for nursing,* King presents an application of her theory of goal attainment that she identifies as the use of a goal-oriented nursing record. Her description of this goal-oriented nursing record closely parallels the steps of the nursing process.

King's Work and the Characteristics of a Theory

King has stated that she has derived a theory of goal attainment from her open system framework of personal, interpersonal, and social systems.

1. **Theories can interrelate concepts in such a way as to create a different way of looking at a particular phenomenon.** King has interrelated the concepts of interaction, perception, communication, transaction, self, role, stress, growth and development, time, and space into a theory of goal attainment. Her theory deals with a nurse-client dyad, a relationship to which each person brings personal perceptions of self, role, and personal levels of growth and development. The nurse and client communicate, first in interaction and then in transaction, to attain mutually set goals. The relationship takes place in space identified by their behaviors and occurs in forward-moving time. In particular, the specification of transaction as dealing with mutual goal attainment is a different way of looking at the phenomenon of nurse-client relationships.

2. **Theories must be logical in nature.** King's theory of goal attainment does describe a logical sequence of events. For the most part, concepts are clearly defined. However, a major inconsistency within her writing is the lack of a clear definition of environment, which is identified as a basic concept for the framework from which she derives her theory. In addition, she indicates that nurses are concerned about the health care of groups but concentrates her discussion on nursing as occurring in a dyadic relationship. Thus, the theory essentially draws on only two of the three systems described in the conceptual framework. The social systems portion of the framework is less clearly connected to the theory of goal attainment than are the personal and inter-

personal systems. The definition of stress indicates that it is both negative and positive, but discussion of stress always implies that it is negative. Finally, King says that the nurse and client are strangers, yet she speaks of their working together for goal attainment and of the importance of health maintenance. Attainment of long-term goals, such as those concerning health maintenance, is not consistent with not knowing each other.

3. **Theories should be relatively simple yet generalizable.** Although the presentation appears to be complex. King's theory of goal attainment is relatively simple. Ten concepts are identified, defined, and their relationships considered; two concepts are identified only. Even though King indicates that many of the concepts are situation dependent, they are not situation specific; that is, they are influenced by the situation but may occur in many different situations. The theory of goal attainment is limited in setting only in regard to "natural environments" and, with growth and development as a major concept, is certainly not limited in age. The theory of goal attainment is generalizable to any dyadic nursing situation with a possible limitation relating to difficulties associated with seeking mutual goal setting with a client who has an external locus of control. The emphasis on mutuality would initially appear to limit the theory to dealing with those clients who can verbally interact with the nurse and physically participate in implementations to meet goals. However, King points to observable behaviors and to both verbal and nonverbal communication. Indeed, even the comatose individual has observable behaviors in the form of vital signs and does communicate nonverbally. The major limitation in relation to this characteristic is the effort required of the reader to sift through the presentation of a conceptual framework and a theory with repeated definitions to find the basic concepts. Another limitation relates to the lack of development of application of the theory in providing nursing care to groups, families, or communities.

4. **Theories can be the bases for hypotheses that can be tested or for theory to be expanded.** King (1990c) presents the following hypotheses that she states are being tested:

   ■ Mutual goal setting will increase ability to perform activities of daily living.

   ■ Mutual goal setting by nurse and patient leads to goal attainment.

   ■ Goal attainment will be greater in patients who participate in goal setting than those who do not participate in goal setting.

   ■ Mutual goal setting will increase elderly patients' morale.

   ■ Perceptual congruence in nurse-patient interactions increases mutual goal setting.

   ■ Goal attainment decreases stress and anxiety in nursing situations.

   ■ Congruence in role expectations and role performance increases transactions in nurse-patient interactions (pp. 81–82).

   These and other hypotheses could be used to test the theory.

5. **Theories contribute to and assist in increasing the general body of knowledge within the discipline through the research implemented to validate them.** King (1981/1990a) reports the results of a descriptive study conducted to test the theory of goal attainment. The study resulted in a classification system to analyze nurse-patient interactions and found that goal attainment is facilitated when the nurse and patient

have accurate perceptions, adequate communication, and set goals mutually. She also states that data about interactions from two separate studies have confirmed the presence of transactions (King, 1990c). Studies reported in the literature include using King's conceptual framework and/or theory of goal attainment to investigate nurses' attitudes toward the elderly, attending behavior and mental status measurements, promoting postoperative participation in self-care (used in conjunction with Orem's theories), and parenting (Brower, 1981; Hanucharunkui & Vinya-nguag, 1991; Norris & Hayer, 1993; Rosendahl & Ross, 1982). These are examples of contributions to the general body of knowledge. The theory of goal attainment needs to be tested further. Such testing will expand the theory's contribution to the discipline.

6. **Theories can be used by practitioners to guide and improve their practice.** As demonstrated in the discussion of nursing process. King's theory of goal attainment can be used to guide and improve practice. Even though this theory in itself can be used as a guide to practice, King (1981/1990a) has also developed the goal-oriented nursing record in an effort to assist the practice of nursing. She presents the goal-oriented nursing record as an application of the theory of goal attainment in nursing. She has also developed a criterion-referenced tool for measuring attainment of health goals (King, 1988). Others have reported the use of King's work in nursing curricula (Daubenmire, 1989).

7. **Theories must be consistent with other validated theories, laws, and principles but will leave open unanswered questions that need to be investigated.** King's theory of goal attainment is not in apparent conflict with other validated theories, laws, and principles. She has clearly documented the sources on which she has based her characteristics and definitions of concepts, and she states that "the major technique used in developing concepts . . . has been a review of the literature in nursing and related fields to identify characteristics of the concept. From this information, an operational definition of the concept is formulated" (King, 1981/1990a, p. 22). Using the review of the literature as a base has helped to avoid being in conflict with others. King shares many similarities with other nursing theorists. As does Peplau (1952/1988), King indicates that the nurse and client usually enter the relationship as strangers when the client has a need. King's basic assumptions about human beings as thinking, sentient decision makers who have a right to information and to participation in decisions about themselves has a humanistic base similar to that of Paterson and Zderad (1976). The emphasis on the right to participate in decisions is similar to that of Orlando (1961/1990a, 1972), among others.

Throughout *A theory for nursing*, King identifies those theories from other fields that support what she is saying. Although there is no apparent conflict, many questions are open for exploration. A few of these are discussed in the hypotheses presented earlier in this section.

S ummary

Imogene King has presented an open systems framework from which she derived a theory of goal attainment. The framework consists of three systems—personal, interpersonal, and social—all of which are in continuous exchange with their environments. The concepts of the personal systems are perception, self, body image, growth and development, time, learning, and space. The concepts of the interpersonal systems are role, interaction, communication, transaction, and stress. Social systems concepts are organization, power, authority, status, decision making, control, and role.

From these systems and their abstract concepts of human beings, health, environment, and society, King derives a theory of goal attainment. The major concepts of the theory of goal attainment are interaction, perception, communication, transaction, role, stress, and growth and development. Each of these is defined, and overall propositions and criteria for determining internal and external boundaries of the theory are presented.

Imogene King has developed a theory of goal attainment that is based on a philosophy of human beings and an open systems framework. She presents the results of some of the research conducted to test the theory and proposes an application of the theory in the form of a goal-oriented nursing record.

The theory is useful, testable, and applicable to nursing practice. Although it is not the "perfect theory," it is widely generalizable and not situation specific. Dr. King's work is solidly based in the literature and provides the reader with a rich set of resources for further study.

References

Brower, H. T. (1981). Social organization and nurses' attitudes toward older persons. *Journal of Gerontological Nursing, 7*, 293–298.

Daubenmire, M. J. (1989). A baccalaureate nursing curriculum based on King's conceptual framework. In J. Riehl-Sisca (Ed.), *Conceptual models for nursing practice* (3rd ed.). Norwalk, CT: Appleton & Lange.

Erikson, E. (1950). *Childhood and society.* New York: Norton. [out of print]

Freud, S. (1966). *Introductory lectures on psychoanalysis.* (J. Strachey, Trans.) New York: Norton. [out of print]

Gesell, A. (1952). *Infant development.* New York: Harper & Row. [out of print]

Hanucharunkui, S. & Vinya-nguag, P. (1991). Effects of promoting patient's participation in self-care on postoperative recovery and satisfaction with care. *Nursing Science Quarterly, 4*, 14–20.

Havinghurst, R. (1953). *Human development and education.* New York: McKay. [out of print]

Inhelder, B. F. & Piaget, J. (1964). *The early growth of logic in the child.* New York: Norton. [out of print]

Jersild, A. T. (1952). *In search of self.* New York: Columbia University Teachers College Press. [out of print]

King, I. M. (1971). *Toward a theory for nursing: General concepts of human behavior.* New York: Wiley. [out of print]

King, I. M. (1983). King's theory of nursing. In I. W. Clements, & F. B. Roberts (Eds.), *Family health: A theoretical approach to nursing care.* New York: Wiley. [out of print]

King, I. M. (1986a). *Curriculum and instruction in nursing.* East Norwalk, CT: Appleton-Century-Crofts. [out of print]

King, I. M. (1986b). King's Theory of Goal Attainment. In P. Winstead-Fry (Ed.), *Case studies in nursing theory.* New York: National League for Nursing.

King, I. M. (1987). *King's theory.* Paper presented at Nurse Theorist Conference, Pittsburgh, PA. (cassette recording).

King, I. M. (1988). Measuring health goal attainment in patients. In C. Waltz, & O. Strickland (Eds.), *Measurement of nursing outcomes* (Vol I, pp. 109–117). New York: Springer.

King, I. M. (1989). King's general systems framework and theory. In J. Riehl-Sisca (Ed.), *Conceptual models for nursing practice* (3rd ed.) (pp. 149–158). Norwalk, CT: Appleton & Lange.

King, I. M. (1990a). *A theory for nursing: Systems, concepts, process.* Albany, NY: Delmar. (Originally published 1981, NY: Wiley.)

King, I. M. (1990b). Health as a goal for nursing. *Nursing Science Quarterly, 3,* 123–128.

King, I. M. (1990c). King's conceptual framework and Theory of Goal of Attainment. In M. E. Parker (Ed.), *Nursing theories in practice.* New York: National League for Nursing.

Norris, D. M., & Hayer, P. J. (1993). Dynamism in practice: Parenting within King's framework. *Nursing Science Quarterly, 6,* 79–85.

Orlando, I. J. (1990). *The dynamic nurse-patient relationship: Function, process and principles.* New York: National League for Nursing. (Originally published 1961, New York: Putnam's)

Orlando, I. J. (1972). *The discipline and teaching of nursing process.* New York: G. P. Putnam's. [out of print]

Peplau, H. E. (1988). *Interpersonal relations in nursing.* London: Macmillan Education. (Original work published 1952, New York: Putnam's)

Paterson, J., & Zderad, L. (1976). *Humanistic nursing.* New York: Wiley. [out of print]

Rosendahl, P. B., & Ross, V. (1982). Does your behavior affect your patient's response? *Journal of Gerontological Nursing, 8,* 572–575.

$\mathcal{B}$ ibliography

Daubenmire, M. J., & King, I. M. (1973). Nursing process model: A systems approach. *Nursing Outlook, 21,* 512–517.

King, I. M. (1964, October). Nursing theory—Problems and prospects. *Nursing Science,* 394–403.

King, I. M. (1968). A conceptual frame of reference for nursing. *Nursing Research, 17,* 27–31.

King, I. M. (1970). Planning for change. *Ohio Nurses Review,* 4–7.

King, I. M. (1976). The health care system: Nursing intervention subsystem. In W. H. Werley, et al. (Eds.), *Health research: The systems approach.* New York: Springer. [out of print]

External Analysis

According to King (1988), knowledge of concepts and relationship in the conceptual framework guides research, education, and practice. Prior to 1988, application and extension of the conceptual framework was limited. Silva (1986) did not include King's framework in her review of research testing nursing theory because it did not meet the inclusion criteria of six published studies (Silva, 1987). In the past 5 or 6 years there has been a notable increase in publications on theory development, testing, and use in practice. A major contribution of new material to the King literature was published in 1995 (Frey & Sieloff, 1995).

Relationship to Nursing Research

King (1988) identifies that research is the link between a conceptual framework and knowledge development. Conceptual framework serve as a basis for development of theories from which research questions and/or hypothesis are formulated and tested. One of the first theories derived from King's framework was the theory of goal attainment (King, 1981). A descriptive study of behaviors in nurse–patient interactions resulted in the transactions and classification system model. King (1981) and Austin and Champion (1983) demonstrated propositions and hypotheses from the theory. Additionally, King (1985, 1986a, 1986b, 1990, 1991a) has reported on continuing activities to refine and test the theory.

Several investigators in addition to King have tested the theory of goal attainment (Hanucharurnkui & Vinya-nguag, 1990; Kameoka & Sugimori, 1993; Kusaka, 1991; Hanna, 1993). Although tested with different populations and various outcomes (goals), the studies all address the underlying hypothesis that nurse–patient interaction leads to goal attainment. Research findings were discussed in relation to the statements derived from the theory. While all are exemplary examples of theory testing research, the study by Kameoka and Sugimori (1993) is especially intriguing because it replicated King's (1981) initial study of nurse–patient interactions in Japan.

Several others have used King's theory of goal attainment to conceptualize research. Research "conceptualized within" is distinguished from research which "tests" theory by the strength of the linkages between concepts and relationship (Whall, 1996). An example of the

Taken from: *Conceptual Models of Nursing: Analysis and Application*, Third Edition by Fitzpatrick and Whall.

former is research which addresses a concern identified as important by a framework. Examples of research "conceptualized within" King's theory of goal attainment are Martin's (1990) educational intervention with male cancer awareness, McGirr et al.'s (1990) cardiac rehabilitation program, and Spees' (1991) intervention with knowledge of medical terms. Levine et al. (1988) conducted a study of personality characteristics of critical care nurses. King's conceptual framework identified as a basis for the study rather than the theory of goal attainment. However, the focus was on nurses as personal systems and on interactions with the environment. All projects were based on nursing's goal to promote or maintain health.

To date, the only other published theory derived from King's conceptual framework is Frey's (1988) formulation of children, families, and chronic illness. The theory has been tested with youths with insulin-_dependent diabetes mellitus and asthma. Refinement has included additional indicators of child health, improved measurement of family systems, inclusion of health and risk behaviors, and explication of concepts for understanding the child as a personal system (Frey, 1993). The goal continues to be on interactions, behavior, and improved health outcome.

Others have demonstrated potential of the theory goal attainment and conceptual framework to guide research. Norris and Hoyer (1993) used the theory of goal attainment to propose a systems framework for family-centered care in a neonatal intensive care unit. Hawks (1991) expanded on King's concept of power. Although not tested, the authors provide testable hypothesis. When implemented, these types of studies can contribute to empirical validity of the theory and provide knowledge for practice with selected clinical populations.

*R*elationship to Nursing Education

King's early work in theory was closely tied to curriculum development. King (1986b) expanded on these ideas in *Curriculum and Instruction in Nursing: Concepts and Process*. The text demonstrates use of the conceptual framework to organize courses, identify objectives, plan instruction, and conduct evaluation. Additional examples of utility of the conceptual framework for curriculum are in the work of Gulitz and King (1988). The Ohio State University has based its baccalaureate curriculum on King's framework. Many of those materials were published by Daubenmire (1989). The framework has also been applied to continuing nursing education (Brown & Lee, 1980).

*R*elationship to Nursing Practice

Huch (1988) defines theory-based practice as nursing care guided by propositions from a nursing framework or theory. There has been an increase in the use of all frameworks and theory to guide practice, and King's are no exception. Examples from the literature include use of the conceptual framework with couples who experience infertility (Davis, 1987), preoperative teaching prior to elective surgery (Swindale, 1989), family therapy (Gonot, 1986), individual psychotherapy (DeHowitt, 1992), group psychotherapy (Laben et al., 1991), care of families with high risk infants (Symanski, 1991), the family impact of cardiac disease (Sirles & Selleck, 1989), psychotic clients with HIV infection (Kemppainen, 1990), the elderly (Kenney, 1990; Kohler, 1988), adults with diabetes (Husband, 1988), and persons with neurofibromatosis (Messner & Smith, 1986). The extent to which these applications contribute to validity of concepts and relationships as proposed by King is dependent on critical evaluation by the authors and others. Unfortunately, evaluation has been inconsistent and often lacking.

In addition, several hospitals have implemented practice based on King's conceptual framework and theory of goal attainment in patient _care departments or units. These include the Centenary Hospital in Scarborough, Ontario, Canada (Coker & Schreiber, 1990), Tampa General Hospital, Tampa, Florida (Messmer, 1993), and Hamilton Civic Hospitals, Hamilton, Ontario, Canada (A. Watson, personal communication, May 28, 1993).

References

Austin, J. K., & Champion, V. L. (1983). King's theory for nursing: Explication and evaluation. In Chinn, P. L. (Ed.), *Advances in nursing theory development* (pp. 49–61). Rockville, MD: Aspen Systems Corporation.

Aydelotte, M. K., & Peterson, K. H. (1987). Keynote address: Nursing taxonomies—state of the art. In McLane, A. M. (Ed.), *Classification of nursing diagnoses: Proceedings of the seventh conference* (pp. 1–16). St. Louis: C. V. Mosby.

Brown, S. T., & Lee, B. T. (1980). Imogene King's conceptual framework: A proposed model for continuing nursing education. *Journal of Advanced Nursing, 5*(5):467–473.

Byrne-Coker, E., Fradley, T., Harris, J., Tomarchio, D., Chan, V., & Caron, C. (1990). Implementing nursing diagnoses within the context of King's conceptual framework. *Nursing Diagnosis, 1*(3):107–114.

Carter, K. F., & Dufour, L. T. (1994). King's theory: A critique of the critiques. *Nursing Science Quarterly, 7*(3), 128–133.

Coker, E. B., & Schreiber, R. (1990). Implementing King's conceptual framework at the bedside. In Parker, M. E. (Ed.), *Nursing theories in practice* (pp. 85–102). New York: National League for Nursing.

Daubenmire M. J. (1989). A baccalaureate nursing curriculum based on King's conceptual framework. In Riehl-Sisca, J. (Ed.), *Conceptual models for nursing practice* (pp. 167–178). Norwalk, CT: Appleton & Lange.

Davis, D. C. (1987). A conceptual framework for infertility. *Journal of Obstetric, Gynecologic, and Neonatal Nursing, Jan/Feb*:30–35.

DeHowitt, M. C. (1992). King's conceptual model and individual psychotherapy. *Perspectives in Psychiatric Care, 28*(4):11–14.

Doornbos, M. M. (1993). *Family health in the families of the young chronically mentally ill.* Unpublished doctoral dissertation. Wayne State University, Detroit, MI.

Ellis, R. (1968). Characteristics of significant theories. *Nursing research, 17*:217–222.

Evans, C. L. (1991). *Imogene King: A conceptual framework for nursing.* Newbury Park, CA: Sage Publications.

Fawcett, J. (1989). *Analysis and evaluation of conceptual models of nursing.* Philadelphia: F. A. Davis.

Frey, M. A. (1988). *Health and social support in families with children with diabetes mellitus* (Doctoral dissertation, Wayne State University, 1987). Dissertation Abstracts International, 48, 4A.

Frey, M. A. (1989). Social support and health: A theoretical formulation derived from King's conceptual framework. *Nursing Science Quarterly, 2*:138–148.

Frey, M. A. (1993). A theoretical perspective of family and child health derived from King's conceptual framework for nursing: A deductive approach to theory building. In Feetham, S. L., Meister, S. B., Bell, J. M. & Gilliss, C. L. (Eds.), *The nursing of families* (pp. 30–37). Newbury Park, CA: Sage.

Frey, M. A., Rooke, L., Sieloff, C., Messmer, P., & Kameoka, T. (1995). King's framework and theory in Japan, Sweden, and the United States. *IMAGE: Journal of Nursing Scholarship.* *27*(2):127–130.

Frey, M. A., & Sieloff, C. (Eds.), 1995. *Advancing King's system framework and theory of nursing.* Newbury Park, CA: Sage.

Gonot, P. W. (1986). Family therapy as derived from King's conceptual model. In Whall, A. (Ed.), *Family therapy theory for nursing: Approaches.* Norwalk, CT: Appleton-Century-Crofts.

Gonot, P. W. (1989). Imogene M. King's conceptual framework of nursing. In J. J. Fitzpatrick & A. L. Whall (Eds.), Conceptual models of nursing: Analysis and application (2nd ed., pp 271–283) Norwalk, CT: Appleton & Lange.

Gultiz, E. A., & King, I. M. (1988). King's general systems model: Application to curriculum development. *Nursing Science Quarterly, 1*(3):128–132.

Hanchett, E. S. (1990, Summer). Nursing models and community as client . . . public health/community health nursing. *Nursing Science Quarterly, 3*(2):67–72.

Hanna, K. M. (1993). Effect of nurse-client transaction on female adolescents' oral contraceptive adherence. *IMAGE: Journal of Nursing Scholarship, 25*(4):285–290.

Hanucharurnkui, S., & Vinya-nguag, P. (1990). Effects of promoting patients' participation in self-care on postoperative recovery and satisfaction with care. *Nursing Science Quarterly, 4*(1):14–20.

Harding, S. (1987). Is there a feminist model? In Harding, S. (Ed.), *Feminism and methodology.* Bloomington, IN: Indiana Univ. Press.

Hawks, J. H. (1991). Power: A concept analysis. *Journal of Advanced Nursing, 16*:754–762.

Huch, M. H. (1988). Theory-based practice: Structuring nursing care. *Nursing Science Quarterly, 1*(1):6–7.

Husband, A. (1988). Application of King's theory of nursing to the care of the adult with diabetes. *Journal of Adanced Nursing, 13*(4):484–488.

Jonas, C. (1987). King's goal attainment theory: Use in gerontological nursing practice. *Perspectives, Winter:* 9–12.

Kameoka, T., & Sugimori, M. (June, 1993). *Application of King's goal attainment theory in Japanese clinical setting.* Paper presented at the meeting of Sigma Theta Tau International Sixth International Nursing Research Congress, Madrid, Spain.

Kemppainen, J. K. (1990). Imogene King's theory: A nursing case study of a psychotic client with human immunodeficiency virus infection. *Archives of Psychiatric Nursing, 4*(6):384–388.

Kenny, T. (1990). Erosion of individuality in care of elderly people in hospital—an alternative approach. *Journal of Advanced Nursing; 15*:571–576.

King, I. M. (1964). Nursing theory—problems and prospects. *Nursing Science, 2*:394–403.

King, I. M. (1968). A conceptual frame of reference for nursing. *Nursing Research, 17*(1):27–31.

King, I. M. (1971). *Toward a theory for nursing.* New York: Wiley.

King, I. M. (1975). A process for developing concepts for nursing through research. In P. J. Verhonick (Ed.), *Nursing research I* (pp. 25–43). Boston: Little, Brown.

King, I. M. (1981). *A theory for nursing: Systems, concept, process.* New York: Wiley; Albany, NY: Delmar.

King, I. M. (1983). King's theory of nursing. In Clements, I. W. & Roberts, F. B. (Eds.), *Family health: A theoretical approach to nursing care.* New York: Wiley.

King, I. M. (1985). Paper presented at the Nursing Theory Conference. Edmonton, Alberta, Canada.

King, I. M. (1986a). King's theory of goal attainment. In Winstead-Fry, P. (Ed.), *Case studies in nursing theories: Curriculum and instruction in nursing* (pp. 192–213). Norwalk, CT: Appleton-Century-Crofts.

King, I. M. (1986b). *Curriculum and instruction in nursing: Concepts and process.* Norwalk, CT: Appleton-Century-Crofts.

King, I. M. (1990). Health as the goal for nursing. *Nursing Science Quarterly, 3*(3):123–128.

King, I. M. (1988). Concepts: Essential elements of theories. *Nursing Science Quarterly, 1*(1):22–25.

King, I. M. (1989a). King's general system framework and theory. In Riehl-Sisca, J. P. (Ed.), *Conceptual models for nursing practice* (pp. 149–158). Norwalk, CT: Appleton & Lange.

King, I. M. (1989b). King's system framework for nursing administration. In Henry, B., Arndt, C., diVincenti, M., Tomey, A. M. (Eds.), *Dimensions of nursing administration: Theory, research, education, practice* (pp. 35–45). Boston, MA: Blackwell Scientific.

King, I. M. (1990a). Health as the goal for nursing. *Nursing Science Quarterly, 3*(3):123–128.

King, I. M. (1990b). King's conceptual framework and theory of goal attainment. In Parker, M. E. (Ed.), *Nursing theories in practice* (pp. 73–84). New York: National League for Nursing.

King, I. M. (July 1990c). *The theory of goal attainment: An update.* Paper presented at Wayne State University College of Nursing 6th Annual Summer Research Conference. Detroit, MI.

King, I. M. (1991a). King's theory of goal attainment. *Nursing Science Quarterly, 5*(1):19–26.

King, I. M. (1991b). Nursing theory 25 years later. *Nursing Science Quarterly, 4*(3):94–95.

King, I. M. (June, 1993). *King's conceptual system and theory of goal attainment.* Paper presented at the meeting of the Sigma Theta Tau International Sixth International Nursing Research Congress, Madrid, Spain.

King, I. M. (1994). Quality of life and goal attainment. *Nursing Science Quarterly, 7*(1):29–32.

Kohler, P. (July, 1988). Model of shared control. *Journal of Gerontological Nursing, 14*(7):21–25.

Kusaka, T. (1991). Application to the King's goal attainment theory in Japanese clinical setting. *Journal of the Japanese Academy of Nursing Education, 1*(1):30–31.

Laben, J. K., Dodd, D., & Sneed, L. (1991). King's theory of goal attainment applied in group therapy for inpatient juvenile sexual offenders, maximum security state offenders, and community parolees, using visual aids. *Issues in Mental Health Nursing, 12*(1):51–64.

Lazarus, R. S., & Folkman, S. (1984). *Stress, appraisal, and coping.* New York: Springer.

Lesnick, M. J., & Anderson, B. E. (1947). *Legal aspects of nursing.* Philadelphia: J. B. Lippincott.

Levine, C. D., Wilson, S. F., & Guido, G. W. (1988). Personality factors of critical care nurses. *Heart and Lung, 17*(4):392–398.

Magan, S. J. (1987). A critique of King's theory. In Parse, R. R. (Ed.), *Nursing science major paradigms, theories, and critiques.* Philadelphia: W. B. Saunders.

Martin, J. P. (1990). Male cancer awareness: Impact of an employee education program. *Oncology Nursing Forum, 17*(1):59–64.

McGirr, M., Rukhomlm, E., Salmoni, A., O'Sullivan, P., & Koren, I. (1990). Perceived mood and exercise behaviors of cardiac rehabilitation programs referrals. *Canadian Journal of Cardiovascular Nursing, 1*(4):14–19.

Meleis, A. (1985). *Theoretical Nursing: Developments and progress.* Philadelphia: J. B. Lippincott.

Meleis, A. (1991). *Theoretical nursing: Developments and progress* (2nd Ed.). Philadelphia: J. B. Lippincott.

Messmer, P. (June, 1993). *Implementation of theory-based nursing practice in a large teaching hospital.* Paper presented at the meeting of Sigma Theta Tau International Sixth International Nursing Research Congress, Madrid, Spain.

Messner, R., & Smith, M. N. (1986). Neurofibromatosis: Relinquishing the masks; a quest for quality of life. *Journal of Advanced Nursing, 11:*459–464.

Morgan, G., & Smircich, L. (1980). The case for qualitative research. *Academic Management Review, 5*(4):491–500.

Norris, D. M., & Hoyer, P. J. (1993). Dynamism in practice: Parenting within King's framework. *Nursing Science Quarterly, 6*(2):79–85.

Rawlins, P. S., Rawlins, T. D., & Horner, M. (1990). Development of the family needs assessment tool. *Western Journal of Nursing Research, 12*(2):201–214.

Rooda, L. A. (1992). The development of a conceptual model for multicultural nursing. *Journal of Holistic Nursing, 10*(4):337–347.

Silva, M. C. (1986). Research testing nursing theory: State of the art. *Advances in Nursing Science, 9:*1–11.

Silva, M. C. (1987). Conceptual models of nursing. In Fitzpatrick, J. J. & Tanunton, R. L. (Eds.), *Annual Review of Nursing Research, Volume 5* (pp. 229–246). New York: Springer.

Sirles, A. T., & Selleck, C. S. (1989). Cardiac disease and the family: Impact, assessment, and implications. *Journal of Cardiovascular Nursing, 3*(2):23–32.

Smith, M. J. (1988). Perspectives on nursing science. *Nursing Science Quarterly, 1*(2):80–85.

Spees, C. M. (1991). Knowledge of medical terminology among clients and families. *IMAGE: Journal of Nursing Scholarship, 23*(4):225–229.

Spratlen, L. P. (1975). Introducing ethnic-cultural factors in models of nursing: Some mental health care applications. *Journal of Nursing Education, 15*(2):23–29.

Swindale, J. E. (1989). The nurse's role in giving pre-operative information to reduce anxiety in patients admitted to hospital for elective minor surgery. *Journal of Advanced Nursing, 14:*899–905.

Symanski, M. E. (1991). Use of nursing theories in the care of families with high-risk infants: Challenges for the future. *Journal of Perinatal and Neonatal Nursing, 4*(4):71–77.

Whall, A. (1989). The influence of logical positivism on nursing practice. *IMAGE: Journal of Nursing Scholarship, 21*(4):243–245.

Whall, A. (1996). In Fitzpatrick, J. J. & Whall, A. L. (Eds.), *Conceptual models of nursing: Analysis and application* (3rd ed.).

SECTION

Dorothy E. Johnson

Marie L. Lobo

Dorothy Johnson was born in Savannah, Georgia, in 1919, the last of seven children. Her Bachelor of Science in Nursing was from Vanderbilt University, Nashville, Tennessee, and her Masters in Public Health from Harvard. She began publishing her ideas about nursing soon after graduation from Vanderbilt. Most of her teaching career was in pediatric nursing at the University of California, Los Angeles. She retired as Professor Emeritus, January 1, 1978, and currently lives in Florida.

Dorothy Johnson has influenced nursing through her publications since the 1950s. Throughout her career, Johnson has stressed the importance of research-based knowledge about the effect of nursing care on clients. Johnson was an early proponent of nursing as a science as well as an art. She also believed nursing had a body of knowledge reflecting both the science and the art. From the beginning, Johnson (1959) proposed that the knowledge of the science of nursing necessary for effective nursing care included a synthesis of key concepts drawn from basic and applied sciences.

In 1961, Johnson proposed that nursing care facilitated the client's maintenance of a state of equilibrium. Johnson proposed that clients were "stressed" by a stimulus of either an internal or external nature. These stressful stimuli created such disturbances, or "tensions," in the patient that a state of disequilibrium occurred. Johnson identified two areas of foci for nursing care that are based on returning the client to a state of equilibrium. First, nursing care

Taken from: *Nursing Theories: The Base for Professional Nursing Practice*, Fourth Edition by George.

should reduce stimuli that are stressors, and second, "nursing care should provide support of the client's 'natural' defenses and adaptive processes" (p. 66).

In 1992, Johnson articulated that much of her thinking was influenced by Florence Nightingale. Johnson related that she was first exposed to Nightingale in the mid-1940s.

While reading Nightingale's (1859/1992) *Notes on nursing* she found that Nightingale focused on the "fundamental needs" of people rather than on the disease process. She also noted that Nightingale focused on the relationship of the person to the environment rather than the disease to the person. In the 1950s and 1960s, as Johnson developed her model, an increasing number of observational studies on child and adult behavior patterns were published. During these same years, general system theory was also discussed frequently. All these experiences influenced Johnson (1992) in the development of her Behavioral Systems Model.

In 1968, Johnson first proposed her model of nursing care as the fostering of "the efficient and effective behavioral functioning in the patient to prevent illness" (Johnson, 1968, April, p. 2). The patient is identified as a behavioral system with multiple subsystems. At this point Johnson began to integrate concepts related to systems models into her work. Johnson's (1968) integration of systems concepts into her work was further illustrated by her statement of belief that nursing was "concerned with man as an integrated whole and this is the specific knowledge of order we require" (p. 207). Not only did nurses need to care for the "whole" client, but the generation of nursing knowledge needed to take a course in the direction of concern with the entire needs of the client.

In the mid- to late-1970s, several nurses published conceptualizations of nursing based on Johnson's behavioral systems model. Some of these were revised in the 1980s. Auger (1976), Damus (1980), Grubbs (1980), Holaday (1980), and Skolny and Riehl (1974) are authors who have interpreted Johnson. Roy (1989), Wu (1973), and others were sharing their beliefs about nursing at the same time, and Johnson's influence, as their professor, is clearly reflected in their works. In 1980, Johnson published her conceptualization of the Behavioral System Model for Nursing. This is the first work published by Johnson that explicates her definitions of the Behavioral System Model. The evolution of this complex model is clearly demonstrated in the progression of Johnson's ideas from works published in the 1950s to her latest available work published in 1980.

Definition of Nursing

Johnson (1980) developed her Behavioral System Model for nursing from a philosophical perspective "supported by a rich, sound, and rapidly expanding body of empirical and theoretical knowledge" (p. 207). From her early beliefs, which focused on the impaired individual, Johnson evolved a much broader definition of nursing. By 1980, she defined nursing as "an external regulatory force which acts to preserve the organization and integration of the patient's behavior at an optimal level under those conditions in which the behavior constitutes a threat to physical or social health, or in which illness is found" (p. 214). Based on this definition, the following four goals of nursing are to assist the patient to become a person:

1. Whose behavior is commensurate with social demands

2. Who is able to modify his behavior in ways that support biologic imperatives

3. Who is able to benefit to the fullest extent during illness from the physician's knowledge and skill

4. Whose behavior does not give evidence of unnecessary trauma as a consequence of illness (p. 207).

*A*ssumptions of the Behavioral System Model

Johnson makes several layers of assumptions in the development of her conceptualization of the Behavioral System Model. Assumptions are made about the system as a whole as well as about the subsystems. Another set of assumptions deals with the knowledge base necessary to practice nursing.

As with Rogers (1970) and Roy (1989), Johnson believes that nurses need to be well grounded in the physical and social sciences. Particular emphasis should be placed on knowledge from both the physical and social sciences that is found to influence behavior. Thus, Johnson believes it would be of equal importance to have information available about endocrine influences on behavior as well as about psychological influences on behavior.

In developing assumptions about behavioral systems, Johnson was influenced by Buckley, Chin, and Rapport, early leaders in the development of systems concepts. Johnson (1980) cites Chin (1961) as the source for her first assumption about systems. In constructing a behavioral system, the assumption is made that there is "'organization, interaction, interdependency, and integration of the parts and elements' (Chin, 1961) of behavior that go to make up the system" (p. 208). It is the interrelated parts that contribute to the development of the whole.

The second assumption about systems also evolves from the work of Chin. A system "'tends to achieve a balance among the various forces operating within and upon it' (1961), and that man strives continually to maintain a behavioral system balance and steady states by more or less automatic adjustments and adaptations to the 'natural' forces impinging upon him" (p. 208). The individual is continually presented with situations in everyday life that require adaptation and adjustment. These adjustments are so natural that they occur without conscious effort by the individual. Johnson (1980) says:

> The third assumption about a behavioral system is that a behavioral system, which both requires and results in some degree of regularity and constancy in behavior, is essential to man; that is to say, it is functionally significant in that it serves a useful purpose both in social life and for the individual (p. 208).

The patterns of behavior characteristic of the individual have a purpose in the maintenance of homeostasis by the individual. The development of behavioral patterns that are acceptable to both society and the individual foster the individual's ability to adapt to minor changes in the environment.

The final assumption about the behavioral system is that the "system balance reflects adjustments and adaptations that are successful in some way and to some degree" (Johnson, 1980, p. 208). Johnson acknowledges that the achievement of this balance may and will vary from individual to individual. At times this balance may *not* be exhibited as behaviors that are acceptable or meet society's norms. What may be adaptive for the individual in coping with impinging forces may be disruptive to society as a whole. Most individuals are flexible enough, however, to be in some state of balance that is "functionally efficient and effective" for them (p. 209).

The integration of these assumptions by the individual provides the behavioral system with the patterns of action to form "an organized and integrated functional unit that determines and limits the interaction between the person and his environment and establishes the relationship of the person to the objects, events, and situations in his environment" (Johnson, 1980, p. 209). The function of the behavioral system, then, is to regulate the individual's response to input from the environment so that the balance of the system can be maintained.

Four assumptions are made about the structure and function of each sub-system. These four assumptions are the "structural elements" common to each of the seven subsystems. The first assumption is "from the form the behavior takes and the consequences it achieves can be inferred what *drive* has been stimulated or what *goal* is being sought" (Johnson, 1980, p. 210). The ultimate goal for each subsystem is expected to be the same for all individuals. However, the methods of achieving the goal may vary depending on culture or other individual variations.

The second assumption is that each individual has a "predisposition to act, with reference to the goal, in certain ways rather than in other ways" (Johnson, 1980, pp. 210–211). This predisposition to act is labeled "set" by Johnson. The concept of "set" implies that despite having only a few alternatives from which to select a behavioral response, the individual will rank those options and choose the option considered most desirable.

The third assumption is that each subsystem has available a repertoire of choices or "scope of action" alternatives from which choices can be made. Johnson (1980) subsumes under this assumption that larger behavioral repertoires are available to more adaptable individuals. As life experiences occur, individuals add to the number of alternative actions available to them. At some point, however, the acquisition of new alternatives of behavior decreases as the individual becomes comfortable with the available repertoire. The point at which the individual loses the desire or ability to acquire new options is not identified by Johnson.

The fourth assumption about the behavioral subsystems is that they produce observable outcomes—that is, the individual's behavior (Johnson, 1980). The observable behaviors allow an outsider—in this case the nurse—to note the actions the individual is taking to reach a goal related to a specified subsystem. The nurse can then evaluate the effectiveness and efficiency of these behaviors in assisting the individual in reaching one of these goals.

In addition, each of the subsystems has three functional requirements. First, each subsystem must be "*protected* from noxious influences with which the system cannot cope" (Johnson, 1980, p. 212). Second, each subsystem must be "*nurtured* through the input of appropriate supplies from the environment" (p. 212). Finally, each subsystem must be "*stimulated* for use to enhance growth and prevent stagnation" (p. 212). As long as the subsystems are meeting these functional requirements, the system and the subsystems are viewed as self-maintaining and self-perpetuating. The internal and external environments of the system need to remain orderly and predictable for the system to maintain homeostasis or remain in balance. The interrelationships of the structural elements of the subsystem are critical for each subsystem to function at a maximum state. The interaction of the structural elements allows the subsystem to maintain a balance that is adaptive to that individual's needs.

An imbalance in a behavioral subsystem produces tension, which results in disequilibrium. The presence of tension resulting in an unbalanced behavioral system requires the system to increase energy use to return the system to a state of balance (Johnson, 1968, April). Nursing is viewed as a part of the external environment that can assist the client to return to a state of equilibrium or balance.

Johnson's Behavioral System Model

Johnson (1980) believes each individual has patterned, purposeful, repetitive ways of acting that comprise a behavioral system specific to that individual. These actions or behaviors form an "organized and integrated functional unit that determines and limits the interaction between the person and his environment and establishes the relationship of the person to the objects, events, and situations in his environment" (p. 209). These behaviors are "orderly, purposeful and predictable . . . [and] sufficiently stable and recurrent to be amenable to description and explanation" (p. 209). Johnson identifies seven subsystems within the Behavioral System Model, an identification that is at variance with others who have published interpretations of Johnson's model. Johnson (1980) states that the seven subsystems identified in her 1980 publication are the only ones to which she subscribes, and she recognizes they are at variance with Grubbs. These seven subsystems were originally identified in Johnson's 1968 paper presented at Vanderbilt University. The seven subsystems are considered to be interrelated, and changes in one subsystem affect all the subsystems.

Johnson has never produced a schematic representation of her system. Conner, Harbour, Magers and Watt (1994); Loveland-Cherry and Wilkerson (1989); and Torres (1986) have produced similar schematic representations of Johnson's model (see Fig. 4–1).

Johnson's Seven Behavioral Subsystems

The *attachment* or *affiliative* subsystem is identified as the first response system to develop in the individual. The optimal functioning of the affiliative subsystem allows "social inclusion, intimacy, and the formation and maintenance of a strong social bond" (Johnson, 1980, p. 212). Attachment to a significant caregiver has been found to be critical for the survival of an infant. As the individual matures, the attachment to the caretaker continues and there are additional attachments to other significant individuals as they enter both the child's and the adult's network. These "significant others" provide the individual with a sense of security.

The second subsystem identified by Johnson is the *dependency* subsystem. Johnson (1980) distinguishes the dependency subsystem from the attachment or affiliative subsystem. Dependency behaviors are "succoring" behaviors that precipitate nurturing behaviors from other individuals in the environment. The result of dependency behavior is "approval, attention or recognition, and physical assistance" (p. 213). It is difficult to separate the dependency subsystem from the affiliative or attachment subsystem because without someone invested in or attached to the individual to respond to that individual's dependency behaviors, the dependency subsystem has no animate environment in which to function.

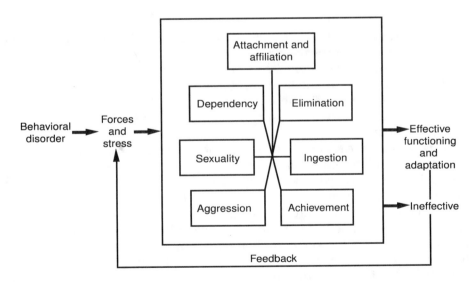

FIGURE 4–1

Johnson's Model. *(From Torres, G. (1986).* Theoretical foundations of nursing. *Norwalk, CT: Appleton-Century-Crofts, p. 121. Used with permission.)*

The *ingestive* subsystem relates to the behaviors surrounding the intake of food. It is related to the biological system. However, the emphasis for nursing, from Johnson's (1980) perspective, is the meanings and structures of the social events surrounding the occasions when food is eaten. Behaviors related to the ingestion of food may relate more to what is socially acceptable in a given culture than to the biological needs of the individual.

The *eliminative* subsystem relates to behaviors surrounding the excretion of waste products from the body. Johnson (1980) admits this may be difficult to separate from a biological system perspective. However, as with behaviors surrounding the ingestion of food, there are socially acceptable behaviors for the time and place for humans to excrete waste. Human cultures have defined different socially acceptable behaviors for excretion of waste, but the existence of such a pattern remains from culture to culture. Individuals who have gained physical control over the eliminative subsystem control those subsystems rather than behave in a socially unacceptable manner. For example, biological cues are often ignored if the social situation dictates that it is objectionable to eliminate wastes at a given time.

The *sexual* subsystem reflects behaviors related to procreation (Johnson, 1980). Both biological and social factors affect behaviors in the sexual sub-system. Again, the behaviors are related to culture and vary from culture to culture. Behaviors also vary according to the gender of the individual. The key is that the goal in all societies has the same outcome—behaviors acceptable to society at large.

The *aggressive* subsystem relates to behaviors concerned with protection and self-preservation. Johnson (1980) views the aggressive subsystem as one that generates defensive responses from the individual when life or territory is threatened. The aggressive subsystem does not include those behaviors with a primary purpose of injuring other individuals, but rather those whose purpose is to protect and preserve self and society.

Finally, the *achievement* subsystem provokes behaviors that attempt to control the environment. Intellectual, physical, creative, mechanical, and social skills are some of the areas that Johnson (1980) recognizes. Other areas of personal accomplishment or success may also be included in this subsystem.

Johnson's Behavioral System Model and Nursing's Metaparadigm

Johnson views *human beings* as having two major systems: the biological system and the behavioral system. It is the role of medicine to focus on the biological system, whereas nursing's focus is the behavioral system. There is recognition of the reciprocal actions that occur between the biological and behavioral systems when some type of dysfunction occurs in one or the other of the systems.

Society relates to the environment in which an individual exists. According to Johnson, an individual's behavior is influenced by all the events in the environment. Cultural influences on the individual's behavior are viewed as profound. However, it is felt that there are many paths, varying from culture to culture, that influence specific behaviors in a group of people, although the outcome for all the groups or individuals is the same.

Health is an elusive state that is determined by psychological, social, biological, and physiological factors (Johnson, 1978). Johnson's behavioral model supports the idea that the individual is attempting to maintain some balance or equilibrium. The individual's goal is to maintain the entire behavioral system efficiently and effectively but with enough flexibility to return to an acceptable balance if a malfunction disrupts the original balance.

Nursing's primary goal is to foster equilibrium within the individual, which allows for the practice of nursing with individuals at any point in the health-illness continuum. Nursing implementations may focus on alterations of a behavior that is not supportive to maintaining equilibrium for the individual. In earlier works, Johnson focused nursing on impaired individuals. By 1980, she stated that nursing is concerned with the organized and integrated whole, but that the major focus is on maintaining a balance in the behavioral system when illness occurs in the individual.

Johnson's Behavioral System and the Nursing Process

Johnson's Behavioral System Model easily fits the nursing process model. Grubbs (1980) developed an assessment tool based on Johnson's seven sub-systems, plus a subsystem she labeled "restorative," which focused on activities of daily living. Activities of daily living are considered to include such areas as patterns of rest, hygiene, and recreation. A diagnosis can be made related to insufficiencies or discrepancies within a subsystem or between sub-systems. Planning for the implementation of nursing care should start at the subsystem level with the ultimate goal of effective behavioral functioning of the entire system. Implementations by the nurse present to the client an external force for the manipulation of the subsystem back to the state of equilibrium. Evaluation of the result of this implementation is readily possible if the state of balance that is the goal has been defined during the planning phase before the implementation.

Assessment

In the assessment phase of the nursing process, questions related to specific subsystems are developed. Holaday (1980), Damus (1980), and Small (1980) propose that the assessment focus on the subsystem related to the presenting health problem. An assessment based on the behavioral subsystems does not easily permit the nurse to gather detailed information about the biological system. Assessment questions related to the affiliative subsystem might focus on the presence of a significant other or on the social system of which the individual is a member. In the assessment of the dependency subsystem, attention is placed on understanding how the individual makes needs known to significant others so that the significant others in the environment can assist the individual in meeting those needs. Assessment of the ingestive subsystem examines patterns of food and fluid intake, including the social environment in which the food and fluid are ingested. The eliminative subsystem generates questions related to patterns of defecation and urination and the social context in which the patterns occur. The sexual subsystem assessment includes information about sexual patterns and behaviors. The aggressive subsystem generates questions about how individuals protect themselves from perceived threats to safety. Finally, the achievement subsystem allows for assessment of how the individual changes the environment to facilitate the accomplishment of goals.

There are many gaps in information about the whole individual if only Johnson's Behavioral System Model is used to guide the assessment. There are few physiological data on the individual's present or past health status. The exception might be when an impaired health state is demonstrated in the ingestive or eliminative subsystems. Family interaction and patterns are touched on only in the affiliative and dependency subsystems. Basic information relating to education, socioeconomic status, and type of dwelling is tangentially related to most of the subsystems. However, these factors are not clearly identified as an important aspect of any of the subsystems.

Diagnosis

Diagnosis using Johnson's Behavioral System Model becomes cumbersome. Diagnosis tends to be general to a subsystem rather than specific to a problem. Grubbs (1980) has proposed four categories of nursing diagnoses derived from Johnson's Behavioral System Model, as follows:

1. *Insufficiency*—a state "which exists when a particular subsystem is not functioning or developed to its fullest capacity due to inadequacy of functional requirements. . .

2. *Discrepancy*—a behavior that does not meet the intended goal. The incongruity usually lies between the action and the goal of the subsystem, although the set and choice may be strongly influencing the ineffective action . . .

3. *Incompatibility*—the goals or behaviors of two subsystems in the same situation conflict with each other to the detriment of the individual . . .

4. *Dominance*—the behavior in one subsystem is used more than any other subsystem regardless of the situation or to the detriment of the other subsystems" (pp. 240–241).

Since Johnson has never written about the use of nursing diagnosis with her model, it is difficult to know whether these diagnostic classifications are Johnson's or if they are an extension of Johnson's work by Grubbs.

Planning and Implementation

Planning for implementation of the nursing care related to the diagnosis may be difficult because of the lack of client input into the plan. The plan focuses on the nurse's action to modify client behavior. These plans, then, have a goal: to bring about homeostasis in a subsystem that is based on the nurse's assessment of the individual's drive, set, behavioral repertoire, and observable behavior. The plan may include protection, nurturance, or stimulation of the identified subsystem.

Planning and implementation for clients that are based on Johnson's Behavioral System Model focus on maintaining or returning an individual's subsystem to a state of equilibrium. Implementation focuses on achieving the goals of nursing as identified by Johnson (1980). Although Johnson refers to the biological system in her goals of nursing, it is not included in her Behavioral System Model and can and does produce incongruities for the planning and implementation of nursing care in relation to a specific diagnosis.

Evaluation

Evaluation is based on the attainment of a goal of balance in the identified subsystems. If baseline data are available for the individual, the nurse may have a goal for the individual to return to the baseline behavior. If the alterations in behavior that are planned do occur, the nurse should be able to observe the return to previous behavior patterns.

There is little or no recognition by either Johnson (1980) or Grubbs (1980) of the client's input into plans for nursing implementation. They use the term *nursing intervention*. Holaday's (1980) example of implementation also does not contain strong client input. Using Johnson's Behavioral System Model with the nursing process is a nurse-centered activity, with the nurse determining the client's needs and the state of behavior appropriate to those needs.

Holaday (1980) demonstrates the flexibility available in the use of the Johnson Behavioral System Model with the nursing process by using a very specific assessment tool to determine appropriate interventions. Holaday uses tests of cognitive development developed by

Piaget to determine the level of information to present to a child during a preoperative teaching session.

Situation. An example of the use of the nursing process with Johnson's Behavioral System Model is demonstrated with Johnny Smith, age 6 weeks, brought into the clinic for a routine checkup. He presents with no weight gain since his checkup at age 2 weeks. His mother states that she feeds him but that he does not seem to eat much. He sleeps 4 to 5 hours between feedings. His mother holds him in her arms without making trunk-to-trunk contact. As the assessment is made, the nurse notes that Mrs. Smith never looks at Johnny and never speaks to him. She states that he was a planned baby but that she never "realized how much work an infant could be." She says her mother has told her she was not a good mother because Johnny is not gaining weight as he should. She states that she has not called the nurse when she knew Johnny was not gaining weight because she thought the nurse would think she was a "bad mother" just as her own mother thought she was a "bad mother."

Based on the information available and using the Johnson Behavioral System Model, assessment focuses on the affiliative and dependency subsystems between mother and Johnny. Further assessment of Mrs. Smith's relationship with her own mother needs to be done. The critical need is for Johnny to begin gaining weight. The secondary need is for Mrs. Smith to resolve her conflict with her own mother. The assessment of the affiliative subsystem focuses on the specific behaviors manifested by Johnny to indicate attachment to his mother. The assessment of the dependency subsystem focuses on the specific behaviors manifested by Johnny to cue his mother to his needs. Because of the nature of his problem, a decision is made to use a tool that specifically focuses on parent-infant interaction during a feeding situation. Thus, the Nursing Child Assessment Feeding Scale (Barnard, 1978) is used during a feeding that takes place at a normal feeding time for Johnny. Johnny cries at the beginning of the feeding and turns toward his mother's hand when she touches his cheek. Mrs. Smith does not speak to Johnny or in any verbal way acknowledge his hunger. When Johnny slightly chokes on some formula, she does not remove the bottle from his mouth. Mrs. Smith does not describe any of the environment to Johnny, nor does she stroke his body or make eye contact with him. Johnny does not reach out to touch his mother nor does he make any vocalizations. The assessment scale indicates that both mother and baby are not cueing each other at a level at which they can respond appropriately.

The diagnoses based on this assessment, using Johnson's Behavioral System Model, are, "insufficient development of the affiliative subsystem" and "insufficient development of the dependency subsystem." Based on these diagnoses, nursing implementation focuses on increasing Mrs. Smith's awareness of the meaning of Johnny's infrequent cues. By increasing her awareness of the meaning of his cues, she can begin to reinforce them so that he begins to know there is someone in the environment who cares about him, thus fostering his attachment to her. Further assistance needs to be given in helping Mrs. Smith in communicating with her infant. If further assessment indicates Mrs. Smith is uncomfortable talking with an infant who does not respond with words, it may be suggested that she read to Johnny from a book, thus providing him with needed verbal stimulation. Another implementation may include the nurse placing herself in Johnny's role and "talking" for him to his mother. The nurse may sit, watching Mrs. Smith hold Johnny, and say such things as "I like it when you pat me," "It feels good when you cuddle me," "When I turn my head like this, I'm hungry."

Evaluation of these implementations are based on two criteria. First, Johnny's weight gains or losses are carefully assessed. Not gaining weight places him in a life-threatening situation; therefore, it is critical that a pattern of weight gain be initiated. Second, the mother-infant interaction can be reassessed, again using the Nursing Child Assessment Feeding Scale

(Barnard, 1978), which allows for comparison of the first observation with a series of subsequent observations.

$\mathcal{Q}$ ohnson's Work and the Characteristics of a Theory

Johnson states that she is presenting a model related to subsystems of the human being that have observable behaviors leading to specific outcomes, although the method of attaining the specific outcomes may vary according to the culture of the individual. Johnson's Behavioral System Model is based on general system concepts. However, the definitions related to the terms used to label her concepts have not been made explicit by Johnson. Grubbs (1980) has presented her definitions of Johnson's terms, and those are the definitions most often reflected in the literature of other investigators claiming to use Johnson's model.

1. **Theories can interrelate concepts in such a way as to create a different way of looking at a particular phenomenon.** Johnson does not clearly interrelate her concepts of subsystems that comprise the Behavioral System Model.

2. **Theories must be logical in nature.** The lack of clear interrelationships among the concepts creates difficulty in following the logic of Johnson's work. The definitions of the concepts are so abstract that they are difficult to use. For example, intimacy is identified as an aspect of the affiliative subsystem, but the concept is not defined or described. An advantage of the abstract definition is that individuals using the model may identify an assessment tool that most specifically fits a problem and use it in their work. There are two major disadvantages. First, the abstract level and multiplicity of definitions make it difficult to compare the same subsystem across studies. Second, the lack of clear definitions for the interrelationships among and between the subsystems makes it difficult to view the entire behavioral system as an entity.

3. **Theories should be relatively simple yet generalizable.** Johnson's behavioral model can be generalized across the lifespan and across cultures. However, the focus on the behavioral system may make it difficult for nurses working with physically impaired individuals to use the model. Johnson's model is also very individual oriented, so that nurses working with groups of individuals with similar problems would have difficulty using the model. The subsystems in Johnson's Behavioral System Model are individual oriented to such an extent that the family can be considered only as the environment in which the individual presents behaviors and not as the focus of care.

4. **Theories are the bases for hypotheses that can be tested or for theory to be expanded,** and

5. **Theories contribute to and assist in increasing the general body of knowledge within the discipline through the research implemented to validate them.** It is difficult to test Johnson's model by the development of hypotheses. Subsystems of the model can be examined because relationships within the subsystems can be identified. The lack of definitions and connections between the subsystems creates a barrier for staling relationships in the form of hypotheses to be tested. Although such relationships may be predicted, the lack of definitions in the original work makes impossible to identify whether it is Johnson's work or someone's interpretation of her work that is being tested.

6. **Theories can be used by practitioners to guide and improve practice.** Johnson does not clearly define the expected outcomes when one of the subsystems is being

affected by nursing implementation. An implicit expectation is made that all humans in all cultures will attain the same outcome—homeostasis. Because of the lack of definitions, the model does not allow for control of the areas of interest, so it is difficult to use the model to guide practice. The authors reportedly using the model to guide practice have not integrated the subsystems to the degree necessary to label this model a theory.

7. **Theories must be consistent with other validated theories, laws, and principles but will leave open unanswered questions that need to be investigated.** Johnson's Behavioral System Model provides a framework for organizing human behavior. However, it is a different framework from that provided by other nursing theorists, such as Roy (1989) or Rogers (1970). Johnson believes that she is the first person to view "man as a behavioral system." Others have viewed the behavioral subsystem as just one piece of the biopsychosocial human being. Johnson's framework does contribute to the general body of nursing knowledge but needs further development. Johnson's Behavioral System Model is based on principles of general system theory. Her statements on the multiple modes of attaining the same subsystem goal, regardless of culture, are an example of the principle of "equifinality." As with Rogers (1970), this allows individuals to develop and change through time at unique rates but with the same outcomes at the end of the process: mature, adult behaviors that are culturally acceptable.

Johnson's Behavioral System Model is not as flexible as Rogers' (1970) concept of homeodynamics or Roy's (1989) adaptation model. Rogers' concepts are so broadly applicable that nursing care can take place at any level: individual, family, or community. All systems within the human being can be considered for the focus of nursing implementations. With Roy's model, the focus is still at the individual level, but the total human being can be considered. Roy's assumptions include that the human being is a biopsychosocial being, which allows for all the subsystems of a human being to be included for nursing assessment and implementation.

Johnson's Behavioral System Model is congruent with many of the nursing models in the belief that the individual is influenced by the environment. Since Nightingale (1859) first presented her beliefs about nursing, nurses have been concerned with the individual's relationship with the environment. In practice, nurses often have the necessary control over the environment to promote a healthier state for the individual.

In general, the Johnson Behavioral System Model does not meet the criteria for a theory. However, it must be stressed that Johnson does not suggest that she has developed a theory, although other nurse scholars have identified and used Johnson as a theorist.

Summary

Although Johnson's Behavioral System Model has many limitations, she does provide a frame of reference for nurses concerned with specific client behaviors. It must also be noted that Johnson, through her work at the University of California, Los Angeles, has had a profound influence on the development of nursing models and nursing theories. Through her position as a faculty member she influenced Roy, Grubbs, Holaday, and others. As a peer, she influenced Riehl, Neuman, Wu, and others, scholars who have generated many ideas about nursing concepts and theories.

Johnson's Behavioral System Model is a model of nursing care that advocates the fostering of efficient and effective behavioral functioning in the patient to prevent illness. The patient is identified as a behavioral system composed of seven behavioral subsystems: affiliative, dependency, ingestive, eliminative, sexual, aggressive, and achievement. Each subsystem is composed of four structural characteristics: drive, set, choices, and observable behaviors. The three functional requirements for each subsystem include protection from noxious influences, provision for a nurturing environment, and stimulation for growth. An imbalance in any of the behavioral subsystems results in disequilibrium. It is nursing's role to assist the client to return to a state of equilibrium.

References

Auger, J. R. (1976). *Behavioral systems and nursing*. Englewood Cliffs, NJ: Prentice-Hall.

Barnard, K. E. (1978). *Nursing Child Assessment Feeding Scale*. Seattle: University of Washington.

Chin, R. (1961). The utility of system models and developmental models for practitioners. In K. Benne, W. Bennis, & R. Chin (Eds.), *The planning of change*. New York: Holt.

Conner, S. S., Harbour, L. S., Magers, J. A., & Watt, J. K. (1994). Dorothy E. Johnson: Behavioral System Model. In A. Marriner-Tomey (Ed.), *Nursing theorists and their work* (3rd ed.) (pp. 231–245). St Louis: Mosby.

Damns, K. (1980). An application of the Johnson Behavioral System Model for Nursing Practice. In J. P. Riehl, & C. Roy (Eds.), *Conceptual models for nursing practice* (2nd ed.) (pp. 274–289). New York: Appleton-Century-Crofts.

Grubbs, J. (1980). An interpretation of the Johnson Behavioral System Model for nursing practice. In J. P. Riehl, & C. Roy (Eds.), *Conceptual models for nursing practice* (2nd ed.) (pp. 217–254). New York: Appleton-Century-Crofts.

Holaday, B. (1980). Implementing the Johnson Model for Nursing Practice. In J. P. Riehl, & C. Roy (Eds.), *Conceptual models for nursing practice* (2nd ed.) (pp. 255–263). New York: Appleton-Century-Crofts.

Johnson, D. E. (1959). The nature of a science of nursing. *Nursing Outlook, 7*, 291–294.

Johnson, D. E. (1961). The significance of nursing care. *American Journal of Nursing, 61*, 63–66.

Johnson, D. E. (1968, April). *One conceptual model of nursing*. Paper presented at Vanderbilt University, Nashville, Tennessee.

Johnson, D. E. (1968). Theory in nursing: Borrowed and unique. *Nursing Research, 17*, 206–209.

Johnson, D. E. (1974). Development of theory: A requisite for nursing as a profession. *Nursing Research, 23*, 372–377.

Johnson, D. E. (1978). State of the art of theory development in nursing. In *Theory development: What, why, how?* (pp. 1–10). New York: National League for Nursing.

Johnson, D. E. (1980). The Behavioral System Model for Nursing. In J. P. Riehl, & C. Roy (Eds.), *Conceptual models for nursing practice* (2nd ed.) (pp. 207–216). New York: Appleton-Century-Crofts.

Johnson, D. E. (1992). The origins of the Behavioral Systems Model. In F. Nightingale, *Notes on nursing: What it is and what it is not* (Com. ed.). Philadelphia: Lippincott. (Originally published, 1859).

Loveland-Cherry, C., & Wilkerson, S. A. (1989). Dorothy Johnson's Behavioral System Model. In J. Fitzpatrick, & A. Whall (Eds.), *Conceptual models of nursing: Analysis and application* (2nd ed.) (pp. 147–164). Norwalk, CT: Appleton & Lange.

Nightingale, F. (1992). *Notes on nursing: What it is, and what it is not* (Com. ed.). Philadelphia: Lippincott. (Originally published, 1859).

Rogers, M. (1970). *The theoretical basis for nursing*. Philadelphia: Davis.

Roy, C. (1989). The Roy Adaptation Model. In J. Riehl-Sisca (Ed.), *Conceptual models for nursing practice* (3rd ed.) (pp. 105–114). Norwalk, CT: Appleton & Lange.

Skolny, M. A., & Riehl, J. P. (1974). Hope: Solving patient and family problems by using a theoretical framework. In J. P. Riehl, & C. Roy (Eds.), *Conceptual models for nursing practice* (pp. 206–217). New York: Appleton-Century-Crofts.

Small, B. (1980). Nursing visually impaired children with Johnson's Model as a conceptual framework. In J. P. Riehl, & C. Roy (Eds.), *Conceptual models for nursing practice* (2nd ed.) (pp. 264–273). New York: Appleton-Century-Crofts.

Torres, G. (1986). *Theoretical foundations of nursing*. Norwalk, CT: Appleton-Century-Crofts.

Wu, R. (1973). *Behavior and illness*. Englewood Cliffs, NJ: Prentice-Hall.

$\mathcal{B}$ ibliography

Hardy, M. E. (1974). Theories: Components, development, evaluation. *Nursing Research, 23,* 100–107.

Johnson, D. E. (1978). *Behavioral System Model for Nursing*. Supplemental materials for Nursing Theorists General Session, the Second Annual Nurse Education Conference.

Neuman, B. (1995). *The Neuman Systems Model* (3rd ed.). Norwalk, CT; Appleton & Lange.

External Analysis

Relationship to Nursing Research

Research in nursing has been used to verify conceptual models and has led toward the goals of establishing the scientific base of nursing. Johnson (1974) states that nursing in the past was not based upon a scientific foundation, and this situation allows the nurse-researcher many choices that are not available to researchers in other fields. It is the nurse-researcher who will influence the development of both the scientific discipline and the professional practice of nursing. By choosing one of the nursing models for the basis of research, the researchers not only influence the profession, but also determine the direction of their own research. The behavioral system model leads the researcher in at least two directions. One person might choose to concentrate on the basic sciences, which are investigating the functioning of the subsystems as well as the functioning of the whole behavioral system. Another researcher may choose instead to investigate problems related to the behavioral system and methods of solving those problems. The area of applied research that deals with identification and solution of problems would be more closely linked to the practice of nursing as stated by Johnson (1959).

Nurse-researchers have demonstrated the usefulness of Johnson's model in clinical practice in a variety of ways. The nursing process and assessment have been studied in relation to the behavioral system model. When using the Johnson model, nursing assessments are based on the patterns that individuals have for meeting their needs. This requires that nurses determine patterns that the clients have rather than merely basing assessment of needs on the diagnosis (Crawford, 1982). Fawz (1979) employed Johnson's model to examine the behavioral characteristics of patients in isolation and found it useful. Damus (1980) developed a classification system for nursing diagnosis based on behavioral subsystems and effectively tested the model with serum hepatitis patients. In 1980, Grubbs also developed a patient assessment tool and described how the Johnson model is congruent with nursing process. Based on the Johnson model, a patient classification system was developed by Auger and Dee (1983). In the psychiatric setting, this patient classification system was found to increase communication as

Taken from: *Conceptual Models of Nursing: Analysis and Application*, Third Edition by Fitzpatrick and Whall.

well as help nurses identify their role. Their classification system was found to be applicable to most clinical settings and to all ages (Dee & Auger, 1983).

Johnson's behavioral system model has also been used as a framework for nursing intervention. Norris (1970) developed a framework that is compatible with the behavioral system approach and adapts itself to the individual patterns of the client, thus allowing "personalization" of nursing intervention. A combination of the behavioral system model and body image theory was found effective in providing nursing care to an amputee patient (Rawls, 1980). Broncatello (1980) applied Auger's (1975) expanded version of Johnson's behavioral system model to the care of patients receiving hemodialysis. She found that this model permitted the personalization of care and also provided the basis of support for adaptive behavior while identifying maladaptive behavior. Derdiarian (1983a) investigated cancer patients' behavioral changes in relation to Johnson's behavioral system model. She developed an instrument to measure behavioral changes (Derdiarian, 1983b), and her research supported the contention that behavioral instability results from illness. In recent works, Derdiarian (1990; 1991) further analyzed Johnson's premise of open and interactive subsystems in cancer patients. Derdiarian concluded that while all the subsystems should be considered, changes in the aggressive-protective subsystem may be the more important indicator for early intervention needs in cancer patients. On the other side of the issue, Reynolds and Comack (1991) report that nursing practice in their institution is based on Johnson's model, and it has been found to be very useful in making nursing diagnoses but can only provide "hints rather than specifics" about nursing interventions.

Johnson's model has also been researched in the nursing care of children and their families. Holaday (1974) compared the achievement behavior of chronically ill and healthy children. The achievement subsystem of the behavioral system model was used as a framework for this study. She used Johnson's concept of "behavioral set" to help ascertain how mothers of chronically ill infants develop responses to their children's crying (Holaday, 1981a, 1981b, 1982). Skolny and Riehl (1974) found the model useful in developing a plan of action to help the mother of a dying young man maintain hope. Johnson's model was used to explain the findings of a study of handicapped preschool children whose body image and spatial awareness was compared with those of normal children (Small, 1980). An assessment tool of family functioning based on the behavioral system model was developed by Lovejoy (1983) and was evaluated in a study of leukemic children. She found that these children were affected by their perceptions of family behavioral disturbances that demonstrated an interaction between systems. Following the description of Campbell and Bunting (1991) of research in the study of emancipation, Cox (1994) based her work on Johnson's model and did not use "triangulation" just as a methodological technique but as an attempt to identify the client system interdependence in her study of mothers and their newborns. All these research studies have tested the behavioral model system and have in-creased nursing's body of knowledge.

*R*elationship to Nursing Education

Nursing education based on the behavioral system model would have definite goals, and course planning would be relatively straightforward. A background in biology, psychology, and sociology would be necessary for complete understanding of the behavioral system. The primary focus of nursing education would be the study of the person as a behavioral system. Behavioral subsystems could be identified as areas for nursing specialization (Rogers, 1973). Also included would be the study of behavioral system problems that would require the use of the nursing process in relation to disruptions in behavioral system functioning. Johnson states that the study of behavioral system problems presents difficulties for curriculum content development because "the knowledge base tends to be disorganized and more intuitive and speculative than scientific" (Johnson, 1980, p. 215).

Relationship to Professional Nursing Practice

Nursing practice is operationalized by its definition in the behavioral system model. The model itself states the "end product," which is the goal of nursing practice (Johnson, 1968c). Nursing's objective is to maintain or restore the person's behavioral system balance and stability or to help the person achieve an optimum level of function. Change of any magnitude toward recovery from illness or toward more desirable health practices depends upon the periodic achievement and maintenance, perhaps for only a short time, of this stable state.

An example of practice based on Johnson's model would be preoperative teaching. By giving patients information concerning their surgery and what they can expect to have happen both preoperatively and postoperatively and by providing support by listening to their concerns and questions, their tension, anxiety, and fatigue would be reduced. This reduction would help them to develop attitudes and behaviors leading to the achievement of equilibrium. Assessment of the effectiveness of preoperative teaching would be included in the nursing process.

With the goal of maintaining or restoring balance to an individual's behavioral system clearly stated, nursing can develop precise measurements for evaluating the efficacy of nursing action. Patient indicators of nursing care based on Johnson's model were developed by Majesky, Brester, and Nishio (1978) and tested with a number of patients with a variety of diagnoses. This tool is considered one measure of quality nursing care. Glennin (1980) specifically classified standards of nursing practice with the concepts of Johnson's model and found it useful. Holaday (1981b) also wrote of the use of this model as a measure of quality health care. Using the operational indices of behavior developed by Auger and Dee (1983) from Johnson's model, nurses in a California neuropsychiatric hospital have been able to actively evaluate outcomes of nursing inter-ventions (Reynolds & Cormack, 1991). In addition to this application of the behavioral system model as a measure of quality, numerous research studies cited above (Auger & Dee, 1983; Broncatello, 1980; Damus, 1980; Derdiarian, 1983a; Holaday, 1974; Lovejoy, 1983; Rawls, 1980) have demonstrated the usefulness of this model in nursing practice in a variety of settings.

References

Auger, J. A. (1975). *Behavioral systems and nursing.* Englewood Cliffs, NJ: Prentice-Hall.

Auger, J. A., & Dee, V. (1983). A patient classification system based on the behavioral system model of nursing: Part 1. *The Journal of Nursing Administration, 13,* 38–43.

Broncatello, K. F. (1980). Auger in action: Application of the model. *Advances in Nursing Science, 2*(2), 13–24.

Bush, H. A. (1979). Models for nursing. *Advances in Nursing Science, 1,* 13–20.

Campbell, J., & Bunting, S. (1991). Voices and paradigms: Perspectives on critical and feminist theory in nursing. *Advances in Nursing Science, 13*(3), 1–15.

Chinn, P. L., & Jacobs, M. K. (1983). *Theory and nursing: A systematic approach.* St. Louis: C. V. Mosby.

Crawford, G. (1982). The concept of patterns in nursing: Conceptual development and measurement. *Advances in Nursing Science, 5,* 1–6.

Cox, M. (1994). *Statistical analysis triangulation of infant outcomes of a nurse managed obstetrical clinic.* Paper presented at the Texas Medical Center National Nursing Research Conference, Houston, TX.

Damus, K. (1980). An application of the Johnson behavioral system model for nursing practice. In J. P. Riehl & S. C. Roy (Eds.), *Conceptual models for nursing practice* (2nd ed.). New York: Appleton-Century-Crofts.

Dee, V., & Auger, J. A. (1983). A patient classification system based on the behavioral system model of nursing: Part 2. *The Journal of Nursing Administration, 13,* 18–23.

Dee, V., & Randell, B. (1989). *N.P.H. Patient classification system: theory-based nursing practice model for staffing.* Nursing Department, UCLA Neuro-Psychiatric Institute and Hospital, Los Angeles.

Derdiarian, A. K. (1983a). An instrument for theory and research development using the behavioral system model for nursing: The cancer patient: Part 1. *Nursing Research, 32*(4), 196–201.

Derdiarian, A. K. (1983b). An instrument for theory and research development using the behavioral system model for nursing: The cancer patient: Part 2. *Nursing Research, 32*(5), 260–266.

Derdiarian, A. K. (1990). The relationships among the subsystems of Johnson's behavioral system model. *IMAGE: Journal of Nursing Scholarship, 22*(4), 219–225.

Derdiarian, A. K. (1991). Effects of using a nursing model-based assessment instrument on quality of nursing care. *Nursing Administration Quarterly, 15*(3), 1–16.

Dubin, R. (1978). *Theory building.* New York: The Free Press.

Ellis, R. (1968). Characteristics of significant theories. *Nursing Research, 17,* 217–222.

Fawz, N. W. (1979). *Development of methodology and examination of characteristics of isolation patients utilizing the Johnson model.* Unpublished master's thesis, University of California.

Glennin, C. (1980). Formulation of standards of nursing practice using a nursing model. In J. P. Riehl & S. C. Roy (Eds.), *Conceptual models for nursing practice* (2nd ed.). New York: Appleton-Century-Crofts.

Grubbs, J. (1980). An interpretation of the Johnson model for nursing practice. In J. P. Riehl & S. C. Roy (Eds.), *Conceptual models for nursing practice* (2nd ed.). New York: Appleton-Century-Crofts.

Hardy, M. E. (1974). Theories: Components, development, evaluation. *Nursing Research, 23,* 99–106.

Holaday, B. (1974). Achievement behavior in chronically ill children. *Nursing Research, 23,* 25–30.

Holaday, B. (1980). Implementing the Johnson model for nursing practice. In J. P. Riehl & S. C. Roy (Eds.), *Conceptual models for nursing practice* (2nd ed.). New York: Appleton-Century-Crofts.

Holaday, B. (1981a). Maternal response to their chronically ill infants' attachment behavior of crying. *Nursing Research, 30,* 343–348.

Holaday, B. (1981b). The Johnson behavioral system model for nursing and the pursuit of quality health care. In G. E. Lasker (Ed.), *Applied systems and cybernetics,* Vol. 4, *Systems research in health care, biocybernetics and ecology.* New York: Pergamon.

Holaday, B. (1982). Maternal conceptual set development: Identifying patterns of maternal response to chronically ill infant crying. *Maternal–Child Nursing Journal, 11,* 47–59.

Jacox, A. (1974). Theory construction in nursing: An overview. *Nursing Research, 23,* 4–13.

Johnson, D. E. (1959a). A philosophy of nursing. *Nursing Outlook, 7,* 198–200.

Johnson, D. E. (1959b). The nature of a science of nursing. *Nursing Outlook 7,* 291–294.

Johnson, D. E. (1961). The significance of nursing care. *American Journal of Nursing, 61*(11), 63–66.

Johnson, D. E. (1968a). Theory in nursing: Borrowed and unique. *Nursing Research, 17*(3), 206–209.

Johnson, D. E. (1968b). Toward a science of nursing. *Southern Medical Bulletin, 56*(4), 13–23.

Johnson, D. E. (1968c). *One conceptual model of nursing*. Paper presented at Vanderbilt University.

Johnson, D. E. (1974). Development of theory: A requisite for nursing as a primary health profession. *Nursing Research, 23*(5), 372–377.

Johnson, D. E. (1978a). State of the art of theory development in nursing. In *Theory development: What, why, how?* New York: National League for Nursing.

Johnson, D. E. (1978b). *Behavioral system model for nursing*. Presented at the 2nd Annual Nurse Educator Conference.

Johnson, D. E. (1980). The behavioral system model for nursing. In J. P. Riehl & S. C. Roy (Eds.), *Conceptual models for nursing practice* (2nd ed.). New York: Appleton-Century-Crofts.

Lovejoy, N. (1983). The leukemic child's perceptions of family behaviors. *Oncology Nursing Forum, 10*(4), 20–25.

Majesky, S. J., Brester, M. H., & Nishio, K. T. (1978). Development of a research tool: Patient indicators of nursing care. *Nursing Research, 27*(6), 365–371.

Norris, C. M. (1970). The professional nurse and body image. In C. E. Carlson (Ed.), *Behavioral concepts and nursing intervention*. Philadelphia: J. B. Lippincott.

North American Nursing Diagnosis Association (1986). *NANDA nursing diagnosis taxonomy I*. St. Louis: North American Nursing Diagnosis Association, St. Louis University School of Nursing.

Rapoport, A. (1968). Foreword. In W. Buckley (Ed.), *Modern systems research for the behavioral scientist*. Chicago: Aldine.

Rawls, A. C. (1980). Evaluation of the Johnson behavioral model for clinical practice. Report on a test and evaluation of the Johnson theory. *IMAGE: Journal of Nursing Scholarship 12*(1), 13–16.

Reynolds, W., & Cormack, D. (1991). An evaluation of the Johnson behavioral system model of nursing. *Journal of Advanced Nursing, 16*, 1122–1130.

Rogers, C. G. (1973). Conceptual models as guides to clinical nursing specialization. *The Journal of Nursing Education, 12*, 2–6.

Silva, M. C. (1977). Philosophy, science, theory: Interrelationships and implications for nursing research. *IMAGE: Journal of Nursing Scholarship, 9*, 59–63.

Skolny, M. A., & Riehl, J. P. (1974). Hope: Solving patient and family problems by using a theoretical framework. In J. P. Riehl & S. C. Roy (Eds.), *Conceptual models for nursing practice*. New York: Appleton-Century-Crofts.

Small, B. (1980). Nursing visually impaired children with Johnson's model as a conceptual framework. In J. P. Riehl & S. C. Roy (Eds.), *Conceptual models for nursing practice*. New York: Appleton-Century-Crofts.

Stevens, B. (1979). *Nursing theory—Analysis, applications, evaluation*. Boston: Little Brown.

Walker, L. O., & Avant, K. C. (1983). *Strategies for theory construction in nursing*. East Norwalk, CT: Appleton-Century-Crofts.

Callista Roy

Julia Gallagher Galbreath

Callista Roy, RN, PhD (b. 1939) is a nurse theorist at Boston College, Massachusetts. Before this appointment, Roy was a Post-Doctoral Fellow and Robert Wood Johnson Clinical Nurse Scholar at the University of California, San Francisco. Roy has served in many positions, including Chair of the Department of Nursing, Mount Saint Mary's College, Los Angeles; Adjunct Professor, Graduate Program, School of Nursing, University of Portland; and Acting Director and Nurse Consultant, Saint Mary's Hospital, Tucson, Arizona. Roy earned her BS in nursing in 1963 from Mount Saint Mary's College, Los Angeles; her MS in nursing in 1966 and doctorate in sociology in 1977 from the University of California, Los Angeles. She is a Fellow of the American Academy of Nursing and active in many nursing organizations including Sigma Theta Tau and the North American Nursing Diagnosis Association (NANDA). She is the author or co-author of a number of works including Introduction to nursing: An adaptation model; Essentials of the Roy Adaptation Model; Theory construction in nursing: An Adaptation Model; *and* The Roy Adaptation Model: The definitive statement.

The Roy Adaptation Model has evoked much interest and respect since its inception in 1964 by Roy as part of her graduate work at the University of California, Los Angeles, under the guidance of Dorothy E. Johnson. In 1970, the faculty of Mount Saint Mary's College in Los Angeles adopted the Roy Adaptation Model as the conceptual framework of the undergraduate nursing curriculum. A text was written by Roy and fellow faculty describing the Roy

Taken from: *Nursing Theories: The Base for Professional Nursing Practice*, Fourth Edition by George.

Adaptation Model and presenting nursing assessment and intervention reflective of the distinctive focus of the Model. In 1991 Roy and Andrews wrote a clinical practice text, *The Roy adaptation model: The definitive statement*. It presents the collective experiences of several contributing authors who have taught and practiced using the Roy model for the past 20 years. Based upon four earlier books, it includes the diagrammatic conceptualizations of the model developed at the Royal Alexandra Hospitals School of Nursing, Edmonton, Alberta, Canada, and published in *Essentials of the Roy adaptation model* (Andrews & Roy, 1986).

Further, Roy and Roberts (1981) wrote *Theory construction in nursing: An adaptation model* to discuss the use of the Roy model to construct nursing theory. The reader who is excited by the model will find that a rich response has been made and continues to be made by nurse practitioners, educators, and researchers in the analysis, testing, and application of the model for nursing (Gaertzen, 1991; Rambo, 1983; Randell, Tedrow, & Van Landingham, 1982; Riehl-Sisca, 1989).

The Roy Adaptation Model

Roy credits the works of von Bertalanffy's (1968) general system theory and Helson's (1964) adaptation theory as forming the basis of the scientific assumptions underlying the Roy model. The philosophic assumptions flow, according to Roy, from humanism and veritivity. The term *veritivity* was coined by Roy to identify the common purposefulness of human existence (Roy & Andrews, 1991). Table 4–1 identifies the assumptions underlying the Roy Model.

The four essential elements of the Roy Adaptation Model are the following:

TABLE 4–1   Assumptions Underlying the Roy Adaptation Model

Scientific	
Systems Theory	Adaptation-Level Theory
Holism	Behavior as adaptive
Interdependence	Adaptation as a function of stimuli and adaptation level
Control processes	
Information feedback	Individual, dynamic adaptation levels
Complexity of living systems	Positive and active processes of responding

Philosophic	
Humanism	Veritivity
Creativity	Purposefulness of human existence
Purposefulness	Unity of purpose
Holism	Activity, creativity
Interpersonal process	Value and meaning of life

(From Roy, C., & Andrews, H. A. (Eds.). (1991). The Roy adaptation model: The definitive statement (p. 5). Norwalk, CT: Appleton & Lange. Used with permission.)

1. The person who is the recipient of nursing care

2. The concept of environment

3. The concept of health

4. Nursing (Roy & Andrews, 1991, pp. 5–6).

The model presents concepts related to these four areas, clarifying each and defining their interrelationships.

The Person

The first area of concern is the identity of the recipient of nursing care. Roy (1984) states that the recipient of nursing care may be the person, a family, a group, a community, or a society. Each is considered by the nurse as a holistic adaptive system. The idea of an adaptive system combines the concepts of system and adaptation.

System. First, consider the concept of a system as applied to an individual. Roy conceptualizes the person in a holistic perspective. Individual aspects of parts act together to form a unified being. Additionally, as living systems, persons are in constant interaction with their environments. Between the system and the environment occurs an exchange of information, matter, and energy. Characteristics of a system include inputs, outputs, controls, and feedback. Figure 4–2 illustrates a simple system.

Dunn (1971), a system theorist, calls our attention to the smallest unit of life, the cell. The cell is a living open system. The cell has its inner and outer worlds. From its outer world, it must

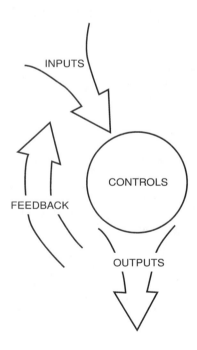

FIGURE 4–2

Diagrammatic representation of a simple system. *(From Roy, C., & Andrews, H. A. (Eds.). (1991).* The Roy adaptation model: The definitive statement *(p. 7). Norwalk, CT: Appleton & Lange. Used with permission.)*

draw forth the substances it needs to survive. Within itself, the cell must maintain order over its vast numbers of molecules. System openness, therefore, implies the constant exchanging of information, matter, and energy between the system and the environment. These system qualities are held by the person.

Adaptation. Figure 4-3 is used by Roy to represent the adaptive system of a person. The adaptive system has inputs of stimuli and adaptation level, outputs as behavioral responses that serve as feedback, and control processes known as coping mechanisms (Roy & Andrews, 1991). The adaptive system has input coming from the external environment as well as from the person. Roy identifies inputs as stimuli and adaptation level. Stimuli are conceptualized as falling into three classifications: focal, contextual, and residual. The stimulus most immediately confronting the person is the *focal stimulus*. The focal stimulus normally constitutes the greatest degree of change impacting upon the person. *Contextual stimuli* are all other stimuli of the person's internal and external world that can be identified as having a positive or negative influence on the situation. *Residual stimuli* are those internal or external factors whose current effects are unclear.

Along with stimuli, the adaptation level of the person acts as input to that person as an adaptive system. The focal, contextual, and residual stimuli combine and interface to set the adaptation level of the person at a particular point in time. This range of response is unique to the individual; each person's adaptation level is constantly changing. Significant stimuli that comprise the focal, contextual, and residual stimuli include factors such as the degree of change, past experiences, knowledge level, strengths, and/or limitations. Roy used Helson's (1964) work to develop this construct.

Outputs of the person as a system are the responses of the person (see Fig. 4–3). Output responses can be both external and internal. Thus, these responses are the person's behaviors. They can be observed, intuitively perceived by the nurse, measured and subjectively reported

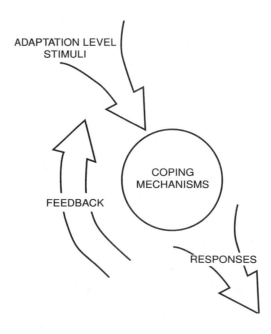

FIGURE 4–3

The person as a system. *(From Roy, C., & Andrews, H. A. (Eds.). (1991). The Roy adaptation model: The definitive statement (p. 8). Norwalk, CT: Appleton & Lange. Used with permission.)*

by the person. Output responses become feedback to the person and to the environment. Roy has categorized outputs of the system as either adaptive responses or ineffective responses. *Adaptive responses* are those that promote the integrity of the person. The person's integrity, or wholeness, is behaviorally demonstrated when the person is able to meet the goals in terms of survival, growth, reproduction, and mastery. *Ineffective responses* do not support these goals (Roy & Andrews, 1991).

Roy has used the term *coping mechanisms* to describe the control processes of the person as an adaptive system. Some coping mechanisms are inherited or genetic, such as the white blood cell defense system against bacteria that seek to invade the body. Other mechanisms are learned, such as the use of antiseptics to cleanse a wound. Roy presents a unique nursing science concept of control mechanisms that are called the *regulator* and the *cognator*. Roy's model considers the regulator and cognator coping mechanisms to be subsystems of the person as an adaptive system.

The *regulator subsystem* has the components of input, internal process, and output. Input stimuli may originate externally or internally to the person. The transmitters of the regulator system are chemical, neural, or endocrine in nature. Autonomic reflexes, which are neural responses originating in the brain stem and spinal cord, are generated as output responses of the regulator subsystem. Target organs and tissues under endocrine control also produce regulator output responses. Finally, Roy presents psychomotor responses originating from the central nervous system as regulator subsystem responses (Roy & Roberts, 1981). Many physiological processes can be viewed as regulator subsystem responses. For example, several regulatory feedback mechanisms of respiration have been identified. One of these is increased carbon dioxide, the end product of metabolism, which stimulates chemoreceptors in the medulla to increase the respiratory rate. Strong stimulation of these centers can increase ventilation six- to sevenfold (Guyton, 1971).

An example of a regulator process is when a noxious external stimulus is visualized and transmitted via the optic nerve to higher brain centers and then to lower brain autonomic centers. The sympathetic neurons from these origins have multiple visceral effects, including increased blood pressure and increased heart rate. Roy's schematic representation of the regulator processes is seen in Figure 4–4.

The other control subsystem original to the Roy model is the *cognator subsystem* (Roy & Andrews, 1991). Stimuli to the cognator subsystem are also both external and internal in origin. Output responses of the regulator subsystem can be feedback stimuli to the cognator subsystem. Cognator control processes are related to the higher brain functions of perception or information processing, judgment, and emotion. Perception, or information processing, is related to the internal processes of selective attention, coding, and memory. Learning is correlated to the processes of imitation, reinforcement, and insight. Problem solving and decision making are the internal processes related to judgment; and finally, emotion has the processes of defense to seek relief, affective appraisal, and attachment. A schematic presentation by Roy of the cognator subsystem is presented in Figure 4–5.

In maintaining the integrity of the person, the regulator and cognator are postulated as frequently acting together. The adaptation level of the person as an adaptive system is influenced by the individual's development and use of these coping mechanisms. Maximal use of coping mechanisms broadens the adaptation level of the person and increases the range of stimuli to which the person can positively respond.

Situation. A decrease in the oxygen supply to Albert Smith's heart muscle stimulates pain receptors that transmit the message of pain along sympathetic afferent nerve fibers to his central nervous system. The autonomic centers of his lower brain then stimulate the sympathetic efferent nerve fibers, and there is an increase in heart and respiratory rates. The result is an

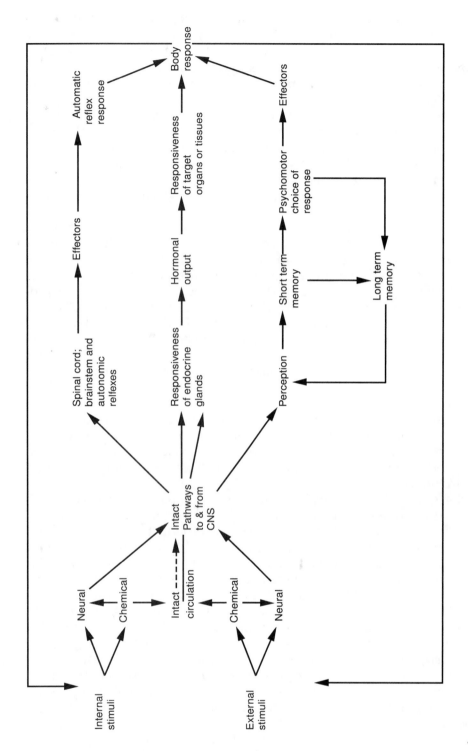

FIGURE 4–4

The **Regulator.** *(From Roy, C., & McLeod, D. (1984). Theory of the person as an adaptive system. In Roy, C., & Roberts, S. L. Theory construction in nursing: An adaptation model (p. 61). Englewood Cliffs, NJ: Prentice-Hall. Used with permission.)*

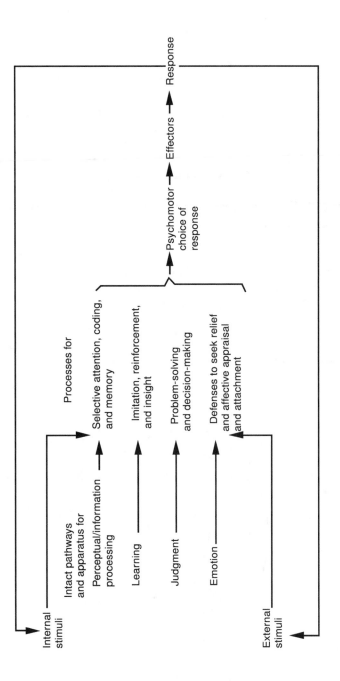

The Cognator. *(From Roy, C., & McLeod, D. (1984). Theory of the person as an adaptive system. In Roy, C., & Roberts, S. L., Theory construction in nursing: An adaptation model (p. 64). Englewood Cliffs, NJ: Prentice-Hall. Used with permission.)*

FIGURE 4–5

increase in the oxygen supply to the heart muscle. This increase can be viewed as regulator subsystem action.

The cognator subsystem also receives the internal pain stimuli as input. Mr. Smith has learned from past experiences that the left chest and arm pain is related to his heart. His judgment is activated in deciding what action to take. He decides to go inside to air conditioning, to sit with his legs elevated, and to take slow, deep breaths. He also decides not to call for emergency help. Certainly, he believes an adaptive response secondary to these actions will occur. However, he may be increasingly alert for further regulator sub-system output responses that might cause him to question his decision. This represents the cognator process of selective attention and coding. Following the episode of pain, Mr. Smith may attempt to gain further insight into the cause of the episode. He may decide that the 90°F weather was causal and remember to limit his activities during extreme heat. In this example, Mr. Smith used the cognator subsystem processes of perception, learning, and judgment.

Although cognator and regulator processes are essential to the adaptive response of the person, these processes are not directly observable. Only the responses of the person can be observed, measured, or subjectively reported. Roy has identified four *adaptive modes* or categories for assessment of behavior that results from the regulator and cognator mechanism responses. These *adaptive modes* are the physiological, self-concept, role function, and interdependence modes (Roy & Andrews, 1991). Behavior related to the modes is the manifestation of the *stimuli*: the person's adaptation level and coping processes. By observing the person's behavior in relation to the adaptive modes, the nurse can identify adaptive or ineffective responses in situations of health and illness. Figure 4-6 diagrammatically conceptualizes the person as an adaptive system that includes the four adaptive modes for assessment.

The four adaptive modes require further explanation. They are as follows.

> *Physiological Mode.* The physiological mode represents physical response to environmental stimuli and primarily involves the regulator subsystem. The basic need of this mode is physiologic integrity and is composed of the needs associated with oxygena-

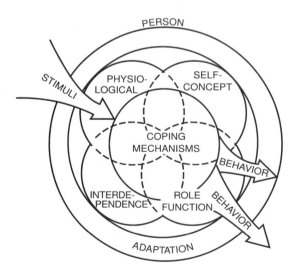

FIGURE 4–6

The person as an adaptive system. *(From Roy, C., & Andrews, H. A. (Eds.). (1991). The Roy adaptation model: The definitive statement (p. 17). Norwalk, CT: Appleton & Lange. Used with permission.)*

tion, nutrition, elimination, activity and rest, and protection. The complex processes of this mode are associated with the senses, fluid and electrolytes, neurological function, and endocrine function (Andrews & Roy, 1991). These needs and processes may be defined as follows:

- *Oxygenation:* The pattern of oxygen use related to respiratory and cardiovascular physiology and pathophysiology (Thompson, 1991).

- *Nutrition:* Patterns of nutrient use for maintaining human functioning, promoting growth, and repairing injured tissue (Servonsky, 1991b).

- *Elimination:* Patterns of elimination of waste products (Servonsky, 1991a).

- *Activity and Rest:* Patterns of activity and rest (Roy, 1991a).

- *Protection:* Patterns related to skin integrity and immunity (Sato, 1991).

- *Senses:* The input channel of the person through which sensory-perceptual information is processed (Roy, 1991c).

- *Fluids and Electrolytes:* The complex process of maintaining body fluids and electrolytes in balance for the person (Jensen, 1991).

- *Neurological function:* Key neural processes and the complex relationship of neural function to regulator and cognator coping mechanisms (Roy, 1991b).

- *Endocrine function:* Patterns of endocrine control and regulation that act in conjunction with the nervous system to maintain control of body processes (Chalifoux, 1991).

Self-Concept Mode. The self-concept mode relates to the basic need for psychic integrity. Its focus is on the psychological and spiritual aspects of the person. Attention is given to the subcategories of physical self and personal self. The physical self has the components of body sensation and body image. The personal self has the components of self-consistency, self-ideal, and moral-ethical-spiritual self. Body sensation is how the person experiences the physical self, and body image is how the person views the physical self. Self-consistency represents the person's efforts to maintain self-organization and to avoid disequilibrium. Self-ideal represents what the person expects to be and do, and the moral-ethical-spiritual self represents the person's belief system and self-evaluator (Andrews, 1991b).

Role Function Mode. The role function mode identifies the patterns of social interaction of the person in relation to others reflected by primary, secondary, and tertiary roles. The basic need met is social integrity (Andrews, 1991a). The primary role determines the majority of a person's behaviors and is defined by the person's sex, age, and developmental stage. Secondary roles are assumed to carry out the tasks required by the stage of development and primary role. Tertiary roles are temporary, freely chosen, and may include activities related to hobbies. Behaviors in this mode are described as instrumental or expressive. Instrumental behaviors are usually physical, have a long-term orientation, and focus on role mastery. Expressive-behaviors represent feelings or attitudes, are usually emotional, and seek immediate response.

Interdependence Mode. The interdependence mode is where affectional needs are met. Strongly reflective of the humanistic values held by Roy, the interdependence mode identifies patterns of human value, affection, love, and affirmation. These processes occur through interpersonal relationships on both individual and group levels (Tedrow, 1991).

Environment

Stimuli from within the person and stimuli from around the person represent the element of environment, according to Roy. Environment is specifically defined by Roy as "all conditions, circumstances, and influences that surround and affect the development and behavior of persons and groups" (Roy & Andrews, 1991, p. 18).

Commonly occurring internal and external stimuli of the environment are an area of study for nursing. For example, when an elderly client is institutionalized, significant external environmental stimuli have impinged upon him or her. The study of this environmental condition aids nurses in promoting adaptation to this change or, perhaps more ideally, defining interventions that minimize the risk of institutionalization for the elderly. Similarly, nurses are increasing their involvement in the institutions of our nation: health, education, industry, and politics. By their involvement, they are altering the environmental stimuli related to situations of health and illness in a broad and often far-reaching manner at a community system level.

Health

Previously, the Roy model defined health as a continuum from death to high-level wellness. This continuum is not used in the present model. Instead, Roy defines health as "a state and a process of being and becoming an integrated and whole person" (Roy & Andrews, 1991, p. 19). The integrity of the person is expressed as the ability to meet the goals of survival, growth, reproduction, and mastery. The aim of the nurse practicing under the Roy model is to promote the health of the person by promoting adaptive responses.

Goal of Nursing

Roy defines the *goal of nursing* as the promotion of adaptive responses in relation to the four adaptive modes. *Adaptive responses* are those that positively affect health. Stimuli and the person's adaptation level are inputs to the person as an adaptive system. The person's adaptation level determines whether a positive response to internal or external stimuli will be elicited. Nursing seeks to reduce ineffective responses and promote adaptive responses as output behavior of the person. The nurse, therefore, promotes health in all life processes, including dying with dignity (Roy & Andrews, 1991).

In the example of the person experiencing chest pain, the stimulus immediately confronting Albert Smith, the focal stimulus is the deficit of oxygen supply to his heart muscle. The contextual stimuli include the 90°F temperature, the sensation of pain, and Mr. Smith's age, weight, blood sugar level, and degree of coronary artery patency. The residual stimuli include his history of cigarette smoking and work-related stress.

For Mr. Smith, the stimuli, adaptation level, and coping processes have resulted in an ineffective response. The deficit of oxygen to his heart is a threat to his physiologic integrity and will not maintain his survival. This response became feedback to the system and a focal stimulus. Mr. Smith used the cognator mechanism to adjust the total stimuli by going indoors to a cooler room and decreasing his oxygen needs by sitting down and elevating his legs. After the adjustment of the stimuli, the oxygen needs of his heart muscle were met, and the pain stopped.

A person's ability to cope varies with the state of the person at different times. For example, the person who has suffered major trauma has a narrowed zone of adaptation and may not survive exposure to a bacterial infection. That same person before the injury may have tolerated exposure to the same bacteria without developing any symptoms of illness.

Nursing activities or intervention are delineated by the model as those that promote adaptive responses in situations of health and illness. As a rule, these approaches are identified as actions taken by the nurse to manage the focal, contextual, or residual stimuli impinging on the person. By making these adjustments, the total stimuli fall within the adaptation level of the person. Whenever possible, the focal stimulus—that which represents the greatest degree of change—is the focus of nursing activity. For a person with chest pain, the focal stimulus is the imbalance between the demand for oxygen by the body and the supply of oxygen that the heart can provide. To alter the focal stimuli, the nurse manages the stimuli of demand so that an adaptive response can be made. In turn, when focal stimuli cannot be altered, the nurse promotes an adaptive response by altering contextual stimuli (Roy & Andrews, 1991).

Additionally, the nurse may anticipate that the person has a potential for ineffective responses secondary to stimuli likely to be present in a particular situation. The nurse acts to prepare the person for the anticipated changes through strengthening regulator and cognator coping mechanisms. Plans that broaden the person's adaptation level correlate with the ideas of health promotion currently found in the literature. Finally, nursing actions suggested by the model include approaches aimed at maintaining adaptive responses that support the person's efforts to creatively use his or her coping mechanisms.

The Nursing Process

The Roy Adaptation Model offers guidelines to the nurse in application of the nursing process. The elements of the Roy nursing process include assessment of behavior, assessment of stimuli, nursing diagnosis, goal setting, intervention, and evaluation (Roy & Andrews, 1991). The six elements of Roy's nursing process parallel the five phases of the nursing process identified in an earlier section.

Behavioral Assessment

Behavioral assessment is considered to be the gathering of responses or output behaviors of the person as an adaptive system in relation to each of the four adaptive modes: physiological, self-concept, role function, and interdependence. The specific data are gathered by the nurse through the processes of observation, careful measurement, and skilled interview techniques.

Assessment of the client in each of the four adaptive modes enhances a systematic and holistic approach. Such assessment clarifies the focus that the nurse or nursing team will take in caring for the client. Ideally, thoroughly conducted and recorded nursing assessment in the four adaptive modes sets the tone of understanding for an entire health care team of the particular situation of a client. Proficiency in the practice of nursing requires skilled assessment of behaviors and the knowledge to compare the person to specific criteria to evaluate behavioral response as adaptive or ineffective. Behavior that varies from expectations, norms, and guidelines frequently represents ineffective responses. Roy has identified frequently occurring signs of pronounced regulator activity and cognator ineffectiveness (see Table 4–2). The presence of these behaviors also suggests ineffective responses.

TABLE 4–2   Indications of Adaptation Difficulty

Signs of pronounced regulator activity:
1. increase in heart rate or blood pressure
2. tension
3. excitement
4. loss of appetite
5. increase in serum cortisol

Signs of cognator ineffectiveness include:
1. faulty perception/information processing
2. ineffective learning
3. poor judgment
4. Inappropriate affect

(From Roy, C., & Andrews, H. A. (Eds.). (1991). The Roy adaptation model: The definitive statement (p. 32). Norwalk, CT: Appleton & Lange. Used with permission.)

Assessment of Stimuli

After a behavioral assessment, the nurse analyzes the emerging themes and patterns of client behavior to identify ineffective responses or adaptive responses requiring nurse support. When ineffective behaviors or adaptive behaviors requiring support are present, the nurse makes an assessment of internal and external stimuli that may be affecting behavior. In this phase of assessment, the nurse collects data about the focal, contextual, and residual stimuli impacting on the client. This process clarifies the etiology of the problem and identifies significant contextual and residual factors. Common influencing stimuli have been identified by Roy and her colleagues and are listed in Table 4–3.

TABLE 4–3   Common Stimuli Affecting Adaptation

Culture—Socioeconomic status, ethnicity, belief system

Family—Structure, tasks

Developmental stage—Age, sex, tasks, heredity, and genetic factors

Integrity of adaptive modes—Physiological (including disease pathology), self-concept, role function, interdependence

Cognator effectiveness—Perception, knowledge, skill

Environmental considerations—Change in internal or external environment, medical management, use of drugs, alcohol, tobacco

(From Roy, C., & Andrews, H. A. (Eds.). (1991). The Roy adaptation model: The definitive statement (p. 32). Norwalk, CT: Appleton & Lange. Used with permission.)

Nursing Diagnosis

Roy describes three methods of making a nursing diagnosis (Roy & Andrews, 1991). One method is to use a typology of diagnoses developed by Roy and related to the four adaptive modes. Table 4–4 is a list of common adaptation problems using this typology. In applying this method of diagnosis to the example of Albert Smith, the diagnosis would be: "Hypoxia."

TABLE 4–4 Typology of Commonly Recurring Adaptation Problems

Physiological Mode

1. Oxygenation
   hypoxia/shock
   ventilatory impairment
   inadequate gas exchange
   inadequate gas transport
   altered tissue perfusion
   poor recruitment of compensatory processes
      for changing oxygen need
2. Nutrition
   weight 20/25% above/below average
   nutrition more/less than body requirements
   anorexia
   nausea and vomiting
   ineffective coping strategies for altered means
      of ingestion
3. Elimination
   diarrhea
   bowel/bladder incontinence
   constipation
   urinary retention
   flatulence
   ineffective coping strategies for altered
      elimination
4. Activity and Rest
   inadequate pattern of activity and rest
   restricted mobility, gait, and/or coordination
   activity intolerance
   immobility
   disuse consequences
   potential for sleep pattern disturbance
   fatigue
   sleep deprivation
5. Protection
   disrupted skin integrity
   pressure sores
   itching
   delayed wound healing
   infection

   potential for ineffective coping with allergic
      reaction
   ineffective coping with changes in immune
      status
6. Senses
   impairment of a primary sense
   potential for injury/loss of self-care abilities
   potential for distorted communication
   stigma
   sensory monotony/distortion
   sensory overload/deprivation
   acute pain
   chronic pain
   perceptual impairment
   ineffective coping strategies for sensory
      impairment
7. Fluid and Electrolytes
   dehydration
   edema
   intracellular water retention
   shock
   hyper or hypo calcemia, kalemia, or natremia
   acid/base imbalance
   ineffective buffer regulation for changing pH
8. Neurological Function
   decreased level of consciousness
   defective cognitive processing
   memory deficits
   instability of behavior and mood
   ineffective compensation for cognitive deficit
   potential for secondary brain damage
9. Endocrine Function
   ineffective hormone regulation, reflected in
      fatigue, irritability, heat intolerance
   ineffective reproductive development
   instability of hormone system loops
   instability of internal cyclical rhythms
   stress

(Continued)

TABLE 4–4 Typology of Commonly Recurring Adaptation Problems (Continued)

Self-Concept Mode

1. Physical Self	2. Personal Self
body image disturbance	anxiety
sexual dysfunction	powerlessness
rape trauma syndrome	guilt
loss	low self-esteem

Role Function Mode

role transition
role distance
role conflict
role failure

Interdependence Mode

ineffective pattern of giving and receiving nurturing
ineffective pattern of aloneness and relating
separation anxiety
loneliness

_____

(From Roy, C., & Andrews, H. A. (Eds.). (1991). The Roy adaptation model: The definitive statement (pp. 41–42). Norwalk. CT: Appleton & Lange. Used with permission.)

The second method is to make a diagnosis by stating the observed response within one mode along with the most influential stimuli. Using this method, a diagnosis for Mr. Smith could be stated as: "Chest pain caused by a deficit of oxygen to the heart muscle associated with an overexposure to hot weather."

The third method summarizes responses in one or more adaptive modes related to the same stimuli. For example, if the person experiencing chest pain is a farmer, working outside in hot weather is necessary for success in his or her work. In this case, an appropriate diagnosis might be: "Role failure associated with limited physical (myocardial) ability to work in hot weather."

On the other hand, a nursing diagnosis using any of the foregoing methods can also be a statement of adaptive responses that the nurse wishes to support. For example, if Mr. Smith is seeking help through vocational counseling to adapt to his physical limitation, the nurse may diagnose a need to support this behavior. In this case, an appropriate diagnosis would be: "Adaptation to role failure by seeking an alternative career." Roy and others also have developed a typology of indicators of positive adaptation (see Table 4–5).

Goal Setting

Goals are the end-point behaviors that the person is to achieve. They are recorded as client behaviors indicative of resolution of the adaptation problem. The goal statement includes the behavior, the change expected, and a time frame. Long-term goals reflect resolution of adaptive problems and the availability of energy to meet other goals (survival, growth, reproduction, and mastery). Short-term goals identify expected client behaviors after management of focal or contextual stimuli. As well, they state client behaviors that indicate cognator or regulator coping. Whenever possible, goals are set mutually with the person. Mutual goal setting respects the privileges and rights of the person (Roy & Andrews, 1991).

Plans for Implementation

Nursing interventions are planned with the purpose of altering or managing the focal or contextual stimuli. Implementation may also focus on broadening the person's coping ability, or adaptation level, so that the total stimuli fall within that person's ability to adapt. The nurse plans specific activities to alter the selected stimuli appropriately (Roy & Andrews, 1991).

TABLE 4–5 Typology of Indicators of Positive Adaptation

Physiological Mode

1. Oxygenation
    stable processes of ventilation
    stable pattern of gas exchange
    adequate transport of gases
    adequate processes of compensation
2. Nutrition
    stable digestive processes
    adequate nutritional pattern for body
        requirements
    metabolic and other nutritive needs met
        during altered means of ingestion
3. Elimination
    effective homeostatic bowel processes
    stable pattern of bowel elimination
    effective processes of urine formation
    stable pattern of urine elimination
    effective coping strategies for altered
        elimination
4. Activity and Rest
    integrated processes of mobility
    adequate recruitment of compensatory
        movement processes during inactivity
    effective pattern of activity and rest
    effective sleep pattern
    effective environmental changes for altered
        sleep conditions
5. Protection
    intact skin
    effective processes of immunity
    effective healing response

adequate secondary protection for changes in
    skin integrity and immune status
6. Senses
    effective processes of sensation
    effective integration of sensory input into
        information
    stable patterns of perception, i.e., interpretation and appreciation of input
    effective coping strategies for altered sensation
7. Fluid and Electrolytes
    stable processes of water balance
    stability of salts in body fluids
    balance of acid/base status
    effective chemical buffer regulation
8. Neurological Function
    effective processes of arousal/attention; sensation/perception; coding, concept formation,
        memory, language; planning, motor response
    integrated thinking and feeling processes
    plasticity and functional effectiveness of developing, aging, and altered nervous system
9. Endocrine Function
    effective hormonal regulation of metabolic and
        body processes
    effective hormonal regulation of reproductive
        development
    stable patterns of closed loop negative feedback hormone systems
    stable patterns of cyclical hormone rhythms
    effective coping strategies for stress

(Continued))

TABLE 4–5 Typology of Indicators of Positive Adaptation (Continued)

Self-Concept Mode

1. Physical Self
   positive body image
   effective sexual function
   psychic integrity with physical growth
   adequate compensation for bodily changes
   effective coping strategies for loss
   effective process of life closure

2. Personal Self
   stable pattern of self-consistency
   effective integration of self-ideal
   effective processes of moral-ethical-spiritual growth
   functional self-esteem
   effective coping strategies for threats to self

Role Function Mode

effective processes of role transition
integration of instrumental and expressive role behaviors
integration of primary, secondary, and tertiary roles
stable pattern of role mastery
effective processes for coping with role changes

Interdependence Mode

stable pattern of giving and receiving nurturing
affectional adequacy
effective pattern of aloneness and relating
effective coping strategies for separation and loneliness

(From Roy, C., & Andrews, H.A. (Eds.). (1991). The Roy adaptation model: The definitive statement (pp. 41–42). Norwalk, CT: Appleton & Lange. Used with permission.)

Evaluation

The nursing process is completed by evaluation. Goal behaviors are compared to the person's output responses, and movement toward or away from goal achievement is determined. Readjustments to goals and interventions are made on the basis of evaluation data (Roy & Andrews, 1991).

The Roy Nursing Process Applied to Nursing in a Recovery Room

The Roy model can be applied to nursing assessment and interventions in various clinical situations. In the following case study, the Roy model is applied to a person during the period of immediate recovery from surgery and anesthesia.

Behavioral assessment focuses on the physiological mode responses during the first hour of recovery time after a person experiences surgery and general anesthesia. By applying the Roy model, significant behaviors can be conceptualized as regulator output responses. Increased sympathetic or parasympathetic system activity can signal regulator system activity. Regulator output responses that vary from baseline values determined for the person may be the first warning of an ineffective response to postoperative stimuli. Key baseline values are the person's presurgery measures of heart rate, blood pressure, and respiratory rate. Immediately upon observation of changes from the baseline, assessment of stimuli is done. Goals are set with the basic survival of the person as a priority. Interventions are taken so that focal and contextual stimuli are altered and adaptation is promoted. The evaluation of goal achievement is made, and further actions are taken as necessary.

Situation. Mrs. Reed is received from surgery after a major abdominal operation. Before surgery, her baseline vital signs were: heart rate, 80 beats per minute; blood pressure, 120/.80 mm Hg; and respiratory rate, 16 per minute. After 45 minutes in recovery, her vital signs are: heart rate, 150 beats per minute; blood pressure, 90/60 mm Hg; respiratory rate, 32 per minute. Increased regulator output response is signaled by sympathetic nervous system stimulation of the heart in response to decreased blood pressure. The nurse decides that Mrs. Reed is showing an ineffective response. Therefore, assessment of stimuli is done.

The focal stimulus is a decrease of arterial blood pressure secondary to an unknown underlying cause. The contextual stimuli are: age 45 years, cool extremities, poor nail blanching, no food or drink for 12 hours, intravenous infusion (IV) of dextrose 5 percent in water with lactated Ringer's solution at 100 cc per hour. Also, contextual stimuli include 200 cc of IV fluids infused during surgery, 10 cc of urine excreted during the first 45 minutes in recovery, 1½ hours of general anesthesia, estimated blood loss of 500 cc during surgery, no operative site bleeding, and level of consciousness slow to respond to tactile stimuli after 45 minutes in recovery. The residual stimuli include history of renal infections.

The nursing diagnosis of a decreased arterial blood pressure secondary to fluid volume deficit is made. A fluid volume loss is suggested both by the contextual data and by the changes in the baseline heart rate, blood pressure, and urine output. The nurse then intervenes by altering contextual stimuli so that an adaptive response is promoted. The goal of a circulatory volume adequate to maintain a blood pressure of plus or minus 20 mm Hg of baseline levels within 15 minutes is set. The nurse plans and then takes the following intervention steps. The IV rate is increased to 300 cc per hour. The foot of the bed is elevated to increase venous return. Forty percent oxygen is given by mask. Mrs. Reed is verbally and tactilely stimulated and told to take slow deep breaths. The nurse prepares vasopressor medications for immediate use and applies an external continuous blood pressure cuff for constant blood pressure monitoring. The nurse also consults with other team members as to Mrs. Reed's clinical presentation.

A constant evaluation of the effectiveness of the nursing actions is made. The nurse holds Mrs. Reed in recovery until the goal of adequate circulation volume is met. Evaluation criteria include urine output greater than 30 cc per hour, mental alertness, rapid nail bed blanching, blood pressure plus or minus 20 mm Hg of presurgery levels, pulse plus or minus 20 beats per minute of baseline, and respirations plus or minus 5 per minute of presurgery levels.

*R*oy's Work and the Characteristics of a Theory

1. **Theories can interrelate concepts in such a way as to create a different way of looking at a particular phenomenon.** The Roy model does interrelate concepts in such a way as to present a new view of the phenomenon being studied. It identifies the key concepts relevant to nursing: the person, environment, health, and nursing. The person is viewed as constantly interacting with internal and external stimuli. The person is active and reactive to these stimuli. Stimuli are defined as focal, that which invokes the greatest degree of change; contextual; and residual. The theory suggests the influence of multiple causes in a situation, which is a strength when dealing with multifaceted human beings. Adaptation is a positive response made by the person to

the experience being encountered. Adaptation is facilitated by the use of the regulator and cognator coping mechanisms. The adaptation level represents the range of stimuli that the person can tolerate and continue to maintain adaptive responses. The areas of response where the effects of coping are evidenced include the four adaptive modes: physiological, self-concept, role function, and interdependence. Thus, by a quick review of the concept of the person who is the recipient of nursing care, one sees that a very specific perspective or image has been defined by the Roy model. Beginning work in the development of theory related to these concepts has been done by Roy, Roberts, and others (Roy & Roberts, 1981). The view suggests a holistic framework as opposed to a view of the ill person as a biological entity with a disease process. It reflects a view of nursing that is concerned with many aspects of the person—physiological, self-concept, role function, and interdependence.

2. **Theories must be logical in nature.** The sequence of concepts in the Roy model follows logically. In the presentation of each of the key concepts there is the recurring idea of adaptation to maintain integrity. The definition of health is based on the idea of integrity, which in turn is operationalized to mean responses that meet the person's goals of survival, growth, reproduction, and mastery. Promoting adaptive responses in situations of health and illness is the goal of nursing. The person is conceptualized as a holistic, adaptive system.

3. **Theories should be relatively simple yet generalizable.** The concepts of the Roy model are stated in relatively simple terms. However, the concept of the person as an adaptive system does present a challenging use of specific terms, including cognator and regulator mechanisms and adaptation level. The four adaptive modes may be the first aspect of the model that the student or nurse is able to assimilate. Based upon nursing tradition, assessment of fluid and electrolytes, elimination, oxygenation, roles, and such evoke familiar images. As one nurse studying the theory stated, "It's what we've always done. I don't know what the big deal is!" Perhaps she failed to realize that such a statement was complimentary of the model's fit to clinical practice.

   Let us also consider the generalizability of the model in various settings. Use of the Roy model to organize curriculum has been demonstrated by the faculty at Mount Saint Mary's College in Los Angeles. Similarly, extensive use of the model as well as pictorial representations of it have been made by the faculty and students of the Royal Alexandra Hospitals School of Nursing (Andrews & Roy, 1986). Use of the model for the care of various client populations is exemplified by the works of Farkas (1981), Giger, Bower, & Miller (1987), and Janelli (1980). Research studies examining the use of the model in nursing practice include the work of Fredrickson et al., (1991), Hoch (1987), Limandri (1986), and Pollock (1993).

4. **Theories can be the bases for hypotheses that can be tested or for theory to be expanded,** and

5. **Theories contribute to and assist in increasing the general body of knowledge of a discipline through the research implemented to validate them.** The testing of a theory in practice is the basis for scientific development of a profession. Because Roy presents her work as a model, subtheorizing is present when application of the model is made for predictive understanding in a clinical situation. The model must be able to clearly identify the connecting relationships between underlying theories. Testable hypotheses are thus generated. Hill and Roberts (1981) discuss "relevant theory derivations" in their study of nursing interventions to promote the health of children with birth defects who are in need of habilitation. Developmental and social learning concepts related to the Roy premises and hypotheses for testing are pro-

posed (see Table 4–6). Multiple examples of hypotheses for testing are generated by Roy and Roberts (1981). Because the model is an umbrella that can link theories, its contributions in the future to the body of nursing knowledge may be considerable.

TABLE 4–6 Relevant Theory Derivations		
Roy's Premises	**Developmental Unit—Child Habilitation**	**Social Learning Unit—Maternal Locus of Control**
Man is an adaptive being.	Habilitation is an adaptation problem.	Generalized expectancy of control is directional towards internality or externality.
If man is an adaptive being, he has an adaptation level. The adaptation level is a function of the interaction between adaptation mechanisms and the environment.	The greater the adaptation level, the greater the habilitation level. The habilitation level is a function of the interaction between adaptation mechanisms and the environment. The greater the deficits in habilitation, the greater the impairment of adaptation level. The greater the impairment of adaptation level, the greater the impairment in activities of daily living. The greater the impairment of adaptation level, the greater the significance of the environment.	A significant stimulus in a child's environment is the mother. The greater the maternal internal locus of control, the greater the parenting patterns fostering independence of a child. The greater the maternal external locus of control, the less the parenting patterns fostering independence of a child.
Nursing intervention is directed towards manipulation of the environment.	The less the habilitation level of the child, the greater the need for nursing intervention.	The less the parenting patterns foster independence of a child, the less the habilitation level of the child.

(From Roy, C., & Roberts, S. L. (1981). Theory construction in nursing: An adaptation model (pp. 36–37). Englewood Cliffs, NJ: Prentice-Hall. Used with permission.)

6. **Theories can be used by practitioners to guide and improve their practice.** Perhaps the most important aspect of a theory is its usefulness in practice. How does application of the Roy model guide and improve the work of the practitioner? A major strength of the model is that it guides nurses to use observation and interviewing skills in doing an individualized assessment of each person. Behavior related to the four adaptive modes is collected during behavioral assessment. In considering all the adaptive modes—physiological, self-concept, role function, and interdependence—the nurse is likely to have a comprehensive view of the person.

   The concepts of the Roy model are applicable within many practice settings of nursing. Literature cited throughout this section reflects application of the model by nurse educators, practitioners, and researchers in a variety of educational and clinical settings.

   The use of the model may demand a change in the allocation of time and resources. Painstaking application of the model requires significant input of time and effort. The benefit to the client of complete assessment and implementations in areas of concern, however, justifies the effort and allocation of resources. Even in practice settings that require quick action, the elements of the model are still compatible with quality care. Especially useful is the guide for the assessment of stimuli which helps identify focal, contextual, and residual stimuli. The development by Roy of a typology of nursing diagnoses of common adaptation problems is an exciting outflow of the model. Further integration of Roy's work with that of NANDA is to be seen. Compatibility of the model to the work related to nursing diagnosis by NANDA is discussed in many chapters in the latest text (Roy &c Andrews, 1991).

   Goal setting and achievement in nursing are likely to be facilitated by application of commonly defined concepts and direction of focus. Because the model encourages identification of the focal, contextual, and residual stimuli within a situation, it immediately indicates the course of nursing action. Nursing actions are geared to altering these stimuli. This aspect of the model helps the practitioner in making specific decisions about what actions to take. In another way, practitioners can see the importance of their actions in influencing the adaptation of the person. For example, the nurse can view nursing actions such as maintaining bed rest or relieving pain or fears as significant in maintaining an adaptive response for the person.

7. **Theories must be consistent with other validated theories, laws, and principles but will leave open unanswered questions that need to be investigated.** By its structure, the Roy model requires the integration of further theorizing for explanatory and predictive information in clinical situations. The concept of adaptation as developed by the model appears to have good linkage qualities. Theory development has been undertaken by Roy, her co-authors, and others as cited throughout this section. Future nursing research and field application will continue to validate and adjust the Roy model.

Summary

The Roy model consists of the four elements of person, environment, health, and nursing. Persons are viewed as living adaptive systems whose behaviors may be classified as adaptive responses or ineffective responses. These responses are derived from the regulator and cognator mechanisms. The assessment of behavior is done in the four adaptive modes: physiological, self-concept, role function, and interdependence. The environment consists of the person's internal and external stimuli. Health is a process of becoming integrated and able to meet the goals of survival, growth, reproduction, and mastery. The goal of nursing is to promote adaptive responses in relation to the four adaptive modes, using information about the person's adaptation level and focal, contextual, and residual stimuli. Nursing activities involve the manipulation of these stimuli to promote adaptive responses.

These elements are in a nursing process that consists of assessment of behaviors and stimuli, nursing diagnosis, goal setting, intervention, and evaluation. Behavioral assessment deals with the four adaptive modes, whereas assessment of stimuli focuses on focal, contextual, and residual stimuli. Nursing diagnosis consists of stating the problem. Goals are set in relation to the problem and are written in behavioral terms. Interventions are planned to manipulate the stimuli, and evaluation compares the person's output responses with the desired behaviors established in the goals.

Roy's model is seen as applicable in the nursing process presented in an earlier section. The characteristics of a theory are also met. There is need for continued research that centers on hypotheses generated by the model.

References

Andrews, H. A. (1991a). Overview of the role function mode. In C. Roy, & H. A. Andrews (Eds.), *The Roy adaptation model: The definitive statement* (pp. 347–361). Norwalk, CT: Appleton & Lange.

Andrews, H. A. (1991b). Overview of the self-concept mode. In C. Roy, & H. A. Andrews (Eds.), *The Roy adaptation model: The definitive statement* (pp. 269–279). Norwalk, CT: Appleton & Lange.

Andrews, H. A., & Roy, C. (1986). *Essentials of the Roy adaptation model.* Norwalk, CT: Appleton-Century-Crofts.

Andrews, H. A., & Roy, C. (1991). Overview .of the physiological mode. In C. Roy, & H. A. Andrews (Eds.), *The Roy adaptation model: The definitive statement* (pp. 57–66). Norwalk, CT: Appleton & Lange.

Chalifoux, Z. (1991). Endocrine function. In C. Roy, & H. A. Andrews (Eds.), *The Roy adaptation model: The definitive statement* (pp. 237–259). Norwalk, CT: Appleton & Lange.

Dunn, H. L. (1971). *High level wellness.* Arlington, VA: Beatty.

Farkas, L. (1981). Adaptation problems with nursing home application for elderly persons: An application of the Roy adaptation nursing model. *Journal of Advanced Nursing, 6,* 363–368.

Fredrickson, K., Jackson, B. S., Strauman, T., & Strauman, J. (1991). Testing hypotheses derived from the Roy adaptation model. *Nursing Science Quarterly, 4,* 168–174.

Gaertzen, I. E. (Ed.). (1991). *Differentiating nursing practice into the twenty-first century.* Kansas City, MO: American Academy of Nursing.

Giger, J. A., Bower, C. A., & Miller, S. W. (1987). Roy adaptation model: ICU adaptation model: ICU application. *Dimensions of Critical Care Nursing, 6,* 215–224.

Guyton, A. C. (1971). *Basic human physiology: Normal function and mechanisms of disease.* Philadelphia: Saunders.

Helson, H. (1964). *Adaptation level theory.* New York: Harper & Row.

Hill, B. J., & Roberts, C. S. (1981). Formal theory construction: An example of the process. In C. Roy, & S. L. Roberts, *Theory construction in nursing: An adaptation model* (pp. 30–39). Englewood Cliffs, NJ: Prentice-Hall.

Hoch, C. C. (1987). Assessing delivery of nursing care. *Journal of Gerontological Nursing, 13,* 10–17.

Janelli, L. M. (1980). Utilizing Roy's adaptation model from a gerontological perspective. *Journal of Gerontological Nursing, 6*, 140–150.

Jensen, K. (1991). Fluids and electrolytes. In C. Roy, & H. A. Andrews (Eds.), *The Roy adaptation model: The definitive statement* (pp. 191–204). Norwalk, CT: Appleton & Lange.

Limandri, B. J. (1986). Research and practice with abused women: Use of the Roy adaptation model as an explanatory framework. *Advances in Nursing Science, 8*, 2–61.

Pollock, S. E. (1993). Adaptation to chronic illness: A program of research for testing nursing theory. *Nursing Science Quarterly, 6*, 86–92.

Rambo, B. (1983). *Adaptation nursing: Assessment and intervention*. Philadelphia: Saunders.

Randell, B., Tedrow, M. P., & Van Landingham, J. (1982). *Adaptation nursing: The Roy conceptual model applied*. St. Louis: Mosby.

Riehl-Sisca, J. P. (1989). *Conceptual models for nursing practice* (3rd ed.). New York: Appleton & Lange.

Roy, C. (1976). *Introduction to nursing: An adaptation model*. Englewood Cliffs, NJ: Prentice-Hall. [out of print]

Roy, C. (1984). *Introduction to nursing: An adaptation model* (2nd ed.). Englewood Cliffs, NJ: Prentice-Hall.

Roy, C. (1991a). Activity and rest. In C. Roy, & H. A. Andrews (Eds.), *The Roy adaptation model: The definitive statement* (pp. 117–147). Norwalk, CT: Appleton & Lange.

Roy, C. (1991b). Neurological function. In C. Roy, & H. A. Andrews (Eds.), *The Roy adaptation model: The definitive statement* (pp. 205–235). Norwalk, CT: Appleton &: Lange.

Roy, C. (1991c). Senses. In C. Roy, & H. A. Andrews (Eds.), *The Roy adaptation model: The definitive statement* (pp. 165–189). Norwalk, CT: Appleton & Lange.

Roy, C., & Andrews, H. A. (1991). *The Roy adaptation model: The definitive statement*. Norwalk, CT: Appleton & Lange.

Roy, C., & Roberts, S. (1981). *Theory construction in nursing: An adaptation model*. Englewood Cliffs, NJ: Prentice-Hall.

Sato, M. K. (1991). Protection. In C. Roy, & H. A. Andrews (Eds.), *The Roy adaptation model: The definitive statement* (pp. 149–164). Norwalk, CT: Appleton & Lange.

Servonsky, J. (1991a). Elimination. In C. Roy, & H. A. Andrews (Eds.), *The Roy adaptation model: The definitive statement* (pp. 99–116). Norwalk, CT: Appleton & Lange.

Servonsky, J. (1991b). Nutrition. In C. Roy, & H. A. Andrews (Eds.), *The Roy adaptation model: The definitive statement* (pp. 81–98). Norwalk, CT: Appleton & Lange.

Tedrow, M. P. (1991). Overview of the interdependence mode. In C. Roy, & H. A. Andrews (Eds.), *The Roy adaptation model: The definitive statement* (pp. 385–403). Norwalk, CT; Appleton & Lange.

Thompson, C. (1991). Oxygenation. In C. Roy, & H. A. Andrews (Eds.), *The Roy adaptation model: The definitive statement* (pp. 67–79). Norwalk, CT: Appleton & Lange.

von Bertalanffy, L. (1968). *General system theory*. New York: Braziller.

External Analysis

$\mathcal{R}$elationship to Nursing Research

The usefulness of a model for research depends on its ability to guide all phases of a study. It should provide a perspective for research by suggesting the subject matter or phenomena to be studied, identifying the nature of the problems to be studied or the research questions to be asked, and identifying appropriate methods of inquiry (Barnum, 1994; Fawcett & Tulman, 1990; Roy, 1991a). The elements and assumptions of the adaptation model provide such a perspective for research in both the basic and clinical science of nursing. The phenomena of study, as identified by the model, are persons, both individuals and groups. The distinctive nature of the problems to be studied or the research questions to be asked are related to basic life processes and patterns, coping with health and illness, and enhancing adaptive coping (positive life processes and patterns) (Roy, 1987b, 1988, 1990, 1991a). According to Roy (1991a), multiple methods are appropriate and desirable when conducting research based on the model.

The concepts Roy (1970) articulated provide a model for the long-term process of observation and clarification of facts leading to postulates regarding (1) the occurrence of adaptation problems; (2) coping mechanisms; and (3) interventions based on laws derived from factors composing the response potential, that is, focal, contextual, and residual stimuli. Using this framework typologies of adaptation problems or nursing diagnoses have been developed as well as typologies of indicators of positive adaptation (Andrews & Roy, 1991b; Roy & Andrews, 1991). In 1981, Roy and Roberts noted the need to develop an organization of categories of interventions that would fit within the model. Some research has been done in this area. Data on cognitive deficits have been used to design intervention protocols for cognitive recovery from head injury (Roy, 1991a). Other have used the framework to develop and test interventions to help promote adaptation based on managing stimuli (Fawcett, 1990; Smith, 1988; Thornbury & King, 1992).

Within the tradition of logical empiricism, to be useful for research, a model must be able to generate testable hypotheses (Silva & Rothbart, 1984). This is consistent with the verificationist perspective of logical positivism, where the meaning of propositions depend on their method of verification. To be meaningful propositions must be verifiable, and this can occur

---

Taken from: *Conceptual Models of Nursing: Analysis and Application*, Third Edition by Fitzpatrick and Whall.

only when phenomena are observable (Whall, 1989). A number of general propositions have been developed from the adaptation model (Roy & McLeod, 1981; Roy & Roberts, 1981). From these general propositions, specific propositions or testable hypotheses can be developed. Roy (Roy &Roberts, 1981) has cited examples of such testable hypotheses which she has stated are relevant for specifying prescriptions for practice. Others also have demonstrated the development of testable hypotheses from the model. Testing of these hypotheses has provided data to validate or support the model (Frederickson et al., 1991; Hill & Roberts, 1981; Smith, 1988; Thornbury & King, 1992).

The model has been used as a framework for research by Roy and others (see Table 4–7 for a partial listing of uses of the adaptation model in research). Roy (1991a) has provided research examples from both basic and clinical nursing science. In basic nursing science the model has been used as a framework for exploring how the cognator coping mechanism acts to promote adaptation and its relationship to the four adaptive modes and for examining the relationship of adaptation to health. In clinical nursing science the model has been used in a program of research related to cognitive recovery of patients with head injury. Specifically, this research focused on gaining an understanding of basic human cognitive processes and how nurses can assist persons to positively affect their health by use of these processes.

Scholars who have used the adaptation model as the conceptual basis for their research have found it to be useful in identifying the concepts and variables to study and in selecting instruments to measure or operationalize these variables (Calvillo & Flaskerud, 1993; Fawcett, 1990; Fawcett & Tulman, 1990; Limandri, 1986; Vicenzi & Thiel, 1992). In addition, it has been found to be useful in suggesting the design or methodology for research studies (Fawcett & Tulman, 1990; Roy, personal communication, March 6, 1986) and in structuring and organizing data into themes and categories (Nyqvist & Sjödén, 1993; Silva, 1987). The model also is useful for deriving testable hypotheses and propositions. The model has clearly demonstrated its usefulness in research.

 **elationship to Nursing Education**

The adaptation model has demonstrated its usefulness in education. As a theoretical framework for nursing education, it is one the most widely used models in this country and is being used increasingly in other countries (Roy, 1982; Roy & Andrews, 1991). A combination of nurs-

---

TABLE 4–7 Use of the Adaptation Model in Research

Focus of Research	Researcher
Cross-cultural pain	Calvillo & Flaskerud (1993)
Caesarean birth	Fawcett (1990)
Child-bearing women	Fawcett & Tulman (1990)
Cancer patients	Frederickson et al. (1991)
Abused women	Limandri (1986)
Breast-feeding women	Nyqvist & Sjödén (1993)
Spouses of surgical patients	Silva (1987)
Elderly persons	Smith (1988)
Persons with Alzheimer's disease	Thornbury & King (1992)

ing process and adaptation problems provide the framework for nursing curricula based on the model and form the units and strands of knowledge and practice which are developed throughout the educational program (Roy, 1973).

The model is currently the basis for the nursing curricula at Mount Saint Mary's College, Los Angeles, and the Royal Alexandra Hospitals School of Nursing, Edmonton, Alberta, Canada (Roy & Andrews, 1991). The model also has been used in a geriatric nurse-practitioner program (Brower & Baker, 1976), and in the first-year nursing course of a generic baccalaureate program at the University of Ottawa School of Nursing, Ottawa, Ontario, Canada (Morales-Mann & Logan, 1990).

According to Roy (1973, 1976b, 1979), the curriculum at Mount Saint Mary's has clearly demonstrated the relationship of nursing theory to nursing education. The model allows for increasing knowledge in the areas of both theory and practice, and it helps students test theory and develop new theoretical insights. In addition, the model distinguishes between nursing science and medical science. Brower and Baker (1976) stated that the adaptation model for nursing integrated nursing theory, thereby decreasing students' anxiety. They also stated that the model provided some distinction between nursing and medicine, although there was some overlap.

Although the model has demonstrated its usefulness in education, challenges faced by educators when implementing the model have been identified. These challenges include (1) developing/adapting courses to be congruent with the model; (2) developing teaching tools which are consistent with the model and suitable for student learning; (3) sequencing content to facilitate student learning about the model, course content, and the relationship between them; and (4) obtaining competent role models in the application of the model (Morales-Mann & Logan, 1990).

*R*elationship to Professional Nursing Practice

Providing direction to the practice of nursing is one of the purposes of a nursing model. The adaptation model provides this direction based on its well-developed guidelines for the use of the nursing process, especially in the steps of assessment and nursing diagnosis. The two-level assessment process focuses on the assessment of behaviors and stimuli and leads to the identification of nursing diagnoses (behaviors related to stimuli) and the establishment of goals (behavioral outcomes). The model provides the framework for intervention which is focused on the management of stimuli. Evaluation assesses the effectiveness of the intervention by examining behavior relative to the goals. As the model has been developed, there has been a refinement of the approaches to nursing diagnosis, an identification of major stimuli for each mode, and development of intervention protocols based on the model (Andrews & Roy, 1991b; Gray, 1991; Roy & Andrews, 1991).

The usefulness of the adaptation model in practice has been demonstrated in a variety of clinical settings with various populations (see Table 4–8). In addition, the model has been adopted by a number of health care agencies in the United States and abroad, where it serves as a basis for practice (Frederickson, 1991; Nyqvist & Sjödén, 1993; Roy, 1986).

Use of the model in practice has been found to expand the scope of assessment by providing a comprehensive framework, which includes psychosocial aspects as well as physiological aspects (Doyle & Rajacich, 1991; Galligan, 1979; Gerrish, 1989; Hamner, 1989; Smith, 1988; Thornbury & King, 1992). Its holistic approach may foster earlier identification of problems (Frederickson, 1993). Despite its usefulness in expanding the scope of assessment, application of the nursing process based on the model can be lengthy, repetitious, and time-consuming, especially during the assessment phase. This has been found to be most

TABLE 4–8   Use of the Adaptation Model in Practice

Occupational health, work environment	Doyle & Rejacich (1991)
Patients with anxiety	Frederickson (1993)
Hospitalized children	Galligan (1979), Starn & Niederhauser (1990)
Patients with Hodgkin's disease	Gerrish (1989)
Coronary care unit	Hamner (1989)
Abused women	Limandri (1986)
Patients with alcoholism	McIver (1987)
Patients with Kawaski disease	Nash (1987)
Home care	Schmitz (1980)
Elderly in apartment complexes	Smith (1986)
Patients with Alzheimer's disease	Thornbury & King (1992)

problematic in intensive care units, where there are rapid changes in patient's conditions, and least problematic in outpatient and long-term care settings (Gerrish, 1989; McIver, 1987; Wagner, 1976).

Some of the difficulty in using the model in practice arises from the overlap in modes, which can make it difficult to structure the assessment to cover one mode at a time and/or to decide which mode is the appropriate one for a given behavior (Gerrish, 1989; Limandri, 1986; Nyqvist & Sjödén, 1993; Wagner, 1976). Because of the overlap in modes, Nyqvist and Sjödén (1993) expressed doubt about the appropriateness of the model for daily patient assessment. Another difficulty in using the model can be the identification and classification of relevant stimuli (Gerrish, 1989). The adaptation model has been used in practice to design nursing interventions based on the management or manipulation of specific stimuli, focal and contextual, which were identified during assessment and formulation of nursing diagnoses. Generally interventions were found to be effective. This approach to intervention, which is specific to the individual and the diagnosis, helps individualize care and may be more effective than more general, standardized approaches to care (Frederickson, 1993; Smith, 1988; Starn & Niederhauser, 1990; Thornbury & King, 1992).

References

Andrews, H. A., & Roy, C. (1986). *Essentials of the Roy adaptation model.* East Norwalk, CT: Appleton-Century-Crofts.

Andrews, H. A., & Roy, C. (1991a). Essentials of the Roy Adaptation Model. In C. Roy & H. A. Andrews (Eds.), *The Roy adaptation model: The definitive statement.* Norwalk, CT: Appleton & Lange.

Andrews, H. A., & Roy, C. (1991b). The nursing process according to the Roy Adaptation Model. In C. Roy & H. A. Andrews (Eds.), *The Roy adaptation model: The definitive statement.* Norwalk, CT: Appleton & Lange.

Barnum, B. J. S. (1994). *Nursing theory: Analysis, application, evaluation* (4th ed.). Philadelphia: J. B. Lippincott.

Benner, P., & Wrubel, J. (1989). *The primacy of caring: Stress and coping in health and illness.* Menlo Park, CA: Addison-Wesley.

Brower, H. T. F., & Baker, B. J. (1976). The Roy Adaptation Model: Using the adaptation model in a practitioner curriculum. *Nursing Outlook,* 24:686–689.

Calvillo, E. R., & Flaskerud, J. H. (1993). The adequacy and scope of Roy's Adaptation Model to guide cross-cultural pain research. *Nursing Science Quarterly,* 6:118–129.

Carpenito, L. H. (1993). *Nursing diagnosis: Application to clinical practice.* Philadelphia: J. B. Lippincott.

Dohrenwend, B. P. (1961). The social psychological nature of stress: A framework for causal inquiry. *Journal of Abnormal and Social Psychology,* 62:294–302.

Doyle, R., & Rajacich, D. (1991). The Roy Adaptation Model: Health teaching about osteoporosis. *AAOHN Journal,* 39:508–512.

Ellis, R. (1978). Characteristics of significant theories. *Nursing Research* 17:217–222.

Fawcett, J. (1990). Preparation for Caesarean childbirth: Derivation of a nursing intervention from the Roy Adaptation Model. *Journal of Advanced Nursing,* 15: 1418–1425.

Fawcett, J., & Tulman, L. (1990). Building a programme of research from the Roy Adaptation Model of nursing. *Journal of Advanced Nursing,* 15:720–725.

Frederickson, K. (1991). Nursing theories—a basis for differentiated practice: Application of the Roy Adaptation Model in nursing practice. In I. E. Goertzen (Ed.), *Differentiating nursing practice into the twenty-first century,* Kansas City, MO: American Academy of Nursing.

Frederickson, K. (1993). Using a nursing model to manage symptoms: Anxiety and the Roy Adaptation Model. *Holistic Nurse Practitioner,* 7(2):36–43.

Frederickson, K., Jackson, B. S., Strauman, T., & Strauman, J. (1991). Testing hypotheses derived from the Roy Adaptation Model. *Nursing Science Quarterly,* 4:168–174.

Galligan, A. C. (1979). Using Roy's concept of adaptation to care for young children. *MCN: The American Journal of Maternal-Child Nursing,* 4:24–28.

Gerrish, C. (1989). From theory to practice. *Nursing Times,* 85(30):42–45.

Gray, J. (1991). The Roy Adaptation Model in nursing practice. In C. Roy & H. A. Andrews (Eds.), *The Roy adaptation model: The definitive statement.* Norwalk, CT: Appleton & Lange.

Hamner, J. B. (1989). Applying the Roy Adaptation Model to the CCU. *Critical Care Nurse,* 9:51–52, 54–61.

Hardy, M. E. (1974). Theories: Components, development, evaluation. *Nursing Research,* 23:100–107.

Helson, H. (1964). *Adaptation-level theory: An experimental and systematic approach to behavior.* New York: Harper & Row.

Hill, B. J., & Roberts, C. S. (1981). Formal theory construction: An example in process. In C. Roy & S. L. Roberts (Eds.), *Theory construction in nursing: An adaptation model.* Englewood Cliffs, NJ: Prentice-Hall.

Jacox, A. (1974). Theory construction in nursing: An overview. *Nursing Research,* 23:4–13.

Lazarus, R. S. (1966). *Psychological stress and the coping process.* New York: McGraw-Hill.

Limandri, B. J. (1986). Research and practice with abused women: Use of the Roy Adaptation Model as an explanatory framework. *Advances in Nursing Science,* 8(4):52–61.

Logan, M. (1990). The Roy Adaptation Model: Are nursing diagnoses amenable to independent nurse functions? *Journal of Advanced Nursing,* 15:468–470.

McIver, M. (1987). Putting theory into practice. *Canadian Nurse,* 83(10):36–38.

Mechanic, D. (1970). Some problems in developing a social psychology of adaptation to stress. In J. McGrath (Ed.), *Social and psychological factors in stress.* New York: Holt, Rinehart & Winston.

Meleis, A. I. (1991). *Theoretical nursing: Development and progress* (2nd ed.). Philadelphia: J. B. Lippincott.

Morales-Mann, E. T., & Logan, M. (1990). Implementing the Roy model: Challenges for nurse educators. *Journal of Advanced Nursing,* 15:142–147.

Nash, D. J. (1987). Kawasaki disease: Application of the Roy Adaptation Model to determine interventions. *Journal of Pediatric Nursing,* 2:308–315.

Nyqvist, K. H., & Sjödén, P. (1993). Advice concerning breastfeeding from mothers of infants admitted to a neonatal intensive care unit: The Roy Adaptation Model as a conceptual structure. *Journal of Advanced Nursing,* 18:54–63.

Roy, C. (1970). Adaptation: A conceptual framework for nursing. *Nursing Outlook,* 18:42–45.

Roy, C. (1973). Adaptation: Implications for curriculum change. *Nursing Outlook,* 21:163–168.

Roy, C. (1976a). *Introduction of nursing: An adaptation model.* Englewood Cliffs, NJ: Prentice-Hall.

Roy, C. (1976b). The Roy Adaptation Model: Comment. *Nursing Outlook* 24:690–691.

Roy, C. (1979). Relating nursing theory to nursing education. A new era. *Nurse Educator,* IV(2):16–21.

Roy, C. (1982). Foreward. In B. Randall, M. P. Tedrow & J. Landingham (Eds.), *Adaptation nursing: The Roy conceptual model applied.* St Louis: C. V. Mosby.

Roy, C. (1983). Roy Adaptation Model. In I. M. Clements & B. R. Roberts, (Eds.), *Family health: A theoretical approach to nursing.* Englewood Cliffs, NJ: Prentice-Hall.

Roy, C. (1984). *An introduction to nursing: An adaptation model* (2nd ed.). Englewood Cliff, NJ: Prentice-Hall.

Roy, C. (August, 1986). *Overview of the Roy Adaptation Model and its contributions to nursing as a practice discipline.* Paper presented at meeting of Nursing Theory Conference. Toronto, Ontario, Canada.

Roy, C. (1987a). Response to "needs of spouses of surgical patients: A conceptualization within the Roy Adaptation Model." *Scholarly Inquiry for Nursing Practice: An International Journal,* 1:45–50.

Roy, C. (1987b). Roy's Adaptation Model. In R. R. Parse (Ed.), *Nursing science: Major paradigms, theories, and critiques.* Philadelphia: W. B. Saunders.

Roy, C. (1988). An explication of the philosophical assumptions of the Roy Adaptation Model. *Nursing Science Quarterly,* 1:26–34.

Roy, C. (1990). Strengthening the Roy Adaptation Model through conceptual clarification—response: Conceptual clarification. *Nursing Science Quarterly,* 3:64–66.

Roy, C. (1991a). The Roy Adaptation Model in nursing research. In C. Roy & H. A. Andrews (Eds.), *The Roy adaptation model. The definitive statement.* Norwalk, CT: Appleton & Lange.

Roy, C. (1991b). Structure of knowledge: Paradigm, model, and research specifications. In I. E. Goertzen (Ed.), *Differentiating nursing practice into the twenty-first century.* Kansas City, MO: American Academy of Nursing.

Roy, C., & Andrews, H. A. (1991). *The Roy Adaptation Model: The definitive statement.* Norwalk: CT: Appleton & Lange.

Roy, C., & Anway, J. (1989). Roy's Adaptation Model: Theories for nursing administration. In B. Henry, C. Arndt, M. DiVincenti & A. Marriner-Tomey (Eds.), *Dimensions of nursing administration: Theory, research, education, practice.* Boston: Blackwell Scientific.

Roy, C., & McLeod, D. (1981). Theory of person as an adaptive system. In C. Roy & S. L. Roberts (Eds.), *Theory construction in nursing: An adaptation model.* Englewood Cliffs, NJ: Prentice-Hall.

Roy, C., & Roberts, S. L. (1981). *Theory construction in nursing: An adaptation model.* Englewood Cliffs, NJ: Prentice-Hall.

Schmitz, M. (1980). The Roy Adaptation Model: Application to a community setting. In J. P. Riehl & C. Roy (Eds.), *Conceptual models for nursing practice* (2nd ed.). New York: Appleton-Century-Crofts.

Selye, H. (1978). *The stress of life.* New York: McGraw-Hill.

Silva, M. C. (1987). Needs of spouses of surgical patients. A conceptualization within the Roy Adaptation Model. *Scholarly Inquiry for Nursing Practice: An International Journal,* 1:29–43.

Silva, M. C., & Rothbart, D. (1984). An analysis of changing trends in philosophies of science on nursing theory development and testing. *Advances in Nursing Science,* 6(2):1–13.

Smith, M. C. (1988). Roy's Adaptation Model in practice. *Nursing Science Quarterly,* 1:97–98.

Starn, J. & Niederhauser, V. (1990). An MCN model for nursing diagnosis to focus intervention. *MCN: The American Journal of Maternal-Child Nursing.* 13:180–183.

Thornbury, J. M. & King, L. D. (1992). The Roy Adaptation Model and care of persons with Alzeheimers disease. *Nursing Science Quarterly,* 5:129–133.

Tiedeman, M. E. (1989). The Roy Adaptation Model. In J. J. Fitzpatrick & A. L. Whall (Eds.), *Conceptual models of nursing: Analysis and application* (2nd ed). Norwalk, CT: Appleton & Lange.

Vicenzi, A. E., & Thiel, R. (1992). AIDS education on the college campus: Roy's Adaptation Model directs inquiry. *Public Health Nursing,* 9:270–276.

von Bertalanffy, L. (1968). *General systems theory.* New York: Braziller.

Wagner, P. (1976). The Roy Adaptation Model: Testing the application of the model in practice. *Nursing Outlook,* 24:661–685.

Whall, A. L. (1989). The influence of logical positivism on nursing practice. *IMAGE: Journal of Nursing Scholarship,* 21:243–245.

Whall, A. L. (1992). Book review: Roy, C., & Andrews, H. A. (1991). *The Roy Adaptation Model: The definitive statement.* Norwalk, CT: Appleton & Lange. *Nursing Science Quarterly,* 5:190–191.

Ziegler, S. M., Vaughn-Wrobel, B. C., & Erlen, J. A. (1986). *Nursing process, nursing diagnosis, nursing knowledge:Avenues to autonomy.* Norwalk, CT:Appleton-Century-Crofts.

*A*dditional References

Roy, C. (1971). Adaptation: A basis for nursing practice. *Nursing Outlook.* 19:254–257.

Roy, C. (1975a). A diagnostic classification system for nursing. *Nursing Outlook.* 23:90–94.

Roy, C. (1975b). The impact of nursing diagnosis. *AORN Journal,* 21:1023–1030.

Roy, C. (1976a). The impact of nursing diagnosis. *Nursing Digest,* 4:67–79.

Roy, C. (1976b). The Roy Adaptation Model: Past, present, and future. Taped at Wayne State University, Detroit, MI.

Roy, C. (1980). The Roy Adaptation Model. In J. P. Riehl & C. Roy (Eds.), *Conceptual models for nursing practice* (2nd ed.). New York: Appleton-Century-Crofts.

Betty Neuman

Julia B. George

Betty Neuman was born in 1924 on a 100-acre farm in Ohio; she was the middle of three children and the only daughter. When she was 11, her father died after six years of intermittent hospitalizations for treatment of chronic kidney disease. His praise of his nurses influenced Neuman's view of nursing and her commitment to becoming an excellent bedside nurse. Her mother's work as rural midwife was also a significant influence.

After graduation from high school, Neuman could not afford nursing education. She worked as an aircraft instrument repair technician, as draftsperson for an aircraft contracting company, and as a short-order cook in Dayton, Ohio, while saving for her education and helping support her mother and younger brother. The creation of the Cadet Nurse Corps Program expedited her entrance into a hospital school of nursing.

In 1947 Neuman graduated from the diploma program of Peoples Hospital (now General Hospital Medical Center), Akron, Ohio. She received a BS in public health nursing (1957) and an MS as a public health-mental health nurse consultant (1966) from the University of California, Los Angeles, in 1985 she was granted a PhD in clinical psychology by Pacific Western University. She has practiced bedside nursing as a staff, head, and private duty nurse in a wide variety of hospital settings. Her work in community settings has included school and industrial nursing, office nurse in her husband Kree's private practice in obstetrics, and counseling and crisis intervention in community mental health settings. In 1967, six months after completion of her MS degree, she became the faculty chair of the program from which she graduated and began her contributions as teacher, author, lecturer, and consultant in nursing and interdisciplinary health care.

Taken from: *Nursing Theories: The Base for Professional Nursing Practice*, Fourth Edition by George.

In 1973 she and her family returned to Ohio. Since then she has worked as a state mental health consultant, provided continuing education programs, and continued the development of her model. She was one of the first California Nurse Licensed Clinical Fellows of the American Association of Marriage and Family Therapy and has maintained a limited private counseling practice. She is also a licensed real estate agent and obtained a private pilot's license in California. In addition to her professional activities, she has exercised her interest in personal property management and other investments.

The Neuman Systems Model was originally developed in 1970 in response to the request of graduate students at the University of California, Los Angeles, for an introductory course that would provide an overview of the physiological, psychological, sociocultural, and developmental aspects of human beings (Neuman, 1995). The model was developed to provide structure for the integration of this material in a wholistic manner. After a two-year evaluation, the model was first published in Nursing Research (Neuman & Young, 1972).

Neuman (1982, 1989, 1995) has published three editions of *The Neuman Systems Model*. She has also had chapters in all editions of *Conceptual models for nursing practice*, the latest being the third edition edited by Riehl-Sisca (1989), and in Parker's (1990) *Nursing theories in practice*. Neuman continues work on the model but also incorporated The Neuman Systems Model Trustees Group in 1988. Neuman (1995) states that the trustees group was established for the perpetuation, preservation, and protection of the integrity of the model. Any future permanent changes in the original Neuman Systems Model diagram (see Fig. 4–7) other than those made by Neuman herself, must have unanimous approval from the trustees.

Development of the Neuman Systems Model

Neuman (1995) says that her personal philosophy of *helping each other live* was supportive in developing the wholistic systems perspective of the Neuman Systems Model. She drew upon her clinical experiences from a variety of health care and community settings and the theoretical perspectives of stress and systems. Caplan's (1964) levels of prevention were also incorporated into the model. Others whose works were drawn upon include de Chardin (1955), Cornu (1957), Edelson (1970), Emery (1969), Laszlo (1972), Lazarus (1981), Selye (1950), and von Bertalanffy (1968).

Nursing is considered a system because nursing practice contains elements in interaction with one another (Neuman, 1995). Advantages of an open systems perspective in nursing include the use of systems as a unifying force across various scientific fields as well as the increasing complexity of nursing, which calls for an organizational system that can respond to change. A systems perspective supports recognition of the complex whole while valuing the importance of the parts. The relationships between the parts and the interactions of the parts or the whole with the environment provide a mechanism for viewing the system-environment exchanges, which support the dynamic and constantly changing nature of the system.

Neuman (1995) views wholism as both a philosophical and a biological concept. Wholism includes relationships that arise from wholeness, dynamic freedom, and creativity as the system responds to stressors from the internal and external environments.

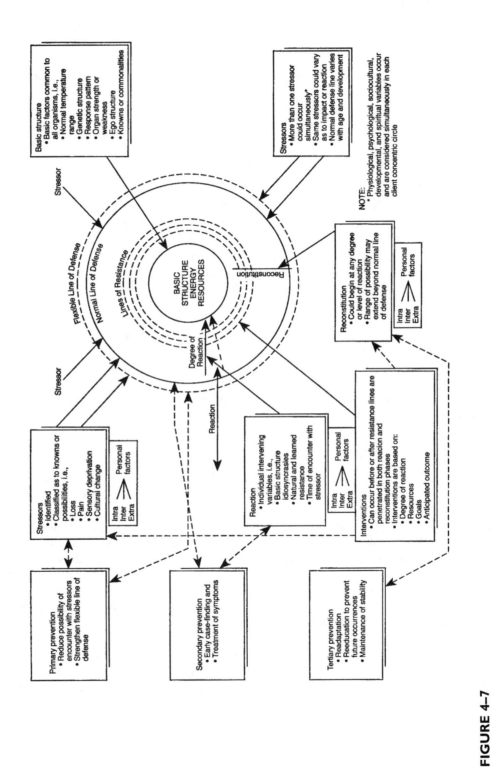

*T*he Neuman Systems Model

The Neuman Systems Model's two major components are stress and the reaction to stress (Neuman, 1995). The client in the Neuman Systems Model is viewed as an open system in which repeated cycles of input, process, output, and feedback constitute a dynamic organizational pattern. Using the systems perspective, the client may be an individual, a group, a family, a community, or any aggregate. In their development toward growth and survival, open systems continuously become more differentiated and elaborate or complex. As they become more complex, the internal conditions of regulation become more complex. Exchanges with the environment are reciprocal; both the client and the environment may be affected either positively or negatively by each other. The system may adjust to the environment or adjust the environment to itself. The environmental influences are identified as intra-, inter-, and extrapersonal.

The ideal is to achieve optimal system stability. Neuman agrees with Heslin (1986) that when a system achieves stability a revitalization occurs. As an open system, the client system has a propensity to seek or maintain a balance among the various factors, both within and outside the system, that seek to disrupt it (Neuman, 1995). Neuman labels these forces as stressors and views them as capable of having either positive or negative effects. Reactions to the stressors may be possible, or not yet occurring, or actual, with identifiable responses and symptoms.

The Neuman Systems Model diagram (see Fig. 4–7) presents the major aspects of the model: the *physiological, psychological, sociocultural, developmental, and spiritual variables; basic structure and energy resources; lines of resistance; normal line of defense; flexible line of defense; stressors; reaction; primary, secondary, and tertiary prevention; intra-, inter-, and extrapersonal factors;* and *reconstitution.* The *environment, health,* and *nursing* are inherent parts of the model, although they are not labeled within the model. The client system is represented in the diagram by a basic structure surrounded by a series of concentric circles.

Basic Structure and Energy Resources

The basic structure, or central core, is made up of those basic survival factors common to the species (Neuman, 1995). These factors include the system variables, genetic features, and strengths and weaknesses of the system parts. If the client system is a human being, the basic structure contains such features as the ability to maintain body temperature within a normal range, genetic characteristics such as hair color and response to stimuli, and the functioning of various body systems and their interrelationships. There are also the baseline characteristics associated with each of the five variables, such as physical strength, cognitive ability, and value systems.

Neuman (1995) identifies system stability or homeostasis as occurring when the amount of energy that is available exceeds that being used by the system. This stability preserves the character of the system. Since the system is an open system, the stability is dynamic. As output becomes feedback and input, the system seeks to regulate itself. A change in one direction is countered by a compensating movement in the opposite direction. When the system is disturbed from its normal, or stable, state there is a rapid surge in the amount of energy needed to deal with the disorganization that results from the disturbance.

Client Variables

Neuman (1995) views the individual client wholistically and considers the variables (physiological, psychological, sociocultural, developmental, and spiritual) simultaneously and comprehensively. In the ideal situation, these variables function in harmony with stability in relation to internal and external environmental stressors. Each of the variables should be considered when assessing system reaction to stressors for each of the concentric circles in the model diagram. It is vital to avoid fragmentation if optimum stability of the client system is to be promoted through nursing care.

The *physiological* variable refers to the structure and functions of the body. The *psychological* variable refers to mental processes and relationships. The *sociocultural* variable refers to system functions that relate to social and cultural expectations and activities. The *developmental* variable refers to those processes related to development over the lifespan. The *spiritual* variable refers to the influence of spiritual beliefs.

Neuman (1995) indicates that the first four variables are commonly understood by nursing. Because the spiritual variable has been more recently added to the model, she discusses it in more detail. This variable is viewed as an innate component of the basic structure that may or may not be acknowledged or developed by the client. Neuman views it as permeating all the other variables of the client system and existing on a developmental continuum from complete unawareness of the presence and potential of the variable to a highly developed spiritual understanding that supports optimal wellness. The continuum includes denial of the existence of the spiritual variable.

Lines of Resistance

The lines of resistance protect the basic structure and become activated when the normal line of defense is invaded by environmental stressors. An example of a response involving lines of resistance is the activation of the immune system mechanisms. If the lines of resistance are effective in their response, the system can reconstitute; if the lines of resistance are not effective, the resulting energy depletion may lead to death.

Normal Line of Defense

In terms of system stability, the normal line of defense represents stability over time (Neuman, 1995). It is considered to be the usual level of stability for the system or the normal wellness state and is used as the baseline for determining deviation from wellness for the client system. The normal line of defense has changed over time as a result of coping with a variety of stressors. The stability represented by the normal line of defense is actually a range of responses to the environment.

Any stressor may invade the normal line of defense when the flexible line of defense offers inadequate protection. When the normal line of defense is invaded or penetrated, the client system reacts. The reaction will be apparent in symptoms of instability or illness and may reduce the system's ability to withstand additional stressors.

Flexible Line of Defense

The flexible line of defense is represented in the model diagram as the outer boundary and initial response, or protection, of the system to stressors. The flexible line of defense serves as a cushion and is described as accordion-like as it expands away from or contracts closer to the normal line of defense (Neuman, 1995). It protects the normal line of defense and acts as a buffer for the client system's usual stable state. Ideally, the flexible line of defense prevents stressors from invading the system. As the distance between the flexible and normal lines of defense increases, so does the degree of protection available to the system.

The flexible line of defense is dynamic rather than stable and can be altered over a relatively short period by factors such as inadequate nutrition or sleep. Either single or multiple stressors may invade the flexible line of defense.

Environment

Neuman (1995) defines environment as all the internal and external factors or influences that surround the client or client system. The influence of the client on the environment and the environment on the client may be positive or negative at any time. Variations in both the client system and the environment can affect the direction of the reaction. For example, individuals who experience sleep deprivation are more susceptible to viruses of the common cold from the environment than those who are well rested.

The *internal* environment exists within the client system. All forces and interactive influences that are solely within the boundaries of the client system make up this environment.

The *external* environment exists outside the client system. Those forces and interactive influences that are outside the system boundaries are identified as external.

Neuman (1989, 1990, 1995) identifies a third environment, the *created environment*. The created environment is developed unconsciously by the client and is symbolic of system wholeness. It represents the open system exchange of energy with both the internal and external environments. It is dynamic and depicts the unconscious mobilization of all system variables but particularly the psychological and sociocultural variables. The purpose of this mobilization is the integration, integrity, and stability of the system. Based on Lazarus's (1981) work, its function is seen as a protective coping shield that encompasses both the internal and external environments. Because it serves as an insulator, the created environment may change the client system's response to stressors. A major objective of the created environment is to provide a positive stimulus toward health for the client. The created environment is developed to be protective but may have a negative effect on the system if it uses energy needed to react to environmental stressors.

To assess the created environment, the caregiver needs to identify three aspects. First, what has been created, what is the nature of the created environment? Second, to what extent is it used and what value does the client place upon it, what are the outcomes? Third, what protection is needed or is possible, what is the ideal that is yet to be created? The created environment is a process-based concept of perpetual adjustment that may increase or decrease the client's state of wellness (Neuman, 1995).

Stressors

Neuman (1995) defines stressors as stimuli that produce tensions and have the potential for causing system instability. The system may need to deal with one or more stressors at any given time. It is important to identify the type, nature, and intensity of the stressor; the time of the system's encounter with the stressor; and the nature of the system's reaction or potential reaction to that encounter, including the amount of energy needed. The reaction may occur in one or more subparts of the system. A reaction in one subsystem may in turn affect the original stressor. Outcomes may be positive with the potential for beneficial system changes that may be temporary or permanent.

Stressors are present both within or outside of the system. Neuman (1995) classifies stressors as intra-, inter-, or extrapersonal in nature. *Intrapersonal* stressors are those that occur within the client system boundary and correlate with the internal environment. An example for the individual client system is the autoimmune response. *Interpersonal* stressors occur outside the client system boundary, are proximal to the system, and have an impact on the system. An example is role expectations. *Extrapersonal* stressors also occur outside the system boundaries but are at a greater distance from the system than are interpersonal stressors. An example is social policy. Interpersonal and extrapersonal stressors correlate with the external environment. The created environment includes intra-, inter-, and extrapersonal stressors.

Health

Neuman (1995) identify health as optimal system stability, or the optimal state of wellness at a given time. Health is seen as a continuum from wellness to illness (see Fig. 4–8). Health is also described as dynamic, with changing levels occurring within a normal range for the client system over time. The levels vary because of basic structure factors and the client system's response and adjustment to environmental stressors. Wellness may be determined by identifying the actual or potential effects of invading stressors on the system's available energy levels. The client system moves toward illness and death (entropy) when more energy is needed than is available and toward wellness (negentropy) when more energy is available, or can be generated, than is needed.

Reaction

Although reaction is identified within Figure 4–8, Neuman does not discuss it separately. She points out that reactions and outcomes may be positive or negative, and she discusses system movement toward negentropy or entropy.

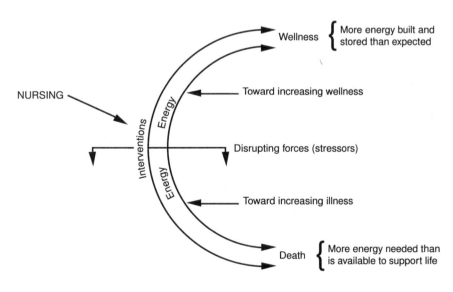

FIGURE 4–8

Wellness-illness based on the systems concept. *(Adapted from Neuman, B., (1982). The Neuman systems model: Applications to nursing education and practice (p. 11). Norwalk, CT: Appleton-Century-Crofts. Used with permission.)*

Prevention

Primary, secondary, and tertiary prevention as interventions are used to retain, attain, and maintain system balance. More than one prevention mode may be used simultaneously.

Primary prevention occurs before the system reacts to a stressor; it includes health promotion and maintenance of wellness. Primary prevention focuses on strengthening the flexible line of defense through preventing stress and reducing risk factors. This intervention occurs when the risk or hazard is identified but before a reaction occurs. Strategies that might be used include immunization, health education, exercise, and life style changes.

Secondary prevention occurs after the system reacts to a stressor and is provided in terms of existing symptoms. Secondary prevention focuses on strengthening the internal lines of resistance and, thus, protects the basic structure through appropriate treatment of symptoms. The intent is to regain optimal system stability and to conserve energy in doing so. If secondary prevention is unsuccessful and reconstitution does not occur, the basic structure will be unable to support the system and its interventions, and death will occur.

Tertiary prevention occurs after the system has been treated through secondary prevention strategies. Its purpose is to maintain wellness or protect the client system reconstitution through supporting existing strengths and continuing to conserve energy. Tertiary prevention may begin at any point after system stability has begun to be reestablished (reconstitution has begun). Tertiary prevention tends to lead back to primary prevention.

Reconstitution

Reconstitution begins at any point following initiation of treatment for invasion of stressors. Neuman (1995) defines reconstitution as the increase in energy that occurs in relation to the degree of reaction to the stressor. Reconstitution may expand the normal line of defense beyond its previous level, stabilize the system at a lower level, or return it to the level that existed before the illness. It depends on successful mobilization of client resources to prevent further reaction to the stressor, and it represents a dynamic state of adjustment.

Nursing

Neuman (1995) also discusses nursing as part of the model. The major concern of nursing is to help the client system attain, maintain, or retain system stability. This may be accomplished through accurate assessment of both the actual and potential effects of stressor invasion and assisting the client system to make those adjustments necessary for optimal wellness. In supporting system stability, the nurse provides the linkage between the client system, the environment, health, and nursing.

Propositions of the Neuman Systems Model

Neuman (1974) presented the assumptions that she identified as underlying the Neuman Systems Model. She has now labeled these as propositions (Neuman, 1995). These propositions follow:

1. Although each individual client or group as a client system is unique, each system is a composite of common known factors or innate characteristics within a normal, given range of response contained within a basic structure.

2. Many known, unknown, and universal environmental stressors exist. Each differs in its potential for disturbing a client's usual stability level, or normal line of defense. The

particular interrelationships of client variables—physiological, psychological, socio-cultural, developmental, and spiritual—at any point in time can affect the degree to which a client is protected by the flexible line of defense against possible reaction to a single stressor or a combination of stressors.

3. Each individual client/client system has evolved a normal range of response to the environment that is referred to as a normal line of defense, or usual wellness/stability state. It represents change over time through coping with diverse stress encounters. The normal line of defense can be used as a standard from which to measure health deviation.

4. When the cushioning, accordion-like effect of the flexible line of defense is no longer capable of protecting the client/client system against an environmental stressor, the stressor breaks through the normal line of defense. The interrelationships of variables—physiological, psychological, sociocultural, developmental, and spiritual—determine the nature and degree of the system reaction or possible reaction to the stressor.

5. The client, whether in a state of wellness or illness, is a dynamic composite of the interrelationships of variables—physiological, psychological, sociocultural, developmental, and spiritual. Wellness is on a continuum of available energy to support the system in an optimal state of system stability.

6. Implicit within each client system is a set of internal resistance factors known as lines of resistance, which function to stabilize and return the client to the usual state of wellness (normal line of defense) or possibly to a higher level of stability following an environmental stressor reaction.

7. Primary prevention relates to general knowledge that is applied to client assessment and intervention in identification and reduction or mitigation of possible or actual risk factors associated with environmental stressors to prevent possible reaction. The goal of health promotion is included in primary prevention.

8. Secondary prevention relates to symptomatology following a reaction to stressors, appropriate ranking of intervention priorities, and treatment to reduce their noxious effects.

9. Tertiary prevention relates to the adjustive processes taking place as reconstitution begins and maintenance factors move the client back in a circular manner toward primary prevention.

10. The client as a system is in dynamic, constant energy exchange with the environment (pp. 20–21).

The Neuman Systems Model and Nursing's Metaparadigm

The four major concepts in nursing's metaparadigm are identified by Neuman as part of her model and have been discussed. A brief summary of each follows.

The *human being* is viewed as an open system that interacts with both internal and external environmental forces or stressors. The human is in constant change, moving toward a dynamic state of system stability or toward illness of varying degrees.

The *environment* is a vital arena that is germane to the system and its function; it includes internal, external, and created environment (Neuman, 1995). The environment may be viewed as all factors that affect and are affected by the system.

Health is defined as the condition or degree of system stability and is viewed as a continuum from wellness to illness (Neuman, 1995) (see Fig. 4–8). Stability occurs when all the system's parts and subparts are in balance or harmony so that the whole system is in balance. When system needs are met, optimal wellness exists. When needs are not satisfied, illness exists. When the energy needed to support life is not available, death occurs.

The primary concern of *nursing* is to define the appropriate action in situations that are stress-related or in relation to possible reactions of the client or client system to stressors. Nursing interventions are aimed at helping the system adapt or adjust and to retain, restore, or maintain some degree of stability between and among the client system variables and environmental stressors with a focus on conserving energy.

The Neuman Systems Model and the Nursing Process

Neuman (1982, 1995) presents a three step nursing process format (see Table 4–9). The first step is entitled "Nursing Diagnosis" and includes the use of a data base to identify variances from wellness and development of hypothetical interventions. The second step, "Nursing Goals," includes caregiver-client negotiation of intervention strategies to retain, attain, or maintain system stability. The third step, "Nursing Outcomes," includes nursing intervention using the prevention modes, confirming that the desired change has occurred or reformulating the nursing goals, using the outcomes of short-term goals to determine longer-term goals, and validating the nursing process through client outcomes. Neuman's first step parallels the assessment and diagnosis phases of the five-phase nursing process. Her second step equates to the planning phase, and her third step equates to the implementation and evaluation phases.

Using the Neuman Systems Model in the assessment phase of the nursing process, the nurse focuses on obtaining a comprehensive client data base to determine the existing state of wellness and the actual or potential reaction to environmental stressors. A more specific guide to assessment is presented in Table 4–10, "An Assessment and Intervention Tool." The collected data are prioritized and compared to, or synthesized with, relevant theories to explain the client's condition. Variances from the usual state of wellness are identified and a summary of impressions developed. The summary includes intra-, inter-, and extrapersonal factors.

The synthesis of data with theory also provides the basis for the *nursing diagnosis*. In the Neuman model, the diagnostic statement should reflect the entire client condition.

Planning involves negotiation between the caregiver and the client, or recipient of care. The overall goal of the caregiver is to guide the client to conserve energy and to use energy as a force to move beyond the present, ideally in a way that preserves or enhances the client's wellness level. More specific goals will be derived from the nursing diagnoses. The perceptions of both the client and the caregiver must be considered in setting goals.

According to Neuman (1995), nursing actions (*implementation*) are based on the synthesis of a comprehensive data base about the client and the theory(ies) that are appropriate in light of the client's perceptions and possibilities for functional competence within the environment. The modes for identifying these actions are the levels of prevention as intervention. Table 4–11 presents a guide to nursing actions using prevention as intervention.

Evaluation is implied in the discussion of reassessment in Table 4–10. It is more explicitly identified in the "Nursing Outcomes" step of Neuman's three-step nursing process (see Table 4–9). According to this third step, evaluation confirms that the anticipated or prescribed change

TABLE 4–9 The Neuman Nursing Process Format

Nursing Diagnosis

Data base

Variances from wellness are determined by correlations and constraints

Hypothetical interventions are determined for prescriptive change

I. Nursing Diagnosis
    A. Database—determined by
        1. Identification and evaluation of potential or actual stressors that pose a threat to the stability of the client/client systems.
        2. Assessment of condition and strength of basic structure factors and energy resources.
        3. Assessment of characteristics of the flexible and normal lines of defense, lines of resistance, degree of potential reaction, reaction, and/or potential for reconstitution following a reaction.
        4. Identification, classification, and evaluation of potential and/or actual intra-, inter-, and extra-personal interactions between the client and environment, considering all five variables.
        5. Evaluation of influence of past, present, and possible future life process and coping patterns on client system stability.
        6. Identification and evaluation of actual and potential internal and external resources for optimal state of wellness.
        7. Identification and resolution of perceptual differences between caregivers and client/client system.

Note: In all the above areas of consideration the caregiver simultaneously considers five variables (dynamic interactions in the client/client system)—physiological, psychological, sociocultural, developmental, and spiritual.

Continued

TABLE 4–9 The Neuman Nursing Process Format (Continued)

Nursing Diagnosis

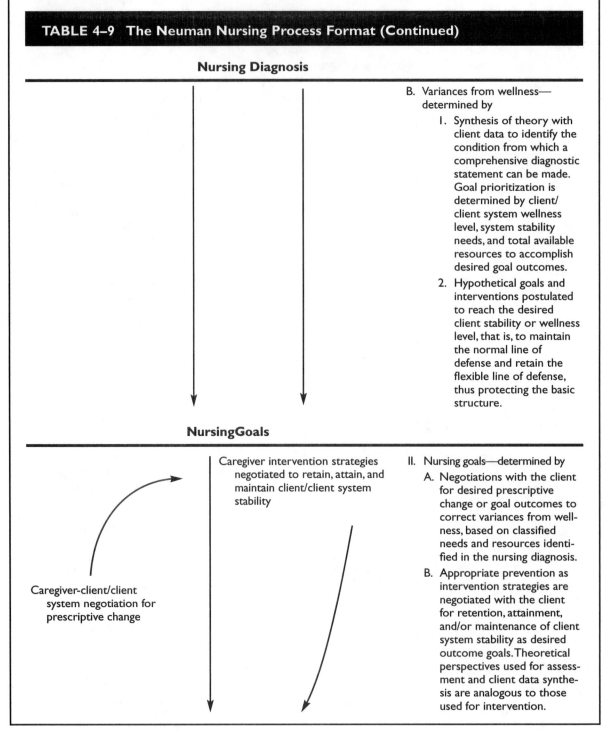

B. Variances from wellness—determined by

1. Synthesis of theory with client data to identify the condition from which a comprehensive diagnostic statement can be made. Goal prioritization is determined by client/ client system wellness level, system stability needs, and total available resources to accomplish desired goal outcomes.

2. Hypothetical goals and interventions postulated to reach the desired client stability or wellness level, that is, to maintain the normal line of defense and retain the flexible line of defense, thus protecting the basic structure.

NursingGoals

Caregiver intervention strategies negotiated to retain, attain, and maintain client/client system stability

Caregiver-client/client system negotiation for prescriptive change

II. Nursing goals—determined by

A. Negotiations with the client for desired prescriptive change or goal outcomes to correct variances from wellness, based on classified needs and resources identified in the nursing diagnosis.

B. Appropriate prevention as intervention strategies are negotiated with the client for retention, attainment, and/or maintenance of client system stability as desired outcome goals. Theoretical perspectives used for assessment and client data synthesis are analogous to those used for intervention.

Continued

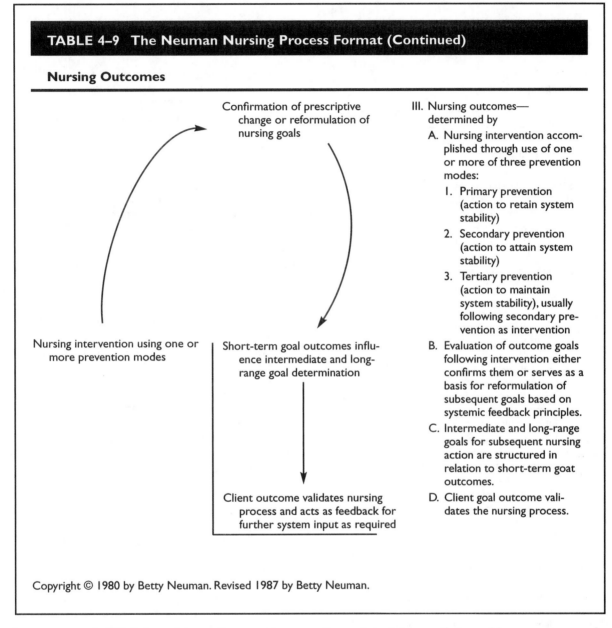

TABLE 4–9 The Neuman Nursing Process Format (Continued)

Nursing Outcomes

Confirmation of prescriptive change or reformulation of nursing goals

Nursing intervention using one or more prevention modes

Short-term goal outcomes influence intermediate and long-range goal determination

Client outcome validates nursing process and acts as feedback for further system input as required

III. Nursing outcomes— determined by

A. Nursing intervention accomplished through use of one or more of three prevention modes:

   1. Primary prevention (action to retain system stability)

   2. Secondary prevention (action to attain system stability)

   3. Tertiary prevention (action to maintain system stability), usually following secondary prevention as intervention

B. Evaluation of outcome goals following intervention either confirms them or serves as a basis for reformulation of subsequent goals based on systemic feedback principles.

C. Intermediate and long-range goals for subsequent nursing action are structured in relation to short-term goat outcomes.

D. Client goal outcome validates the nursing process.

Copyright © 1980 by Betty Neuman. Revised 1987 by Betty Neuman.

has occurred. If this is not true, then goals are reformulated. Immediate and long-range goals are then structured in relation to the short-range outcomes.

*S*trengths and Weaknesses of the Neuman Systems Model

The major strength of the Neuman Systems Model is its flexibility for use in all areas of nursing—administration, education, and practice. The third edition of *The Neuman Systems Model* includes many chapters that discuss the use of the model in all of these areas throughout the United States and in Australia, Canada, England, Holland, Sweden, and Wales. This widespread acceptance supports the essentially universal applicability of the model.

TABLE 4-10 An Assessment and Intervention Tool

A. Intake Summary
   1. Name _____
      Age _____
      Sex _____
      Marital status _____
   2. Referral source and related information _____
      _____

B. Stressors as Perceived by Client
   (If client is incapacitated, secure data from family or other resources.)
   1. What do you consider your major stress area, or areas of health concern? (Identify these areas.)
   2. How do present circumstances differ from your usual pattern of living? (Identify lifestyle patterns.)
   3. Have you ever experienced a similar problem? If so, what was that problem and how did you handle it? Were you successful? (Identify past coping patterns.)
   4. What do you anticipate for yourself in the future as a consequence of your present situation? (Identify perceptual factors, that is, reality versus distortions—expectations, present and possible future coping patterns.)
   5. What are you doing and what can you do to help yourself? (Identify perceptual factors, that is, reality versus distortions—expectations, present and possible future coping patterns.)
   6. What do you expect caregivers, family, friends, or others to do for you? (Identify perceptual factors, that is, reality versus distortions—expectations, present and possible future coping patterns.)

C. Stressors as Perceived by Caregiver
   1. What do you consider to be the major stress area, or areas of health concern? (Identify these areas.)
   2. How do present circumstances seem to differ from the client's usual pattern of living? (Identify life style patterns.)
   3. Has the client ever experienced a similar situation? If so, how would you evaluate what the client did? How successful do you think it was? (Identify past coping patterns.)
   4. What do you anticipate for the future as a consequence of the client's present situation?

(Identify perceptual factors, that is, reality versus distortions—expectations, present and possible future coping patterns.)
   5. What can the client do to help him- or herself? (Identify perceptual factors, that is, reality versus distortions—expectations, present and possible future coping patterns.)
   6. What do you think the client expects from caregivers, family, friends, or other resources? (Identify perceptual factors, that is, reality versus distortions—expectations, present and possible future coping patterns.)

Summary of Impressions
Note any discrepancies or distortions between the client's perception and that of the caregiver related to the situation.

D. Intrapersonal Factors
   1. Physical (examples: degree of mobility, range of body function)
   2. Psycho-sociocultural (examples: attitudes, values, expectations, behavior patterns, and nature of coping patterns)
   3. Developmental (examples: age, degree of normalcy, factors related to present situation)
   4. Spiritual belief system (examples: hope and sustaining factors)

E. Interpersonal Factors
   Examples are resources and relationship of family, friends, or caregivers that either influence or could influence Area D.

F. Extrapersonal Factors
   Examples are resources and relationship of community facilities, finances, employment, or other area which either influence or could influence Areas D and E.

G. Formulation of a Comprehensive Nursing Diagnosis
   This is accomplished by identifying and ranking the priority of needs based on total data obtained from the clients perception, the caregiver's perception, or other resources, such as laboratory reports, other caregivers, or agencies. Appropriate theory is related to the above data.

   With this format, reassessment is a continuous process and is related to the effectiveness of intervention based upon the prior stated goals. Effective reassessment would include the following as they relate to the total client situation:

Continued

TABLE 4–10 An Assessment and Intervention Tool (Continued)

1. Changes in nature of stressors and priority assignments
2. Changes in intrapersonal factors
3. Changes in interpersonal factors
4. Changes in extrapersonal factors

In reassessment it is important to note the change of priority of goals in relation to the primary, secondary, and tertiary prevention as intervention categories. An assessment tool of this nature should offer a current, progressive, and comprehensive analysis of the clients total circumstances and relationship of the five client variables (physiological, psychological, sociocultural, developmental, and spiritual) to environmental influences.

From Neuman, B. (1995). The Neuman Systems Model. (pp. 59 – 61). Norwalk, CT: Appleton & Lange.

TABLE 4–11 Format for Prevention as Intervention

Nursing Action

Primary Prevention	Secondary Prevention	Tertiary Prevention
1. Classify stressors that threaten stability of the client/client system. Prevent stressor invasion.	1. Following stressor invasion, protect basic structure.	1. During reconstitution, attain and maintain maximum level of wellness or stability following treatment.
2. Provide information to retain or strengthen existing client/client system strengths.	2. Mobilize and optimize internal/external resources to attain stability and energy conservation.	2. Educate, reeducate, and/or reorient as needed.
3. Support positive coping and functioning.	3. Facilitate purposeful manipulation of stressors and reactions to stressors.	3. Support client/client system toward appropriate goals.
4. Desensitize existing or possible noxious stressors.	4. Motivate, educate, and involve client/client system in health care goals.	4. Coordinate and integrate health service resources.
5. Motivate toward wellness.	5. Facilitate appropriate treatment and intervention measures.	5. Provide primary and/or secondary preventive intervention as required.
6. Coordinate and integrate interdisciplinary theories and epidemiological input.	6. Support positive factors toward wellness.	
7. Educate or reeducate.	7. Promote advocacy by coordination and integration.	
8. Use stress as a positive intervention strategy.	8. Provide primary preventive intervention as required.	

Note: *A first priority for nursing action in each of the areas of prevention as intervention is to determine the nature of stressors and their threat to the client/client system, some general categorical functions for nursing action are initiation, planning, organization, monitoring, coordinating, implementing, integrating, advocating, supporting, and evaluating. An example of a limited classification system for stressors is illustrated by the following four categories: (1) deprivation, (2) excess, (3) change, and (4) intolerance.*

Copyright © 1980 by Betty Neuman. Revised 1987 by Betty Neuman.

Neuman (1995) reports that the model was designed for nursing but can be used by other health disciplines, which can be viewed as either a strength or weakness. As a strength, if multiple health disciplines use the model, a consistent approach to client care would be facilitated. If all disciplines use similar data collection techniques based upon the assessment tool presented by Neuman, perhaps the client would not have to tell his or her story so many different times—at least once to each health care discipline. As a weakness, if the model is useful to a variety of disciplines, it is not specific to nursing and thus may not differentiate the practice of nursing from that of other disciplines.

The major weakness of the model is the need for further clarification of terms used. Interpersonal and extrapersonal stressors need to be more clearly differentiated. It may be that interpersonal stressors occur between two people and extrapersonal stressors occur between a group or society and the person. This differentiation is not clearly made. Other areas that require greater specification are how to identify variances of wellness and levels of wellness. Reaction also needs to be defined.

The Neuman Systems Model and the Characteristics of a Theory

1. **Theories can interrelate concepts in such a way as to create a different way of looking at a particular phenomenon.** Neuman has presented a view of the client that is equally applicable to an individual, a family, a group, a community, or any other aggregate. The systems view she presents, in conjunction with the prevention modalities as intervention, are a unique way of viewing health care phenomena. The interaction of the client system and its environments as they relate to health provide a useful view of the world. The emphasis on primary prevention, including health promotion, is specific to this model and increasingly important in today's health care environment.

2. **Theories must be logical in nature.** The Neuman Systems Model, particularly as presented in the model diagram, is logically consistent. The three-step nursing process is also logical, with its emphasis on a comprehensive data base, mutual decision making between caregiver and client system, and use of outcomes. However, there are some inconsistencies between the diagram and the verbal presentation of the model. The diagram includes reaction that is not specifically discussed in the text. Conversely, the verbal presentation incorporates health, environment, and nursing, which do not appear in the diagram. It is inferred that the diagram is considered to be the most important representation of the model because it is changes in the diagram that require unanimous agreement of the Neuman Trustees. Logically, based upon this inference, the concepts in the verbal presentation should be derived from the diagram.

    Other inconsistencies relate to Neuman's emphasis on a wholistic approach and a comprehensive view of the client system and her discussion of health and illness. The wholistic and comprehensive view is associated with an open system. Health and illness are presented on a continuum with movement toward health described as negentropic and toward illness as entropic. Entropy is a characteristic of a closed, rather than an open, system. She does speak of levels of wellness, rather than levels of illness, but does not make it clear if health and illness are dichotomous.

3. **Theories should be relatively simple yet generalizable.** Once understood, the Neuman Systems Model is relatively simple, and has readily acceptable definitions of its

components. Its generalizability is supported by the more than three dozen chapters in the third edition of *The Neuman Systems Model* that discuss the use of the model in curriculum, nursing practice, and nursing administration in the United States and internationally. Neuman (1995) also indicates that although the model was designed for nursing, it can be used by other health care providers.

An initial drawback to simplicity is the diagram of the model (see Figure 4–7). In its efforts to represent multiple relationships and components, the diagram has become awesome. With a guide to the diagram, the components can be clearly understood, and the initial sense of overwhelming complexity overcome.

4. **Theories can be the bases for hypotheses that can be tested or for theory to be expanded,** and

5. **Theories contribute to and assist in increasing the general body of knowledge within the discipline through the research implemented to validate them.** Hypotheses can be and have been derived from the Neuman Systems Model and the relationships within the model. The third edition of *The Neuman Systems Model* cites multiple published research articles, doctoral dissertations, and masters theses that have reported research based on the model. The areas of research have included client systems of individuals, families, and groups of practicing nurses and nursing students in educational settings, hospitals, and the community.

6. **Theories can be used by practitioners to guide and unprove their practice.** Neuman has provided tools that are specifically designed to assist practitioners in using the model in practice (see Table 4–10 and Table 4–11). The model is congruent with the increasing emphases on home health care and health promotion. It has been widely used by practitioners in nursing education, practice, and administration nationally and internationally.

7. **Theories must be consistent with other validated theories, laws, and principles but will leave open unanswered questions that need to be investigated.** Neuman identifies the theories upon which she drew to develop the systems model. Her work appears to be consistent with these theories, and there is no apparent conflict with other theories. There are many questions yet to be answered, including: Does the created environment more often have a positive or negative system outcome? Does the use of the Neuman Systems Model increase the effectiveness of communication with other health care providers? What is the most effective way to identify a client system's optimal level of wellness?

The Neuman Systems Model does not fully meet all the characteristics of a theory. Since it is presented as a model, this is not surprising. Neuman (1995) reports that she and A. Koertvelyessy have found that the major theory of the model is that of optimal client system stability. This theory is that the health of the client system is represented by stability. Neuman cites an unpublished paper as the only reference for the theory.

$\mathcal{S}$ummary

The Neuman Systems Model was developed to help teach graduate students an integrated approach to client care. The model is based in general system theory and views the client as an open system that responds to stressors in the environment. The client variables are physiological, psychological, sociocultural, developmental, and spiritual. The client system consists of a basic or core structure that is protected by lines of resistance. The usual level of health is identified as the normal line of defense that is protected by a flexible line of defense. Stressors are intra-, inter-, and extrapersonal in nature and arise from the internal, external, and created environments. When stressors break through the flexible line of defense, the system is invaded and the lines of resistance are activated and the system is described as moving into illness on a wellness-illness continuum. If adequate energy is available, the system will be reconstituted with the normal line of defense restored at, below, or above its previous level. Nursing interventions occur through three prevention modalities. Primary prevention occurs before the stressor invades the system; secondary prevention occurs after the system has reacted to an invading stressor; and tertiary prevention occurs after secondary prevention as reconstitution is being established.

This model has been widely used in all areas of nursing practice. Its flexibility and universality are documented in the many publications that describe its use in nursing education, research, administration, and direct patient care. Further definition of some of the concepts in the model will serve to strengthen it further.

References

Caplan, G. (1964). *Principles of preventive psychiatry.* New York: Basic Books. [out of print]

Cornu, A. (1957). *The origin of Marxist thought.* Springfield, IL: Thomas. [out of print]

de Chardin, P. T. (1955). *The phenomenon of man.* London: Collins. [out of print]

Edelson, M. (1970). *Sociotherapy and psychotherapy.* Chicago: University of Chicago. [out of print]

Emery, F. (Ed.). (1969). *Systems thinking.* Baltimore: Penguin Books. [out of print]

Heslin, K. (1986). *A systems analysis of the Betty Neuman model.* Unpublished student paper. University of Western Ontario, London, Ontario, Canada.

Laszlo, E. (1972). *The systems view of the world: The natural philosophy of the new development in the sciences.* New York: Braziller. [out of print]

Lazarus, R. (1981). The stress and coping paradigm. In C. Eisdorfer, D. Cohen, A. Kleinman, & P. Maxim (Eds.), *Models for clinical psychopathology* (pp. 177–214). New York: SP Medical and Scientific Books.

Neuman, B. (1974). The Betty Neuman health-care systems model: A total person approach to patient problems. In J. P. Riehl, & C. Roy (Eds.), *Conceptual models for nursing practice* (pp. 99–114). New York: Appleton-Century-Crofts. [out of print]

Neuman, B. (1982). *The Neuman Systems Model.* Norwalk, CT: Appleton-Century-Crofts. [out of print]

Neuman, B. (1989). *The Neuman Systems Model* (2nd ed.). Norwalk, CT: Appleton & Lange. [out of print]

Neuman, B. (1990). Health on a continuum based on the Neuman Systems Model. *Nursing Science Quarterly, 3,* 129–135.

Neuman, B. (1995). *The Neuman Systems Model* (3rd ed.). Norwalk, CT: Appleton & Lange.

Neuman, B. M., & Young, R. J. (1972). A model for teaching total person approach to patient problems. *Nursing Research, 21,* 264–269.

Parker, M. E. (Ed.). (1990). *Nursing theories in practice.* New York: National League for Nursing.

Riehl-Sisca, J. (1989). *Conceptual models for nursing practice* (3rd ed.). Norwalk, CT: Appleton & Lange.

Selye, H. (1950). *The physiology and pathology of exposure to stress.* Montreal, Quebec, Canada: ACTA. [out of print]

External Analysis

The overall goals of the model, i.e., holistic care, prevention, health promotion, and systems concepts, are congruent with current societal values held by the World Health Organization, the American Nurses' Association (Neuman, 1989, p. 10), and the focus on primary prevention and interdisciplinary care being promoted in the health care industry today. In addition, given the current complexities of health care and the need for health care providers to rapidly and easily assimilate change, the expansive characteristic of systems models becomes an essential component of effective practice (Neuman, 1989, p. 5).

Relationship to Nursing Research

As evidenced by the model's increased empirical utilization through research, the Neuman systems model is being used as a guide for conceptualization of research problems. The findings of a 1986–1987 survey of graduate nursing programs regarding use of the Neuman model in research identified 38 studies (Louis & Koertvelyessy, 1989). The vast majority of these ($N=20$) were descriptive in nature and studied adult populations. The only Neuman model concept not being investigated was that of the spiritual variable. The authors present the 38 study citations and abstracts in an appendix to their chapter.

The most frequently cited example of research based on the Neuman model is the work of Ziemer (1983), who examined the effects of providing patients with selected types of information preoperatively on their ability to cope postoperatively. The empirical indicators for the model concept of stressor was that of surgery, lines of defense were measured by frequency of coping behavior, the primary prevention intervention was provision of preoperative information, and stressor impact was operationalized by development of physiological symptoms postoperatively.

While Ziemer concluded that the Neuman systems model may be faulty because none of the six study hypotheses was supported, the study did have several major limitations. Among those were the lack of a power analysis to determine if the sample size obtained for the study was large enough to detect statistical significance. Secondly, as identified by Ziemer (1983), the scale used to measure the coping responses of postoperative surgical patients was developed

Taken from: *Conceptual Models of Nursing: Analysis and Application*, Third Edition by Fitzpatrick and Whall.

using healthy students as the normative group. And finally, the notion that provision of information preoperatively would prevent or reduce physiological symptoms such as nausea, vomiting, or difficulty voiding postoperatively seems faulty.

Lancaster's (1991/1992) study examined how women with family histories of breast cancer appraise and cope with their increased risk of developing the disease. A middle-range theory of breast cancer prevention was formulated from the Neuman model and proposed relationships among stressors (breast cancer risk factors), stressor appraisal (breast cancer threat appraisal), and primary prevention interventions (primary prevention coping behaviors) were hypothesized and tested. The work of Lazarus and Folkman (1984) is also reflected in the middle-range theory in an effort to incorporate a more dynamic view of coping as well as to assist in the development of a typology of primary prevention interventions.

Based on a power analysis, a sample of 120 subjects was needed to detect a moderate effect size. The final sample consisted of 209 women. All measures were reliable and valid. Both study hypotheses were supported.

Bueno et al. (1992) also based their study of risk behaviors of motor vehicle crash victims on the Neuman model. The motor vehicle accidents were conceptualized as the stressors that threaten wellness. Risk behaviors such as driving under the influence of alcohol and failing to wear safety belts were proposed to be behaviors that weakened the lines of defense. Data from this study provided the foundation for developing and testing tertiary prevention interventions that would decrease risk behavior of motor vehicle crash victims.

The concepts of stressors, client system variables, interpersonal social factors, and created environment were the focus for the pilot study on ventilator dependent patients by Lowry and Anderson (1993). Also using the Lazarus theory of stress and coping to support the Neuman model, this descriptive exploratory study sought to identify the patient's perceptions of their ventilator experiences. Although the sample size was very small ($N=4$) and does not permit one to draw conclusions from the study, it does provide further evidence of researcher's abilities to operationalize and test the abstract Neuman model concepts.

In addition to these four studies, literature searches of CINAHL, MEDLINE, and the Sigma Theta Tau International library revealed numerous other published and unpublished research related to the Neuman model ($N=87$). For example, Blank et al. (1989) uses the Neuman systems model stressor typology to identify the perceived home care needs of caregivers and patients who underwent cancer treatment. Grant and Bean (1992) used the Neuman model typology for stressors to categorize the self-identified needs of informal caregivers of head-injured adults. Using this study as an example, Grant et al. (1993) demonstrate how conceptual frameworks can guide the research process.

The literature search revealed that a wide range of populations and topics were studied using the model as a framework. However, the vast majority of these works were brief statements identifying the model as the study's conceptual framework or providing an overview of the model's major concepts. Some researchers did not cite the 1989 Neuman text (Koku, 1992; Freiberger et al., 1992; Kahn, 1992) or reference Neuman as a primary source (Radwanski, 1992).

Recommendations for further development of the model through the research process would include the following. Conceptual, theoretical, and empirical structures as identified by Fawcett and Downs (1986) need to be included in all research reports along with appropriate narrative to describe it. Proposed research based on the model needs to be made explicit as middle-range theory. Findings of studies may be used to establish or refute the credibility of the Neuman model and may be included in the next edition of the Neuman text in a section devoted to research and testing of the model. All research should use the most current model conceptualization as the basis for their studies.

Relationship to Nursing Education

The model was originally designed as a teaching aide and later used as curriculum guide (Neuman, 1972). Since 1972, it has been used in nursing curriculums at the University of Pittsburgh; Saint Xavier College; Northwestern State University; California State University, Fresno; University of Ottawa, Canada; University of Saskatchewan, Canada; Neumann College; Saint Anselm College; and the Universities of Nevada, Las Vegas, Wyoming, Missouri-Kansas City, and Minnesota, as well as others.

These universities and colleges have used various approaches to use the model to guide baccalaureate education. These approaches are discussed in detail by Kilchenstein and Yakulis (1984), Bourbonnais and Ross (1985), Stittich et al. (1989), Mrkonich et al. (1989), Nelson et al. (1989), and others. The sheer number of academic programs across the United States and in other countries that have utilized the Neuman model in curriculum efforts speaks well of the model's versatility and breadth of application.

Master's education in nursing has also been guided by the Neuman model. Texas Woman's University currently uses the model as the basis for their master's curriculum. Faculty have used it to develop courses in a variety of specialty areas such as psychiatric–mental health, community health, maternal–child health, nursing administration, as well as medical–surgical nursing (Johnson et al., 1982). Stittich et al. (1989) describes how California State University at Fresno applied the model to their master's and nurse-practitioner programs.

The model has also been applied in community-based education programs. Dunn and Trepanier (1989) describe their efforts to develop three high-risk perinatal courses as well as workshops, in-services, and conferences based on the Neuman model.

Relationship to Nursing Practice

Like its application to nursing education, the Neuman model has been applied to a wide variety of nursing practice arenas. Model application has been facilitated through the development and testing tools designed to facilitate incorporation of model terminology and assist in model implementation in the practice arena. Such tools include the Neuman nursing process and the prevention as intervention formats (Neuman, 1989, p. 17).

Examples of clinical practice areas that have found the model helpful are reflected in the work of Waters (1993), who used the model to assist her in dealing with clients with disturbances in self-esteem. Similarly, Davies (1989) incorporated the model into her community psychiatric nursing practice in Wales.

The model was used by Piazza et al. (1992) in pediatric oncology nursing practice to assess, plan, and evaluate care of the 8-year-old child with leukemia; and Galloway (1993) used the model to assist her to cope with a mentally and physically impaired infant.

In the maternal–child health arena, Bullock's (1993) efforts to systematically assess the health effects that battering has on mothers and infants in an effort to improve their quality of life were guided by model concepts. Unfortunately, Bullock cited the 1972 version of the Neuman model and thus did not address how Neuman's newer concepts would be related to this population.

Derstine (1992) examined the use of nursing theory to guide rehabilitation nursing practice and reviewed how others have applied the Neuman model to assist them to care for this patient population. Schlentz (1993) described how the Neuman model, in tandem with the Nursing minimum data set, may be used to effectively plan care for a geriatric population.

Primary, secondary, and tertiary interventions for patients suffering from hypermetabolism in multisystem organ failure are presented by Bergstrom (1992) as one example of model application to the critical care area.

Walker (1994) is pioneering the use of the model to evaluate the quality of client-centered care and demonstrate the cost/benefit ratio of primary prevention as compared to secondary and tertiary interventions. To achieve these outcomes, she has blended concepts from total quality management, the Neuman systems model, and Gil's (1990) model for social policy analysis adapted for health care. Work such as this assures the continued development and use of the model well into the 21st century.

References

Allen, C. J. (1989). Incorporating a wellness perspective for nursing diagnosis in practice. In R. M. Caroll-Johnson (Ed.), *Classification of nursing diagnoses: Proceedings of the eighth conference.* Philadelphia: J. B. Lippincott.

Anderson, E., McFarlane, J., & Helton, A. (1986). Community as client: A model for practice. *Nursing Outlook, 34*(5), 220–224.

Beddome, G. (1989). Application of the Neuman systems model to the community-as-client. In B. Neuman (Ed.), *The Neuman systems model* (2nd ed.). Norwalk, CT: Appleton & Lange.

Bergstrom, D. (1992). Hypermetabolism in multisystem organ failure: A Neuman systems perspective. *Critical Care Nursing Quarterly, 15*(3), 63–70.

Blank, J. J., Clark, L., Longman, A. J., & Atwood, J. (1989). Perceived homecare needs of cancer patients and their caregivers. *Cancer Nursing, 12*(2), 78–84.

Bourbonnais, F. F., & Ross, M. M. (1985). The Neuman systems model in nursing education: Course development and implementation. *Journal of Advanced Nursing, 10,* 117–123.

Bueno, M. M., Redeker, N., & Norman, E. M. (1992). Analysis of motor vehicle crash data in an urban trauma center: Implications for nursing practice and research. *Heart and Lung, 21*(6), 558–567.

Bullock, L. F. (1993). Nursing interventions for abused women on obstetrical units. *AWHONN's Clinical Issues, 4*(3) 371–377.

Caplan, G. (1964). *Principles of preventive psychiatry.* New York: Basic Books.

de Chardin, P. Teilhard (1955). *The phenomenon of man.* London: Collins.

Cornu, A. (1957). *The origins of Marxist thought.* Springfield, IL: Charles C Thomas

Davies, P. (1989). In Wales: Use of the Neuman systems model by community psychiatric nurses. In B. Neuman (Ed)., *The Neuman systems model* (2nd ed.) (pp. 375–383). Norwalk, CT: Appleton & Lange.

Delunas, L. R. (1990). Prevention of elder abuse: Betty Neuman health care systems approach. *Clinical Nurse Specialist, 4*(1), 54–58.

Derstine, J. B. (1992). Theory-based advanced rehabilitation nursing: Is it a reality? *Holistic Nursing Practice, 6*(2), 1–6.

Dubin, R. (1978). *Theory building.* New York: Free Press.

Dunn, S. I., & Trepanier, M-J. (1989). Application of the Neuman systems model to perinatal nursing. In B. Neuman (Ed.), *The Neuman systems model* (2nd ed.), (pp. 407–419). Norwalk, CT: Appleton & Lange.

Edelson, M. (1970). *Sociotherapy and psychotherapy.* Chicago: University of Chicago Press.

Ellis, R. (1968). Characteristics of significant theories. *Nursing Research, 17*(3), 217–222.

Emery, F. (Ed.) (1969). *Systems thinking.* Baltimore: Penguin.

Fawcett, J. (1989). *Analysis and evaluation of conceptual models in nursing* (2nd ed.). Philadelphia: F. A. Davis.

Fawcett, J., & Downs, F. S. (1986). *The relationship of theory and research.* Norwalk, CT: Appleton-Century-Crofts.

Freiberger, D., Bryant, J., & Marino, B. (1992). The effects of different central venous line dressing changes on bacterial growth in a pediatric oncology population. *Journal of Pediatric Oncology, 9*(1), 3–7.

Fulton, R. A. B. (1995). The spiritual variable: Essential to the client system. In B. Neuman (Ed), *The Neuman Systems Model* (3rd ed.) (pp. 77–91). Norwalk, CT: Appleton & Lange.

Galloway, D. A. (1993). Coping with a mentally and physically impaired infant: A self-analysis. *Rehabilitation Nursing, 18*(1), 34–36.

Gil, D. G. (1990). *Unravelling social policy* (4th ed.). Rochester, VT: Schenkman.

Grant, J. S., & Bean, C. A. (1992). Self-identified needs of informal caregivers of head-injured adults. *Family and Community Health, 15*(2), 49–58.

Grant, J. S., Kinney, M. R., Davis, L. L. (1993). Using conceptual frameworks or models to guide nursing research. *Journal of Neuroscience Nursing, 25*(1), 52–56.

Gray, W., Rizzo, N. D., & Duhl, F. D. (Eds.) (1969). *General systems theory and psychiatry.* Boston: Little, Brown.

Hardy, M. (1974). Theories: Components, development, evaluation. *Nursing Research, 23*(2), 100–107.

Hill, R. (1966). Contemporary developments in family theory. *Journal of Marriage and Family, 28,* 3–6.

Hoffman, M. K. (1982). From model to theory construction: An analysis of the Neuman health care systems model. In B. Neuman (Ed.), *The Neuman systems model.* Norwalk, CT: Appleton-Century-Crofts.

Hoskins, L. M., Fitzpatrick, J. J., Warren, J. J., Carpenito, L. J., Jakob, D., & Mills, W. C. (1992). Axes: Focus of Taxonomy II. *Nursing Diagnosis, 3*(2), 117–123.

Johnson, M. N., Vaughn-Wrobel, B., Ziegler, S. M., Hough, L., Bush, H. A., & Kurtz, P. (1982). Use of the Neuman health-care systems model in the master's curriculum: Texas Woman's University. In B. Neuman (Ed.), *The Neuman systems model.* Norwalk, CT: Appleton-Century-Crofts.

Kahn, E. C. (1992). A comparison of family needs based on the presence or absence of DNR orders. *Dimensions of Critical Care Nursing, 11*(5), 286–292.

Kilchenstein, L., & Yakulis, I. (1984). The birth of a curriculum: Utilization of the Betty Neuman health-care systems model in an integrated baccalaureate programme. *The Journal of Nursing Education, 23,* 126–127.

Klir, G. J. (1972). Preview: The polyphonic general systems theory. In G. J. Klir (Ed.), *Trends in general systems theory.* New York: Wiley.

Koku, R. V. (1992). Severity of low back pain. *AAOHN Journal, 40*(2), 84–89.

Lancaster, D. R. (1991/1992). Coping with appraised threat of breast cancer. Primary prevention coping behaviors utilized by women at increased risk. *Dissertation Abstracts International, 53*(1), 202B (DAI order #DA9215110).

Lazarus, R. S. (1966). *Psychological stress and coping response.* New York: McGraw-Hill.

Lazarus, R. S., & Folkman, S. (1984). *Stress, appraisal, and coping.* New York: Springer.

Lazlo, E. (1972). *The systems view of the world: The natural philosophy of the new development in the sciences.* New York: Braziller.

Louis, M., & Koertvelyessy, A. (1989). The Neuman model in nursing research. In B. Neuman (Ed.), *The Neuman systems model* (2nd ed) (pp. 93–113). Norwalk, CT: Appleton & Lange.

Lowry, L. W., & Anderson, B. (1993). Neuman's framework and ventilator dependency: A pilot study. *Nursing Science Quarterly, 6*(4), 195–200.

Miller, J. (1965). Living systems: structure and process. *Behavioral Science, 10,* 337–379.

Mrkonich, D., Miller, M., & Hessian, M. (1989). Cooperative baccalaureate education: The Minnesota intercollegiate nursing consortium. In B. Neuman (Ed.), *The Neuman Systems Model* (2nd ed.) (pp. 175–182). Norwalk, CT: Appleton & Lange.

Mynatt, S. L., & O'Brien, J. (1993). Partnership to prevent chemical dependency in nursing: Using Neuman's systems model. *Journal of Psychosocial Nursing, 31*(4), 27–34.

Nelson, L. F., Hansen, M., McCullagh, M. (1989). A new baccalaureate North Dakota–Minnesota nursing education consortium. In B. Neuman (Ed.), *The Neuman systems model* (2nd ed.) (pp. 183–192). Norwalk, CT: Appleton & Lange.

Neuman, B. (1972). The Betty Neuman model: A total person approach to viewing patient problems. *Nursing Research, 21*(3), 264–269.

Neuman, B. (1980). The Betty Neuman health-care systems model: A total approach to patient problems. In J. Riehl & C. Roy (Eds.), *Conceptual models for nursing practice* (2nd ed.). New York: Appleton-Century-Crofts.

Neuman, B. (Ed.) (1982). *The Neuman systems model: Application to nursing education and practice.* New York: Appelton-Century-Crofts.

Neuman, B. (1983). Family intervention using the Betty Neuman health-care systems model. In I. Clements & F. Roger (Eds.), *Family health: A theoretical approach to nursing care* (pp. 161–176). New York: John Wiley.

Neuman, B. (Ed.) (1989). *The Neuman systems model* (2nd ed.). Norwalk, CT: Appleton & Lange.

Neuman, B. (1990). Health as a continuum based on the Neuman systems model. *Nursing Science Quarterly, 3,* 129–135.

Neuman, B. (1995). The Neuman Systems Model. In B. Neuman (Ed), *The Neuman Systems Model* (3rd ed.) (pp. 3–62). Norwalk, CT: Appleton & Lange.

Pearls, F. (1973). *The Gestalt approach: Eyewitness to therapy.* Palo Alto, CA: Science and Behavior Books.

Piazza, D., Foote, A., Wright, P., & Holcombe, J. (1992). Neuman systems model used as a guide for the nursing care of an eight year old child with leukemia. *Journal of Pediatric Oncology Nursing, 9*(1), 17–24.

Putt, A. (1972). Entropy, evolution and equifinality in nursing. In J. Smith (Ed.), *Five years of cooperation to improve curricula in western schools of nursing.* Boulder, CO: Western Interstate Commission for Higher Education.

Radwanski, M. (1992). Self-medicating practices for managing chronic pain after spinal cord injury. *Rehabilitation Nursing, 17*(6), 312–318.

Reed, K. (1982). The Neuman systems model: A basis for family psychosocial assessment and intervention. In B. Neuman (Ed.), *The Neuman systems model* (pp. 188–193). Norwalk, CT: Appleton-Century-Crofts.

Reed, K. S. (1989). Family theory related to the Neuman systems model. In B. Neuman (Ed.), *The Neuman systems model* (2nd ed.) (pp. 385–395). Norwalk, CT: Appleton & Lange.

Reed, K. S. (1993a). *Betty Neuman: The Neuman systems model.* (Notes on nursing theories Monograph No. 11.) Newbury Park, CA: Sage.

Reed, K. S. (1993b). Adapting the Neuman systems model for family nursing. *Nursing Science Quarterly, 6*(2), 93–97.

Schlentz, M. D. (1993). The minimum data set and the levels of prevention in the long-term care facility. *Geriatric Nursing, 14*(2), 79–83.

Seyle, H. (1950). *The physiology and pathology of exposure to stress.* Montreal: ACTA.

Stevens, B. J. (1979). *Nursing theory: Analysis, application, and evaluation.* Boston: Little, Brown.

Stittich, E. M., Avent, C. L., & Patterson, K. (1989). Neuman-based baccalaureate and graduate nursing programs. California State University, Fresno. In B. Neuman (Ed.), *The Neuman systems model* (2nd ed.) (pp. 163–174). Norwalk, CT: Appleton & Lange.

von Bertalanffy, L. (1968). *General systems theory.* New York: George Braziller.

Waddell, K. L., & Demi, A. S. (1993). Effectiveness of an intensive partial hospitalization program for treatment of anxiety disorders. *Archives of Psychiatric Nursing, 7*(1), 2–10.

Walker, P. H. (1994). Dollars and sense in health reform: Interdisciplinary practice and community nursing centers. *Nursing Administration Quarterly, 19(1),* 1–11.

Walker, P. H. (1995). TQM and the Neuman Systems Model: Education for health care administration. In B. Neuman (Ed), *The Neuman Systems Model* (3rd ed.) (pp. 365–376). Norwalk, CT: Appleton & Lange.

Waters, T. (1993). Self-efficacy, change, and optimal client stability. *Addictions Nursing Network, 5*(2), 48–51.

Ziegler, S. M. (1982). Taxonomy for nursing diagnosis derived from the Neuman systems model. In B. Neuman (Ed.), *The Neuman systems model.* Norwalk, CT: Appleton-Century-Crofts.

Ziemer, M. M. (1983). Effects of information on postsurgical coping. *Nursing Research, 32*(5), 282–287.

SECTION 5

Jean Watson

Barbara Talento

Jean Watson (b. 1940) received her nursing diploma from Lewis Gale Hospital, Roanoke, VA; her BS in nursing from the University of Colorado, Boulder; her MS in psychiatric-mental health nursing from the University of Colorado, Denver; and her PhD in Educational Psychology from the University of Colorado, Boulder. She is currently Distinguished Professor, Director, Center for Human Caring, School of Nursing, University of Colorado Health Science Center, Denver. She has practiced nursing in private practice, as a clinical consultant, nurse researcher, faculty member, and educational administrator. She is a fellow in the American Academy of Nursing and has received numerous other awards and honors, including a Visiting Kellogg Fellowship at Western Australia Institute of Technology and an International Fulbright Award. She holds honorary doctorates from Assumption College, Worcester, MA, and the University of Akron, OH. Watson has been an invited distinguished lecturer in numerous countries such as Israel, Canada, Japan, Australia, and Taiwan as well as in the United States. She is the author of numerous articles, book chapters, and two books. Her research has been in the area of human caring and loss.

The foundation of Jean Watson's theory of nursing was published in 1979 in *Nursing: The philosophy and science of caring.* In 1985, with a re-release in 1988, her theory was published in *Nursing: Human science and human care.* Watson believes that the main focus in nursing is on carative factors that are derived from a humanistic perspective combined with a scientific knowledge base. For nurses to develop humanistic philosophies and value systems, a strong

Taken from: *Nursing Theories: The Base for Professional Nursing Practice*, Fourth Edition by George.

liberal arts background is necessary. This philosophy and value system, in turn, provides a solid foundation for the science of caring. A liberal arts base can assist nurses to expand their vision and views of the world and to develop critical thinking skills. An expanded world view and critical thinking skills are needed in the science of caring, which focuses on health promotion rather than on cure of disease.

According to Watson (1979), curing disease is the domain of medicine. She asserts that the caring stance that nursing has always held is being threatened by the tasks and technology demands of the curative factors. In Watson's works, one finds reference to existential humanists such as Erikson (1963), Heidegger (1962), Maslow (1954), and Rogers (1967). In addition, she uses the theories of Selye (1956) and Lazarus (1966) to delineate stress and caring, and the theories of Leininger (1981) and Henderson (1964) for nursing knowledge. Overall, a humanistic value system undergirds her construction of the science of caring.

Watson's Theory

Watson (1979) proposes seven assumptions about the science of caring and ten primary carative factors to form the framework of her theory. The basic assumptions are the following:

1. Caring can be effectively demonstrated and practiced only interpersonally.

2. Caring consists of carative factors that result in the satisfaction of certain human needs.

3. Effective caring promotes health and individual or family growth.

4. Caring responses accept a person not only as he or she is now but as what he or she may become.

5. A caring environment is one that offers the development of potential while allowing the person to choose the best action for himself or herself at a given point in time.

6. Caring is more "healthogenic" than is curing. The practice of caring integrates biophysical knowledge with knowledge of human behavior to generate or promote health and to provide ministrations to those who are ill. A science of caring is therefore complementary to the science of curing.

7. The practice of caring is central to nursing (pp. 8–9).

Watson (1985/1988) views caring as the most valuable attribute nursing has to offer to humanity, yet caring has, over time, received less emphasis than other aspects of the practice of nursing. She states:

> The human care role [in nursing] is threatened by increased medical technology, bureaucratic-managerial institutional constraints in a nuclear age society. At the same time there has been a proliferation of curing and radical treatment cure techniques often without regard to costs (p. 33).

In today's world, nursing seems to be responding to the various demands of the machinery with less consideration of the needs of the person attached to the machine. In Watson's view, the disease might be cured, but illness would remain because without caring health is not attained. Caring is the essence of nursing and connotes responsiveness between the nurse and the person; the nurse co-participates with the person, Watson contends that caring can assist the person to gain control, become knowledgeable, and promote health changes. In Watson's humanistic value system, there is a high regard for autonomy and freedom of choice, which leads to an emphasis on client self-knowledge and self-control and client as the person in charge.

The structure for the science of caring is built upon the following ten carative factors:

1. The formation of a humanistic-altruistic system of values

2. The instillation of faith-hope

3. The cultivation of sensitivity to one's self and to others

4. The development of a helping-trust relationship

5. The promotion and acceptance of the expression of positive and negative feelings

6. The systematic use of the scientific problem-solving method for decision making

7. The promotion of interpersonal teaching-learning

8. The provision for a supportive, protective, and(or) corrective mental, physical, socio-cultural, and spiritual environment

9. Assistance with the gratification of human needs

10. The allowance for existential-phenomenological forces (Watson, 1979, pp. 9–10).

Of these ten carative factors, the first three form the "philosophical foundation for the science of caring" (Watson, 1979, p. 10). *The formation of a humanistic-altruistic value system* (carative factor 1) begins developmentally at an early age with values shared with parents. This value system is mediated through one's own life experiences, the learning one gains, and exposure to the humanities. Watson (1979) suggests that caring that is based on humanistic values and altruistic behavior can be developed through examination of one's own views, beliefs, interactions with various cultures, and personal growth experiences. These are all perceived as necessary to the nurse's own maturation, which then promotes altruistic behavior toward others.

Faith-hope (carative factor 2) is essential to both the carative and the curative processes. Nurses need to transcend the push toward acceptance of only Western medicine and assist the person in an understanding of alternatives such as meditation or the healing power of belief in self or in the spiritual (Watson, 1979). Watson's (1985/1988) emphasis on the spiritual, with the inclusion of the soul, is unusual in theory development. When modern science has nothing further to offer the person, the nurse can continue to use faith-hope to provide a sense of well-being through those beliefs that are meaningful to the individual.

Cultivation of sensitivity to self and others (carative factor 3) explores the need of the nurse to begin to feel an emotion as it present itself. It is only through development of one's own feelings that one can genuinely and sensitively interact with others. As nurses strive to increase their own sensitivity, they become more authentic. Becoming authentic encourages self-growth and self-actualization in both the nurse and those with whom the nurse interacts. A basic premise of Watson's (1985/1988) is that:

> A person's mind and emotions are windows to the soul. Nursing care can be and is physical, procedural, objective, and factual, but at the highest level of nursing the nurses' human care responses, the human care transactions, and the nurses' presence in the relationship transcend the physical material world, bound in time and space, and make contact with the person's emotional and subjective world as the route to the inner self and the higher sense of self (p. 50).

Furthermore, she contends that nurses promote health and higher level functioning only when they form person-to-person relationships as opposed to manipulative relationships (Watson, 1979).

To appreciate the remaining seven carative factors, one needs to understand that they spring from the foundation developed by these first three. Therefore, the nurse develops a humanistic-altruistic value system, believes in the instillation of faith-hope, and cultivates sensitivity to self and to others to develop a helping-trust relationship and the rest of the carative factors. One of the strongest tools the nurse can use in *establishing a helping-trust relationship* (carative factor 4) is a mode of communication that establishes rapport and caring. Watson uses the works of Rogers (1962), Carkhuff (1971), and Gazda (1975) to define the characteristics needed in the helping-trust relationship. These characteristics are congruence, empathy, and warmth. Congruence implies that nurses are genuine in their interactions and do not put up facades; that nurses act in an open and honest manner. Empathy refers to the attempt that nurses make to tune into the feelings of their clients. Empathy may be described as "walking in another's moccasins" in that it allows the nurse to accept the client's feelings without responding defensively with anger or fear. Warmth refers to the positive acceptance of another. It is expressed most often by open body language, touch, and tone of voice.

Communication in this context includes verbal and nonverbal communication and listening in a manner that connotes empathetic understanding. It is through this intense focus on communication that the nurse can center on clues and themes that can lead to an even greater depth of awareness for the person. One barrier in this process is that thoughts are often substituted for feelings, which precludes the ability to reach deeper levels of awareness. *The expression of feelings, both positive and negative* (carative factor 5) ought to be facilitated because, according to Watson (1979), such expression improves one's level of awareness. "Feelings alter thoughts and behavior, and they need to be considered and allowed for in a caring relationship" (p. 44). Indeed, if one can become aware of the feeling, one can often understand the behavior it engenders.

In carative factor 6, the issue of *research and systematic problem solving* is presented. Because nurses are occupied with the tasks of nursing (i.e., treatments, procedures, charts), they often fail to address the larger issues of conducting research, defining the discipline, or developing a scientific base for nursing. However, Watson (1979) believes that:

> Without the systematic use of the scientific problem-solving method, effective practice is accidental at best and haphazard or harmful at worst. The scientific problem-solving method is the only method that allows for control and prediction, and that permits self-correction (pp. 55–56).

Watson makes a strong argument for the need for the absolutism of the scientific method, but she also values the relative nature of nursing and makes an equally strong argument for the need to examine and develop other methods of knowing to provide a holistic perspective. The science of caring should not always be neutral and objective, two important characteristics of the scientific method.

Promotion of interpersonal teaching-learning (carative factor 7) is the factor that affords people the most control over their own health because it provides them with both information and alternatives. The caring nurse focuses on the learning process as much as the teaching process, for learning offers the best way to individualize the information to be disseminated. Understanding the person's perceptions of the situation assists the nurse to prepare a cognitive plan that works within the person's framework and alleviates the stress of the event (Watson, 1979).

Carative factor 8 deals with the daily, routine functions that the nurse uses to promote health, restore to health, or prevent illness. It is the factor labeled as *provision for a supportive, protective and(or) corrective mental, physical, socio-cultural, and spiritual environment.* Watson (1979) divides these functions into external variables, such as the physical, safety, and environmental factors, and internal variables, such as mental, spiritual, or cultural activities, which the nurse manipulates in order to provide support and protection for the person's mental and physical well-being.

There is an interdependence between the external and the internal environments because it is the person's perceptions that render the environment as threatening or nonthreatening.

Although the subjective appraisal of threat can be a distortion of reality, the perception of threat is still a stressful event to the person. Events such as change of job, divorce, illness, and loss of a loved one can arouse a sense of threat. Through assessment, the nurse can determine the person's appraisal of the situation and abilities to cope. Then the nurse can supply situational support, help the person develop a more accurate perception, or provide the cognitive information that can strengthen the patient's own coping mechanisms. Watson (1979) suggests that the nurse also must provide comfort, privacy, and safety as part of this carative factor. In addition, she believes that a basic element is a clean-esthetic environment. While clean, sterile surroundings might not be health promoting, esthetics can improve health through promotion of increased self-worth and dignity. A pleasant environment improves the affective state, facilitates interactions with others, and promotes a sense of satisfaction with life.

Carative factor 9, *assistance with the gratification of human needs,* is grounded in a hierarchy of needs similar to that of Maslow (1954). However, Watson has created a hierarchy that she considers to be relevant to the science of caring in nursing. The following are Watson's (1979) ordering of needs:

1. **Lower Order Needs (Biophysical Needs)**   **Survival Needs**
   The need for food and fluid
   The need for elimination
   The need for ventilation

2. **Lower Order Needs (Psychophysical Needs)**   **Functional Needs**
   The need for activity-inactivity
   The need for sexuality

3. **Higher Order Needs (Psychosocial Needs)**   **Integrative Needs**
   The need for achievement
   The need for affiliation

4. **Higher Order Need (Intrapersonal-Interpersonal Need)**   **Growth-seeking Need**
   The need for self-actualization (p. 108).

Establishing hierarchical needs does not preclude the necessity to view each person in the context of the whole. Meeting only lower order needs may not assist the complex human being toward self-actualization. Each need is viewed in the context of all the others, and all are valued. Watson (1979) also says:

> Keeping in mind the holistic-dynamic framework for viewing the human needs, the carative factor assistance with the gratification of human needs leads to a more complete development of each human need. Some needs are more familiar and concrete because of the tangible ways in which they manifest themselves. Others are more abstract and elusive. They are equally important for quality nursing care and the promotion of optimal health (pp. 109–111).

Overall, the theme is that, despite the hierarchical nature in which they are presented, the needs all deserve to be attended to and valued. Research finding have established a correlation between emotional distress and illness. Therefore, an assessment that uses an holistic approach that examines the "dynamic, symbolic aspects of each need" (Watson, 1979, p. 117) provides a more balanced portrait of the person* Watson states:

> The current thinking about holistic care emphasizes (1) that etiological components that have many factors interact and produce change through complex neurophysiological and neurochemical pathways, (2) that each psychological function has a physiological correlate, and (3) that each physiological function has a psychological correlate (pp. 117–118).

As an example, disturbances found in the biophysical need for food and fluid demonstrate the requirement for holistic care. Bulimia, anorexia, and gastrointestinal ulcers are just a few of the disorders that indicate the complex interaction between the physiological and the psychological. Watson's work delineates the interrelationship in each area of her hierarchy (see Table 5–1).

Allowance for existential phenomenological factors is carative factor 10. Phenomenology is a way of understanding people from the way things appear to them, from their frame of reference (Watson, 1979). Existential psychology is the study of human existence using phenomenological analysis. For the nurse, this factor helps to reconcile and mediate the incongruity of viewing the person holistically while at the same time attending to a hierarchical ordering of needs. Incorporating these factors into the science of nursing assists the nurse to understand the meaning the person finds in life or to help the person find meaning in difficult life events, or both. Because life, illness, and death are basically irrational, the nurse using carative factor 10 may assist the person to find the strength or courage to confront life or death. Watson suggests that each nurse must turn inward to face his or her own existential questions before being able to assist others to cope with the human predicament.

*W*atson's Theory and Nursing's Metaparadigm

Human Being

Although in Watson's earlier writings she refers to her work as a philosophy and science of nursing, in her later book she clearly states that the work represents a nursing theory (Watson, 1985/1988). In that context, and using nursing's heritage, she adopts a view of the human being as:

> . . . a valued person in and of him- or herself to be cared for, respected, nurtured, understood, and assisted; in general a philosophical view of a person as a fully functional integrated self. The human is viewed as greater than, and different from, the sum of his or her parts (p. 14).

TABLE 5–1 Holistic Care Needs in Bulimia and Anorexia

Watson's Hierarchy	Application to Bulimia and Anorexia
Higher Order Need (interpersonal)	Self-actualization retarded
	Unrealistic sense of perfection never achieved
Higher Order Needs (psychosocial)	Diminished sense of achievement secondary to distorted body image
	Self-involvement leads to diminished affiliative activity, possibly impaired sexual relationships
Lower Order Needs (psychophysical)	Purge or binge or self-imposed starvation depletes cellular nutrition, leading to decreased activity
	Body image distortion may impair sexuality
Lower Older Needs (biophysical)	Food and fluids restricted

She believes that humans are best viewed in a developmental conflicts frame and that "systematic attention to developmental conflicts of individuals and their families is necessary for health care" (Watson, 1979, p. 246). These conflicts, based upon Erikson's model, are primarily psychosocial and represent crises and turning points encountered throughout the human life cycle. Commonly occurring, these conflicts can elicit a stress reaction that requires a coping response. The nurse must understand human beings when they are sick, well, or under stress.

Health

Although acknowledging the World Health Organization's definition of health as the positive state of physical, mental, and social well-being, Watson (1979) believes that other factors need to be included. She adds the following three elements:

1. A high level of overall physical, mental, and social functioning.

2. A general adaptive-maintenance level of daily functioning.

3. The absence of illness (or the presence of efforts that lead to its absence) (p. 220).

Watson states that what has traditionally been called health care is a myth. That which has been called health care, the diagnosing of disease, treatment of illness, and prescription of drugs, is medical care. True health care focuses on life style, social conditions, and environment. Watson (1985/1988) adds:

> Health refers to unity and harmony within the mind, body, and soul. Health is also associated with the degree of congruence between the self as perceived and the self as experienced (p. 48).

One major factor affecting health is stress or stress-related activities that are also associated with life style, social conditions, and environment. Illness, on the other hand, may not be disease but may be a disharmony between body, soul, and spirit that may lead to stress. In addition, Watson believes the individual should define his or her own state of health or illness, since she prefers to view health as a subjective state within the mind of the person.

Environment/Society

One of the variables that affects society in today's world is the social environment. Society provides the values that determine how one should behave and what goals one should strive toward. These values are affected by change in the social, cultural, and spiritual arenas, which in turn affects the perception of the person and can lead to stress. People also have an intrinsic need to belong, to be part of a group(s) and of society as a whole. Furthermore, each person has a need for affection, a need to love and be loved. Stress or illness can separate the person from those who meet such affiliative or affectional needs. It is within the practice of caring that nursing can assist in meeting these needs. Watson (1979) states:

> Caring (and nursing) has existed in every society. Every society has had some people who have cared for others. A caring attitude is not transmitted from generation to generation by genes. It is transmitted by the culture of the profession as a unique way of coping with its environment (p. 8).

Nursing

According to Watson (1979), "nursing is concerned with promoting health, preventing illness, caring for the sick, and restoring health" (p. 7). Nursing focuses on health promotion as well as treatment of disease. She sees nursing as having to move educationally in the two areas of stress and developmental conflicts to provide holistic health care, which she believes is central to the practice of caring in nursing. One of Watson's (1985/1988) assumptions is that "nursing's social, moral, and scientific contributions to humankind and society lie in its commitment to human care ideals in theory, practice, and research" (p. 33).

In further writings Watson (1985/1988) defines nursing as ". . . a human science of persons and human health-illness experiences that are mediated by professional, personal, scientific, esthetic, and ethical human care transactions" (p. 54). Nursing in this context is rooted in the humanities as well as in the natural sciences. Nursing's goal, through the caring process, is to help people gain a high degree of harmony within the self in order to promote self-knowledge and self-healing, or to gain insight into the meaning of the happenings in life. Yet nursing is faced with the explosion of technology, the increase in the acuity of patients along with a decrease in the length of hospital stay. All these factors have an impact on the practitioner's ability to focus beyond the cure factor to the care factor. The relationship between the nurse and the patient/client entails several unique features based upon mutual expectations. The client certainly expects the nurse to follow whatever orders there are for treatment but also expects the nurse to be humane and caring. The nurse values caring but is often willing to sacrifice that valued attribute in order to accomplish the tasks of the technological age. The struggle within the practice of nursing will be that of reinforcing humanistic studies and the knowledge that to be humane, caring practitioners we must believe in the dignity and worth of each patient/client. Nursing must reinforce the values that are held as a profession and insist on those values as the linchpin upon which to build the priorities of patient care.

*W*atson's Theory and the Nursing Process

Watson recommends a broad approach to nursing that searches out connections rather than separations between the parts that make up the whole of the person. To accomplish this, nurses employ a scientific problem-solving method by which they can draw from a data base and basic nursing principles to make nursing judgments and decisions. Watson (1979) points out that the nursing process contains the same steps as the scientific research process. The rationales for these processes are identical in that both try to solve a problem or answer a question. Both try to discover the best solution. However, she believes nurses tend to be frightened by the scientific research processes. If nurses could learn that the processes are basically the same and that they provide a framework for decision making, then nurses would derive comfort from the order established by using the scientific process. This might best be accomplished by teaching the two processes, nursing and research, at the same time, to practice them together, and to recognize that the ultimate goal in nursing is high quality patient care that can be achieved by using this systematic approach.

Watson (1979) further elaborates the two processes as follows (Italics indicate the research process interwoven in the nursing process):

Assessment

- Assessment involves *observation, identification,* and *review* of the *problem; use* of the applicable *knowledge in literature.*

- It includes conceptual knowledge for the *formulation* and *conceptualization* of a *framework* in which to view and assess the problem.

- It also includes the *formulation of hypotheses* about relationships and factors that influence the problem.

- Assessment also includes *defining variables* that will be examined in solving the problem.

Plan

- The plan helps to determine how *variables will be examined* or measured.

- It includes a *conceptual approach* or design for solving problems that is referred to as the nursing care plan.

- It also includes determining what data will be collected and on what person and how the data will be collected.

Intervention

- Intervention is direct action and implementation of the plan.

- It includes the collection of data.

Evaluation

- Evaluation is the method of and the process for *analyzing data* as well as the examination of the effects of intervention based on the data.

- It includes *interpretation* of the *results*, the degree to which a positive outcome occurred, and whether the results can be generalized beyond the situation, (pp. 65–66).

Beyond that, according to Watson, evaluation may also generate additional hypotheses or possibly even lead to the generation of a nursing theory based on the problem studied and the solutions. An application of Watson's work in the nursing process is seen through the case study of Anthony M. (see Table 5–2).

Situation. Anthony M. was a 14-year-old with a slender, almost cachectic, appearance. He weighed 85 pounds and was 5 feet 6 inches tall. Both his mother and father were deeply concerned about his weight loss of almost 30 pounds and were upset by daily battles related to eating. Anthony was equally upset since he felt he was at just the right weight. He felt that his parents had no right to control what or how much he ate. He was admitted to an adolescent psychiatric unit where the family's problem could be addressed.

Anthony complained that his parents were demanding and tried to control his life. He felt that they did not understand him and probably did not love him. When discussing his weight, he denied being hungry, so therefore he felt that he was eating enough. He stated, "Look, I'm fat and ugly, can't they see that? Girls don't like me, I've never been invited to a boy-girl party. The guys think I'm O.K., especially since I help with their homework, but I don't hang around with anyone special."

Anthony's weight was not within the norm for his age or height. At his height, his optimal weight should have ranged between 115 and 130 pounds. His skin appeared dry and flaky. His bones were clearly visible; there seemed to be no flesh covering them. He was listless and taciturn. His approach to food was marked by extreme disinterest.

TABLE 5–2 Watson's Theory in Nursing Process Applied to Anthony M.

Nursing Process	Application of Theory
ASSESSMENT	
Lower Order Needs (biophysical)	How does Anthony M. view his body? Is he within norms for his height, weight, and age? Does he consume enough calories to maintain normal growth? Does a physical assessment indicate all systems are functioning at normal levels?
Lower Order Needs (psychophysical)	Is his body image realistic? Is he participating in the usual activities of his age? Does evaluation of laboratory tests indicate nutritional deficiencies?
Higher Order Needs (psychosocial)	Are his relationships with peers satisfactory? How does he view his nascent sexuality? Has starvation retarded puberty? Does his environment appear facilitive of personal growth? Does he feel loved or lovable? Has he established a sense of autonomy from his parents?
Higher Order Needs (intrapersonal)	How does Anthony M. feel about himself? Does he like his world? Does he feel he is accomplishing his goals?
NURSING DIAGNOSES	Disturbances in self-concept related to: Body image disturbance Powerlessness Impaired social interaction Unresolved independence or dependence
PLANNING AND IMPLEMENTATION	
Use carative factors	Establish a caring environment through empathetic understanding. Develop a helping-trust relationship by encouraging expression of feeling of fear of weight gain, anger at treatment plan, resentment of authority figures. Use warmth, empathy, and congruence to establish open communication. Promote interpersonal teaching-learning by involving patient in nutritional plan. Teach patient how to deal with conflict, issue of autonomy. Facilitate relationship within the family that foster autonomy. Encourage identification of stress factors. Assist in dealing with sexual identity. Encourage Anthony M. to assess his social interactions and develop satisfying ones. Emphasize personal satisfaction rather than perfection.
EVALUATION	Has a trusting relationship been established? Is Anthony M. developing normally In the areas assessed: biophysically, psychophysically, psychosocially, and intrapersonally? Has Anthony M. learned the skills necessary to grow and mature successfully?

*W*atson's Work and the Characteristics of a Theory

According to Watson (1985/1988), "a theory is an imaginative grouping of knowledge, ideas, and experience that are represented symbolically and seek to illuminate a given phenomenon" (p. 1). She rejects traditional, quantifiable methodology when such methodology sacrifices the pursuit of new knowledge of human behavior. She sees nursing as being increasingly involved in procedures and variable manipulation while it might best be involved in a search for alternative views to study human caring, health-illness, and health promotion. She states that she views nursing as ". . . both a human science and an art, and as such it cannot be considered qualitatively continuous with traditional, reductionistic, scientific methodology" (p. 2). Watson suggests that nursing might want to develop its own science that would not be related to the traditional sciences but rather would develop its own concepts, relationships, and methodology. Table 5–3 illustrates her ideas of nursing's context as opposed to the traditional view.

1. **Theories can interrelate concepts in such a way as to create a different way of looking at a particular phenomenon.** The use of the term *caring* is not unique to Watson. What is unique is her basic assumptions for the science of caring in nursing and the ten carative factors that form the structure for that concept. She describes caring in both philosophical and scientific terms. Caring is placed in a hierarchical context, meeting lower order biophysical needs first and moving toward higher order psychosocial and intrapersonal needs. Watson also says that the needs are interrelated. For example, food and fluid needs are lower order biophysical needs that must be met, yet intake of food and fluids is strongly related to love, security, culture, and self-concept. The science of caring suggests that the nurse recognize and assist with each of the client's interrelated needs in order to help the client reach the highest order need of self-actualization.

2. **Theories must be logical in nature.** Watson's work is logical in that the carative factors are based on broad assumptions that provide a supportive framework. She uses these carative factors to help delineate nursing from medicine. The carative factors are logically derived from the assumptions and related to the hierarchy of needs.

3. **Theories should be relatively simple yet generalizable.** Watson's theory is relatively simple because it does use theories from other disciplines that are familiar to nurses. It becomes more complex when entering the area of existential-phenomenology, for many nurses may not have the liberal arts background to provide the proper foundation for understanding this area. On the other hand, nurses do have the empirical knowledge of human nature, including working with persons who are dealing with pain, loss, and suffering. The theory is relatively simple, but the fact that it de-emphasizes the pathophysiological for the psychosocial diminishes its ability to be generalizable. Watson (1979) discusses this problem in the preface of her book when she speaks of the "trim" and "core" of nursing. She defines trim as the clinical focus, the procedures and techniques. The core of nursing is that which is intrinsic to the nurse-client interaction that produces a therapeutic result. Core mechanisms are the carative factors. Unfortunately, those are the very factors that seem to be most often sacrificed in today's technological world.

TABLE 5–3   Differing Perspectives Between Traditional Science and Human Science

Traditional Medical Natural Science Context	Emerging Alternative Nursing Human Science and Context of Caring
Normative	Ipsative
Reductionistic	Transactional
Mechanistic	Metaphysical
Humanistic—contextual	
Method centered	Phenomena centered
Neutrality of values	Value laden; values acknowledged, clarified
Disease centered on pathology—physiology, the physical body	Human responses to illness and personal meanings of human condition
Ethics of "science"	Human-social ethics—morality
More quantitative	More qualitative
Absolutes, givens, laws	Relativism, probabilism
Human as object	Human as subject
Objective experiences	Subjective—intersubjective experiences
Facts	Experience, meaning
Nomothetic	Idiographic +/ nomothetic
Concrete—observable	Abstract—may or may not "be seen"
Analytical	Dialectical, philosophical, metaphysical
Science as product	Science as creative process of discovery
Human = sum of parts ex. (bio-psycho-socio-cultural-spiritual-being)	Human = mind-body-spirit gestalt of whole being (not only more than sum of parts, but different)
Physical, materialistic	Existential-phenomenological-spiritual
"Real" is that which is measurable, observable, and knowable	"Real" is abstract, largely subjective as well as objective, but it may or may not ever be fully known, observable, fully measured, what is "real," holds mystery and unknowns yet to be discovered.

Used with permission from Watson, J. (1988) Nursing: Human science and human care (p. 10). New York: National League for Nursing.

4. **Theories can be the bases for hypotheses that can be tested or for theory to be expanded.** Watson's work is based upon phenomenological studies that generally ask questions rather than state hypotheses. Its purpose is to describe the phenomena, to analyze, and to gain an understanding.

5. **Theories contribute to and assist in increasing the general body of knowledge within the discipline through research implemented to validate them.** Watson has suggested that the best method for testing her theory is through field study. One example is her work in the area of loss and caring that took place in Cundeelee, Western Australia, and involved a tribe of aborigines. She first had the aborigines describe the phenomena of loss. They then defined what caring meant to them. Through analy-

sis of the descriptive data, Watson (1985/1988) was able to develop a theory of transpersonal caring, which states that loss creates a disharmony, in three spheres: mind, body, and spirit. The nurse can enter into the process of transpersonal caring by comforting, listening, and allowing for free expression of feelings based on the culturally relevant norms of the person. Because the carative factors , expand on theories learned from other disciplines and mold them into uniquely nursing knowledge, continued research that involves the carative factors should increase the general body of knowledge in nursing.

Since Watson did her early work, many theorists and researchers have extended the concept of caring into the areas of nursing philosophy/ethics, practice, and education. Currently, five categories of caring are being researched or written about: caring as a human trait, caring as a moral imperative, caring as an affect, caring as an interpersonal relationship, and caring as a therapeutic intervention (Morse, Solberg, Neander, Botorff, & Johnson, 1990). Bishop and Scudder (1991), Gadow (1988), Gaut (1993), and Leininger (1988) all discuss caring within the context of one of these categories. Benner and Wrubel (1988) are researching caring as a nursing outcome and find that both patient and nurse benefit. Morse, Botoroff, Neander and Solberg (1991) did a comparative analysis of the newer concepts in the theories of caring and found that further refinement in both theory construction and in research methodology needs to be made. However, while urging continued research, Watson (1990) passionately extols her readers to look beyond traditional methods of knowing. She states, "If our aim for caring knowledge in nursing is higher than achieving machine-like knowledge, if our aim is to express and to reflect life and life forces, it is not enough to be technically correct. Much of nursing contains caring knowledge that enriches the soul. . . . How does any one way to knowledge development exemplify the wonder of humanity and human caring processes of nursing?" (p. 17). In an effort to quantify "caring," researchers may lose sight of the intangibles. Qualitative research methodologies may well capture the ephemeral characteristics of caring but are time intensive. In an era of fiscal stringency, when time on task is valued, nurses need the research to prove that caring is as efficacious, if not more so, as the technology they use.

6. **Theories can be used by practitioners to guide and improve their practice.** Watson's work can be used to guide and improve practice. It can provide the nurse with the most satisfying aspects of practice and can provide the client with the holistic care so necessary for human growth and development.

7. **Theories must be consistent with other validated theories, laws, and principles but will leave open unanswered questions that need to be investigated.** Watson's work is supported by the theoretical work of numerous humanists, philosophers, developmentalists, and psychologists. She clearly designates the theories of stress, development, communication, teaching-learning, humanistic psychology, and existential phenomenology that provide the foundation for the science of caring. She presents these in a way that provides a uniquely nursing view, that leads to further questions to be investigated.

nalysis and Conclusions

The strength of Watson's work is that it not only assists in providing the quality of care that clients ought to receive but also provides the soul-satisfying care for which many nurses enter the profession. Because the science of caring ranges from the biophysical through the intrapersonal, each nurse becomes an active co-participant in the client's struggle toward self-actualization. In addition, the client is placed in the context of the family, the community, and the culture. All of this encourages the nurse to make the client, rather than the technology, the focus of practice. Along with that comes the nurse's responsibility and opportunity for personal growth.

The limitations may very well be the same issues. Given the acuity of illness that leads to hospitalization, the short length of stay, and the increasingly complex technology, such quality of care may be deemed impossible to give in a hospital. Bureaucratic structures are not known for their attention to much beyond the cost-benefit ratio. The rewards from within that structure are for the "trim" and not for the "core" of nursing, often placing the practitioner in an untenable position. Nurses who function in any bureaucratic structure that focuses on task accomplishment, whether that structure be in a hospital, home health or official public health agency, visiting nurse association, or any other location, are subject to the same limitations in relation to Watson's theory.

Although Watson acknowledges the need for a biophysical base to nursing, this area receives little attention in her writings. The ten carative factors primarily delineate the psychosocial needs of the person. In addition, while the carative factors have a sound foundation based on other disciplines, they need further research in nursing to demonstrate their application to practice.

S ummary

Watson provides many useful concepts for the practice of nursing. She ties together many theories commonly used in nursing education and does so in a manner helpful to practitioners of the art and science of nursing. The detailed descriptions of the carative factors can give guidance to those who wish to employ them in practice or research. Using her theory can add a dimension to practice that is both satisfying and challenging.

R eferences

Benner, P., & Wrubel, J. (1988). *The primacy of caring: Stress and coping in health and illness.* Menlo Park: Addison-Wesley.

Bishop, A. H., & Scudder, J. R. (1991). *Nursing: The practice of caring.* New York: National League for Nursing.

Carkhuff, R. (1971). *The development of human resources in education and psychology and social change.* New York: Holt, Rhinehart & Winston.

Erikson, E. (1963). *Childhood and society* (2nd ed.). New York: Norton.

Gadow, S. (1988). Covenant without cure. In J. Watson, & M. Ray (Eds.), *The ethics of care and the ethics of cure.* New York: National League for Nursing.

Gaut, D. A. (1993). *A global agenda for caring.* New York: National League for Nursing.

Gazda, G. (1975). *Basic approaches to group psychotherapy and group counseling.* Springfield, IL; Thomas.

Heidegger, M. (1962). *Being and time.* New York: Harper & Row. [out of print]

Henderson, V. (1964). *The nature of nursing.* American Journal of Nursing, 64, 62–68.

Lazarus, R. S. (1966). *Psychological stress and the coping process.* New York: McGraw Hill. [out of print]

Leininger, M. (Ed.). (1981). *Caring.* Thorofare, NJ: Charles B. Slack.

Leininger, M. (1988). History, issues and trends in discovery and uses of care in nursing. In M. Leininger (Ed.), *Care: Discovery and uses in clinical and community nursing.* Thorofare, NJ: Slack.

Maslow, A. (1954). *Motivation and personality.* New York: Harper & Bros. [out of print]

Morse, J. M., Botorff, J. L., Neander, W., & Solberg, S. (1991). Comparative analysis of conceptualizations and theories of caring. *Image, Journal of Nursing Scholarship, 23,*199–126.

Morse, J. M., Solberg, S. M., Neander, W. L., Botorff, J. L., & Johnson, J. L. (1990). Concepts of caring and caring as a concept. *Advances in Nursing Science, 13*(1), 1–14.

Rogers, C. (1962). The interpersonal relationship: The core of guidance. *Harvard Educational Review, 32,* 416.

Rogers, C. (1967). *Person to person: The problem of being human.* Lafayette, CA: Real People Press, [out of print]

Selye, H. (1956). *The stress of life.* New York: McGraw Hill. [out of print]

Watson, J. (1979). *Nursing: The philosophy and science of caring.* Boston: Little, Brown.

Watson, J. (1988). *Nursing: Human science and human care, A theory of nursing.* New York: National League for Nursing (Originally published 1985, Appleton-Century-Crofts).

Watson, J. (1990). Caring knowledge and informed moral passion. *Advances in Nursing Science, 13*(1), 15–24.

B ibliography

Chinn, P. (1988). *Ethical issues in nursing.* Rockville, MD: Aspen.

Gaines, B., Saunders, J., & Watson, J. (1984). Philosophy of nursing: A national survey. *Western Journal of Nursing Research, 6,*401–404.

Sakalys, J., & Watson, J. (1986). Professional educational post-baccalaureate education for professional nursing . . . Reintegration of the classical liberal arts model. *Journal of Professional Nursing, 2,* 91–97.

Schroeder, C., & Maeve, M. X. (1992). Nursing care partnerships at the Denver Nursing Project in Human Caring: An application and extension of caring theory in practice. *Advances in Nursing Science, 35*(2), 25–38.

Watson, J. (1981). The lost art of nursing. *Nursing Forum, 20,*244–249.

Watson, J. (1981). Professional identity crisis—Is nursing finally growing up? *American Journal of Nursing, 81,* 1488–1490.

Watson, J. (1985). Nursing's scientific quest. *Nursing Outlook, 29,*413–416.

Watson, J. (1987). Academic and clinical collaboration: Advancing the art and science of human caring. *Community Nursing Research, 20,* 1–16.

Watson, J. (1987). Nursing on the caring edge—Metaphorical vignettes. *Advances in Nursing Science, 30,*10–18.

Watson, M. J. (1988). New dimensions of human caring theory. *Nursing Science Quarterly, 1,* 175–181.

External Analysis

𝒩ursing Research

One of the goals of the Center for Human Caring at the University of Colorado School of Nursing is to develop knowledge of human caring and healing. Research activities at the Center include the development and testing of practice modalities that enhance human integrity and health. For example, colleagues at the Center have worked collaboratively, using similar designs, to develop a cohesive knowledge base about caring needs and behaviors across the life span (Clayton, 1989). The human care model also has been used to guide studies by nurse–scientists who are not connected to the Center for Human Care, and by students in master's and doctoral programs. In addition, the Center for Human Care offers a summer visiting fellowship program for academics who want to be mentored in caring–healing theory and research methods.

It is important to note that Watson (1985b) thinks that "traditional" research methods are not adequate for knowledge development in the human care model. Given the focus on knowledge of caring–healing for the human spirit, human phenomenal fields, and meanings related to health–illness experiences, Watson (1985b) suggests qualitative–naturalistic–phenomenological methods. Descriptive phenomenological approaches are proposed as the best methods for understanding the human predicament and the meaning attached to health–illness given current knowledge of scientific methods (Watson, 1985b). It also may be appropriate to consider the usefulness of feminist theory and constructivism (Guba & Lincoln, 1989), which engage the "subject/stakeholder" as a coparticipant in the research process.

𝒩ursing Education

Watson has suggested that the nursing discipline needs to develop new paradigms for educational preparation (Watson & Phillips, 1992). To this end the human care model has been used as the basis for curricula in the nursing doctoral (ND) program at the University of Colorado and in at least four nursing education programs in the United States and Canada

---

Taken from: *Conceptual Models of Nursing: Analysis and Application,* Third Edition by Fitzpatrick and Whall.

(Watson, personal communication, 1994). An advanced postgraduate program of study is available through the Center for Human Care that includes mentored study of caring–healing for educators.

An educational process based on the human care model requires knowledge of the humanities, art, basic sciences, ethics, and discipline-specific caring–healing (Watson & Phillips, 1992). An academic program guided by the philosophy and ethics of the human care model has the potential to develop a nursing professional who is self-aware and spiritually aware as a way of being professionally. As noted by Boyd and Mast (1989), "the emphasis on art, discovery, esthetics, wholeness, and spirituality offers a refreshing alternative" for academic preparation in nursing.

Nursing Practice

The human care model is being used as a clinical practice model in the United States and Canada in acute, community, and long-term care settings (Watson, personal communication, 1994). Dissemination and implementation of a human care practice model is supported by direct consultation with Watson and her colleagues at the Center for Human Care and indirectly through video tapes and electronic bulletin boards. Clinicians also can study caring praxis at the Center and obtain a certificate in caring skills.

The moral ideal and transpersonal care process delineated by Watson in the human care model provide a welcomed frame of reference for contemporary nursing practice. At a time when the disease–cure-for-profit health care system seems to be more dehumanizing and nihilistic, a return to the philosophical roots of modern nursing is needed to guide practice. The emphasis on an intention to care and recognition of the healing potential of the human spirit (nurse and patient) offer an opportunity to enter a new century with optimism about human "becoming."

References

Adam, E. (October 1989). *Levels of abstraction in nursing content development.* Paper presented at the Second Annual Rosemary Ellis Scholars' Retreat. Frances Payne Bolton School of Nursing, Case Western Reserve University, Cleveland, OH.

Boyd, C, & Mast, D. (1989). Watson's model of human care. In J. J. Fitzpatrick and A. Whall (Eds.). *Conceptual models of nursing: Analysis and application* (2nd ed.) (pp. 371–383). Norwalk, CT: Appleton & Lange.

Clayton, G. M. (1989). Research testing Watson's theory. The phenomenon of caring in an elderly population. In J. Riehl-Sisca (Ed.), *Conceptual models for nursing practice* (pp. 245–252). Norwalk, CT: Appleton & Lange.

Dubin, R. (1978). *Theory building.* New York: Macmillan.

England, M. (1989). Nursing diagnosis: A conceptual framework. In J. J. Fitzpatrick & A. Whall (Eds.), *Conceptual models of nursing. Analysis and application* (2nd ed.) (pp. 347–369). Norwalk, CT: Appleton & Lange.

Fawcett, J. (1984). The metaparadigm of nursing: Present status and future refinements. IMAGE, *16*(3), 84–87.

Fawcett, J. (1993). *Analysis and evaluation of nursing theories.* Philadelphia: F. A. Davis.

Flaskerud, J. H., & Halloran, E. J. (1980). Areas of agreement in nursing theory development. *Advances in Nursing Science, 3*(1), 1–7.

Guba, E. G., & Lincoln, Y. S. (1989). *Fourth generation evaluation.* Newbury Park, CA: Sage.

Hardy, M. (1974). Theories: Components, development, evaluation. *Nursing Research, 23*:100–107.

Leonard, V. W. (1989). A Heideggarion phenomenologic perspective on the concept of the person. *Advances in Nursing Science, 11*(4), 40–55.

Mitchell, G. J., & Cody, W. K. (1992). Nursing knowledge and human science: Ontological and epistemological considerations. *Nursing Science Quarterly, 5*(2).

Moritz, D. A. (1982). Nursing diagnosis in relation to the nursing process. In M. J. Kim & D. A. Moritz (Eds.), *Classification of nursing diagnoses: Proceedings of the third and fourth national conferences* (pp. 53–57). New York: McGraw-Hill.

Newman, M. (1979). *Theory development in nursing.* Philadelphia: F.A. Davis.

Nightingale, F. (1969). *Notes on Nursing: What it is and what it is not.* New York: Dover (originally published 1859).

Roy, C. (1982). Theoretical framework for classification of nursing diagnoses. In M. J. Kim & D. A. Moritz (Eds.), *Classification of nursing diagnoses: Proceedings of the third and fourth national conferences.* (pp. 215–221) New York: McGraw-Hill.

Smith, J. A. (1981). The idea of health: A philosophical inquiry. *Advances in Nursing Science, 3*:53–60.

Watson, J. (1979). *Nursing: The philosophy and science of caring.* Boston: Little, Brown.

Watson, J. (1985a). *Nursing: The philosophy and science of caring.* Boulder, CO: Colorado Associated Univ. Press.

Watson, J. (1985b). *Nursing: Human science and human care: A theory of nursing.* Norwalk, CT: Appleton-Century-Crofts.

Watson, J. (1987). Nursing on the caring edge: Metaphorical vignettes. *Advances in Nursing Science, 10*(1):10–18.

Watson, M. J. (1988). New dimensions of human caring theory. *Nursing Science Quarterly, 1*(4), 175–181.

Watson, J. (1989). Watson's philosophy and theory of human caring in nursing. In J. Riehl-Sisca (Ed.), *Conceptual models for nursing practice* (pp. 219–236). Norwalk, CT: Appleton & Lange.

Watson, J. (1990). The moral failure of the patriarchy. *Nursing Outlook, 38*(2):62–66.

Watson, J. (1992). Window on theory of human caring. In M. O'Toole (Ed.), *Miller-Keane encyclopedia & dictionary of medicine, nursing, & allied health* (5th ed.) (p. 1481). Philadelphia: W.B. Saunders.

Watson, J. (1993). *A guide to applying the art & science of human caring: A consultation with Jean Watson and colleagues* (Videotape). New York: National League for Nursing.

Watson, J., G., Phillips, S. (1992). A call for educational reform: Colorado nursing doctorate model as exemplar. *Nursing Outlook, 40*:20–26.

Madeleine M. Leininger

Julia B. George

Madeleine M. Leininger received her basic nursing education at St. Anthony's School of Nursing, Denver, CO, and graduated in 1948. In 1950 she earned a bachelor of science from Benedictine College, Atchison, KS; in 1953 a master of science in nursing from Catholic University, Washington, DC; and in 1965 a PhD in anthropology from the University of Washington, Seattle. She is a Fellow in the American Academy of Nursing and holds an LhD from Benedictine College.

Dr. Leininger is the founder of the transcultural subfield of nursing. She is Professor of Nursing and Anthropology and Human Care Research, College of Nursing and Liberal Arts, Wayne State University. She has held both faculty and administrative appointments in nursing education and has published extensively.

In the 1940s Leininger (1991) recognized the importance of caring to nursing. Statements of appreciation for nursing care made by patients alerted her to caring values and led to her longstanding focus on care as the dominant ethos of nursing. During the mid-1950s, she experienced what she describes as cultural shock while she was working in a child guidance home in the midwestern United States. While working as a clinical nurse specialist with disturbed children and their parents, she observed recurrent behavioral differences among the children and concluded that these differences had a cultural base. She identified a lack of knowledge of the children's cultures as the missing link in nursing to understand the variations in care of clients. This experience led her to become the first professional nurse in the world to earn a

Taken from: *Nursing Theories: The Base for Professional Nursing Practice*, Fourth Edition by George.

doctorate in anthropology, and led to the development of the new field of transcultural nursing as a subfield of nursing.

Leininger first used the terms "transcultural nursing," "ethnonursing," and "cross-cultural nursing" in the 1960s. In 1966, at the University of Colorado, she offered the first transcultural nursing course with field experiences and has been instrumental in the development of similar courses at a number of other institutions (Leininger, 1979). In 1979, Leininger defined transcultural nursing as:

> a learned subfield or branch of nursing which focuses upon the comparative study and analysis of cultures with respect to nursing and health-illness caring practices, beliefs, and values with the goal to provide meaningful and efficacious nursing care services to people according to their cultural values and health-illness context (p. 15).

At the same time she defined ethnonursing as:

> the study of nursing care beliefs, values, and practices as cognitively perceived and known by a designated culture through their direct experience, beliefs, and value system (p. 15).

The term "transcultural nursing" (rather than "cross-cultural") is used today to refer to the evolving knowledge and practices related to this new field of study and practice. Leininger (1991) stresses the importance of knowledge gained from direct experience or directly from those who have experienced and labels such knowledge as *emic*, or people-centered. This is contrasted with *etic* knowledge, which describes the professional perspective. She contends that *emically* derived care knowledge is essential to establish nursing's epistemological and ontological base for practice.

Leininger built her theory of transcultural nursing on the premise that the peoples of each culture not only can know and define the ways in which they experience and perceive their nursing care world but also can relate these experiences and perceptions to their general health beliefs and practices. Based upon this premise, nursing care is derived and developed from the cultural context in which it is to be provided.

Leininger (1991) asserts that human care is central to nursing as a discipline and as a profession. She, and others, have studied the phenomena of care for over four decades. They recognize and are proponents of the preservation of care as the essence of nursing. With this increasing recognition of care as essential to nursing knowledge and practice, Leininger labeled her theory Culture Care. She drew upon anthropology for the culture component and upon nursing for the care component. Her belief that cultures have both health practices that are specific to one culture and prevailing patterns that are common across cultures led to the addition of the terms "diversity" and "universality" to the title of her theory. Thus, the most current title of Leininger's theory is Culture Care or Culture Care Diversity and Universality.

ᴸeininger's Theory

In 1985, Leininger published her first presentation of her work as a theory, and in 1988 and 1991 she presented further explication of her ideas. In the 1991 presentation, she provided orientational definitions for the concepts of culture, cultural care, cultural care diversity, cultural care universality, nursing, worldview, cultural and social structure dimensions, environmental context, ethnohistory, generic (folk or lay) care system, professional care system, cultural congruent nursing care, health, care/caring, cultural care preservation, cultural care accommodation, and cultural care repatterning. Some of these definitions were from earlier works and some were original to the 1991 work. Leininger points out that these definitions are provisional guides that may be altered as a culture is studied.

In addition to the definitions, she presented assumptions which support her prediction that "different cultures perceive, know, and practice care in different ways, yet there are some commonalities about care among all cultures of the world" (Leininger, 1985, p. 210). She refers to the commonalities as universality and to the differences as diversity.

Culture is the "learned, shared and transmitted values, beliefs, norms, and lifeways of a particular group that guides their thinking, decisions, and actions in patterned ways" (Leininger, 1991, p. 47). A related assumption is that the values, beliefs, and practices for culturally related care are shaped by, and often embedded in, "the worldview, language, religious (or spiritual), kinship (social), political (or legal), educational, economic, technological, ethnohistorical, and environmental context" of the culture (p. 45).

Cultural care diversity indicates "the variabilities and/or differences in meanings, patterns, values, lifeways, or symbols of care within or between collectives that are related to assistive, supportive, or enabling human care expressions" (Leininger, 1991, p. 47). In contrast, cultural care universality indicates the "common, similar, or dominant uniform care meanings, patterns, values, lifeways or symbols that are manifest among many cultures and reflect assistive, supportive, facilitative, or enabling ways to help people" (p. 47). It is assumed that, while human care is universal across cultures, caring may be demonstrated through diverse expressions, actions, patterns, lifestyles, and meanings. *Cultural care* is defined as "the subjectively and objectively learned and transmitted values, beliefs, and patterned lifeways that assist, support, facilitate, or enable another individual or group to maintain their well-being, health, improve their human condition and lifeway, or to deal with illness, handicaps or death" (p. 47). A related assumption is that cultural care is "the broadest holistic means to know, explain, interpret, and predict nursing care phenomena to guide nursing care practices" (p. 44).

Worldview is the way in which people look at the world, or at the universe, and form a "picture or value stance" about the world and their lives (Leininger, 1991, p. 47). *Cultural and social structure dimensions* are defined as involving "the dynamic patterns and features of interrelated structural and organizational factors of a particular culture (subculture or society) which includes religious, kinship (social), political (and legal), economic, educational, technologic and cultural values, ethnohistorical factors, and how these factors may be interrelated and function to influence human behavior in different environmental contexts" (p. 47). *Environmental context* is "the totality of an event, situation, or particular experience that gives meaning to human expressions, interpretations, and social interactions in particular physical, ecological, sociopolitical and/or cultural settings" (p. 48). *Ethnohistory* includes "those past facts, events, instances, experiences of individuals, groups, cultures, and institutions that are primarily people-centered (ethno) and which describe, explain, and interpret human lifeways within particular cultural contexts and over short or long periods of time" (p. 48). "Knowledge of meanings and practices derived from world views, social structure factors, cultural values, environmental context, and language uses are essential to guide nursing decisions and actions in providing cultural congruent care" (Leininger, 1988, p. 155).

Generic (folk or lay) care systems are "culturally learned and transmitted, indigenous (or traditional), folk (home-based) knowledge and skills used to provide assistive, supportive, enabling, or facilitative acts toward or for another individual, group, or institution with evident or anticipated needs to ameliorate or improve a human lifeway, health condition (or well-being), or to deal with handicaps and death situations" (Leininger, 1991, p. 48). Generic or folk knowledge is emic. *Professional care system(s)* are defined as "formally taught, learned, and transmitted professional care, health, illness, wellness, and related knowledge and practice skills that prevail in professional institutions usually with multidisciplinary personnel to serve consumers" (p. 48). Professional care knowledge is etic. *Health* is "a state of well-being that is culturally defined, valued, and practiced, and which reflects the ability of individuals (or groups) to perform their daily role activities in culturally expressed, beneficial, and patterned lifeways"

(p. 48). The related assumptions are that all cultures have generic or folk health care practices, that professional practices usually vary across cultures, and that in any culture there will be cultural similarities and differences between the care receivers (generic) and the professional care-givers.

Care as a noun is defined as those "abstract and concrete phenomena related to assisting, supporting, or enabling experiences or behaviors toward or for others with evident or anticipated needs to ameliorate or improve a human condition or lifeway" (Leininger, 1991, p. 46). Care is assumed to be a distinct, dominant, unifying and central focus of nursing, and, while curing and healing cannot occur effectively without care, care may occur without cure. *Care* as a verb is defined as "actions and activities directed toward assisting, supporting, or enabling another individual or group with evident or anticipated needs to ameliorate or improve a human condition or lifeway or to face death" (p. 46). Assumptions related to care and caring include that they are essential for the survival of humans, as well as for their growth, health, well-being, healing, and ability to deal with handicaps and death. The expressions, patterns, and lifeways of care have different meanings in different cultural contexts. The phenomenon of care can be discovered or identified by examining the cultural group's view of the world, social structure, and language.

Along with the universal nature of human beings as caring beings, the cultural care values, beliefs, and practices that are specific to a given culture provide a basis for the patterns, conditions, and actions associated with human care. Knowledge of these provides the base for three modes of nursing care decisions and actions, all of which require the coparticipation of the nurse and clients. *Cultural care preservation* is also known as maintenance and includes those "assistive, supporting, facilitative, or enabling professional actions and decisions that help people of a particular culture to retain and/or preserve relevant care values so that they can maintain their well-being, recover from illness, or face handicaps and/or death" (Leininger, 1991, p. 48). *Cultural care accommodation,* also known as negotiation, includes those "assistive, supporting, facilitative, or enabling creative professional actions and decisions that help people of a designated culture to adapt to or negotiate with others for a beneficial or satisfying health outcome with professional care providers" (p. 48). *Cultural care repatterning,* or restructuring, includes "those assistive, supporting, facilitative, or enabling professional actions and decisions that help a client(s) reorder, change, or greatly modify their lifeways for new, different, and beneficial health care pattern [sic] while respecting the client(s) cultural values and beliefs and still providing a beneficial or healthier lifeway than before the changes were coestablished with the client(s)" (p. 49). Repatterning requires the creative use of an extensive knowledge of the client's culture base and must be done in a way that is sensitive to the client's lifeways while using both generic and professional knowledge.

Nursing is defined as "a learned humanistic and scientific profession and discipline which is focused on human care phenomena and activities in order to assist, support, facilitate, or enable individuals or groups to maintain or regain their well-being (or health) in culturally meaningful and beneficial ways, or to help people face handicaps or death" (Leininger, 1991, p. 47). *Professional nursing care (caring)* is defined as "formal and cognitively learned professional care knowledge and practice skills obtained through educational institutions that are used to provide assistive, supportive, enabling, or facilitative acts to or for another individual or group in order to improve a human health condition (or well-being), disability, lifeway, or to work with dying clients" (p. 38). *Cultural congruent (nursing) care* is defined as "those cognitively based assistive, supportive, facilitative, or enabling acts or decisions that are tailor-made to fit with individual, group, or institutional cultural values, beliefs, and lifeways in order to provide or support meaningful, beneficial, and satisfying health care, or well-being services" (p. 49). Related assumptions include that nursing, as a transcultural care discipline and profession, has a central purpose to serve human beings in all areas of the world; that when culturally based nursing care is beneficial and healthy it contributes to the well-being of the client(s)—whether individuals, groups, families, communities, or institutions—as they function within the context of their environments. Also, nursing care will be culturally congruent or beneficial only when the clients are known by the nurse and the clients' patterns, expressions, and cultural values are used in appropriate and meaningful ways by the nurse with the clients. Finally, it is assumed that if clients receive nursing care that is not at least reasonably culturally congruent (that is, compatible with and respectful of the clients' lifeways, beliefs, and values), the client will demonstrate signs of stress, noncompliance, cultural conflicts, and/or ethical or moral concerns.

Leininger named her theory Culture Care Diversity and Universality and depicts it in the Sunrise Model (see Figure 5–1). This model may be viewed as a cognitive map that moves from the most abstract to the least abstract. The top of the model is the worldview and social system level, which directs the study of perceptions of the world outside of the culture—the suprasystem in general system terms. Leininger (1985) states this level leads to the study of the nature, meaning, and attributes of care from three perspectives. Values and social structure could be a part of each of the perspectives. The microperspective studies individuals within a culture; these studies typically would be on a small scale. The middle perspective focuses on more complex factors in one specific culture; these studies are on a larger scale than micro-studies. The macro-studies investigate phenomena across several cultures and are large in scale.

The cultural care worldview flows into knowledge about individuals, families, groups, communities, and institutions in diverse health care systems. This knowledge provides culturally specific meanings and expressions in relation to care and health. The next focus is on the generic or folk system, professional care system(s), and nursing care. Information about these systems includes the characteristics and the specific care features of each. This information allows for the identification of similarities and differences or cultural care universality and cultural care diversity.

Next are nursing care decisions and actions which involve cultural care preservation/maintenance, cultural care accommodation/negotiation and cultural care repatterning/restructuring. It is here that nursing care is delivered. Within the Sunrise Model, culture congruent care is developed. This care is both congruent with and valued by the members of the culture.

Leininger (1991) points out that the model is not the theory but a depiction of the components of the theory of Culture Care Diversity and Universality. The purpose of the model is to aid the study of how the components of the theory influence the health status of, and care provided to, individuals, families, groups, communities, and institutions within a culture. She presents cogent arguments for the use of the model to guide discovery research that uses qualitative and ethnographic methods of study. She speaks strongly against the use of operational definitions and preconceived notions, and the use of causal or linear perspectives in studying cultural care diversity and universality. She supports the importance of finding out what is, of exploring and discovering the essence and meanings of care.

*L*eininger's Theory and Nursing's Metaparadigm

Leininger defines health but does not specifically define the major concepts of human being, society/environment, and nursing. However, her view of these concepts can be derived from her conceptual definitions and assumptions. She also presents an argument for care as the central concept in nursing's metaparadigm (Leininger, 1991).

Human beings are best represented in her assumptions. Humans are believed to be caring and to be capable of being concerned about the needs, well-being, and survival of others.

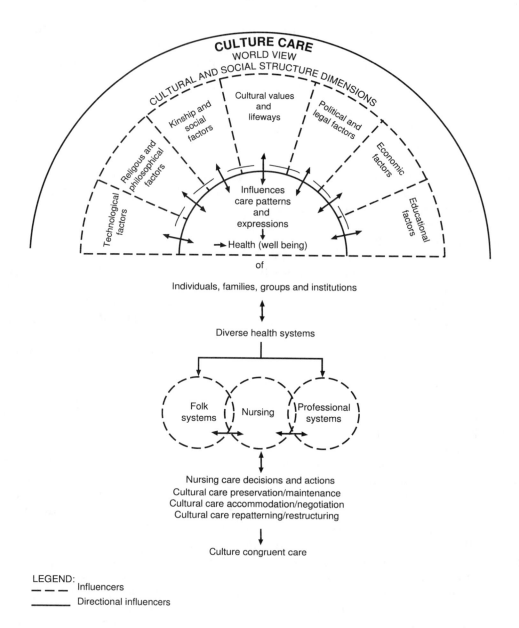

FIGURE 5-1

Leininger's Sunrise Model depicts dimensions of Cultural Care Diversity and Universality. (*From Leininger, M. (1991). Culture Care Diversity & Universality: A theory of nursing (p. 43). New York: National League for Nursing. Used with permission.*)

Human care is universal, that is, seen in all cultures. Humans have survived within cultures and through place and time because they have been able to care for infants, children, and the elderly in a variety of ways and in many different environments. Thus, humans are universally caring beings who survive in a diversity of cultures through their ability to provide the universality of care in a variety of ways according to differing cultures, needs, and settings. Leininger (1991) also indicates that nursing as a caring science should focus beyond traditional nurse-patient interactions and dyads to include "families, groups, communities, total cultures, and institutions" (p. 22) as well as worldwide health institutions and ways to develop international nursing care policies and practices. She points out that in many non-Western cultures family and institutions dominate. In these cultures, person is not an important concept. Indeed, there may be no term in the language for person.

Leininger defines *health*; this definition appears earlier in this section. She speaks of health systems, health care practices, changing health patterns, health promotion, and health maintenance. Health is an important concept in transcultural nursing. Because of the emphasis on the need for nurses to have knowledge that is specific to the culture in which nursing is being practiced, it is presumed that health is viewed as being universal across cultures but defined within each culture in a manner that reflects the beliefs, values, and practices of that particular culture. Thus, health is both universal and diverse.

Society/environment are not terms that are defined by Leininger; she speaks instead of worldview, social structure, and environmental context. However, society/environment, if viewed as being represented in culture, are a major theme of Leininger's theory. Environmental context is defined as being the totality of an event, situation, or experience. Leininger's (1991) definition of culture focuses on a particular group (society) and the patterning of actions, thoughts, and decisions that occurs as the result of "learned, shared, and transmitted values, beliefs, norms, and lifeways" (p. 47). This learning, sharing, transmitting, and patterning occur within a group of people who function in an identifiable setting or environment. Therefore, although Leininger does not use the specific terms of society or environment, the concept of culture is closely related to society/environment, and is a central theme of her theory.

Nursing is defined by Leininger; this definition appears earlier in this section. She expresses concern that nurses do not have adequate preparation for a transcultural perspective and that they neither value nor practice from such a perspective to the fullest extent possible. She presents three types of nursing actions that are culturally based and thus congruent with the needs and values of the clients. These are cultural care preservation/maintenance, cultural care accommodation/negotiation, and cultural care repatterning/restructuring and have been defined earlier in this section. These three modes of action can lead to the delivery of nursing care that best fits with the client's culture and thus decreases cultural stress and potential for conflict between client and caregiver.

Culture Care Diversity and Universality and the Nursing Process

After careful review of the Sunrise Model, it becomes apparent that there are parallels between the model and the nursing process. This is true, in part, because both represent a problem solving process. The focus of the nursing process is the client who is the recipient of nursing care. The client is also a focus of the Sunrise Model, but the importance of knowledge and understanding of the client's culture is a major shaping force in the Model.

Gaining knowledge and understanding of another's culture may be very time consuming for the nurse who is not familiar with that culture. Leininger (1978) speaks with concern about the possibility of the nurse being involved in culture shock or cultural imposition. *Culture shock* may result when an outsider attempts to comprehend or adapt effectively to a different cultural group. The outsider is likely to experience feelings of discomfort and helplessness and some degree of disorientation because of the differences in cultural values, beliefs, and practices. Culture shock may lead to anger and can be reduced by seeking knowledge of the culture before encountering that culture. *Cultural imposition* refers to efforts of the outsider, both subtle and not so subtle, to impose his or her own cultural values, beliefs, behaviors upon an individual, family, or group from another culture. Cultural imposition has been particularly prevalent in efforts to impose Western health care practices upon other cultures.

The upper portions of the Sunrise Model involve the development of knowledge about cultures, people, and care systems. When appropriately used, they could help prevent culture shock and cultural imposition. These levels are similar to the *assessment* and *diagnosis* phases of the nursing process. However, in the Sunrise Model, knowledge of the culture could be gained before identifying a specific client who would be the focus of the nursing process. First, one is assessing or gathering knowledge and information about the social structure and worldview of the client's culture. Other information that is needed includes the language and environmental context of the client as well as the factors of technology, religion, philosophy, kinship, social structure, cultural values and beliefs, politics, legal system, economics, and education. Much of this knowledge could be gathered before the identification of a particular client and would be useful in preventing both culture shock and cultural imposition.

Worldview and social structure knowledge needs to be applied to the situation of the client, whether that client is an individual, a family, a group, a community, or a sociocultural institution. Next, it is recognized that the client exists within a health system and the values, beliefs, and behaviors of the generic (folk), professional, and nursing care portions of that health system need to be identified. Throughout this assessment process, it is important to recognize and identify those characteristics which are universal or common across cultures and those which are diverse or specific to the culture being assessed. After identifying the cultural care diversities and universalities for the culture, a nursing diagnosis can be developed based upon those areas in which the client is not meeting a cultural expectation of the client's culture.

Once the diagnosis has been established, *planning* and *implementation* occur within Nursing Care Decisions and Actions. Again, the nursing care decisions and actions need to be culturally based to best meet the needs of the client and provide culture congruent care. The three modes of action are cultural care preservation/maintenance, cultural care accommodation/ negotiation, and cultural care repatterning/restructuring. In cultural care preservation/maintenance, the professional actions focus on supporting, assisting, facilitating, or enabling clients to preserve or retain favorable health, to recover from illness or to face handicaps or death. An example would be facilitating an elderly person's access to grocery shopping so that the individual can continue to prepare healthy meals—or encouraging the sharing of those meals with another in a manner which is culturally acceptable.

Cultural care accommodation/negotiation create professional efforts to facilitate, enable, assist, or support actions which represent ways to negotiate with or adapt or adjust to the client's health and care patterns for a beneficial or satisfying health outcome. For example, in planning for prenatal classes for multigravidas in a Hispanic community, provision for child care needs to be included as Hispanic mothers place very high value on caring for their children and do not use babysitters as freely as do many mothers in American society. The Hispanic mother's care pattern is to provide care for her child and to have the child near her. She will choose to not attend the class rather than leave her child at home with a babysitter. Those who do not understand this may become involved in cultural imposition and label the mother as not caring when she does not attend meetings at which child care is not available.

Cultural care repatterning/restructuring refers to professional actions that seek to help clients change meaningful health or life patterns to patterns that will be healthier for them while respecting the client's cultural values. For example, Charles Sanders, whose dietary pattern has been to eat fried and salted foods at every meal, is found to have hypertension and elevated blood cholesterol levels. Fried chicken with a salty batter is an important element in Mr. Sanders' diet—it is a food which appears on the menu at family celebrations and one which is frequently packed in the brown bag meal he carries to work. Fortunately, the chicken itself is one of the forms of protein which is recommended in low cholesterol diets. The repatterning which can occur relates to the way in which the chicken is prepared. The food preparer in the Sanders family could be taught to skin the chicken (helps lower the cholesterol), use a coating of herbs (rather than salt to help with the hypertension), and bake in the microwave oven with no added fat rather than fry with a salty batter (helps with both cholesterol and hypertension). Such change would repattern the preparation of a favorite food into a way that could provide for the continued inclusion of this food in the diet on a regular basis. At the same time, important changes in the way in which Mr. Sanders eats would be supported. Similar repatterning could occur with other foods, for example, instead of cooking green beans with salt pork, the beans could be cooked with herbs and a little polyunsaturated or mono-saturated oil.

The Sunrise Model does not include an area identified as *evaluation*. However, in Leininger's (1991) discussion of transcultural nursing, she places a great deal of importance upon the need for nursing care to provide ways in which care will benefit the client and on the need to systematically study nursing care behaviors to determine which care behaviors are appropriate to the lifeways and behavioral patterns of the culture for healing, health, or well-being. Such study certainly is the equivalent of evaluation. Without evaluation of the outcomes of a particular plan of care that used the nursing process, or a series of such plans, the systematic study that Leininger advises cannot be completed.

*C*ulture Care Diversity and Universality and the Characteristics of a Theory

Beginning with the identification of a need to understand the culture of clients, through the introduction of the terms transcultural nursing and ethnonursing care, to the presentation of the Sunrise Model, Madeleine Leininger has developed the theory she calls Culture Care Diversity and Universality.

1. **Theories can interrelate concepts in such a way as to create a different way of looking at a particular phenomenon.** Leininger has developed the Sunrise Model to demonstrate the interrelationships of the concepts in her theory of Culture Care Diversity and Universality. The worldview and social structure portion of the model does not differ significantly from any other view of culture and its interaction with human beings, with the possible exception of the inclusion of care and health patterns. The Model focuses on individuals, families, groups, communities, and socio-cultural institutions which is similar to other theories of nursing. The inclusion of the term "cultural" does provide a distinguishing feature since no other nursing theory has this emphasis on culture. Health systems include generic, professional, and nursing care systems. The inclusion of the generic system is unique to the cultural care theory. Nursing care decisions and actions are identified as supporting, accommodating to, or repatterning current health and care practices. The focus of nursing care decisions and actions is shared with many other theories. The division of actions into supporting, accommodating, or repatterning is specific to this theory. The Sunrise Model of Culture Care Diversity and Universality in itself supports the concepts of diversity and universality. The worldview, social structure, and description of individuals, families, groups, communities, and institutions are essentially universal as they have much in common with many other theories. The identified care systems and types of nursing care actions are diverse, or more specific and unique to this particular theory. Overall, the theory of Culture Care was the first to focus specifically on human care from a transcultural perspective (Leininger, 1991). It provides a holistic

rather than a fragmented view of people. This view includes "worldview; biophysical state; religious (or spiritual) orientation; kinship patterns; material (and nonmaterial) cultural phenomena; the political, economic, legal, educational, technological, and physical environment; language; and folk and professional care practices" (p. 23). Thus, Leininger has interrelated concepts in a way which provides a different way of looking at the phenomenon of nursing care.

2. **Theories must be logical in nature.** There is an inherent logic in the thought that as more is known about a client, the opportunity to provide care that meets that client's needs increases. Leininger has focused on a particular area of knowledge as being important—that area is the culture of the client with culture having a broad definition. The Sunrise Model has a logical order to it. This order is reflected in the movement from a worldview through language and environmental context, care patterns and expressions of individuals, families, groups, communities, and institutions into diverse health systems to nursing care decisions and actions to culture congruent nursing care (see Figure 5–1).

3. **Theories should be relatively simple yet generalizable.** Leininger's theory is essentially parsimonious in that the necessary concepts are incorporated in such a manner that the theory and its model can be applied in many different settings. The theory and model are not simple in terms of being easily understood upon first contact. However, Leininger's presentations of the theory and model support the need for each of the concepts and demonstrate how the concepts are interrelated. Once the interrelationships are grasped, simplicity is more apparent. The theory and model are excellent examples of being generalizable. The concepts and relationships that are presented are at a level of abstraction which allows them to be applied in many different situations. They provide a guide for knowledge that moves from initial generation of knowledge through affirmation of substantive knowledge to application of that knowledge in a caring process. While the knowledge is to be specific to the situation in which the nursing care is to occur, the process of generating and applying the knowledge is universal.

4. **Theories can be the bases for hypotheses that can be tested or for theory to be expanded.** During the development of the Culture Care Diversity and Universality theory many studies have been conducted that demonstrate the theory can be the basis for research. A number of these studies were presented during four national transcultural nursing conferences held from 1975 to 1978 at the College of Nursing, University of Utah. The proceedings of these conferences are presented in *Transcultural Nursing* (Leininger, 1979). These proceedings reflect the importance of ethnographic research in the development of this theory. Leininger (1985) presented a number of relational statements that provide a foundation for further study (see Table 5–4). In addition, Leininger (1991) developed a method of study which she labelled ethnonursing research method. She includes examples of ethnonursing research studies of Filipino and Anglo-American nurses, old order Amish, urban Mexican-Americans, Ukrainian pregnancy and childbearing, the Gadsup Akuna, dying patients, and Greek Canadian widows.

It is important to note that the theory of Culture Care Diversity and Universality is based upon, and calls for, qualitative rather than quantitative research. The development of hypotheses is characteristic of positivistic, quantitative research. The development of research questions, and of relational statements, is characteristic of qualitative research. Leininger (1991) states that nursing science should be defined

> ### TABLE 5–4 Hypotheses Derived from Leininger's Theory
>
> - There is an identifiable, positive relationship between the way people of different cultures define, interpret, and know care with their recurrent patterns of thinking and living.
> - The *emic* (inside views) of cultural care values, beliefs, and practices of cultures will show a close relationship to their daily life care patterns.
> - The meaning and use of cultural care concepts varies cross-culturally and influences nursing caregiver and care-receiver practices.
> - There is a meaningful relationship between social structure factors and worldview with generic (folk) and professional care practices.
> - Nursing care subsystems are closely related to professional health care systems but differ markedly from generic health care systems.
> - Nursing care decisions or actions that reflect the use of the client's cultural care values, beliefs, and practices will be positively related to client's satisfactions with nursing care.
> - Nursing care actions or decisions that are based upon the use of cultural care preservation, accommodation, and/or repatterning in client care will be positively related to beneficial nursing care.
> - Signs of intercultural care conflicts and stresses will be evident if caregivers fail to use cultural care values and beliefs of clients.
> - Marked differences between the meanings and expressions of care givers and care recipients lead to dissatisfactions for both.
> - High dependency of the clients upon technological nursing care activities will be closely related to cultural care that reflects decreased personalized care actions.
> - Religion and kinship care factors will be more resilient to change than technological factors.
> - Western views of cultural care values will be markedly different from non-Western care values.
> - Self-care practices will be evident in cultures that value individualism and independence; other care practices will be evident in cultures that support human interdependence.
> - Anglo-American nurse-client teaching methods will be dysfunctional with clients of non-Western cultural value orientations.
>
> (*Adapted from Leininger, M. M. (1985). Transcultural Care Diversity and Universality: A theory of nursing. Nursing and Health Care, 6, 210, 212.*)

"as the creative study of nursing phenomena which reflects the systematization of knowledge using rigorous and explicit research methods within either the qualitative or quantitative paradigm in order to establish a new or to advance nursing's discipline knowledge" (p. 30). Therefore, from the viewpoint of qualitative research, this criterion is met.

5. **Theories contribute to and assist in increasing the general body of knowledge within the discipline through the research implemented to validate them.** The research that has been conducted on transcultural nursing has contributed to the general body of knowledge within the discipline of nursing. One of the outcomes of this research is the identification of major cultural care constructs. Leininger indicates that, as of 1991, ethnonursing research identified 172 care constructs from 54 cultures. These constructs have more diversity than universality of meaning. Included in these constructs are anticipation of, attentiveness to, comfort, compassion, coping,

empathy, engrossment, helping, nurturance, protection, restoration, support, stimulation, stress alleviation, succorance, surveillance, tenderness, touch, and trust (Leininger, 1979, 1985).

Leininger (1991) has directed her research for the last three decades in the epistemological search to establish care as the essence of, and a distinct construct of, nursing. She has sought to explicate the illusive and embedded diverse culture specific and cultural universals of care. The goal of her theory is to provide *culturally congruent care* for the health or well-being of individuals, families, communities, and institutional environments. She views transcultural nursing as the arching framework for all nursing education, theory, research, and practice as nurses are expected to *care* for all people of diverse cultures worldwide. Her ideas have moved nursing beyond unicultural reference to a multicultural perspective.

6. **Theories can be utilized by the practitioners to guide and improve their practice.** In her presentation of the theory, Leininger presents examples of research findings which can guide and improve the practice of nursing. One example presents the differences in the interpretations of care by American nurses in several general hospitals, Canadian nurses, and Polynesian nurses in Hawaii. The American nurses interpreted care as first dealing with stress alleviation and then comfort. Canadian nurses reported care as being primarily support. Polynesian nurses in Hawaii first identified care as sharing with others in personalized cultural ways and then added being generous to others to achieve signs of harmony among people and their environment. Knowing the diversity in nurses' interpretation of care supports the diversity which will be present in clients and reinforces the need to be knowledgeable about this diversity. Care is universal, the meaning of care is diverse. Leininger (1991) also presents the use of the theory in nursing administration. She states that "the goal of the theory is to improve and to provide culturally congruent care to people that is beneficial, will fit with, and be useful to the client, family, or culture group healthy lifeways" (p. 39).

7. **Theories must be consistent with other validated theories, laws, principles but will leave open unanswered questions that need to be investigated.** Leininger's theory is certainly consistent with all theories that include the concept of the importance of knowing the client as a person rather than as a problem. Leininger's discussion of the seriousness of unintentional cultural imposition practices by nurses, and of the nurse's need to be aware of his or her own culture and its implications for the nurse-client situation, is very similar to King's (1981) emphasis on the importance of perceptions and the need for the nurse to be alert to both client and personal perceptions. This is but one example of areas of agreement with other theories. It is important to note that while Leininger, Watson (1988), and Boykin and Schoenhofer (1993) all speak of the importance of caring, they approach caring differently.

The unanswered questions that remain to be investigated are greater in number than those that have been answered. Since cultures are diverse not only among cultures but within them, and individuals, even within the same culture, respond differently to the same stimuli, each nurse-client situation provides new questions to be explored.

Strengths and Limitations

A major strength of Leininger's theory is the recognition of the importance of culture and its influence on everything that involves the recipients and providers of nursing care. The development of this theory over a number of years has allowed its concepts and constructs to be tested by a number of people in a variety of settings and cultures. The Sunrise Model provides guidance for the areas in which information needs to be collected.

Some limitations, as identified by Leininger (1991), include the limited number of graduate nurses who are academically prepared to conduct the investigations needed to provide transcultural nursing care. While there has been some increase in the number of nurses prepared in transcultural nursing, it is important to note the danger of cultural biases and cultural imposition occurring with nurses' personal cultural values. An associated concern is that too few nursing programs include courses and planned learning experiences that provide a knowledge base for transcultural nursing practice. There is also a need for research funds to support continued study of caring practices—both those that are universal and those that are particular to a culture.

In some of her writings, Leininger is not consistent in her terminology. For example, in *Transcultural Nursing* (1979), she refers to ethnocultural care constructs and then to ethnonursing care constructs. In her theory presentation she refers to these same constructs as major cultural care constructs (Leininger, 1988). Since the constructs are listed it is relatively easy to be aware that these terms all refer to the same constructs. However, the reader's mental energy could be conserved for understanding the theory and model if the terminology were more consistent.

The complexity of the Sunrise Model can be viewed as both a strength and a limitation. The complexity is a strength in that it emphasizes the importance of the inclusion of anthropological and cultural concepts in nursing education and practice. On the other hand, the complexity can lead to misinterpretation or rejection, both of which are limitations.

Summary

Madeleine Leininger has been working since the 1950s on the development of her theory of Culture Care Diversity and Universality. In the 1960s, she first began to use the terms transcultural nursing and ethnonursing. While she has slightly different definitions of these terms, she often uses them interchangeably, an action that can be confusing to the reader.

The major concepts of her theory are culture, cultural care diversity and universality, cultural care, nursing, worldview, cultural and social structure dimensions, environmental context, ethnohistory, generic (folk) care system, professional care system, health, care, caring, cultural care preservation, cultural care accommodation, cultural care repatterning, and cultural congruent nursing care. She defines each of these concepts and presents assumptions that are related to them. The concepts and their interrelationships provide the basis for the Sunrise Model of this theory.

The Sunrise Model presents a cognitive model which, when viewed from the top down, moves from the cultural and social structure through individuals, families, groups, communities, and institutions in generic, professional, and nursing care systems to nursing care decisions and actions that are cultural care preserving, accommodating, and repatterning. The Model also indicates the need to move from knowledge generation through substantive knowledge to application of the knowledge. In discussing the Model, Leininger (1991) presents the idea that care patterns and processes may be universal or diverse. Universal care indicates care patterns, values, and behaviors that are common across cultures. Care diversities represent those patterns and processes that are unique or specific to an individual, family, or cultural group. Leininger believes, and research has supported, that care diversities are greater in number than are universal care patterns.

The theory of Culture Care Diversity and Universality is of significance in a society that is becoming more and more aware of the cultural diversity within its boundaries. While this theory does not provide specific directions for nursing care, it does provide guidelines for the gathering of knowledge and a framework for the making of decisions about what care is needed or would be of the greatest benefit to the client. Leininger has clearly identified what has been a major deficit in our provision of nursing care and provided a road map to begin to fill the gaps created by that deficit.

References

Boykin, A., & Schoenhofer, S. (1993). *Nursing as caring: A model for transforming practice.* New York: National League for Nursing.

Leininger, M. (1978). *Transcultural nursing: Concepts, theories, and practices.* New York: Wiley. [out of print]

Leininger, M. (1979). *Transcultural nursing.* New York: Masson. [out of print]

Leininger, M. M. (1985). Transcultural Care Diversity and Universality: A theory of nursing. *Nursing and Health Care, 6,* 209–212.

Leininger, M. M. (1988). Leininger's theory of nursing: Cultural Care Diversity and Universality. *Nursing Science Quarterly, 1,* 152–160.

Leininger, M. M. (1991). *Culture Care Diversity and Universality: A theory of nursing.* New York: National League for Nursing.

King, I. (1981). *A theory for nursing: Systems, concepts, process.* New York: Wiley. [out of print]

Watson, J. (1988). *Nursing: Human science and human care.* New York: National League for Nursing.

Bibliography

Gaut, D., & Leininger, M. M. (1991). *Care: The compassionate healer.* New York: National League for Nursing.

Leininger, M. M. (1970). *Nursing and anthropology: Two worlds to blend.* New York: Wiley.

Leininger, M. M. (1973). *Contemporary issues in mental health nursing.* Boston: Little, Brown.

Leininger, M. M. (Ed.) (1976). *Transcultural health care issues and conditions.* Philadelphia: Davis.

Leininger, M. M. (1980). Caring: A central focus of nursing and health care services. *Nursing & Health Care, 1,* 135–143, 176.

Leininger, M. M. (Ed.) (1980). *Transcultural nursing: Teaching, practice and research.* Salt Lake City: University of Utah College of Nursing.

Leininger, M. M. (Ed.) (1981). *Care: An essential human need.* Thorofare, NJ: Slack.

Leininger, M. M. (1981). Transcultural nursing: Its progress and its future. *Nursing & Health Care, 2,* 365–371.

Leininger, M. M. (Ed.) (1984). *Care: The essence of nursing and health.* Thorofare, NJ: Slack.

Leininger, M. M. (1984). *Reference sources for transcultural health and nursing.* Thorofare, NJ: Slack.

Leininger, M. M. (1984). Transcultural nursing: An overview. *Nursing Outlook, 32,* 72–73.

Leininger, M. M. (Ed.) (1985). *Qualitative research methods in nursing.* Orlando, FL: Grune & Stratton.

Leininger, M. M., & Watson, J. (1990). *The caring imperative in nursing education.* New York: National League for Nursing.

External Analysis

Nursing Research on the Model

Theory can be generated at three levels in the sunrise model: macro, mid, and micro levels. Knowledge gained from research at the macro level will be applicable beyond nursing in that it will explain the totality of human behavior (Leininger, 1985a, p. 42). Research questions conceptualized within the mid and micro levels of the model will involve smaller domains of inquiry. Studies at these levels will focus on individuals, families, or cultural groups as they enter the folk and professional health care systems.

A variety of research methods may be used to test theories derived from the model. To date, the primary methods used have been those of an ethnographic, ethnonursing approach (Leininger, 1992b). Because the theory of Culture Care Diversity and Universality has only recently been presented to nurses (primarily because of the lack of a cadre of nurses sufficiently prepared to deal with cultural concepts), studies grounded in the theory have only begun to emerge.

Leininger utilized the theory to describe, explain, and predict the health and care life-styles and patterns of 10 cultures in an urban setting (1981–1991). Ray (1984) conducted the first large-scale general hospital ethnocare study in nursing using concepts and methods from Leininger's framework. A number of doctoral studies throughout the United States and Canada have conceptualized research questions within the Culture Care theory. Cameron (1990) investigated the influence of extended caregiving on the health status of elderly Anglo-Canadian wives. Gates (1988) studied the care and cure meanings and experiences of those who were dying in hospice and hospital settings. Care and cultural context of Lebanese Muslims in an urban community was the focus of Luna's (1989) ethnographic and ethnonursing study. Findings from Rosenbaum's (1990) study revealed the meaning and experience of cultural care, cultural care continuity, cultural health and grief phenomena of older Greek-Canadian widows. Wenger (1988) studied the phenomenon of care in a high-context culture with the Old Order Amish. Several master's students have utilized Leininger's theory for conceptualizing research questions: Burns, (1987); Gelazis, (1988); McFarland, (1989); Morgan, (1989); and Stasiak, (1991).

Leininger initiated the establishment of the Committee on Nursing and Anthropology and the Transcultural Nursing Society as organizations for nurses interested in transcultural nurs-

---

Taken from: *Conceptual Models of Nursing: Analysis and Application,* Third Edition by Fitzpatrick and Whall.

ing and human care to share their research and other experiences together. In 1988 the International Association for Human Caring was formed to encourage scholarly exchange of ideas and encourage research (Leininger, 1991, p. 17).

Nursing Education Based on the Model

As founder and developer of the field of transcultural nursing, Leininger has been instrumental in the establishment of master's and doctoral programs in nursing that expose transcultural care perspectives. In the early 1960s, she realized that very little care and cultural nursing content existed in nursing curricula. "Clearly nurses without preparation in transcultural nursing would be greatly handicapped when working with people of diverse cultures" (Leininger, 1991, p. 16). The University of Colorado offered the first course in transcultural nursing in 1966–1967, followed by the Universities of Washington (1969) and Utah (1977), and Wayne State University (1981) in Detroit (Leininger, 1984, p. 43). "By 1980, about 20 percent of nursing programs accredited by the National League for Nursing incorporated cultural concepts and principles into the undergraduate program (Leininger, 1989) and by 1991, 15 percent of graduate nursing programs in the United States had transcultural nursing courses" (Leininger, 1993b, p. 35).

Leininger's publications on the Culture Care theory have played a valuable role in educating nurses about her theory. She held back on the publication of a book on the theory itself until nurses were educated in transcultural nursing, but prepared the way with numerous workshops, presentations, and journal articles. Nursing educators from several countries continue to benefit from Leininger's expert consultation during short-term intensive exchange visits to Wayne State University.

Nursing Practice Based on the Model

Leininger maintains that the coming decade will witness the utilization of transcultural nursing knowledge and research in practice. Because of the dearth of transculturally prepared faculty, much of the potential for the theory of Culture Care Diversity and Universality to influence and guide nursing practice has yet to be realized. She maintains that the time has come ". . . to prevent cultural imposition practices, cultural care negligence, cultural care conflicts, and many other practice . . . problems. . . . Nurses are now keenly feeling and demanding transcultural care knowledge to help them function in a tense multicultural world" (Leininger, 1991, p. 41).

References

Algase, D., & Whall, A. (1993). Rosemary Ellis' views on the substantive structure of nursing. IMAGE: *The Journal of Nursing Scholarship 25*(1), 69–72.

Bodner, A., & Leininger, M. (1992). Transcultural nursing care values, beliefs, and practices of American (USA) gypsies. *Journal of Trans-Cultural Nursing, 4*, 17–28.

Burns, G. (1987). *Ethnocare of the homeless in large urban communities.* Unpublished master's field study, Wayne State University, Detroit.

Cameron, C. (1990). *Health status of elderly Anglo-Canadian wives providing extended caregiving to their disabled husbands within Leininger's theory.* Unpublished doctoral dissertation. Wayne State University. Detroit.

Fawcett, J. (1989). *Analysis and evaluation of conceptual models of nursing.* Philadelphia: F. A. Davis.

Fitzpatrick, J., & Whall, A. (1989). Conceptual models of nursing. Analysis and application. Bowie, MD: Brady.

Gates, M. (1988). *Care and cure meanings, experiences and orientations of persons who are dying in hospital and hospice settings.* Unpublished doctoral dissertation, Wayne State University, Detroit.

Gelazis, R. (1988). *Well-being and humor in Lithuanian Americans.* Unpublished post-master's field study, Wayne State University, Detroit.

Hardy, M. (1974). Theories: Components, development, evaluation. *Nursing Research, 23*(2), 100–106.

Kloosterman, N. (1991). Cultural care: The missing link in severe sensory alteration. *Nursing Science Quarterly, 4*(3), 119–122.

Leininger, M. (1978). *Transcultural nursing: Concepts, theories, and practices.* New York: Wiley.

Leininger, M. (1984). Transcultural nursing: An essential knowledge and practice field for today. *The Canadian Nurse, 80*(11), 41–45.

Leininger, M. (1985a). *Qualitative research methods in nursing.* New York: Grune & Stratton.

Leininger, M. (1985b). Transcultural care diversity and universality: A theory of nursing. *Nursing and Health Care, 6*(4), 209–212.

Leininger, M. (1988). Leininger's theory of nursing. Culture care diversity and universality. *Nursing Science Quarterly, 1*(4), 152–160.

Leininger, M. 1989a). Transcultural nursing trends in schools of nursing in U.S.A. Unpublished manuscript. Detroit, Wayne State University.

Leininger, M. (1989b). Transcultural nursing: Quovadis (where goeth the field). *Journal of Transcultural Nursing, 1*(1), 33–45.

Leininger, M. (1990). Issues, questions, and concerns related to the nursing diagnosis cultural movement from a transcultural nursing perspective. *Journal of Transcultural Nursing, 2*(1), 23–32.

Leininger, M. (1991). *Cultural care diversity & universality: A theory of nursing.* New York: National League for Nursing.

Leininger, M. (1992a). Strange myths and inaccurate facts in transcultural nursing. *Journal of Transcultural Nursing, 4*(2), 39–40.

Leininger, M. (1992b). Current issues, problems, and trends to advance qualitative paradigmatic research methods for the future. *Qualitative Health Research, 2*(4), 392–403.

Leininger, M. (1993a). Gadsup of Papua New Guinea revisited: a three decade view. *Journal of Transcultural Nursing, 5*(1), 21–29.

Leininger, M. (1993b). Assumptive premises of the theory. In C. Reynolds & M. Leininger, *Madeleine Leininger: Cultural care diversity and universality theory* (pp. 15–38). Newbury Park, CA: Sage.

Leininger, M. (1994). *Transcultural nursing: concepts, theory, research, and practice* (2nd ed.). Columbus, OH: McGraw-Hill and Greden.

Luna, L. (1989). *Care and cultural context of Lebanese Muslims in an urban U.S. community: An ethnographic and ethnonursing study conceptualized within Leininger's theory.* Unpublished doctoral dissertation, Wayne State University, Detroit.

McFarland, M. (1989). *Culture care theory and ethnonursing mini-study of care experiences in residential nursing homes and Mexican-American communities.* Unpublished post-master's field study. Wayne State University, Detroit.

Morgan, M. (1989). *Ethnonursing: A study of care in a hospital context using Leininger's theory of culture care.* Unpublished post-master's field study, Wayne State University, Detroit.

Ray, M. (1984). The development of a classification system of institutional caring. In M. Leininger (Ed.), *Care: The essence of nursing and health* (pp. 95–112). Thorofare, NJ: Slack.

Reynolds, C., & Leininger, M. (1993). *Madeleine Leininger: Cultural care diversity and universality theory.* Newburg Park, CA: Sage.

Rosenbaum, J. (1990). *The meaning and experience of cultural care, cultural care continuity, cultural health and grief phenomena of older Greek Canadian widows.* Unpublished doctoral dissertation. Wayne State University, Detroit.

Spangler, Z. (1991). *Nursing care values and practices of Philippine-American and Anglo-American nurses using Leininger's theory.* Unpublished doctoral dissertation, Wayne State University, Detroit.

Stasiak, D. (1991). *Ethnonursing: A study of Mexican-Americans in urban cities.* Unpublished master's field study; Wayne State University, Detroit.

Wenger, A. F. (1988). *Phenomenon of care in a high-context culture: The Old Order Amish.* Unpublished doctoral dissertation, Wayne State University, Detroit.

Rogers' Model:
Science of Unitary Persons

Stephanie I. Muth Quillin

Martha E. Rogers, the woman responsible for modern nursing's focus on the person as a unified whole, died March 13, 1994. She was 79 years of age. While nurses mourned, many outside of nursing were also touched by her passing. Her picture and major accomplishments were printed in the New York Times obituary section 5 days after her death (Tomasson, 1994). Her birth date, May 12, is one she shared with Florence Nightingale (Hektor, 1989). History may judge that the two had comparable influences on the development of nursing as a profession.

Martha E. Rogers began college in 1931 at the University of Tennessee, studying science for 2 years before switching to nursing. She earned a diploma from Knoxville General Hospital School of Nursing in 1936 and completed her nursing preparation with a bachelor of science degree from George Peabody College in 1937. She earned a master's degree in public health nursing from Teacher's College, Columbia University, in 1945. She held numerous leadership positions in public health nursing. In 1952 she earned a master's degree in public health at Johns Hopkins University. In 1954, she earned her doctorate, also from Johns Hopkins University. In the same year, she went to New York University, where she became Professor and Head of the Division of Nurse Education (Safier, 1977). She headed that program until her retirement in 1975, whereupon she became Professor Emerita (Malinski, 1986). She continued to write and lecture, explaining and refining her model nearly until her death. Her last article appeared in the Spring 1994 issue of *Nursing Science Quarterly*.

Rogers received numerous awards, honors, and citations both nationally and internationally, including three honorary doctorates. Her colleagues considered her to be one of the most original thinkers in nursing. For example, Levine stated that Rogers' "view of human

---

Taken from: *Conceptual Models of Nursing: Analysis and Application*, Third Edition by Fitzpatrick and Whall.

beings . . . is a philosophic position of overwhelming importance for nursing (1988, p. 16). Her contributions to the nursing literature are extensively cited. That Rogers valued education, clear and creative thinking, and service to individuals and to society is reflected in her writings. Her abstract conceptual model and more specific theories of nursing grew from her effort to define, defend, and promote the growth of nurses as learned professionals, capable of unique and responsible service to humankind. In her clear delineation of the scientific focus of nursing, Rogers had a most significant influence upon scientific inquiry in nursing and professional nursing practice.

Rogers' abstract conceptual model was first published in 1970 in her book. *An Introduction to the Theoretical Basis of Nursing,* although its antecedents may be found in prior published works (Rogers, 1961). After its publication, in 1970, major clarifications were made as the conceptualizations were further refined. These changes can be found in Rogers' chapter in *Conceptual Models for Nursing Practice* (Rogers, 1980a), in her series of six videotapes entitled *The Science of Unitary Man* (Rogers, 1980b), in *Family Health: A Theoretical Approach to Nursing Care* by Clements and Roberts (Rogers, 1983), and in Violet Malinski's' book, *Explorations on Martha Rogers' Science of Unitary Human Beings* (1986), as well as in two articles in *Nursing Science Quarterly* (Rogers, 1988; Rogers, 1992) and a chapter in E. A. M. Barrett's *Visions of Rogers' Science Based Nursing* (1990). Rogers also explained, discussed, and responded to questions about her conceptual model during her presentations at the annual Rogerian Conferences and the Discovery International Nurse Theorist Conferences (Huch, 1991; M. J. Smith, 1988), and to students and faculty across the country. The model has served as the basis for explication of other nursing conceptualizations, including those of Newman, Parse, and Fitzpatrick, discussed in this volume and in its previous editions.

Much of Rogers' work cited has been collected under one cover, *Martha E. Rogers: Her Life and Her Work,* by V. M. Malinski and E. A. M. Barrett. Their book was released a few months after Rogers death in 1994. Another book released at the same time is *Rogers' Scientific Art of Nursing Practice,* edited by M. Madrid and E. A. M. Barrett. This second new book contains insights regarding nursing practice based on Rogers' science of nursing and personal accounts by nurses using Rogers' model in the art of nursing.

asic Considerations Included in the Model

The basic elements (nursing, person, health, environment), referred to as "commonplaces of the discipline" by Levine (1988), are necessary in any description of nursing. Rogers' definitions and explications of these terms will be presented first, with emphasis on Rogers' view of the nursing profession, after which other elements unique to Rogers' abstract conceptual model will be discussed. These elements are what Rogers called "concepts" or "building blocks" (energy fields, openness, pattern, and pan-dimensionality) and "principles of homeodynamics" (resonancy, helicy, and integrality). Some of the terminology used by Rogers to describe person and environment will be best understood after reading about the elements unique to Rogers' model presented later in this section.

Definitions of Nursing

Rogers stated that the science of nursing is "the science of unitary human beings" (1983). She believed that nursing was unique in that no other science studies the person as a whole. The purpose of nursing is "to promote human betterment wherever people are" (1992, p. 33).

Description of Nursing Activity

Rogers (1970) saw nursing activity as creative and imaginative, rooted in abstract knowledge, intellectual judgment, and compassion. She emphasized the use of the nurse's own self and the safe utilization of nursing skills and technology. Rogers (1992) emphasized the use of noninvasive modalities that are compatible with her model, such as therapeutic touch and meditation, as well as modalities that may be developed, such as color, sound, motion, and humor. She saw nurses as independent practitioners taking the lead in community-based health centers, with hospitals or "sick" centers providing support services. Rogers' conceptual model specifies the person's innovative development and rhythmical complexity. Nursing activity is based upon the wholeness of human beings and "de-rives its safety and effectiveness from a unified concept of human functioning" (1970, p. 124). Nurses help people "design ways to fulfill their different rhythmic patterns" (1992, p. 33).

The nursing process becomes dynamic when viewed within Rogers' framework. Instead of a static process wherein the nurse sets time-limited goals for the person, Rogers proposed that nursing be a continuously evolving process that includes the nurse as an environmental component (Rogers, 1980b). Nurses help individuals, families, and groups, wherever they are (including space as space exploration continues), achieve maximum well-being according to their potential (Rogers, 1992).

Definition and Description of Person

Critical to Rogers' discussion of the element of person is the statement that ". . . the whole cannot be understood when reduced to particulars" (1970, p. 44). Person is understood within her conceptual model as a whole that is more than and different from the sum of its parts (1970, p. 91). This unified view of person has been part of nursing's history, but Rogers explicitly defined this concept in scientific terms. Person was defined by Rogers as an open system, that is, "an irreducible, indivisible, pandimensional energy field identified by pattern and manifesting characteristics that are specific to the whole and which cannot be predicted from knowledge of the parts" (1992, p. 29). She states that the person's fundamental unit is not the cell but the human energy field.

Rogers cautioned against confusing her view of unitary human beings with other contemporary views of holism, which are really the summation of greater numbers of parts. Persons are to be viewed optimistically, taking into account their capacity to change and their ability to participate knowingly and creatively (although not always wisely) in the process of change (Rogers, 1983, 1992).

Definition and Description of Environment

In Rogers' view each unique human field is embedded in its unique environmental field. Person and environment are integral with each other and coextensive with the universe. The boundaries of environment become nonexistent in Rogers' model because they extend to infinity. She defined environment as "an irreducible, energy field identified by pattern and manifesting characteristics different from those of the parts" (1986, p. 5). Through extensive study, Rogers traced the history of human thought regarding the interaction of persons and environment (1970, 1980b). She concluded that the most logical conceptualization is that of a four-dimensional universe of interacting wholes. (The term *four-dimensional* was later changed to *pandimensional*.)

Definition and Description of Health

The word *health* was often used by Rogers but she declined to give it a specific definition. She came to understand that *illness* and *health* are value words, broadly defined by each culture "to denote behaviors that are of high value and low value" (1980b). Rogers conceptualized health and illness as expressions of the interactions of person and environment in the process of unfolding (1970, pp. 42, 51, 85). Her own use of the word in sentences is semantically compatible with definitions connoting well-being and absence of major illness or disease.

Rogers raised an interesting point when she observed that processes considered pathological on earth may "signify health for the space-bound" (1992, p. 27). She specifically mentioned physiological norms, and we speculate that she was referring to vital signs such as blood pressure which might be altered in space. We also know that weightlessness alters calcium content and density of bone. Perhaps certain ailments, such as osteoporosis or arthritis, would not be considered afflictions in an environment of constant weightlessness. We may further speculate that cancer may have a positive role in the evolution of "homo spacialis," as Rogers (1992) refered to future human beings evolving in space, since cancer cells have metabolic rates and temporal qualities different from those of other body cells. Rogers may also have had in mind that people who function best with very short, long, or otherwise unusual sleep patterns on Earth would be well suited for certain functions in space travel or space living.

Interrelationships Among Concepts of Person, Environment, Health, and Nursing

Rogers saw nursing as a "learned profession" with full professional status (1980a, 1980b). This means that nursing not only has a practice component but is also a science. Figure 5–2 illustrates an interpretation by the author of Rogers' view of nursing, including interrelationships among person, environment, health, and nursing. Also represented in the figure are the concepts that are unique to Rogers' model. As shown, concepts derived from study and observation about human beings provide a basis for the conceptual model. The conceptual model (discussed more completely later in this section) provides a stimulus for and gives direction to nursing science. Knowledge generated through model-based research provides a base for practice. Practice provides service to people that will maximize health potential. Rogers perceived service as rendered in all settings and appropriate for all people.

Description of Concepts Unique to the Model: Energy Fields, Openness, Pattern, Pandimensionality

Energy Fields. Rogers (1980a, 1980b) noted that current literature indicated that the fundamental unit of all living and nonliving things is the energy field. Things do not have energy fields, rather they are energy fields. "Fundamental unit" connotes the representative unit of a thing that, if examined, will thoroughly reveal its character or nature. The cell was thought of as the fundamental unit of living things, but current research notes that the sum of all of the information about the functions and interactions of cells does not reveal the full nature of the organism. By describing the energy field as the fundamental unit, Rogers hoped to avoid the "summing of parts" in nursing's study of human beings. Such summing, according to Rogers, results in views of humankind that are not helpful to nurses, such as models in which the body is likened to a machine or closed system (mechanistic models), or models in which the mind and body are viewed separately. Rather, she hoped to promote a conceptualization of person that captures the essence of being in its entirety. According to Sarter (1989), Rogers' concept of an irreducible whole as the primary unit of existence is aligned with the philosophy of Teilhard de Chardin, in which consciousness is seen as coextensive with

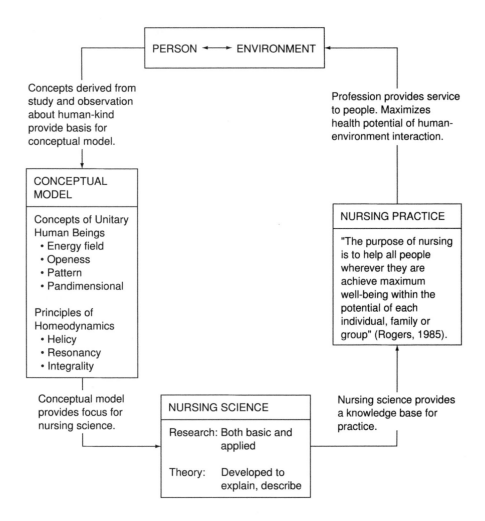

FIGURE 5–2

An interpretation of Rogers' view of nursing, including interrelation among person, environment, health, and nursing.

the universe and persons as centers of energy within the overall pattern. Rogers did not use the term consciousness, possibly because such a usage could imply a mind–body (dualism).

Openness. Rogers (1980a, 1980b) used openness to refer to the qualities exhibited by an open system as opposed to a closed system. Open systems (energy fields) are conceptualized as extending to infinity and as integral with one another. Von Bertalanffy (1968) postulated that living systems are open systems displaying negative entropy (negentropy). In other words, living systems do not run down but instead display increasing diversity or heterogeneity. Rogers expanded this view in her conceptual model to include "a universe of open systems" (1992, p. 29). Sarter (1989) states that Rogers denied existence of closed systems. If all systems are open systems then the concept of openness would extend to the inanimate. Cowling (1993) contrasts a "system perspective" with a "unitary perspective," demonstrating a difference between the two. Rogers continued to use the term "open systems" to describe energy fields through 1992, but Cowling has demonstrated that Rogers' intended focus was on manifestations of wholeness.

Pattern. Pattern (formerly, pattern and organization) is perhaps the most abstract of Rogers' concepts. Rogers stated that it is an abstraction, a single wave that identifies the given energy field (1986, p. 5). The wave pattern is ever changing as an expression of the given unitary human being becoming or evolving. The pattern of the wave form is unique to each individual or group and identifies the uniqueness of each individual or group unfolding, integral with the respective environment.

Pandimensional. Rogers said that pandimensionality (formerly, four-dimensionality and multidimensionality) is a "nonlinear domain without spatial or temporal attributes'" (Rogers, 1992). She stated that words in our language are not sufficient to fully explain this concept. Rogers' concept of four-dimensionality in her model of person and environment was similar to theory proposed by Albert Einstein. Neither Einstein nor Rogers view time separately from the three dimensions of space. Rogers explained that the concept has to do with nonlinear time and nonstatic space, which Einstein called spacetime (Rogers, 1980b). Rogers at first used the term four-dimensionality (1980a, 1980b) then later preferred multidimensionality (1990) and finally pandimensionality (1992) as better capturing her meaning. Rogers explained the relevance of this concept to the model many times. She said that human and environmental energy fields and all reality are pandimensional and that change emerges continuously, evolutionally and unpredictably from nonlinear and nonspatial coordinates. (1980a, 1992).

For a discussion of differences and similarities that may be present in rogerian and einsteinian worldviews the reader is referred to Sarter's 1989 article. *Nonlinearity* describes the pandimensional universe that Rogers envisioned. (*Nonlinear* is also a mathematical term describing formulas for events that are sometimes unpredictable. This context may also be consistent with Rogers' views.) Any present point in Rogers' view is relative, which has implications for the explanation of previously unexplained phenomena (1980a), sometimes referred to as *paranormal events*. Rogers' model is antithetical to the verificationist perspective of the logical positivists. As described by Whall (1989), the verifications value propositions based on observable phenomena and discount statements or propositions based on less observable phenomena. Conversely, Rogers' model encourages us to seriously examine ideas and theories that lack observable "objective" data or connections but may be reported or entertained as reality by clients and others. While Rogers' concepts may be criticized on this basis by some, it is worth noting that "mainstream" scientists are also breaking away from the verificationist perspective. For example, the conservative journal *Scientific American* published an article explaining how quantum physics does *not* negate time travel (Deutsch & Lockwood, 1994).

Relationship of Energy Field, Openness, Pattern, and Pandimensionality to Person, Environment, Health, and Nursing

The four concepts—energy fields, openness, pattern, and pandimensionality—when synthesized by Rogers, comprise "unitary human beings." The major components of the model of unitary human beings are discussed in the following sections. Internal analysis and evaluation of the model will deal with analysis of Rogers' abstract conceptual system, displayed in Figures 5–3 and 5–4, rather than the model of nursing, health, and person displayed in Figure 5–2.

Rogers' (1970, 1980a) definition of nursing is a reflection of her humanistic rather than mechanistic concept of person and nursing (Rogers, 1983). The focus of nursing is compassionate concern for maintaining and promoting health, preventing illness, and caring for and rehabilitating the sick and the disabled (1970, p. vii). Rogers was committed to nursing as both

FIGURE 5–3

Central Components in Rogers' Abstract Conceptual System.

a science, with its abstract body of knowledge, and an art that uses the science's body of knowl-edge. Professional practice in nursing "seeks to promote symphonic interaction between man and environment, to strengthen the coherence and integrity of the human field, and to direct and redirect patterning of the human and environmental fields for realization of maximum health potential" (1970, p. 122). M. C. Smith (1990) interprets Rogers as having meant that the nurse becomes a coparticipant with the client in repatterning the energy field for maximum health potential. Although Rogers' used "repatterning" in her 1970 book, it was not used as a transitive verb (pp. 97–98). Rogers did not use the term *repattern* in her 1992 article, perhaps because the prefix "re" is inconsistent with the principle of helicy, in which rhythmicities are nonrepeating. Barrett (1988, 1990) discusses rogerian nursing practice as "pattern manifesta-tion appraisal and deliberative mutual patterning" (1990, p. 33).

**nternal Analysis**

Underlying Assumptions

Rogers (1970) listed five assumptions underlying her conceptual model. They were derived from a selective review of the literature on humanity, physics, mathematics, and the behavioral sciences.

1. Man is a unified whole possessing his own integrity and manifesting characteristics that are more than and different from the sum of his parts (p. 47).

2. Man and environment are continuously exchanging matter and energy with one another (p. 54).

3. The life process evolves irreversibly and unidirectionally along the space–time con-tinuum (p. 59).

4. Pattern and organization identify man and reflect his innovative wholeness (p. 65).

5. Man is characterized by the capacity for abstraction and imagery, language and thought, sensation and emotion (p. 73).

(Rogers often used the term *man* to refer to human beings in publications prior to 1983; thus, when she is quoted directly above the term *man* is used.) The first four assumptions have relevance for all living systems, as well as to the person (Rogers, 1970, p. 67). The fifth

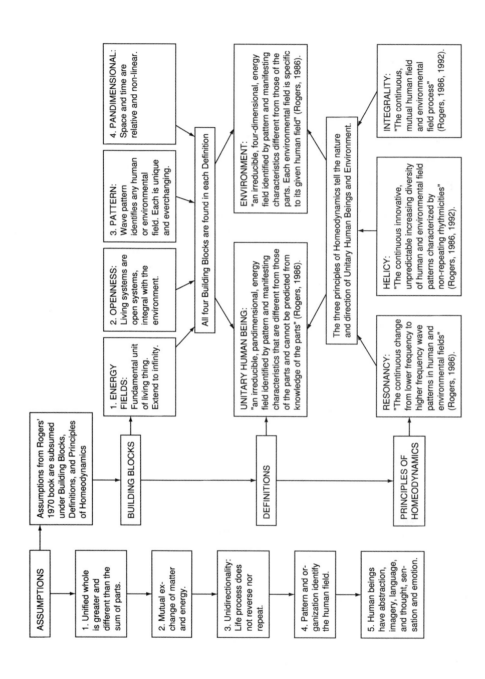

FIGURE 5–4

Summary of Rogers' Model.

assumption applies only to human beings. The fifth assumption differentiates human beings from the rest of the world of living things (1970, p. 67).

These assumptions were not restated in later publications, probably because they were subsumed elsewhere. The first assumption, describing the human being as a unified whole that is more than the sum of parts, was subsumed under the concept of energy fields. The second assumption, that of the mutual exchange of matter and energy, was replaced with the concept of openness and the principle of integrality. Human beings are viewed as integral with their environments, changing process mutually. The third assumption, describing the life process evolving unidirectionally, is actually a part of the principle of helicy. The word *unidirectional* was replaced by *nonrepeating rhythmicities*. The fourth assumption, regarding pattern and organization, became the concept of pattern. It is clear that the concepts also function as assumptions.

The fifth assumption, describing persons as sentient beings capable of abstract imagery and thought, remains as Rogers' statement that hers is not a mechanistic model and that human beings are set apart from other living things. Although she did not restate it in later publications, neither did she recant it. Rogers made an explicit assumption regarding human beings in her 1992 article when she wrote that the principles of homeodynamics (pp. 14–12) "have validity only within the science of unitary human beings" (p. 30). This is an important statement to note, since the energy field is stated to be the fundamental unit of the living and nonliving. The principles of homeodynamics are specific to Rogers' theory regarding human beings and are not meant to be lifted out of this context for the study of other entities or energy fields.

Another statement by Rogers that may be viewed as an assumption is that persons are knowing participants in health care and they are able to make choices (Rogers, 1990, p. 13).

Central Components

The central components of the model are the unitary human being and the environment engaged in the life process. The components are derived from the synthesis of Rogers' four building blocks and comprise, in Rogers' view, nursing's abstract conceptual system. The components are defined earlier in this section but are repeated here for clarity:

- *Unitary human being:* "an irreducible, pandimensional energy field identified by pattern and manifesting characteristics that are different from those of the parts and cannot be predicted from knowledge of the parts" (1986, p. 5).

- *Environment:* "an irreducible, four-dimensional energy field identified by pattern and manifesting characteristics different from those of the parts. Each environmental field is specific to its given human field" (1986, p. 5)

From the abstract conceptual system, Rogers derived the three other components of the model, which she called *principles of homeodynamics;* they are "broad generalizations that postulate the nature and direction of unitary human development" (1980a, p. 333).

- *Resonancy:* The continuous change from lower-frequency to higher-frequency wave patterns in human and environmental fields (Rogers, 1986, p. 6).

- *Helicy:* The continuous innovative, unpredictable increasing diversity of human and environmental field patterns (1992, p. 31) characterized by nonrepeating rhythmicities (Rogers, 1986, p. 6).

- *Integrality:* The continuous, mutual human field and environmental field process (Rogers, 1992, p. 31).

Definitions of Components and Comparison to Chaos Theory

The components person and environment were defined earlier, as were helicy, resonancy, and integrality. Rogers emphasized the noncausal nature of change. She formerly stated that change is probabilistic. A significant change from 1986 is her use of the word *unpredictability* to replace *probability* in the definition of helicy.

Earlier students of Rogers thought that if only we could conceptualize a way to measure or truly appreciate the human–environmental wave pattern we might be able to *predict* an outcome. Rogers herself used the word *prediction* (1970, p. 57, 87, 96, 117) and discussed the concept of probability theory (1970, p. 57). Recently, Rogers stated the term *unpredictable* "transcends the term *probability*" (1992, p. 32; 1990, p. 7).

Unpredictability is compatible with the creativity Rogers viewed as inherent in all development, change, and evolution. This creativity is an *emergent,* different from what went before, neither a sum nor combination of parts. In chaos theory the emergent may be dependent on initial conditions, but is not predictable from initial conditions (Gleick, 1987).

Chaos theory, defined differently by various sciences and disciplines, is the latest scientific motif. The term *chaos* was apparently coined by James Torke, a mathematician, in 1975 and began to stand for what more and more scientists were willing to observe in their respective disciplines: the fact that linearity and predictability apply to only a small fraction of phenomena, and that all the rest need a new or different paradigm. Mathematicians and physicists and others have found that simple systems may breed complexity, and that complexity may yield observable patterns (Gleick, 1987).

Rogers' science of unitary human beings continues to place nursing at the forefront of the most sophisticated scientific thought and theoretical development. Central tenets of chaos theory similar or compatible with those of Rogers' theory are complexity, pattern, unpredictability, and creativity. Nonlinearity is also used in chaos theory, but in the mathematical sense, whereas Rogers used nonlinearity to refer to dimensions of space and time. Some discussion of chaos theory in nursing has taken place, for example, the scholarly dialogue with commentary by Puskar, Hardin, and Updike (1992) and the response by Phillips (1992).

Rogers also derived several theories from the abstract conceptual system: (1) The *theory of accelerating evolution* states that change (evolution) is becoming more and more rapid Rogers cited increasingly complex technology, and changing sleep patterns (1980a, 1992). (2) In her *theories of paranormal events* Rogers explained that when human fields are viewed as pandimensional the relative present for one person is different from that of someone else. This could offer explanations for such phenomena as the well-documented instances of precognition, déjà vu, and clairvoyance (1980a, 1992). The conceptual model has served as a basis for certain nursing theories, including the therapeutic touch theory of Dolores Krieger (Rogers, 1986). (3) The *manifestations of field patterning* theory specifies that wave patterns include sleep/wake patterns, patterns of human field motion, and the developmental process of living and dying. These patterns are characterized by increasing complexity and increasing diversity (1980a, 1992).

Relationships Among Components

Unitary human being appears to be the most important component. Rogers emphasized that unitary human being is the focus of nursing's research and practice (Fig. 5–3). Within the conceptual model the concept human being is defined as an energy field, inseparable from the environment and interchangeable with the life process. In this sense, human being is the only component in the conceptual model; the principles have action definitions that describe human being (Fig. 5–3). Rogers formerly stated that the derived theories were intended to explain, describe, and predict. When she replaced *probability* with *unpredictability* in the helicy definition, she then said that theories and research could provide "description, explanation and vision" (1992, p. 33).

Analysis of Consistency

According to Dubin, "the argument about the adequacy of the theoretical model is always and only an argument about the logic employed in constructing it" (1978, p. 12). Rogers often described her theory as emerging out of creative synthesis (1986) or as an "emergent" (1992, p. 28). Bigge (1976) describes an emergent theory as a genuinely new outlook, novel, different from predecessors and more internally consistent and adequate than its predecessors." An emergent is not a compromise between opposing theories. Rogers not only remained open to change, but invited critique of her model. She progressively refined it until the concepts and terminology describing it became clearer and more succinct. In fact, this emergence of her model in interaction with its "environment" exemplifies rather well the process of innovative change that is described *within* the model. No flaws in logic can be found in the model, hence using Dubin's standard the model is adequate. The definitions are clear. Rogers has carefully attended to the definitions of all the words she uses, except for the term *nonlinear* (see earlier discussion). Concepts are used in consistent ways throughout the model. A possible problem might be the use of the word *system*. Although Rogers (1986) refered to von Bertalanffy (1968) in describing the concept of openness, Cowling (1993), in his article on unitary knowing, illustrates how Rogers' model transcends the open systems framework. A lack of precision may result with continued use of the word *systems,* which when used by scholars other than Rogers, connotes interaction in a nonpandimensional manner.

Analysis of Adequacy

Conceptual models are assessed in a variety of ways. Hardy (1974, 1978) and Ellis (1968) suggest examining scope, complexity, and usefulness. Rogers' model is broad in scope and centered on the life process of human beings. In fact, Rogers (1985) and others (Malinski, 1986) referred to the model as a worldview. According to Ellis, the broader the scope, the greater the significance of a theory. Ellis states that "another characteristic of significant theories is that they have complexity; they treat multiple variables or relationships, or of the complexity of a single variable" (1968, p. 219). Some nurse-scholars have identified the probable philosophical roots of Rogers' model. Sarter (1989) mentions Ludwig von Bertalanffy, Pierre Teilhard de Chardin, Bertrand Russell, Michael Polanyi, Kurt Lewin, Theodosins Dobzhansky, and Albert Einstein. Reeder (1993) compares and contrasts Rogers' views with those of Wilhelm Dilthey and Jurgen Habermas. Hanchett (1992) compares Eastern philosophy as exemplified in Tibetan Buddhist philosophy with several of Rogers' concepts and principles, finding areas of similarity. These quests for deeper understanding testify at once to the model's innovativeness and sophistication, although as a true emergent, Rogers' model will not match any other models or theories exactly. Meleis

(1991) states that the model's "view of humanity and environment and the lack of separation between mind and body is congruent with the Eastern view" (p. 322). She says that the model is "understandable in the international arena" (p. 322) and that its use and influence will spread more than expected during the 1990s.

Rogers' model is based on concepts that are complex and difficult to understand. However, once these concepts are clearly understood, the model itself as depicted in Figure 5–3 is simple and elegant.

Testability is another desirable characteristic of significant theories (Hardy, 1974; Ellis, 1968). Rogers' model in general and in part is not testable, but theorems and hypotheses dervied from the model are. Rawnsley (1990) draws our attention to the fact that the investigator using Rogers' model inductively to derive hypotheses must supply the intermediate propositions that are not specified in Rogers' model. The investigator must use "a personal interpretation of the logical implications of the concepts and principles" (p. 195) used. Hypotheses derived from the model have been tested by many researchers in nursing. As this body of research continues to grow, examination of hypotheses and results are allowing support and modification of the model. However, support of the model itself through quantitative research is equivocal because the results of the research support or refute the hypotheses and not the linkages to the conceptual model. Whether or not the interpretation of linkages between the model and real life is "correct" is still a judgment made either by the investigator or by the scientific community.

Issues identified in use of the model are the complexity of its language, the need for those using the model to develop a noncausal mind-set, and the need to measure the life process of human beings without resorting to measuring parts. Theories are also significant if they are useful for clinical practice (Ellis, 1968), which Rogers' model is. Use of Rogers' model in research and practice is examined in the External Analysis section on page 324.

Rogers's Work and the Characteristics of a Theory

1. **Theories can interrelate concepts in such a way as to create a different way of looking at a particular phenomenon.** Rogers's abstract system clearly creates an alternative view of people and their world. The theoretical statement that nursing is the use of the principles of homeodynamics for the service of humanity compels one to look at nursing in a very different way. An excellent example is the principle of helicy with its emphasis on pattern and rhythmicity.

2. **Theories must be logical in nature.** There is definitely a logical development of the major constructs. This logical development proceeds from the identification of assumptions, through the building blocks, to the principles of homeodynamics.

3. **Theories should be relatively simple yet generalizable.** The theory is generalizable because it is not dependent on any given setting. It has been stated that Rogers's conception of man is elegant in its simplicity (Fawcett, 1989). However, the theory is far from simple in that its level of abstraction and the nature of the terminology contribute to difficulties in understanding. In addition, the theory is based on the use of open systems that are inherently complex.

4. **Theories can be the bases for hypotheses that can be tested or for theory to be expanded,** and

5. **Theories contribute to and assist in increasing the general body of knowledge within the discipline through the research implemented to validate them.** It is clear that the abstract level of the system leads to the generation of a plethora of research questions. Barrett (1990), Fawcett (1989), Ference (1989), Malinski (1986), Madrid and Winstead-Fry (1986), and Rogers (1989) all cite numerous studies ostensibly designed to test this framework. However, research is hampered by the lack of simplicity, operational definitions, and valid instruments to measure outcomes. The complex interrelationships involved in the framework contribute to these difficulties. Qualitative research approaches have been suggested as an effective method for minimizing these problems (Reeder, 1984; Wilson & Fitzpatrick, 1984). These and other efforts designed to minimize these research problems need to be continued so that nursing can truly benefit from Rogers's abstract system.

6. **Theories can be used by practitioners to guide and improve their practice.** Rogers's ideas can be applied to practice. When these ideas are applied to nursing practice, the understanding of the client's behavior takes on new dimensions. Such dimensions include accepting diversity as the norm, empowering both nurse and client, viewing change as positive, and accepting the integral connectedness of life (Malinski, 1986). This changed understanding results in alterations in the focus of nursing actions. The case study of Janie presented in this section provides an example. In addition, nursing interventions such as therapeutic touch and the use of light, color, music, and movement have been derived from Rogers's tenets. However, evidence of positive effects of nursing interventions derived from this model is needed.

7. **Theories must be consistent with other validated theories, laws, and principles but will leave open unanswered questions that need to be investigated.** Rogers's work is consistent with other validated theories, laws, and principles. The abstract nature of the system provides great potential for generating questions for further study and deriving interventions for nursing practice. Rogers's abstract system has also been instrumental in the development of other theories. Newman's (1994) and Parse's (1992) works are two such examples.

S ummary

Building on a broad theoretical base from a variety of disciplines, Rogers developed the principles of homeodynamics. Inherent in the principles are five basic assumptions: (1) the human being is a unified whole, possessing individual integrity and manifesting characteristics that are more than and different from the sum of the parts; (2) the individual and the environment are continuously exchanging matter and energy with each other; (3) the life process of human beings evolves irreversibly and unidirectionally along a space-time continuum; (4) patterns identify human beings and reflect their innovative wholeness; and (5) the individual is characterized by the capacity for abstraction and imagery, language and thought, sensation and emotion. The principles of integrality, helicy, and resonancy are compared to general system theory, developmental theories, and adaptation theories. Ways to use the principles in the nursing process are explored. The difficulty in understanding the principles, the lack of operational definitions, and inadequate instruments for measurement are the major limitations to the effective use of this theory.

References

Barrett, E. A. M. (Ed.). (1990). *Visions of Rogers's science-based nursing.* New York: National League for Nursing.

Burns, N., & Grove, S. K. (1987). *The practice of nursing research: Conduct, critique, and utilization.* Philadelphia: Saunders.

Erikson, E. (1963). *Childhood and society* (2nd ed.). New York: Norton. [our of print]

Fawcett, J. (1989). *Analysis and evaluation of conceptual models of nursing* (2nd ed.). Philadelphia: Davis.

Ference, H. M. (1989). Comforting the dying: Nursing practice according to the Rogerian model. In J. Riehl-Sisca (Ed.), *Conceptual models for nursing practice* (3rd ed.) (pp. 197–205). Norwalk, C T: Appleton & Lange.

Gilligan, C. (1982). *In a different voice: Psychological theory and women's development.* Cambridge, MA: Harvard University Press.

Hardy, M. E. (1974). Theories: Components, development, evaluation. *Nursing Research, 23,* 100–107.

Havinghurst, R. (1972). *Developmental tasks and education* (3rd ed.). New York: McKay. [out of print]

Johnston, R. L. (1986). Approaching family intervention through Rogers's conceptual model. In A. L. Whall (Ed.), *Family therapy theory for nursing: Four approaches.* Norwalk, CT: Appleton-Century-Crofts.

Kim, H. S. (1986). *The nature of theoretical thinking in nursing.* Norwalk, CT: Appleton-Century-Crofts.

Kohlberg, L. (1973). *Collected papers on moral development and moral education.* Cambridge, MA: Moral Education and Research Foundation. [out of print]

Lutjens, L. R. J. (1991). *Martha Rogers: The science of unitary human beings.* Newbury Park, CA: Sage.

Madrid, M., & Winstead-Fry, P. (1986). Rogers's conceptual model. In P. Winstead-Fry (Ed.), *Case studies in nursing theory* (pp. 73–102). New York: National League for Nursing.

Malinski, V. M. (Ed.). (1986). *Explorations on Martha Rogers's science of unitary human beings.* Norwalk, CT: Appleton-Century-Crofts.

Newman, M. A. (1994). *Health as expanding consciousness* (2nd ed.). NY: National League for Nursing.

Parse, R. R. (1987). *Nursing science: Major paradigms, theories, and critiques.* Philadelphia: Saunders.

Parse, R. R. (1992). Human becoming: Parse's theory of nursing. *Nursing Science Quarterly, 5,* 35–42.

Piaget, J., & Inhelder, R. (1969). *The psychology of the child.* New York: Basic Books. [out of print]

Reeder, F. (1984). Philosophical issues in the Rogerian science of unitary human beings. *Advances in Nursing Science, 6,* 14–23.

Rogers, M. E. (1970). *The theoretical basis of nursing.* Philadelphia: Davis. [out of print]

Rogers, M. E. (1971). *Accountability.* Convention address, University of Utah College of Nursing, June 5, 1971.

Rogers, M. E. (1983). Science of unitary human beings: A paradigm for nursing. In I. W. Clements, & F. B. Roberts (Eds.), *Family health: A theoretical approach to nursing care.* New York: Wiley Medical.

Rogers, M. E. (1988). Nursing science and art: A prospective. *Nursing Science Quarterly, 1,* 99–102.

Rogers, M. E. (1989). Nursing: A science of unitary human beings. In J. Riehl-Sisca (Ed.), *Conceptual models for nursing practice* (3rd ed.) (pp. 181–188). Norwalk, CT: Appleton & Lange.

Rogers, M. E. (1990). Space-age paradigm for new frontiers in nursing. In M. E. Parker (Ed.), *Nursing theories in practice* (pp. 105–113). New York: National League for Nursing.

Rogers, M. E. (1992). Nursing science and the space age. *Nursing Science Quarterly, 5,* 27–34.

Roy, C., & Andrews, H. A. (1991). *The Roy Adaptation Model: The definitive statement.* Norwalk, CT: Appleton & Lange.

Smith, M.J. (1988). Perspectives on nursing science. *Nursing Sciences Quarterly, 1,* 80-85

von Bertalanffy, L. (1968). *General system theory.* New York: Braziller. [out of print]

Wilson, L. M., & Fitzpatrick, J. J. (1984). Dialectic thinking as a means of understanding systems-in-development: Relevance to Rogers's principles. *Advances in Nursing Science, 6,* 24–41.

*B*ibliography

Madrid, M., & Barrett, E. A. M. (Eds.). (1994). *Rogers' scientific art of nursing practice.* New York: National League for Nursing.

Malinski, V. M., & Barrett, E. A. M. (1994). *Martha E. Rogers: Her life and her work.* Philadelphia: Davis.

Meleis, A. I. (1985). *Theoretical nursing: Development and progress.* Philadelphia: Lippincott.

Rogers, M. E. (1992). Nightingale's *Notes on nursing*: A prelude to the 21st century. In F. Nightingale. *Notes on nursing: What it is, and what it is not* (Com. ed.). Philadelphia: Lippincott.

Sarter, B. (1988). *The stream of becoming: A study of Martha Rogers's theory.* New York: National League for Nursing.

External Analysis

Relationship to Nursing Research

As shown in Figure 5–2, Rogers' abstract conceptual model is directly related to research and theory development in nursing science. The conceptual model provides the stimulus and direction for these scientific activities. Rogers' model offers a way of looking at reality that is unique to the nursing profession. Researchers whose assumptions and propositions are consistent with the model are able to clearly defend their work as nursing. Rogers' delineation of the science of unitary human beings provides a unique and substantive focus for the discipline.

Rogers (1967) indicated that the critical need in nursing is for basic research in the science of nursing. Rogers expected the theory emerging from her model to ultimately describe and explain phenomena of unitary human beings and life process phenomena (1992). There is a need for both basic and applied research (Rogers, 1980a, 1986, 1992). The model is not testable itself nor is it meant to be. Rather, theories and hypotheses derived from the model are subjected to scientific investigation.

The derivation of testable theories or hypotheses from the model requires understanding and the ability to infer. Some early examples of research related to Rogers' conceptualization include that of Newman (1978), Fawcett (1975), Fitzpatrick (1980), Floyd (1983), and Cowling (1985), as well as several presenters (Moore, Engle, Johnston, and Fromm) at the American Nurses Association (ANA) Council of Nurse Researchers symposium entitled "Research Related to Rogers' Conceptual Model" (ANA Council of Nurse Researchers, Washington, D.C., September 16–18, 1981). Studies by Rawnsley, Ference, Alligood, Gueldner, and Barrett, as well as some of the above, appear in Malinski's *Explorations on Martha Rogers' Science of Unitary Human Beings* (1986).

The number of studies being done and published using Rogers' model is accelerating. Twenty studies were reviewed and analyzed by Dykeman and Loukissa (1993). These included only published studies using Rogers' revised three principles of homeodynamics (post 1980) and specifically using Rogers' model as the conceptual framework. (Early studies may not be consistent with Rogers' model as it has evolved.) Most of these studies contained more than one hypothesis. Overall, less than half of the hypotheses were supported. According to Dykeman and Loukissa (1993), this is most likely a result of measurement problems.

Taken from: *Nursing Theories: The Base for Professional Nursing Practice*, Fourth Edition by George.

Only three instruments have been designed specifically within Rogers' model. Ference (1986) developed the first one, the "human field motion test," in 1978 to study the correlates of human development, later called *manifestation of patterning* by Rogers (1992). The instrument is based on the semantic differential technique. It has been used in several studies framed within Rogers' model, thus accelerating development of the science of unitary human beings. The second instrument to be developed was Barrett's "human field power test" in 1983 (Ference, 1986), later refined and called the *power as knowing participation in change test* (Dykeman & Loukissa, 1993). The third was Paletta's "temporal experience scales" (Dykeman & Loukissa, 1993). All of the above tests are paper and pencil tests that require verbal facility of the client.

Young children and certain other clients cannot use paper and pencil tests to tell us about themselves. Studies of young infants have mainly relied on weight, sleep patterns, and/or vital signs to identify pattern manifestation or expression of the unitary energy field. An interesting concept, applicable to all clients, is energy and energy flow in relation to therapeutic touch (Krieger, 1981). Washington (1987, 1990) developed an instrument for use with infants, called the *Vigere index,* which measures infant vigor. Washington based her theoretical framework on work by Neal (1976). Neal was a student of Rogers' (Rogers, 1970, p. 105). There is concordance with Rogers' model in Washington's assertion that the ability to conserve or expend energy in interaction with the environment is an expression of the person's developmental health.

Some instruments not designed to measure Rogers' concepts may in fact measure something other than the investigator intended. For example, the personal orientation inventory (POI) was used in three studies to measure actualization or self-actualization. However, the POI measures self-actualizing value(s) held by the testee (Shostrom, 1966). The POI may not correspond to the self-actualization that Rogers described as people fulfilling life's potentials.

For a new science, this may be a normal stage of development. Many of the researchers gained insights for revisions of design or instrumentation, but replications have not yet been reported (Dykeman and Loukissa, 1993). Theorists who have extended Rogers' model to make it less vague are Fitzpatrick (1983), Newman (1979), and Parse (1981). These theories have particularly explained the understanding of health in the model, and Parse added a specific research methodology.

Devising methods to measure the life process of human beings without resorting to measuring parts remains a challenge to researchers using the model. Reeder (1983) addressed this issue in Rogers' work and suggested using phenomenology as one possible approach. Phenomenology allows for a holistic interpretation of the phenomenon under study without reducing the object of that study to the sum of its parts. Cowling (1986) addressed this research problem and suggested several designs appropriate to Rogers' model. Experimental or quasiexperimental designs may be appropriate in certain instances to test manifestations of change in the human–environmental process. Other types of research suggested by Cowling are historical research, philosophical studies, and survey's (or survey research). Cowling (1986) also suggested several methodologies, including single-case methods.

*R*elationship to Nursing Education

In 1963, Rogers called for the rebuilding of undergraduate and graduate programs in nursing to reflect the evolution of nursing science (Rogers, 1963). Consistent with her definition of nursing as a learned profession, Rogers called for placement of all nursing education in institutions of higher learning. A learned profession must claim a unique body of knowledge. In

1964 she outlined a doctoral program in nursing at New York University consistent with the science of unitary human beings (Rogers, 1964).

A strength of Rogers' model in education is the conceptualization of nursing as a theory-based science. This conceptualization mandated university-based education for nurses and paved the way for the development of the doctor of philosophy degree in nursing.

Rogers sees nursing more closely related to the liberal arts college than to any of the other colleges of the university. The science of unitary human beings mandates inclusion of courses in physics and philosophy as well as those in the biologic and social sciences. Education, which follows Rogers' framework, prepares a generalist in nursing who views person and environment as interacting and ever changing.

Relationship to Professional Nursing Practice

The model emphasizes the need for individualized nursing care based on the unique situation of any person or group and the unique environment. Malinski (1986) notes seven trends that occur in practice with the use of Rogers' model:

1. Empowering both nurse and client (p. 28).

2. Accepting diversity as the norm (p. 28).

3. Becoming attuned to patterning (p. 29).

4. Recognizing and using wave modalities such as light, music, and movement as integral to the patterning process and thus to health and healing (p. 29).

5. Viewing change as positive (p. 29).

6. Expanding the assessment phase of the nursing process (p. 30).

7. Accepting the integral connectedness of life (p. 30).

Rogers did not relate her model to the nursing process format (assessment, diagnosis, intervention, evaluation). Barrett (1988) used the terms *pattern appraisal* and *deliberative mutual patterning* to describe a nursing process in using Rogers' model. Cowling (1993) explicates these concepts. An important point is that pattern appraisal requires an inclusive perspective of what counts as pattern information. He speaks of using the aspects of human existence that are experience, perception, and expression in appraising client patterns. Assessment is focused on and guided by what the client wants from the encounter with the nurse. Assessment is not restricted to one modality but includes all that are appropriate. Some of these are observation, language, recognizing recurring themes, intuitive inquiry, sharing between nurse and client, physical examination, and reporting of sensations. Pattern appraisal guides deliberative mutual repatterning. Cowling (1993) calls this *mutually derived purposive strategies*. (The term *intervention* has been dropped in many arenas because it implies action by the nurse that may not include the client in the exploratory and decision-making process.)

The nurse practicing within the Rogerian model will realize that "appraisal" and "mutual patterning" are themselves only arbitrarily separated for discussion. The nurse is part of the client's environment during appraisal and thus the patterning will alter. And of course, observation and appraisal go on continuously through purposive patterning. Fawcett extracted elements of the nursing process from Rogers' publications and related these to the nursing process (1984, p. 223). Some of the suggestions, such as assessing "subsystem pathology," are no longer congruent with Rogers' model. Aggleton and Chalmers also did this, providing a brief overview of nursing practice consistent with Rogers' model (1984, p. 38). Whall (1981) elaborates the assessment of families using Rogers' model. While clearly derived from the assumptions, building blocks, and principles in Rogers' model, Whall's focus is on assessment and does not attempt to force an outline of the nursing process from the model. Whall's and later Johnstons's (1986) assessment guideline is very usable, and it is related explicitly to terminology and middle-range theories already present in the literature on family functioning. Falco and Lobo (1980) use helicy, resonancy, and complementarity to derive a care plan (assessment, diagnosis, implementation, and evaluation) for a specific individual.

As depicted in Figure 5–4, Rogers' conceptual model is useful in research and theory development. It is the responsibility of the researcher and theorist to further develop and refine the specific knowledge base for practice. The practitioner uses the knowledge creatively in each client care situation. Other types of knowledge are not discarded but are viewed differently. As Newman points out, "disease conditions can no longer be considered as entities unto themselves but must be regarded as manifestations of the total pattern of the individual in interaction with the environment (1979, p. 21).

Rogers (1980a, 1980b, 1983) envisioned changes in nursing practice based on the theories evolving from her model. She gave several examples. The aging process is perceived not as a running down of the individual but as a growing diversity in field pattern; thus many characteristics of older persons, such as changing sleep patterns, cease to be viewed as abnormal or in need of intervention. Other changes she envisioned are that dying be viewed as a developmental process rather than an event; and that nursing care become even more individualized to specific persons in their own unique situations. *Therapeutic touch* is a practice mode that has been formalized and shown to be efficacious by Krieger (Rogers, 1983; Krieger, 1981; Meehan, 1993; Quinn & Strelkauskas, 1993). This modality has its origin in rogerian theory.

*R*eferences

Aggleton, P., & Chalmers, H. (1984). Rogers' unitary field model. *Nursing Times, 80*(50), 35–39.

Barrett, E. A. M. (1988). Using Rogers' Science of Unitary Human Beings in nursing practice. *Nursing Science Quarterly, 1*(2), 50–51.

Barrett, E. A. M. (Ed.) (1990). *Visions of Rogers' science-based nursing.* New York: National League for Nursing.

Bigge, M. L. (1976). *Learning theories for teachers* (3rd ed.). New York. Harper & Row.

Carpenito, L. J. (1992). *Nursing diagnosis: Application to clinical practice* (4th ed.). Philadelphia: J. B. Lippincott.

Cowling, W. R., III (1985). Relationship of mystical experience, differentiation, and creativity. *Perceptual Motor Skills, 61,* 451–456.

Cowling, W. R., III (1986). The science of unitary human beings: Theoretical issues, methodological challenges, and research realities. In V. M. Malinski (Ed.), *Explorations on Martha Rogers' science of unitary human beings.* (pp. 65–77) Norwalk, CT: Appleton-Century-Crofts.

Cowling, W. R., III (1993). Unitary knowing in nursing practice. *Nursing Science Quraterly, 6*(4), 201–207.

Deutsch, D., & Lockwood, M. (1994). The quantum physics of time travel. *Scientific American. 270,* 68–74.

Dubin, R. (1978). *Theory building.* New York: The Free Press.

Dykeman, M. C., & Loukissa, D. (1993). The Science of Unitary Human Beings: An integrative review. *Nursing Science Quarterly, 6*(4), 179–188.

Ellis, R. (1968). Characteristics of significant theories. *Nursing Research, 17*(3), 217–222.

England, M. (1989). Nursing diagnosis: A conceptual framework. In J. J. Fitzpatrick & A. L. Whall (Eds.), *Conceptual models of nursing.* (2nd ed.). Norwalk, CT: Appleton & Lange.

Falco, S. M. & Lobo, M. L. (1980). Martha E. Rogers. In Nursing Theories Conference Group & J. B. George (Eds.). *Nursing theories: The base for professional nursing practice.* Englewood Cliffs, N.J.: Prentice-Hall.

Fawcett, J. (1975). The family as a living open system: An emerging conceptual framework for nursing. *International Nursing Review, 22*(4), 113–116.

Fawcett, J. (1984). *Analysis and evaluation of conceptual models of nursing.* Philadelphia: F. A. Davis.

Ference, H. M. (1986). The relationship of time experience, creativity traits, differentiation, and human field motion. In V. M. Malinski (Ed.), *Explorations on Martha Rogers' science of unitary human beings* (pp. 95–105). Norwalk, CT: Appleton-Century-Crofts.

Fitzpatrick, J. J. (1980). Patient's perceptions of time: Current research. *International Nursing Review, 27*(5), 148–153.

Fitzpatrick, J. J. (1983). A life perspective rhythm model. In J. J. Fitzpatrick & A. L. Whall (Eds.), *Conceptual models of nursing: Analysis and application* (pp. 295–302) Bowie, MD: Brady.

Floyd, J. A. (1983). Research using Rogers' conceptual systems: Development of a testable theorem. *Advances in Nursing Science, 5*(2), 37–48.

Gleick, J. (1987). *Chaos: Making a new science.* New York: Penguin.

Hanchett, E. S. (1992). Concepts from Eastern philosophy and Rogers' Science of Unitary Human Beings. *Nursing Science Quarterly, 5*(4), 164–170.

Hardy, M. E. (1974). Theories: Components, development, evaluation. *Nursing Research, 23,* 100–107.

Hardy, M. E. (1978). Perspectives on nursing. *Advances in Nursing Science, 1,* 37–48.

Hektor, L. M. (1989). Martha E. Rogers: A life history. *Nursing Science Quarterly, 2*(2), 63–73.

Huch, M. H. (1991). Perspectives on health. *Nursing Science Quarterly, 4*(1), 33–40.

Johnston, R. (1986). Approaching family intervention through Rogers' conceptual model. In A. L. Whall (Ed.), *Family therapy for nursing: Four approaches* (pp. 11–32). East Norwalk, CT: Appleton-Century-Crofts.

Krieger, D. (1981). *Foundations for holistic health nursing practices: The Renaissance nurse.* Philadelphia: J. B. Lippincott.

Levine, M. E. (1988). Antecedents from adjunctive disciplines: Creation of nursing theory. *Nursing Science Quarterly, 1*(1).

Madrid, M., & Barrett, E. A. M. (Eds.). (1994). *Rogers' scientific art of nursing practice.* New York: National League for Nursing.

Malinski, V. M. (Ed.). (1986). *Explorations on Martha Rogers' science of unitary human beings.* Norwalk, CT: Appleton-Century-Crofts.

Malinski, V. M., & Barrett, E. A. M. (Eds.). (1994). *Martha E. Rogers: Her life and her work.* Philadelphia: F. A. Davis.

Meehan, T. C. (1993). Therapeutic touch and postoperative pain: A Rogerian research study. *Nursing Science Quarterly, 6,* 69–78.

Meleis, A. I. (1991). *Theoretical nursing: Development and progress* (2nd ed.), Philadelphia: J. B. Lippincott.

Neal, M. V. (Ed.). (1976). Conceptual basis for MCH nursing practice: A construct. In *Proceedings of Perinatal Conference.* Baltimore: University of Maryland, School of Nursing.

Newman, M. A. (1978). *Application of theory in education and service.* Paper presented at the Nurse Educator Conference at New York University, New York.

Newman, M. A. (1979). *Theory development in nursing.* Philadelphia: F. A. Davis.

Parse, R. R. (1981). *Man-living-health, a theory of nursing.* New York: Wiley.

Parse, R. R. (1987). *Nursing science.* Philadelphia: W. B. Saunders.

Phillips, J. R. (1992). Response. *Nursing Science Quarterly, 5*(3), 107–111.

Puskar, K., Hardin, S. B., Updike, P. (1992). Commentary. *Nursing Science Quarterly, 5*(3), 107.

Quinn, J. F., & Strelkauskas, A. J. (1993). Psychoimmunologic effects of therapeutic touch on practitioners and recently bereaved recipients: A pilot study. *Advanced Nursing Science, 15,* 13–26.

Rawnsley, M. M. (1990). Structuring the gap from conceptual system to research design within a Rogerian world view. In E. A. M. Barrett (Ed.), *Visions of Rogers' science-based nursing.* New York: National League for Nursing.

Reeder, F. (1983). Philosophical issues in the Rogerian science of unitary human beings. *Advances in Nursing Science, 6*(2), 14–23.

Reeder, F. (1993). The Science of Unitary Human Beings and interpretive human science. *Nursing Science Quarterly, 6*(1), 13–24.

Rogers, M. E. (1961). *Educations revolution in nursing.* New York: MacMillan.

Rogers, M. E. (1963). Building a strong educations foundation. *American Journal of Nursing, 63*(6), 94–95.

Rogers, M. E. (1964). *Reveille in nursing.* Philadelphia: F. A. Davis.

Rogers, M. E. (February, 1967). *Nursing science: Research and researchers.* Paper presented at Annual Conference on Research and Nursing, Division of Nursing Education, Teachers College, Columbia University, New York.

Rogers, M. E. (1970). *The theoretical basis of nursing.* Philadelphia: F. A. Davis.

Rogers, M. E. (1980a). A science of unitary man. In J. P. Riehl & C. Roy (Eds.). *Conceptual models for nursing practice* (2nd ed.). New York: Appleton-Century-Crofts.

Rogers, M. E. (Speaker). (1980b). *The science of unitary man* (videotape). New York: Media for Nursing.

Rogers, M. E. (1983). Science of unitary human beings: A paradigm for nursing. In I. W. Clements & F. B. Roberts (Eds.), *Family health: A theoretical approach to nursing care.* New York: Wiley.

Rogers, M. E. (Speaker). (1985). *The science of unitary human beings.* Presented at the Discovery International Conference, Pittsburgh, PA (Audiocassette). Louisville, KY: Meetings Internationale.

Rogers, M. E. (1986). Science of Unitary Human Beings. In V. M. Malinski (Ed.), *Explorations on Martha Rogers' Science of Unitary Human Beings* (pp. 3–8). Norwalk, CT: Appleton-Century-Crofts.

Rogers, M. E. (1988). Nursing science and art: A prospective. *Nursing Science Quarterly, 1*(3), 99–102.

Rogers, M. E. (1990). Nursing: Science of unitary, irreducible human beings. Update 1990. In E. A. M. Barrett (Ed.), *Visions of Rogers' science based nursing* (pp. 5–11). New York: National League for Nursing.

Rogers, M. E. (1992). Nursing science and the space age. *Nursing Science Quarterly, 5*(1), 27–34.

Rogers, M. E. (1994). The Science of Unitary Human Beings: Current perspectives. *Nursing Science Quarterly, 7*(1), 33–35.

Safier, G. (1977). *Contemporary American leaders in nursing: An oral history.* New York: McGraw-Hill.

Sarter, B. (1989). Some critical philosophical issues in the Science of Unitary Human Beings. *Nursing Science Quarterly, 2*(2), 74–78.

Shostrom, E. L. (1966). *Personal orientation inventory, Manual.* San Diego: Educational and Industrial Testing Service.

Smith, M. C. (1990). Pattern in nursing practice. *Nursing Science Quarterly, 3*(2), 57–59.

Smith, M. J. (1988). Perspectives on nursing science. *Nursing Science Quarterly, 1*(2), 80–85.

Tomasson, R. E. (March 18, 1994). Martha Rogers, 79, an author of books on nursing theory. *The New York Times,* p. B8.

von Bertalanffy, L. (1968). *General system theory.* New York: George Braziller.

Washington, C. C. (1987). Infant assessment: The development, validity, and reliability of the Infant Vigere Index for two to eight week old infants. *Dissertation Abstracts International, 49,* 2134 (University Microfilms No. AAG8813460).

Washington, C. C. (1990). A developmental health assessment index for 2–8 week old infants. In J. F. Wang, P. S. Simon & C. L. Nath (eds.), *Vision of excellence: the decade of the nineties.* Charleston, WV: West Virginia Nurses Association Research Conference Group.

Whall, A. L. (1981). Nursing theory and assessment of families. *Journal of Psychiatric Nursing and Mental Health Services, 19*(1), 30–35.

Whall, A. L. (1989). The influence of logical positivism on nursing practice. *IMAGE: Journal of Nursing Scholarship, 21*(4), 243–245.

SECTION

The Health Promotion Model

In the early 1980s, the Health Promotion Model (HPM) first appeared in nursing literature. It was proposed as a framework for integrating nursing and behavioral science perspectives on factors influencing health behaviors. The framework was offered as a guide for exploration of the complex biopsychosocial processes that motivate individuals to engage in behaviors directed toward the enhancement of health.[1] The term "health behavior" was being used with increasing frequency in health literature and there was renewed interest in earlier work by

---

Taken from: *Health Promotion in Nursing Practice*, Third Edition by Pender.

Dunn[2,3] on high-level wellness and related behavior that was motivated by a desire to promote personal health and well-being in the absence of illness.

In the late 1980s, public attention to health promotion continued to escalate and people were intrigued by the idea of health as a positive state. Still, little was understood about what motivated people to seek to express their health potential. In 1987, the HPM, with minor revisions, appeared in the second edition of this book.[4] That version of the model is shown in Figure 6–1. It stimulated a number of studies to determine the power of its component constructs to explain and predict health behaviors. The studies reported here test this version of the model.

The HPM is a competence- or approach-oriented model. Unlike the Health Belief Model and Protection Motivation Theory described in the previous section, the HPM does not include "fear" or "threat" as sources of motivation for health behavior. Although immediate threats to health have been shown to motivate action, threats in the distant future lack the same motivational strength. Thus, avoidance-oriented models of health behavior are of limited usefulness in motivating overall healthy lifestyles in people in youth and early adulthood as well as in other individuals who for varying reasons perceive themselves to be invulnerable to illness.

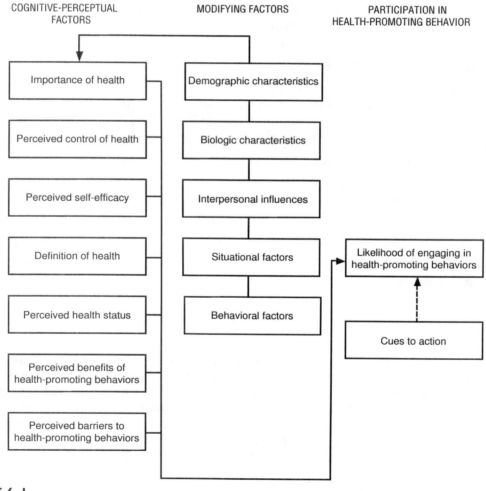

FIGURE 6–I

Health Promotion Model.

Because the HPM does not rely on "personal threat" as a primary source of health motivation, it is a model with potential applicability across the life span. In reality, the sources of health behavior motivation for any given individual have unique combinational properties, from predominantly health-promotion or approach-oriented motives, through mixed motives of both approach *and* avoidance, to predominantly avoidance-oriented or protective motives. The HPM is applicable to any health behavior in which "threat" is not proposed as a major source of motivation for the behavior.

The Theoretical Basis for the Health Promotion Model

The HPM is an attempt to depict the multidimensional nature of persons interacting with their environment as they pursue health. The model integrates a number of constructs from expectancy-value theory and social learning theory (now renamed social cognitive theory), within a nursing perspective of holistic human functioning. Expectancy-value theory and social cognitive theory will be briefly described here

Expectancy-Value Theory

Many conceptions of goal-directed behavior, including social cognitive theory, arc based on the expectancy-value model of human motivation described by Feather.[5] According to the expectancy-value model, behavior is rational and economical. Specifically, a person will engage in a given action and will persist in it to the extent that (a) the outcome of taking action is of positive personal value, and (b) based on available information, taking this course of action is likely to bring about the desired outcome. Thus, individuals will not invest their effort and personal resources in working toward goals that are of little or no value to them. Furthermore, most individuals will not invest their efforts in goals that, despite their attractiveness, are perceived as impossible to achieve. Personal change can best be understood within this theoretical framework by considering the subjective value of the change and the subjective expectancy of achieving it.[6] The motivational significance of the **subjective value of change** is based on the supposition that the more a person is dissatisfied with his or her present situation in a particular domain, the greater will be the rewards or benefits associated with favorable change. This subjective value of change can be viewed as comparable to the perceived benefits of engaging in a given health behavior. The motivational significance of the **subjective expectancy of successfully obtaining the change** or outcome is based on prior knowledge of personal successes or the successes of others in attaining the outcome and the personal confidence that one's success will be the same or even superior to others.[6] This concept is similar to the concept of self-efficacy in social cognitive theory.

Social Cognitive Theory

Social cognitive theory presents an interactional model of causation in which environmental events, personal factors, and behavior act as reciprocal determinants of each other. The theory places major emphasis on self-direction, self-regulation, and perceptions of self-efficacy. Social cognitive theory, proposes that human beings possess the following basic capabilities[7]:

1. Symbolization: processing and transforming transient experiences into internal models that serve as guides for future action

2. Forethought: anticipating likely consequences of prospective actions and planning future courses of action to achieve valued goals

3. Vicarious learning: acquiring rules for the generation and regulation of behavior through observation without the need to engage in extensive trial and error

4. Self-regulation: using internal standards and self-evaluative reactions as a means to motivate and regulate behavior; arranging the external environment to create incentives for action

5. Self-reflection: thinking about one's own thought processes and actively modifying them

Given these basic capabilities, behavior is neither solely driven by inner forces nor automatically shaped by external stimuli. Instead, cognitions and other personal factors, behavior, and environmental events are interactive. Behavior can modify cognitions and other personal factors as well as change the environment. On the other hand, the environment can augment or constrain behavior. This dynamic interactional causality provides a rich array of human possibilities.[8]

According to social cognitive theory, self beliefs formed through self-observation and self-reflective thought powerfully influence human functioning. These self beliefs include: self-attribution, self-evaluation, and self-efficacy. Beliefs concerning self-efficacy are particularly important. Perceived self-efficacy is a judgment of one's ability to carry out a particular course of action. Perceptions of self-efficacy develop through mastery experiences, vicarious learning, verbal persuasion, and somatic responses to particular situations. Marked overestimation of competencies can result in failure and marked underestimation can result in lack of challenge and resultant growth. Efficacy judgments that appear to be most functional are those that slightly exceed present capabilities. Such judgments facilitate undertaking realistically demanding tasks that build competencies and confidence. The greater the perceived efficacy, the more vigorous and persistent individuals will be to engage in a behavior, even in the face of obstacles and aversive experiences. Self-efficacy is a central construct in the HPM. For a comprehensive description of social cognitive theory, the reader is referred to the book, *Social Foundations of Thought and Action*, by Albert Bandura.[7]

ssumptions of the Health Promotion Model

The HPM is based on the following assumptions, which reflect both nursing and behavioral science perspectives:

1. Persons seek to create conditions of living through which they can express their unique human health potential.

2. Persons have the capacity for reflective self-awareness, including assessment of their own competencies.

3. Persons value growth in directions viewed as positive and attempt to achieve a personally acceptable balance between change and stability.

4. Individuals seek to actively regulate their own behavior.

5. Individuals in all their biopsychosocial complexity interact with the environment, progressively transforming the environment and being transformed over time.

6. Health professionals constitute a part of the interpersonal environment, which exerts influence on persons throughout their life span.

7. Self-initiated reconfiguration of person-environment interactive patterns is essential to behavior change.

These assumptions emphasize the **active role** of the client in shaping and maintaining health behaviors and in modifying the environmental context for health behaviors.

Tests of the Health Promotion Model

The HPM as depicted in Figure 6–1 has been used as a framework for research aimed at predicting overall health-promoting lifestyles as well as specific behaviors, such as exercise and use of hearing protection. In some of the studies, a small set of variables has been selected from the model to test as predictors of a given behavior. Other studies have tested the majority of variables in the model. A number of these studies that have been published as articles or government reports are presented here. It is beyond the scope of this section to review the many theses and dissertations that have been based on the HPM.

Explaining and Predicting Health-Promoting Lifestyles

Achieving a healthy lifestyle in major behavioral domains should be the goal of individuals of all ages. In order for nurses to assist clients in accomplishing this, determinants of healthy lifestyles need to be identified.

Health-Promoting Lifestyles of Blue-Collar Workers

Race and ethnicity are viewed as powerful influences on health behaviors. Increasingly in the United States, information is becoming available not only on the morbidity and mortality experiences of racial and ethnic groups but on their risk behaviors and health behaviors. Weitzel[9] in a study of a multicultural population of 179 European-American (51%), Hispanic (27%) and African-American (20%) blue-collar workers examined the prediction of a health-promoting lifestyle using the HPM. Specifically, four of seven cognitive-perceptual variables were tested: importance of health, perceived control of health, perceived self-efficacy, and perceived health status. Modifying factors studied were the demographics of gender, age, education, and income. All variables were assessed by questionnaire.

Both total and subscale scores on the Health-Promoting Lifestyle Profile (HPLP)[10] were regressed on the cognitive-perceptual factors and modifying factors. All of the cognitive-perceptual variables examined were predictive of one or more health-promoting behaviors. Health status, self-efficacy, importance of health, and education were the strongest predictors of total HPLP scores, explaining 20% of the variance. Of the HPLP subscales, the model best predicted nutrition behaviors, with 28% of the variance explained.

Pender and her colleagues conducted a research program funded by the National Center for Nursing Research (now the National Institute of Nursing Research), National Institutes of Health, to evaluate the HPM in four different populations: working adults; older, community-dwelling adults; ambulatory cancer patients; and cardiac rehabilitation patients.[11] The following brief descriptions report the major findings of their work.

Health-Promoting Lifestyle of Worksite Fitness Program Participants

Workplace health-promotion programs have emerged as a prominent component of employer-sponsored health care benefits primarily in response to increasing evidence that lifestyle can positively influence health status. Although many employees initially enroll in workplace health-promotion efforts, the problems of erratic participation and dropouts plague many programs. In this study, researchers evaluated the HPM's explanatory potential for health-promoting lifestyles in a sample of 589 employees enrolled in six employer-sponsored corporate health promotion programs in a large metropolitan area. All cognitive-perpetual factors in the HPM except benefits and barriers were measured in the study. In terms of modifying factors, selected demographic characteristics and the behavioral factor of stage of exercise (acquisition or maintenance) were also measured. Data were collected using questionnaires and the daily exercise records maintained by all the participating fitness programs.

When the data were analyzed using multiple regression analysis, 31% of the variance in current health-promoting lifestyle patterns was explained with personal competence (a proxy for self-efficacy in relation to overall lifestyle), definition of health, health status, control of health, gender, age, and the behavioral factor of stage of exercise being significant explanatory factors.[12]

Causal path modeling using LISREL, a computer program for structural equation analysis, revealed that the majority of indirect and direct paths proposed in the model were significant. However, the demographic characteristics of age and gender had significant direct paths as well as significant indirect paths to health-promoting lifestyles. The direct paths from the modifying factors to health-promoting behavior were not consistent with the HPM suggesting a possible need for modifications in the model.

Health-Promoting Lifestyles Among Community-Dwelling Older Adults

Healthy aging is highly dependent on acceptance of responsibility for initiating and maintaining healthy lifestyles by individuals themselves. Although older adults report a high level of interest in what they can do to promote their own health, only recently have elderly Americans been included in health-promotion programming and research efforts. The purpose of this study was to test the usefulness of selected variables from the HPM (definition of health, importance of health, control of health, perceived health status, and selected demographics) in explaining the frequency of health-promoting lifestyle behaviors among 361 community-dwelling older adults (55 years or above) as well as in predicting health-promoting lifestyles at a later point in time. Quota sampling was used to achieve representation across age ranges. Subjects were recruited from various community settings in a mid-western state. Questionnaire booklets were used for data collection.

Hierarchic multiple regression analysis revealed that the selected cognitive-perceptual and modifying factors from the HPM explained 28% of the variance in lifestyle with definition of health, control of health, gender, and age making statistically significant contributions to the regression equation. Self-motivation, an added exploratory personal characteristic, contributed an additional 6% explained variance for a total explained variance of 34%. This suggests that individual characteristics other than demographics should be considered as potential determinants of health behaviors. The same set of variables predicted 29% of the variance in lifestyle 12 months later. Structural equation modeling using LISREL revealed that only some of the indirect and direct paths proposed in the model were significant. Age had no significant direct paths to any of the cognitive-perceptual variables and gender and socioeconomic status had significant direct paths, as well as the hypothesized indirect paths to health-promoting lifestyle. Perceived health status did not have a significant direct path to health-promoting lifestyle. Thus, some proposed paths were supported, others were not.

Health-Promoting Lifestyles of Cardiac Rehabilitation Program Participants

Cardiac rehabilitation programs began in the 1960s when prescriptions for physical activity and exercise replaced recommendations for long-term rest after myocardial infarction. Many programs now include numerous activities directed toward fostering healthy lifestyles. The purpose of this study was to determine the usefulness of the HPM in explaining the occurrence of health-promoting lifestyles among cardiac rehabilitation participants and predicting lifestyle at a later time. Participants were recruited from individuals enrolled in fifteen Phase II and Phase III cardiac rehabilitation programs in a mid-western state. Each participant identified his or her significant other, who was also invited to participate. Of the volunteer participant-significant-other pairs, 576 pairs, predominantly European-Americans, provided complete data for this study. Participants ranged in age from 30 to 84 years of age. Data were collected using questionnaire booklets.

Hierarchic multiple regression was conducted with four of seven HPM cognitive-perceptual variables (importance of health, control of health, definition of health, and health status), demographic characteristics, interpersonal influences, and behavioral factors entered into the regression. Self-motivation, an individual characteristic not in the HPM, was entered on an experimental basis. Cognitive-perceptual and modifying factors explained 21% of the variance in lifestyle, with self-motivation contributing an additional 6% explained variance. Significant HPM predictors for lifestyle scores were definition of health, control of health, demographics (age, education, gender), interpersonal influences (lifestyle of significant other), and behavioral factors (phase of cardiac rehabilitation). This total set of variables predicted 25% of the variance in health-promoting lifestyle 3 months later. In structural equation modeling using LISREL, only some of the hypothesized direct and indirect paths were supported. The modifying factors of age and socioeconomic status had direct paths to lifestyle as well as the hypothesized indirect paths. Perceived control of health did not have a direct path to lifestyle. This study raised a question concerning the appropriateness of the model for predicting health-related lifestyles among cardiac rehabilitation populations. Although some cardiac rehabilitation patients report a shift in their motivation from fearing recurrence of a coronary event to desire to optimize their personal health, it is possible that disease avoidance still remains a major motivational dynamic underlying health behaviors for these clients. If so, "avoidance models" or a "mixed model" might provide a better framework for explaining and predicting variance in the lifestyle of this group as well as that of other groups in whom a recent occurrence of catastrophic illness may make avoidance motives predominant.

Health-Promoting Lifestyles Among Ambulatory Cancer Patients

Cancer is now routinely treated in the community as people maintain their lifestyles during therapy. Cancer self-help groups that place emphasis on health promotion and wellness also exist throughout the nation. Thus, health professionals should place primary emphasis on working with cancer patients to foster healthy lifestyles and augment their mental and physical well-being. This study tested the HPM as a model to explain and predict the occurrence of health-promoting lifestyles among 385 ambulatory cancer patients receiving chemotherapy and radiation in outpatient settings. The cancer patients were selected from those undergoing treatment in 13 clinical sites in the mid-western United States. HPM variables tested in the study were importance of health, control of health, health definition, health status, and selected demographics. Data were collected via questionnaire.

Multiple regression revealed that 24% of the variance in health-promoting lifestyle was explained by the HPM cognitive-perceptual variables of perceived control of health, definition of health, and perceived health status, and the modifying factors of education, income, age, and employment. All of these variables made significant but modest contributions to the explained variance. Importance of health was not associated with a health promoting lifestyle.[13] Using structural equation modeling, a number of hypothesized indirect and direct paths were significant. However, age and socioeconomic status both had significant direct paths to health-promoting lifestyle. This was inconsistent with the proposed indirect relationships in the HPM.

Health-Promoting Lifestyles of Participants in the National Survey of Personal Health Practices and Consequences 1979–1980

Johnson et al.[14] attempted to evaluate the HPM using secondary analysis on data from 1290 respondents to the National Survey of Personal Health Practices and Consequences 1979–1980, a telephone survey of 3025 individuals between the ages of 20 to 64. Only one to two items from the survey, rather than well-established scales, were used as indicators of each of the HPM variables: control of health, self-efficacy, and perceived health status. Modifying variables of demographics (gender, age, income, marital status, and education) and biologic characteristics (body mass index) were also included in the analysis. Proxy measures of one to three items were selected for five of the six proposed dimensions of a health-promoting lifestyle. These proxy items were not aggregated as a measure of overall health-promoting lifestyle, nor did they capture the multiple dimensions of each lifestyle domain.

Using structural equation analysis (LISREL), all modifying variables were found to have direct paths as well, as the HPM hypothesized indirect paths to the proxy measures of health-promoting behaviors. Three of seven cognitive-perceptual variables and two of five modifying variables were tested. This limited set of variables predicted 5.3% to 12.6% of the variance in the proposed proxy measures of single HPLP subscales. Study findings agree with results of a number of studies that indicate the need to build into the model "direct" effects of the proposed modifying factors on health behavior. The questionable validity and reliability of the cognitive-perceptual and outcome measures used may well have contributed to the extremely low explained variance observed.

Explaining and Predicting Exercise Behavior

Fender and colleagues conducted a series of studies within the same National Institute of Nursing Research (NINR) funded research program to determine if the HPM was useful in explaining or predicting the specific behavior of exercise. These studies are summarized below.

Exercise Among Worksite Fitness Program Participants

The HPM was used as the conceptual framework for exploring the frequency of exercise among 539 predominantly European-American working adults participating in corporate fitness programs in six midwest corporations. All model variables except cues to action were measured in the study. The study participants were divided into two groups by exercise stage, acquisition (N = 208) and maintenance (N = 331). In the first stage of data analysis, hierarchic multiple regression was used, with 3-month exercise frequency regressed on cognitive-perceptual variables entered first and modifying variables entered last. In the acquisition group, 22% of the variance in exercise was explained with exercise efficacy, benefits, and the modifying behavioral factor of prior exercise behavior (measured by a single, self-report item) being significant. In the maintenance group, 21% of the variance in exercise was explained with perceived control of **physical fitness**, exercise efficacy, barriers, control of health, and prior exercise behavior being significant. The acquisition and maintenance groups were combined, and structural equation analysis using LISREL was performed on the data. As predicted, the modifying variables of gender and socioeconomic status had only significant indirect paths to exercise.

Next, actual fitness center exercise records for the previous month (rather than a single, self-report item) were used to measure prior exercise behavior. With refinement in the measure of prior exercise behavior, HPM variables predicted 59% of the variance in exercise frequency. This major increase in variance explained should caution researchers concerning use of single items to measure model variables. Barriers, personal competence (general self-efficacy measure), age, and prior exercise behavior were significant direct predictors, with prior exercise being the most powerful (manuscript submitted for publication). These findings support the existence of a direct "**habit**" effect on exercise rather than the proposed indirect effect of behavioral factors as proposed in the HBM.

Exercise Patterns of Community-Dwelling Older Adults

This study was conducted to determine the extent to which the HPM would explain exercise adherence among older adults in the community. A total of 361 adults aged 55 and over were recruited from urban, suburban, and rural communities in a midwestern state. Study participants had to be ambulatory without assistive devices and able to participate in a program of exercise. Most were of European-American descent. Six cognitive-perceptual factors (importance of health, perceived control of health, definition of health, health status, benefits, and barriers to exercise) were assessed by questionnaire. Self-motivation and preferred level of exertion, not in the HPM, were included as exploratory variables. Modifying factors of demographic and biologic characteristics and behavioral factors were also assessed. Exercise was measured by the exercise subscale of the HPLP. In hierarchic multiple regression analysis, exercise scores were regressed on both cognitive-perceptual variables and modifying variables. The selected HPM variables explained 24% of the variance in exercise. Self-motivation and preferred exertion added an additional 10%. Preferred exertion could be interpreted as an indirect measure of the biologic characteristic of energy reserve for older adults and thus legitimately included as a modifying factor.

Structural equation analysis using LISREL was performed on the data. Benefits and barriers had significant direct paths to exercise but control of health, health status, and definition of health did not.

Exercise Behavior of Cardiac Rehabilitation Program Participants

The purpose of this study was to determine the usefulness of the HPM in explaining the frequency of exercise behaviors among cardiac rehabilitation program participants. Study volunteers were recruited from individuals enrolled in 15 Phase II and Phase III cardiac rehabilitation programs in a mid-western state. The 511 cardiac rehabilitation patients who agreed to participate ranged in age from 31 to 84 years and were predominantly European-American. All variables were measured by questionnaires. All HPM variables were measured except situational factors and cues to action. Exercise frequency was measured over a 12-week period by cardiac rehabilitation program attendance and by the exercise subscale of the HPLP. The significant other's exercise behavior was measured as an indication of interpersonal influence (modeling).

Components of the HPM explained 23% of the variance in exercise behavior measured by the HPLP exercise subscale and 20% when measured by high or low cardiac program attendance. Exercise efficacy, barriers to exercise, importance of health, and phase of exercise had significant beta weights. Structural equation analysis using LISREL revealed that as hypothesized, gender and socioeconomic status has only indirect effects on exercise. However, the direct effects of perceived control of health, perceived health status, and definition of health were not supported.

Exercise Patterns of Ambulatory Cancer Patients

A focus on "wellness" or health promotion rather than on illness has progressively occurred during the last decade among people with cancer. This has been the result of changes in survival, improvement in cancer treatments, and changes in the settings where cancer treatments are delivered. Exercise is one recognized component of healthy lifestyle among cancer patients. Patients who have been sedentary may actually begin exercising during the period of therapy. The purpose of this study was to test the usefulness of the HPM in explaining the occurrence of reported exercise behavior among ambulatory cancer patients receiving chemotherapy and radiation in outpatient settings. Predictor variables were measured by questionnaire administered to 385 predominantly European-American patients undergoing treatment for their disease in 13 clinical sites in the midwestern United States. Two measures of exercise behavior were used, the exercise subscale of the HPLP and the health diary or daily record of health-related events that the individual filled out each day for a month's period of time.

Using hierarchic multiple regression, the exercise subscale of the HPLP was regressed on the cognitive-perceptual factors of importance of health, control of health, definition of health, health status, benefits, and barriers as well as the modifying variables of demographic characteristics (marital status, employment, gender, education, age, and income) and reaction to diagnosis as an additional cancer-specific variable. Cognitive-perceptual variables from the HPM combined to explain 42% of the variance in exercise with modifying factors and reaction to the diagnosis explaining negligible variance. Benefits and barriers alone explained 38% of the variance in exercise. Perceived health status was the only other HPM factor with a significant beta weight in the regression. The direct and indirect paths among the HPM variables were explored using structural equation analysis (LISREL). Both gender and socioeconomic status had the HPM-proposed indirect paths to exercise. However, the HPM-proposed direct paths of perceived control of health and definition of health to exercise were not supported.

Adolescents' Exercise Beliefs and Prediction of Their Exercise Behavior

A team of scientists at the University of Michigan Child/Adolescent Health Behavior Research Center, funded by the NINR, are exploring the determinants of health behaviors and risk behaviors among preadolescents and adolescents. The HPM provides the organizing framework for several of these studies.

Garcia and colleagues[15] examined gender and developmental differences in exercise-related beliefs and exercise behaviors of 286 racially diverse youth: 30% African-Americans, 63% European-Americans, and 7% of other racial heritage. It is well known that physical activity declines almost 50% during adolescence, with females becoming increasingly more sedentary than males. The HPM provided this basis for the model of exercise prediction tested in this study. Those fifth-, sixth-, and eighth-grade students who had parental consent and assented to participate completed the questionnaire designed to assess model variables. The HPM variables assessed were perceived health status, previous exercise, exercise benefits and barriers, exercise self-efficacy, interpersonal influences (exercise models, norms, and social support), and situational influences (sedentary time, and access to facilities and programs). The modifying factors of gender, grade, and race were also assessed. Eight weeks later, students completed an exercise log for 7 consecutive days. They completed the logs at school for the previous day.

Regression analysis revealed that only 19% of the variance in exercise was explained. Although low, this is comparable to the amount of explained variance found in many other adolescent exercise studies. Significant predictors of exercise were gender, the exercise benefits and barriers differential, and access to facilities and programs. Previous exercise came close but failed to reach significance. Surprisingly in an adolescent population, self-efficacy did not directly predict exercise behavior. An exploratory path analysis revealed that the effects of grade, perceived health status, self-efficacy, social support for exercise, and exercise norms indirectly affected exercise through the exercise benefits and barriers differential.

Predicting Use of Hearing Protection

Repetitive exposure to high noise levels can cause psychologic distress and hearing loss. In the United States, 14 million workers are exposed to hazardous noise where they work.[16] Noise-induced hearing loss can be prevented, but once it has occurred it is irreversible. Occupational health nurses can intervene to reduce hearing loss and its associated medical costs and impaired quality of life by motivating employees to regularly use hearing protection devices. However, to optimize the effectiveness of interventions, it is important for nurses to understand those factors that affect hearing protection practices.[17]

Predicting Use of Hearing Protection Among Factory Workers

Lusk et al.[18] tested the HPM as a causal model to predict workers' use of hearing protection devices. This behavior may well represent a mix of both health-protecting and health-promoting motivation. Workers could select personal hearing protection from a variety of earplugs and earmuffs provided by the plant. A convenience sample of 561 workers provided data for the study. The cognitive-perceptual variables of perceived control of health, perceived self-efficacy, definition of health, perceived health status, perceived benefits, and perceived barriers were used as predictors along with the modifying variables of demographic characteristics and situational factors. Use of hearing protection was measured by the workers' self-reports of the percent of time (0% to 100%) they used hearing protection during the past week, the past month, and the past 3 months. Data were analyzed by structural equation modeling. The model implied by the HPM accounted for 49% of the variance in use of hearing protection. Value of use (benefits), barriers, self-efficacy, and health competence were found to have significant direct paths to use of hearing protection. Situational factors (accessibility) and demographic characteristics (gender, age, education, and job category) had significant indirect paths. When exploratory causal modeling including all theoretically specified paths and, in addition, all direct paths from modifying factors was used to examine use of hearing protection, 53% of the variance was explained. Significant predictors of use were self-efficacy, value of use (benefits), perceived barriers, health competence, education, age, gender, and situational factors.

Predicting Use of Hearing Protection Among Construction Workers

Lusk and colleagues used the HPM as a conceptual framework for studying the use of hearing protection among 359 construction workers in the Midwest (unpublished data, 1995). All variables in the model except importance of health, behavioral factors, biologic characteristics, and cues to action were assessed using questionnaires. Use of hearing protection was measured by workers' self-report of percent of time (0% to 100%) that they used hearing protection during the past week, the past month, and the past 3 months in high-noise areas. Structural equation modeling revealed that the path model implied by the HPM fit fairly well, accounting for 36% of the variance in use. Value of use, barriers, self-efficacy, and perceived health status had significant direct paths to use. When an exploratory model was employed, with all predictors having direct paths to use, three of the original predictors (value of use, barriers, and self-efficacy) and two additional ones (interpersonal support for behavior [modeling] and situational influences on behavior [noise exposure]) were found to have significant direct paths to use of protection. This exploratory model with additional direct paths explained over 50% of the variance in use of hearing protection.

Predicting Use of Hearing Protection Among Mexican-American Industrial Workers

Kerr, a member of Lusk's research team, tested the cross-cultural applicability of the HPM in a study that aimed to identify components of the HPM that were most strongly related to use of hearing protection among Mexican-American workers.[19] Mexican-Americans are the largest Hispanic subgroup and fastest growing ethnic and racial minority in the United States, comprising 13.5 million people. Thus, occupational health professionals need to understand the factors influencing the use of hearing protection among Mexican-American workers in order to develop more effective programs to increase use. A sample of 119 workers was recruited from a garment industry in the southwestern United States where Mexican Americans constituted a large portion of the work force. Participants needed to be able to read English, but assistance was provided as needed. Questionnaires and focus group sessions were used for collection of data. The HPM variables included in the study were interpersonal influences (support, norms, models), situational factors, control of health, self-efficacy, definition of health, perceived health status, benefits, value of use, and barriers. Use of hearing protection was measured by the workers self-report of the percent of time (0% to 100%) they actually used hearing protection during the past week, the past month, and the past 3 months when they were in their work areas.

Self-efficacy in the use of hearing protection, a clinical conception (definition) of health, benefits of use of hearing protection, and a higher perceived health status were positively related to use and perceived barriers negatively related to use. A path model consistent with the HPM resulted in explanation of 25% of the variance in use of hearing protection. When a second model was tested allowing direct paths from modifying factors to use of hearing protection, 55% of the variance in use of hearing protection was explained by three variables representing four cognitive-perceptual factors in the model: benefits minus barriers, clinical conception of health, and perceived health. The modifying factor of situational influences (hearing protection requirement and plant site) also contributed to the explained variance.

An overview of all the studies reported in this section appears in Table 6–1. The table reports for each study, the population, dependent variable, and independent variables studied. Significant predictor variables are identified and the percent of variance explained reported. Across the various studies, multiple regression analysis, path analysis, and structural equation analysis were the statistical methods employed.

Implications of Research Findings

In the studies conducted to date to test the HPM, 5 to 12 variables have been studied at any given time. None of the reported studies have tested the effects of "cues to action." In the studies in which most of the HPM variables were tested, the variance explained ranged from 19% to 59%. It should be noted that the predictive performance of the HPM in relation to hearing protection was considerably enhanced when modifying factors were allowed to directly affect the target behavior (36% explained variance increased to 51%; 25% explained variance increased to 55%).

An analysis of the studies reported indicate that the behavior-specific variables of **perceived self-efficacy**, **benefits** and **barriers** were empirically supported as predictors of health behaviors in the majority of studies in which they were included. Self-efficacy and barriers received the strongest support, with benefits receiving moderate support.

On the other hand, the results of the studies indicate that the health-specific variables need to be reevaluated as to their centrality in predicting health-promoting and protecting behaviors. **Importance of health** failed to explain health behavior in 9 of the 11 studies in which it was included. The reason for lack of explanatory power was clear. Participants in all studies ranked "health" so high as a value in relation to other personal values that without variance, this variable was not useful as a predictor. **Perceived control of health** contributed to the explanation of health-promoting lifestyle in a majority of the studies but by and large did not contribute to the explanation of specific health behaviors. When perceived control of health was a significant predictor, the direction of the relationship was sometimes other than that pre-

TABLE 6–1 Summary of Findings From Studies Using the Health Promotion Model

Author	Population	Dependent Variable	Variables Studied	Variance Explained
Health-Specific Outcome Measures				
Weitzel[9]	Blue-collar workers	Health-promoting lifestyle	1,6,7,8,10	20%
Pender et al.[12]	White-collar workers	Health-promoting lifestyle	1,5,6,7,8, 9,10	31%
Walker[11]	Community-dwelling older adults	Health-promoting lifestyle	1,6,7,9,10	28%
Sechrist[11]	Cardiac rehabilitation participants	Health-promoting lifestyle	1,3,5,6,7, 9,10	21%
Frank-Stromborg et al.[13]	Ambulatory cancer patients	Health-promoting lifestyle	1,6,7,9,10	24%
Johnson et al.[14]	National data sample	Health-promoting lifestyle	1,2,7,8,10 (proxy items used)	Not reported for HPLP total score
Behavior-Specific Outcome Measures				
Exercise Pender[11]	White-collar workers	Exercise frequency (acquisition stage)	1,2,3,4,5*,6,7,8,9, 10,11,12	22%
		Exercise frequency (maintenance state)	1,2,3,4,5*,6,7,8,9, 10,11,12	21%
Pender et al. (Unpublished data)	White-collar workers	Exercise frequency (total group with stages combined)	1,2,3,4,5†,6,7,8,9, 10,11,12	59%
Walker[11]	Community-dwelling older adults	Exercise frequency	1,2,5,6,7,9,10, 11,12	24%
Sechrist[11]	Cardiac rehabilitation patients	Exercise frequency	1,2,3,5,6,7,8,9, 10,11,12	23%
Frank-Stromborg[11]	Ambulatory cancer patients	Exercise frequency	1,6,7,9,10,11,12	42%
Garcia et al.[15]	Preadolescents and adolescents	Exercise frequency and intensity	1,3,4,5,8,10,11,12	19%
Use of Hearing Protection Lusk et al.[18]	Factory workers (skilled trades)	Use of hearing protection	1,4,7,8,9,10,11,12 (Modifying factors allowed to have direct paths to use)	49% 53%

Continued

TABLE 6–1 Summary of Findings From Studies Using the Health Promotion Model (Continued)

Author	Population	Dependent Variable	Variables Studied	Variance Explained
Lusk (Unpublished data)	Construction workers	Use of hearing protection	<u>1,3,4</u>,7,<u>8,9,10, 11,12</u> (Modifying factors allowed to have direct paths to use)	36% 51%
Kerr[19]	Mexican-American industrial workers	Use of hearing protection	3,4,7,<u>8,9,10,11,12</u> (Modifying factors allowed to have direct paths to use)	25% 55%

Key   1 = *Demographic characteristics*   7 = *Perceived control of health*
       2 = *Biologic characteristics*   8 = *Perceived self-efficacy*
       3 = *Interpersonal influences*   9 = *Definition of health*
       4 = *Situational factors*   10 = *Perceived health status*
       5 = *Behavioral factors*   11 = *Perceived benefits*
       6 = *Importance of health*   12 = *Perceived barriers*
                                13 = *Cues to action*

Underlined number indicates significant predictor of dependent variable
* Prior exercise measured by self-report on a single item.
† Prior exercise measured by fitness center exercise records from previous month

dicted. This inconsistency of performance has been reported in other studies. **Definition of health** was predictive of health-promoting lifestyle in all the studies reported but was explanatory or predictive in only two of nine studies when specific behaviors were being predicted. **Perceived health status** was a significant predictor of the target behaviors in a number of studies and was predictive both in those studies of health-promoting lifestyle and in studies of specific behaviors such as exercise and use of hearing protection. However, only limited variance was explained. Thus, perceived health status might best be reinterpreted as a psychological personal factor that can either directly or indirectly affect health behavior when current health status is relevant to performance of a given health action. For example, health status may be relevant to vigorous exercising but not relevant to brushing one's teeth.

Given that the HPM evolved from social learning theory, **interpersonal, situational**, and **behavioral influences** on health behaviors are of high theoretical importance. Significant effects of these variables on health behaviors in a number of the studies reported provide empirical evidence that they should be retained but positioned to have direct as well as indirect effects on health-promoting behavior. Repositioning the above three variables does not violate the theoretical integrity of the model and is consistent with social learning theory, in which the environment (situational and interpersonal influences) and prior behavior (behavioral factors) affect subsequent behavior. Development of rigorous measures of these variables relevant to various health behaviors is needed.

Cues to action are transient stimuli that are difficult to identify and measure reliably. Thus, the utility of this variable in the model can be questioned.

In the revised HPM, importance of health, perceived control of health, and cues to action will be deleted from the model. Definition of health, perceived health status, and demographic and biologic characteristics will be repositioned in the model and included in a category of personal factors from which can be selected variables that are considered relevant influences on a particular health behavior in a given target population. The revised HPM is presented in the next portion of this section.

$\mathcal{T}$he Revised Health-Promotion Model

The revised HPM appears in Figure 6–2. The variables in the revised HPM and their interrelationships are described below. Three new variables have been added to the model: activity-related affect, commitment to a plan of action, and immediate competing demands and preferences. It is beyond the scope of this section to describe approaches to measuring each variable, but information regarding measurement of variables that is not already reported in the literature can be obtained from the author.

Individual Characteristics and Experiences

Each person has unique personal characteristics and experiences that affect subsequent actions. The importance of their effect will depend on the target behavior being considered. The aspects of prior behavior or individual characteristics selected for measurement provide flexibility in the HPM to capture variables that may be highly relevant to a particular health behavior but not to all health behaviors or in a particular target population but not in all populations.

Prior Related Behavior

Behavioral factors have been retained in the HPM as "prior related behavior." Empirical studies indicate that often the best predictor of behavior is the frequency of the same or a similar behavior in the past. Prior behavior is proposed as having both direct and indirect effects on the likelihood of engaging in health-promoting behaviors. The direct effect of past behavior on current health promoting behavior may be due to habit formation, predisposing one to engage in the behavior automatically, with little attention to the specific details of its execution. Habit strength accrues each time the behavior occurs and is most facilitated by concentrated, repetitive practice of the behavior.

Consistent with social cognitive theory, prior behavior is proposed as also having an indirect influence on health-promoting behavior through perceptions of self-efficacy, benefits, barriers, and activity-related affect. According to Bandura,[7] actual enactment of a behavior and its associated feedback is a major source of efficacy or "skill" information. Anticipated or experienced benefits from engaging in the behavior are referred to by Bandura as outcome expectations. If desired short-term benefits are experienced early in the course of the behavior, the behavior is more likely to be repeated. Barriers to a given behavior are experienced and stored in memory as "hurdles" that need to be overcome to successfully engage in the behavior. Every incident of a behavior is also accompanied by emotions or affect. Positive or negative affect either before, during, or following the behavior is encoded into memory as information that is retrieved when engaging in the behavior is contemplated at a later point in time. Prior

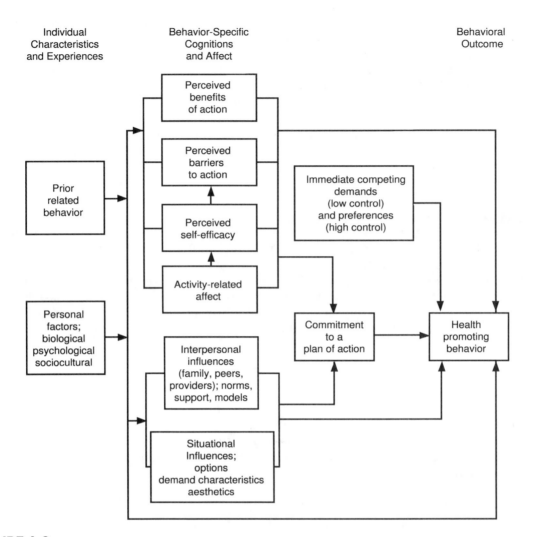

Individual Characteristics and Experiences

Behavior-Specific Cognitions and Affect

Behavioral Outcome

FIGURE 6–2

Revised Health Promotion Model.

behavior is proposed as shaping all of these behavior-specific cognitions and affect. The nurse can help the client shape a positive behavioral history for the future by focusing on the benefits of a behavior, teaching clients how to overcome hurdles to carrying out the behavior, and engendering high levels of efficacy and positive affect through successful experiences of performance and positive feedback.

Personal Factors

The relevant personal factors predictive of a given behavior are shaped by the nature of the target behavior being considered. In the revised HPM, personal factors have been categorized as biologic, psychologic and sociocultural. Personal biologic factors include variables such as age, gender, body mass index, pubertal status, menopausal status, aerobic capacity, strength, agility, or balance. Personal psychologic factors can include variables such as self-esteem, self-motivation, personal competence, perceived health status, and definition of health.

Personal sociocultural factors include variables such as race, ethnicity, acculturation, education, and socioeconomic status. Since numerous personal factors exist, those factors to be included in any given study should be limited to the few that are theoretically relevant to explanation or prediction of a given target behavior. The difference in behavioral relevance of these factors is illustrated by the fact that aerobic capacity may directly influence participation in vigorous exercise but is unlikely to directly influence eating a nutritious diet. Personal factors are proposed as directly influencing both behavior-specific cognitions and affect as well as health-promoting behavior. Although personal factors may influence cognitions and affect and predict health behaviors, some personal factors cannot be changed; thus, they are seldom incorporated into health-behavior change interventions.

Behavior-Specific Cognitions and Affect

This category of variables within the HPM is considered to be of major motivational significance. Furthermore, these variables constitute a critical "core" for intervention, as they are subject to modification through nursing actions.

Perceived Benefits of Action

One's plan to engage in a particular behavior often hinges on the anticipated benefits or outcomes that will occur. Anticipated benefits of action are menial representations of the positive or reinforcing consequences of a behavior. According to expectancy-value theory, the motivational importance of anticipated benefits is based on personal or vicarious experience of outcomes from prior direct experience with the behavior or observational learning from others engaging in the behavior. Beliefs in benefits or positive outcome expectations have generally been shown to be a necessary although not sufficient condition for engagement in a specific health behavior. Individuals tend to invest time and resources in activities with a high likelihood of increasing their experience of positive outcomes. The motivational importance of perceived benefits of action has been supported in the majority of HPM studies in which it has been tested.

Benefits from performance of the behavior may be intrinsic or extrinsic. Examples of intrinsic benefits include increased alertness and decreased feelings of fatigue. Extrinsic benefits can include monetary rewards or social interactions possible as a result of engaging in the behavior. Initially, extrinsic benefits of health behaviors may be of high motivational significance, whereas intrinsic benefits may be more powerful in motivating continuation of health behaviors. The expected magnitude of benefits and the temporal relation of benefits to action impact the potency of anticipated benefits as a determinant of health behavior. In the HPM, perceived benefits are proposed as directly motivating behavior as well as indirectly motivating behavior through determining the extent of commitment to a plan of action to engage in the behaviors from which the anticipated benefits will result.

Perceived Barriers to Action

Anticipated barriers have been repeatedly shown in empirical studies to affect intentions to engage in a particular behavior and the actual execution of the behavior. In relation to health-promoting behaviors, barriers may be imagined or real. They consist of perceptions concerning the unavailability, inconvenience, expense, difficulty, or time-consuming nature of a particular action. Barriers are often viewed as the blocks, hurdles, and personal costs of undertaking a given behavior. Loss of satisfaction from giving up health-damaging behaviors such as smoking or eating high-fat foods to adopt a healthier lifestyle can also constitute a barrier. Earners usually arouse motives of avoidance in relation to a given behavior.

When readiness to act is low and barriers are high, action is unlikely to occur. When readiness to act is high and barriers are low, the probability of action is much greater. Perceived barriers to action as depicted in the revised HPM affect health-promoting behavior directly by serving as blocks to action as well as indirectly through decreasing commitment to a plan of action.

Perceived Self-Efficacy

Self-efficacy, as defined by Bandura,[7] is the judgment of personal capability to organize and execute a particular course of action. It is concerned not with the skill one has but with judgments of what one can do with whatever skills one possesses. Judgments of personal efficacy are distinguished from outcome expectations. Perceived self-efficacy is a judgment of one's abilities to accomplish a certain level of performance, whereas an outcome expectation is a judgment of the likely consequences (eg, benefits, costs) such behavior will produce. Perceptions of skill and competence in a particular domain motivate individuals to engage in those behaviors that they excel in. Feeling efficacious and skilled in one's performance is likely to encourage one to engage in the target behavior more frequently than feeling inept and unskilled.

Personal knowledge about one's self-efficacy is based on four types of information: (1) performance attainments from actually engaging in the behavior and evaluating performance in relation to some self-standard or external feedback given by others, (2) vicarious experiences of observing the performance of others and their related self-evaluation and feedback, (3) verbal persuasion on the part of others that one does possess the ability to carry out a particular course of action, and (4) physiologic states (e.g., anxiety, fear, calm, tranquility) from which people judge their competencies.[20] In the HPM, perceived self-efficacy is proposed as being influenced by activity-related affect. The more positive the affect, the greater the perceptions of efficacy. In turn, self-efficacy is proposed as influencing perceived barriers to action, with higher efficacy resulting in lowered perception of barriers to the performance of the target behavior. Self-efficacy motivates health-promoting behavior directly by efficacy expectations and indirectly by affecting perceived barriers and commitment or persistence in pursuing a plan of action.

Activity-Related Affect

Subjective feeling states occur prior to, during, and following a behavior, based on the stimulus properties of the behavior itself. These affective responses may be mild, moderate, or strong and are cognitively labeled, stored in memory, and associated with subsequent thoughts of the behavior. Affective responses to a particular behavior consist of three components: emotional arousal to the act itself (activity-related), the self acting (self-related), or the environment in which the action takes place (context-related). The resultant feeling state is likely to affect whether an individual will repeat the behavior again or maintain the behavior long-term.[21] Behavior-contingent feeling states have been explored as determinants of health behaviors in recent szudies.[21-25] The affect associated with the behavior reflects a direct emotional reaction or gut-level response to the thought of the behavior, which can be positive or negative—is it fun, delightful, enjoyable, disgusting, or unpleasant? Behaviors associated with positive affect are likely to be repeated, whereas those associated with negative affect are likely to be avoided. For some behaviors, both positive and negative feelings states will be induced. Thus, the relative balance between positive and negative affect prior to, during, and following the behavior is important to ascertain. Activity-related affect is different from the evaluative dimension of attitude as proposed by Fishbein and Ajzen.[20] The evaluative dimension of attitude reflects affective evaluation of the specific outcomes of a behavior rather than the response to the stimulus properties of the behavior itself.

For any given behavior, the full range of negative and positive feelings states should be elaborated so that both are adequately measured. In many instruments proposed to measure affect, negative feelings are elaborated more extensively than positive feelings. This is not surprising since anxiety, fear, and depression have been studied much more than joy, elation, and calm. Based on social cognitive theory, there is a relationship proposed between self-efficacy and activity-related affect. McAuley and Courneya[22] found that positive affective response during exercise was a significant predictor of post exercise efficacy. This is consistent with Bandura's proposal that emotional responses and their induced physiologic states during a behavior serve as sources of efficacy information.[7] Thus, activity-related affect is proposed as influencing health behavior directly as well as indirectly through self-efficacy and commitment to a plan of action.

Interpersonal Influences

According to the HPM, interpersonal influences are cognitions concerning the behaviors, beliefs or attitudes of others. These cognitions may or may not correspond with reality. Primary sources of interpersonal influence on health-promoting behaviors are families (parents or siblings), peers, and health care providers. Interpersonal influences include: norms (expectations of significant others),[20] social support (instrumental and emotional encouragement), and modeling (vicarious learning through observing others engaged in a particular behavior).[7] These three interpersonal processes have been shown to affect individuals' predisposition to engage in health-promoting behaviors in a number of health-related studies. Social norms set standards for performance that individuals can adopt or reject. Social support for a behavior taps the sustaining resources offered by others. Modeling portrays the sequential components of a health behavior and is an important strategy for behavior change in social cognitive theory. Interpersonal influences affect health-promoting behavior directly as well as indirectly through social pressures or encouragement to commit to a plan of action.

Individuals vary in the extent to which they are sensitive to the wishes, examples, and praise of others. However, given sufficient motivation to behave in a way consistent with interpersonal influences, individuals are likely to undertake behaviors for which they will be admired and socially reinforced. In order for interpersonal influences to have an effect, individuals must attend to the behaviors, wishes, and inputs of others; comprehend them; and assimilate them into cognitive representations related to given behaviors. Susceptibility to the influence of others may vary developmentally and be particularly evident in adolescence. Some cultures may place more emphasis on interpersonal influences than others. For example, *familismo* among Hispanic populations may encourage individuals to engage in a particular behavior for the good of the family rather than for personal gain.

Situational Influences

Personal perceptions and cognitions of any situation or context can facilitate or impede behavior. Situational influences on health-promoting behavior include perceptions of options available, demand characteristics, and aesthetic features of the environment in which a given behavior is proposed to take place. Kaplan and Kaplan,[26] in their work on restorative natural environments, have heightened awareness of how environments or situational contexts can impact health and health-related behaviors. Individuals are drawn to and perform more competently in situations or environmental contexts in which they feel compatible rather than incompatible, related rather than alienated, safe and reassured rather than unsafe and threatened. Environments that are fascinating and interesting are also desirable contexts for the performance of health behaviors.

In the revised HPM, situational influences have been reconceptualized as direct and as indirect influences on health behavior. Situations may directly affect behaviors by presenting an environment "loaded" with cues that trigger action. For example, a "no smoking" environment creates demand characteristics for nonsmoking behavior. Company regulations for hearing protection to be worn create demand characteristics that regulations be obeyed. Both situations enforce commitment to health actions.

Situational influences have been given little attention in prior studies of the HPM and are worthy of further exploration as potentially important determinants of health behavior. They may hold an important key to developing new and more effective strategies for facilitating the acquisition and maintenance of health behaviors.

Behavioral Outcome

Commitment to a plan of action initiates a behavioral event. This commitment will propel the individual into and through the behavior unless a competing demand that the individual cannot avoid or a competing preference that the individual does not resist intervenes.

Commitment to a Plan of Action

Human beings generally engage in organized rather than disorganized behavior. According to Ajzen and Fishbein, intentionality is a major determinant of volitional behavior.[27] **Commitment to a plan of action** in the revised HFM implies the underlying cognitive processes: (1) commitment to carry out a specific action at a given time and place and with specified persons or alone, irrespective of competing preferences, (2) identification of definitive strategies for eliciting, carrying out, and reinforcing the behavior. The requirement of identification of specific strategies to be used at different points in the behavioral sequence goes beyond intentionality to further the likelihood that the plan of action developed by nurse and client will be successfully implemented. For example, the strategy of contracting consists of a mutually agreed-on set of actions to which one party commits with the understanding that the other party will provide some tangible reward or reinforcement if the commitment is sustained. Strategies can be selected by clients to energize and reinforce health behaviors according to their own preferences and the stage of change that they are at. Commitment alone without associated strategies often results in "good intentions" but failure to perform a valued health behavior.

Immediate Competing Demands and Preferences

Immediate competing demands or preferences refer to alternative behaviors that intrude into consciousness as possible courses of action immediately prior to the intended occurrence of a planned health-promoting behavior. Competing demands are viewed as those alternative behaviors over which individuals have a relatively low level of control because of environmental contingencies such as work or family care responsibilities. Failure to respond to a demand may have untoward effects for the self or for significant others. Competing preferences are viewed as alternative behaviors with powerful reinforcing properties over which individuals exert a relatively high level of control. They can derail a health-promoting behavior in favor of the competing behavior.[28] The extent to which an individual is able to resist competing preferences depends on his or her ability to be self-regulating. Examples of "giving in" to competing preferences are: selecting a food high in fat rather than low in fat because of taste or flavor preferences; driving past the recreation center where one usually exercises to stop at the mall (a preference for browsing or shopping rather than exercising). Both competing demands and preferences can derail a plan of action to which one has committed. Competing demands can be differentiated from barriers in that the individual must carry out an unanticipated behavior based on external demand or untoward results are likely to occur. Competing preferences can be differentiated from barriers such as lack of time, because competing preferences are last-minute urges based on one's preference hierarchy that derail a plan for positive health action.

Individuals vary in their ability to sustain attention and avoid disruption. Some individuals may be predisposed developmentally or biologically to be more easily swayed from a course of action than others. Inhibiting competing preferences requires the exercise of self-regulation and control capabilities. Strong commitment to a plan of action may sustain dedication to complete a behavior in light of competing demands or preferences. In the HPM, immediate competing demands and preferences directly affect the probability of occurrence of health behavior as well as moderate the effects of commitment.

Health-Promoting Behavior

This variable in the model has been addressed extensively throughout the book so needs little further discussion here. Health-promoting behavior is the end point or action out come in the HPM. However, it should be noted that health-promoting behavior is ultimately directed toward **attaining positive health outcomes** for the client. Health promoting behaviors, particularly when integrated into a healthy lifestyle that pervade all aspects of living, result in a positive health experience throughout the life span.

*D*irections for Research

The revised HPM presented in this section incorporates the outcome expectancies of expectancy-value theory and self-efficacy expectancies for mastery of social cognitive theory. Further, interpersonal, situational, and behavioral factors, as well as cognitive and other personal factors delineated in social learning theory are integral to the HPM. Thus, it is theoretically consistent with these frameworks. The model has been refined to focus on 10 determinants or categories of determinants of behavior rather than the previous 13 determinants. The revised model needs to be tested empirically. Before testing the model with any specific health behavior, it is suggested that rigorous measures of behavior-specific variables be developed if they do not already exist. This may involve eliciting appropriate content for the instruments prior to their design. Relationships among the variables should be tested in predictive studies. Where there is already evidence supporting the predictive validity of constructs in the HPM, such as perceived barriers to action, perceived benefits of actions, perceived self-efficacy, interpersonal influences, and situational influences, health promotion intervention studies should be designed incorporating these variables. The extent to which the revised HPM is useful in explaining, predicting, and altering health-promoting behaviors will be determined through further empirical studies.

*S*ummary

The theoretical underpinnings and assumptions of the HPM have been presented in this section as well as the results of a number of studies testing the HPM. The revisions of the model to increase its potential utility for prediction and intervention are presented with a rationale for the revisions.

References

1. Pender NJ. *Health Promotion in Nursing Practice*. Norwalk, Conn: Appleton-Century-Crofts; 1982.
2. Dunn HL. What high-level wellness means. *Can J Public Health*, 1959;50(11):447–457.
3. Dunn HL. High-level wellness for men and society. *Am J Public Health*. 1959;49 (6):786–792.
4. Pender NJ. *Health Promotion in Nursing Practice*. 2nd ed. Norwalk, Conn: Appleton & Lange; 1987.
5. Feather NT, ed. *Expectations and Actions: Expectancy-Value Models in Psychology*. Hillsdale, NJ: Lawrence Erlbaum Associates Inc; 1982.
6. Klar Y, Nadel A, Mallor TE. Opting to change: student's informal self-change endeavors. In: Klar Y, Fisher JD, Chinsky JM, et al., eds. *Self-change: Social and Psychological Perspectives*. New York, NY: Springer-Verlag; 1992:63–83.
7. Bandura A. *Social Foundations of Thought and Action: A Social Cognitive Theory*. Englewood Cliffs, NJ: Prentice-Hall Inc; 1986.
8. Bandura A. Self efficacy: toward a unifying theory of behavioral change. *Psychol Rev.* 1977;84:191–215.
9. Weitzel MH. A test of the Health Promotion Model with blue collar workers. *Nurs Res.* 1989;38(2);99–104.
10. Walker SN, Sechrist KR, Fender NJ. The Health-Promoting Lifestyle Profile: development and psychometric characteristics. *Nurs Res.* 1987;36(2):76–81.
11. Pender NJ, Walker SN, Sechrist KR, et al. *The Health Promotion Model: Refinement and Validation*. Final Report to the National Center for Nursing Research, National Institutes of Health (Grant no. NRO1121) Dekalb, IL: Northern Illinois University Press; 1990.
12. Pender NJ, Walker SN, Sechrist KR, et al. Predicting health-promoting lifestyles in the workplace. *Nurs Res.* 1990:39(6):326–332.
13. Frank-Stromborg M, Fender NJ, Walker SN. Determinants of health-promoting lifestyles in ambulatory cancer patients. *Soc Sci Med.* 1990;31:1159–1168.
14. Johnson JL, Ratner PA, Bottorff JL, et al. An exploration of Pender's Health Promotion Model using LISREL. *Nurs Res.* 1993;42(3):132–138.
15. Garcia A, Norton-Broda MA, Frenn M, et al. Gender and developmental differences in exercise beliefs among youth and prediction of their exercise behavior. *J School Health.* 1995,65(6):213–219.
16. Occupational Safety and Health Administration. *Noise Control: A Guide for Workers and Employers*. Washington DC: US Department of Labor; 1980.
17. Lusk SL. *Preventing Noise-Induced Hearing Loss*. Final report to the National Institute of Nursing Research, National Institutes of Health, (Grant No. NR02050); 1994.
18. Lusk SL, Ronis D, Kerr MJ, et al. Test of the health promotion model as a causal model of workers' use of hearing protection. *Nurs Res.* 1994;43(3):151–157.
19. Kerr MJ. *Factors Related to Mexican-American Workers' Use of Hearing Protection*. Ann Arbor, Mich: University of Michigan; 1994 *Dissertation Abstracts International*, 1994, University Microfilms No. 9501083.
20. Fishbein M, Ajzen J. *Belief, Attitude, Intention and Behavior: An Introduction to Theory and Research*. Boston, Mass: Addison-Wesley Publishing Co Inc; 1975.
21. Gauvin L, Rejeski WJ. The exercise-induced feeling inventory: development and initial validation. *J Sport Exerc Psychol.* 1993;15:403–423.

22. McAuley E, Courneya KS. Self-efficacy relationships with affective and exertion responses to exercise. *J Appl Soc Psychol.* 1992;22:312–326.
23. Hardy CJ, Rejeski WJ. Not what, but how one feels: the measurement of affect during exercise. *J Sport Exerc Psychol.* 1989;11:304–317.
24. Godin G. Importance of the emotional aspect of attitude to predict intention. *Psychol Rep.* 1987;61:719–723.
25. Rejeski WJ, Gauvin L, Hobson ML, et al. Effects of baseline responses, in-task feelings, and duration of activity on exercise-induced feeling states in women. *Health Psychol.* 1995;14:350–359.
26. Kaplan R, Kaplan S. *The Experience of Nature: A Psychological Perspective.* Cambridge, England: Cambridge University Press; 1989.
27. Ajzen I, Fishbein M. *Understanding Attitudes and Predicting Social Behavior.* Englewood Cliffs, NJ: Prentice-Hall Inc; 1980.
28. Vara LS, Epstein L. Laboratory assessment of choice between exercise or sedentary behaviors. *Res Q Exerc Sport.* 1995;64:356–360.

INDEX

Index